CW00407730

DEVON AND CORNWALL RECORD SOCIETY

New Series

Volume 67

Effigy of Sir Stephen Richard Glynne, 9th Bt, from his funeral monument (1874), St Deiniol's Church, Hawarden (Clwyd): Photo author, reproduced by kind permission of the rector of St Deiniol's, Hawarden.

CORNISH CHURCHES IN THE NINETEENTH CENTURY

The Church Notes of
the Lysons brothers and Sir Stephen Glynne

VOLUME I: CHURCHES A–L

Edited by
Paul Cockerham

DEVON AND CORNWALL RECORD SOCIETY

THE BOYDELL PRESS

Editorial Matter © Devon and Cornwall Record Society 2024

All Rights Reserved. Except as permitted under current legislation
no part of this work may be photocopied, stored in a retrieval system,
published, performed in public, adapted, broadcast,
transmitted, recorded or reproduced in any form or by any means,
without the prior permission of the copyright owner

First published 2024

A publication of the
Devon and Cornwall Record Society
published by The Boydell Press
an imprint of Boydell & Brewer Ltd
PO Box 9, Woodbridge, Suffolk IP12 3DF, UK
and of Boydell & Brewer Inc.
668 Mt Hope Avenue, Rochester, NY 14620–2731, USA
website: www.boydellandbrewer.com

ISBN   978 0 90185 343 1

Series information is printed at the back of this volume

A CIP catalogue record for this book is available
from the British Library

The publisher has no responsibility for the continued existence or accuracy
of URLs for external or third-party internet websites referred to in this book,
and does not guarantee that any content on such websites is,
or will remain, accurate or appropriate

Printed and bound in Great Britain by
TJ Books Limited, Padstow, Cornwall

CONTENTS

Illustrations

Maps

Colour Plates

Tables

Figures

The editor, contributors and publisher are grateful to all the institutions and persons listed for permission to reproduce the materials in which they hold copyright. Every effort has been made to trace the copyright holders; apologies are offered for any omission, and the publisher will be pleased to add any necessary acknowledgement in subsequent editions.

PREFACE AND ACKNOWLEDGEMENTS

The idea for this book germinated some time in 2009/10, when, in common with others interested in the history of church buildings, I wished to consult the mid nineteenth-century church notes compiled by Sir Stephen Glynne. Learning that they had been published in book form for several counties by then, I was frustrated to find that those for Cornwall could be looked at only by thumbing through several volumes of *Notes & Queries* that had appeared in the 1930s, requiring the simultaneous use of both thumbs and many bookmarks. Faced with this inconvenience, I resolved to do better and produce something similar to the volumes published for Derbyshire and Shropshire, or even aspire to a publication in the manner of Somerset and Yorkshire, as an illustrated edition of Glynne's notes. Contact with the Clwyd Record Office in Hawarden, where the notes were then on deposit, was established, and an enormous mass of photocopies of all the Cornish material was despatched to me; in addition, I received not only the blessing of the then county archivist, Claire Harrington, but, crucially, the permission of the owner of the notes, C.A. Gladstone, to publish them. I remain deeply grateful to both individuals.

Whether it was the sheer mass of paper, and (in all honesty) the tedium of transcribing Glynne's writing, or that other research projects intervened, I am not sure, other than the initial flush of enthusiasm faded, and consequent productivity faltered. Such things often happen for the best, however, as knowing that I was part way through my endeavour, my friend and fellow enthusiast on Cornish churches, Jo Mattingly, suggested that I combine Glynne's notes with those of Samuel and Daniel Lysons, compiled as part of their preparation for the publication of the Cornish volume of their series *Magna Britannia*. Most of the Lysons' manuscripts are in the British Library, only briefly catalogued, and in consequence little known; yet Jo had already transcribed their church notes for Cornwall found in Add. Ms. 9462, gave me a copy, and suggested I get on with the job. I found the two sets of notes beautifully complementary, not just chronologically but also from their content. The accounts made by Lysons were generally quite brief, shorthand records of the buildings but frequently illustrated with vignettes of particularly appealing structural or other features, while Glynne's were carefully considered, precise, architectural commentaries.

As I juxtaposed their records of the churches and began to understand the value of their combined first-hand observations, I found myself asking two questions. First, how did these antiquaries physically tour the remote county of Cornwall, and how did their rough fieldnotes contribute to, in the case of Lysons, their *Magna Britannia* project, and for Glynne, the neatly written-up notebook entries? And secondly, subsequent to their accounts, what structural modifications had taken place in the churches to produce the buildings we see today?

Trawling through the Lysons' archive, and the prodigious quantity of their correspondence and other papers in both the British Library and Kresen Kernow (KK), helped me formulate ideas on the Lysons' working methods; and the discovery of Cornish material in Glynne's diaries and one of his notebooks in the National Library of Wales (NLW) provided similar information. And indeed, it was only when I spent lengthy periods of time reading the personalia of these men that I felt I was beginning to understand them: what made them do what they did, how they did it, and with what results. The accolade must go to NLW, Glynne of Hawarden Ms. 185, one of his small, scruffy, field notebooks, which still retains its pencil in a holder on the side. It is a stubby, common thing, and as it had been only roughly sharpened with a knife it had a hard and blunt lead (albeit 175 years old); but it impressed on me as perhaps nothing else did, the sheer physical effort these men had to expend in undertaking their tours and making their careful observations.

The second question was answered, rather more mundanely, by continual devilling in the Devon Heritage Centre (DHC) and KK, sifting through hundreds of diocesan and parochial papers relating to church building projects and other endeavours, enlivened, meanwhile, by the running commentaries made over two centuries and more, by a decanter of rural deans, on the sometimes parlous material state of the churches in their purlieu.

Presented in this – the first of two volumes – are the fruits of this research. The Introduction aims to place both sets of church notes within the context of the survival of Cornish church buildings in the first half of the nineteenth century, their subsequent adaptation and restoration, and associated ecclesiological viewpoints; in addition, I hope it answers the self-imposed questions outlined above. I am very grateful to the Devon & Cornwall Record Society for the opportunity to publish this material, which I hope will prove to be of value to 'church crawlers' and local historians alike, not least in opening up the diversity and depth of the primary sources available in the record offices of Cornwall and Devon.

Any work that has been many years in the gestation usually involves a large number of individuals and organisations, and this book is no exception. The staff in the manuscripts department of the British Library have always been most helpful, and, I think, became resigned to repeatedly delivering up the large, and very heavy, volumes of the Lysons' notes and correspondence. In addition, the members of the imaging department of the library, whilst struggling with the aftermath of a severe cyberattack in the autumn of 2023, have assisted me as well as they were able, and I am deeply grateful to them for allowing me to use my own images of the manuscripts while the department was unable to function. Equal kindness has been shown to me by Alexandra Foulds, archivist at Gladstone's Library, Hawarden, who has been a most helpful correspondent, and enthusiastically aided my research into the Glynne archive there. The staff at the Bodleian Library, Clwyd Record Office, Morrab Library, NLW, and the Society of Antiquaries of London have been very supportive and happily facilitated requests for images of material they hold. Three repositories deserve special mention, however, namely the DHC, Kersen Kernow, and the Courtney Library of the Royal Institution of Cornwall, where the archivists and librarians never blinked in fielding my applications to see all manner of books, documents, photographs, glass slides, and assorted ephemera, and I am deeply indebted to them all.

As indicated in the list of illustrations, apart from the institutional copyright holders, the publishers and I are also very grateful to Charlie Gladstone, Jacqui-Pollard Enys, and Michael Warner, for permission to reproduce material for which they hold the copyright; and the rector of St Deiniol's church Hawarden, and the Parochial Church Council of St Wynwallow's church Landewednack, for allowing me to include photographs of items in their churches. Every effort has been made to trace copyright holders; apologies are offered for any omission, and the publishers will be pleased to add any necessary acknowledgements in subsequent editions.

Many friends and colleagues have also assisted me with this project, and to them I extend my grateful thanks, namely Colin Bradley, Angela Broome (†), Kim Cooper, Christine Edwards, Lydia Fisher, Paul Holden, Alex Hooper (†), Ellie Jones, Catherine Lorigan, Oliver Padel, Nigel Saul, and David Thomas; but I owe special debts of gratitude to Andrew Langdon and Ann Preston-Jones for imparting to me some of their immense knowledge of Cornish medieval crosses; Christian Steer, for photographing the Lysons manuscripts for me; Maxine Symons, for much encouragement and making many transcriptions of documents in the DHC; and both Stuart Blaylock and Michael Warner, for reading and commenting constructively on the Introduction. My editor, Catherine Rider, has been a pleasure to work with, and I have enjoyed responding to her insightful thoughts on my writing, which have greatly improved the text. I am also very grateful to the Trustees of the Yorkist History Trust, and those of the 'Q'-Fund, for awarding generous grant aid towards the costs of illustrations in this volume.

Lastly, however, I owe most of all to Jo Mattingly, not only for facilitating this work and believing in me to bring it to fruition, but for putting her encyclopaedic knowledge of Cornish churches freely at my disposal. In addition, she has read the entirety of the church notes and made numerous corrections and amendments – far too many to acknowledge individually. Without her input, this work would probably never have got off the ground; the fact that it has is a fitting tribute to her consummate understanding of the subject, which is all that needs to be said.

BIBLIOGRAPHIC ABBREVIATIONS

Beacham and Pevsner, *Cornwall*

P. Beacham and N. Pevsner, *The Buildings of England: Cornwall* (New Haven/London, 2014).

Bizley, *Slate Figures*

A.C. Bizley, *The Slate Figures of Cornwall* (Marazion, 1965).

Blight, *West Cornwall*

J.T. Blight, *Churches of West Cornwall; With Notes of Antiquities of the District, etc.* (Oxford/London, 1865).

Cockerham, *Continuity and Change*

P.D. Cockerham, *Continuity and Change: Memorialisation and the Cornish Funeral Monument Industry, 1497–1660* (Oxford, 2006).

Gilbert, *Historical Survey*

C.S. Gilbert, *An Historical Survey of the County of Cornwall, to Which Is Added a Complete Heraldry of the same; With Numerous Engravings*, 2 vols (Plymouth Dock, 1817–20).

Gray, *Gazetteer*

T. Gray, *A Gazetteer of Ancient Bench Ends in Cornwall's Parish Churches* (Exeter, 2016).

Henderson Ms. 'East Cornwall'

C. Henderson, Ms. 'Materials for a Parochial History of East Cornwall, Vizt. of the Hundreds of Trigg, Lesnewth, Stratton, East and West […] from Original Sources, Begun July 1924', Courtney Library, Truro.

Henderson, *Cornish Church Guide*

C. Henderson, *The Cornish Church Guide* (Truro, 1928).

Holden (ed.), *Celebrating Pevsner*

P. Holden (ed.), *Celebrating Pevsner: New Research on Cornish Architecture* (London, 2017).

Holden (ed.), *The Distinctiveness of Cornish Buildings*

P. Holden (ed.), *The Distinctiveness of Cornish Buildings: Conference Papers Marking the Fiftieth Anniversary of the Cornish Buildings Group Presented at St Austell in 2019* (Donington, 2023).

Langdon, *North Cornwall*

A. Langdon, *Stone Crosses in North Cornwall* (*s.l.*, 1992).

Langdon, *Mid-Cornwall*

A. Langdon, *Stone Crosses in Mid-Cornwall* (*s.l.*, 1994).

Langdon, *East Cornwall*

A. Langdon, *Stone Crosses in East Cornwall* (*s.l.*, 1996).

Langdon, *West Penwith*

A. Langdon, *Stone Crosses in West Penwith* (*s.l.*, 1997).

Langdon, *West Cornwall*

A. Langdon, *Stone Crosses in West Cornwall (Including The Lizard)* (*s.l.*, 1999).

Lysons, *Cornwall*

D. and S. Lysons, *Magna Britannia, Being a Concise Topographical Account of the Several Counties of Great Britain: Volume the Third, Containing Cornwall* (London, 1814).

Maclean, *Trigg Minor*

Sir J. Maclean, *The Parochial and Family History of the Deanery of Trigg Minor in the County of Cornwall*, 3 vols (London, 1873–9).

Mattingly, 'Pevsner'

J. Mattingly, 'If Only Pevsner Had Started in the Midlands: Making Sense of Cornwall's Perpendicular Church Architecture', in Holden (ed.), *Celebrating Pevsner*, 74–82.

Mattingly, 'Distinctiveness by Omission'

J. Mattingly, 'Distinctiveness by Omission: Whatever Happened to Cornwall's Chancel Arches?', in Holden (ed.), *The Distinctiveness of Cornish Buildings*, 137–58.

Mattingly, 'Rood Loft Construction'

J. Mattingly, 'Rood Loft Construction, Decoration, and Cult Focus in Ashburton (Devon) and Cornwall from the 1450s to 1548', in J. Barry, J.G. Clark, and W. Richardson (eds), *Education and Religion in Medieval and Renaissance England: Essays in Honour of Nicholas Orme* (Donington, 2023), 74–110.

Mattingly, *Churches of Cornwall*

J. Mattingly, *Churches of Cornwall* (Stroud, 2023).

Orme, *Religious History to 1560*

N. Orme, *A History of the County of Cornwall: Vol.2, Religious History to 1560* (Woodbridge, 2010).

Polsue, *Parochial History*

[J. Polsue], *A Complete Parochial History of the County of Cornwall: Compiled from the Best Authorities & Corrected and Improved from Actual Survey*, 4 vols (Truro/London, 1867–72).

Rogers, 'Church Towers'

J.J. Rogers, 'On the Church Towers of the Lizard district', *TEDAS* 4 (1853), 185–8.

Roscoe *et al.*, *Dictionary*

I. Roscoe, E. Hardy, and M.G. Sullivan (eds), *A Biographical Dictionary of Sculptors in Britain, 1660–1851* (New Haven/London, 2009).

Sedding, *Norman Architecture*

E.H. Sedding, *Norman Architecture in Cornwall: A Handbook to Old Cornish Ecclesiastical Architecture, with Notes on Ancient Manor-Houses* (London, 1909).

Warner, *A Time to Build*

M. Warner, *A Time to Build: Signposts to the Building, Restoration, Enhancement, and Maintenance of Cornwall's Anglican Churches and Mission Rooms 1800–2000* (s.l., 2022).

ABBREVIATIONS

BL	British Library
BVM	Blessed Virgin Mary
CCS	Cambridge Camden Society
CDP	*Cornish and Devon Post*
CL	Courtney Library
CRSBI	Corpus of Romanesque Sculpture in Britain and Ireland
CT	*Cornish Telegraph*
CTimes	*Cornish Times*
DCRS	Devon and Cornwall Record Society
DHC	Devon Heritage Centre
DR	Diocesan Records
EDAS	Exeter Diocesan Architectural Society
FP	*Lake's Falmouth Packet & Cornwall Advertiser*
GL	Gladstone's Library
ICBS	Incorporated Church Building Society
JRIC	*Journal of the Royal Institution of Cornwall*
KK	Kresen Kernow (Cornwall Record Office)
LPL	Lambeth Palace Library
NDJ	*North Devon Journal*
NLW	National Library of Wales
NS	New Series
OED	*Shorter Oxford English Dictionary*
RCG	*Royal Cornwall Gazette*
RIC	Royal Institution of Cornwall
s.l.	*sine loco* [without location of publishing]
TC	*The Cornishman*
TEDA(A)S	*Transactions of the Exeter Diocesan Architectural (and Archaeological) Society*
WB	*The West Briton*
WBCA	*The West Briton and Cornish Advertiser*
WDM	*Western Daily Mercury*

Introduction

On 5 December 1812, the Rev. Charles Mayson, rector of Lezant in Cornwall, wrote to his fellow clergyman Rev. Daniel Lysons, rector of Rodmarton (Gloucestershire), responding to his enquiry about the manor house of Trecarrell, standing in Mayson's parish:

> Sir, a fine Gothick Hall is the only remaining part of the Mansion of Trecarrell, which reaches to the lofty and carved roof; within that there is yet a consider-able portion of the Screen. The Chapel is not a great distance from the house, & when I came to the Parish, part of the Cloister was standing. The Trecarrell arms are carved, or rather cut on the Moor stone (Cornish granite) over the ex-terior entrance of the Hall. Those on the tomb in the Church are the arms of the Trefusis family. I am sorry to add, that the painted glass in the East window was removed, together with the mullions, by a former Rector of Lezant, to introduce a modern sash.[1]

The quantity and variety of information thus related was doubtless very helpful to Daniel and his brother Samuel, in their joint quest for parochial, dynastic, and antiquarian data on the manors and parishes of Cornwall. The two men were working together to accumulate as many particulars as they could, in the preparation of a county volume to be published as part of their nationwide topographical and historical survey, entitled *Magna Britannia* (1806–22). Fundamental to their work was an understanding of a parish and its history, which, for their purposes, was underpinned by a detailed knowledge of the church, its architecture, fixtures, fittings, and monumental antiquities. They painstakingly collected such evidence during expeditions in the field and augmented their findings using antiquarian and documentary sources, leading them to deeper insights into the inter-relationships between the parish, manors, dynasties, and the wider topographical landscape.[2]

Mayson's letter, detailing changes in the church fabric that had occurred within living memory, contained historical nuggets previously unknown to Samuel and Daniel, despite Samuel's own visit to Lezant in 1807. His record of the church is brief, barely more than 'Handsome moor-stone Church', yet for most other parishes Samuel's descriptions are more extensive. The entire corpus of church notes remains in manuscript and is published here for the first time as a valuable, and virtually untapped, historical resource, not least as so many of the brothers' observations were never published.

Alongside the Lysons' collections, this volume places the church notes of Sir Stephen Glynne, a well-heeled baronet with a family seat at Hawarden Castle (Clwyd), who visited Cornwall periodically from the late 1830s to 1870. Glynne's motives for recording churches *in extenso* – principally their architecture, but with a mild interest in their fixtures and fittings – could not have been in more contrast

---

[1]   BL, Add. Ms. 9419, fol. 18r.
[2]   Their church notes for Cornwall are now BL, Add. Mss 9445, 9462.

to those of the Lysons. Simply put, his notes are the fruits of a personal passion for visiting churches – a pastime that took him all over the kingdom and abroad – which were neatly written up in an extended series of notebooks. They were never intended for publication, and although in his lifetime their existence was well known, as a personal archive they were rarely, if ever, used for research by others; there is, for instance, virtually no evidence of input by others in surviving correspondence. Glynne's notes for many counties have since appeared in print, and they are frequently quarried for their detailed – perhaps obsessive – architectural information. Those for Cornwall have previously been published in short instalments in *Notes & Queries* of the 1930s, but that series was incomplete, and reference to them today is not straightforward (Table 1).[3]

Table 1. List of parishes visited by Glynne, and concordance of his manuscript notes and their publication in *Notes & Queries.*

Parish	Dedication (Glynne)	Date of visit	Notebook	Foliation	*Notes & Queries*
Antony	St Anthony & St John	23 Feb. 1849	13	55–6	167, p. 364
Antony	St John	23 Feb. 1849	13	56–7	168, p. 152
Boconnoc		23 Jan. 1842	17	130–1	167, pp. 400–1
Bodmin	St Petroc	21 Feb. 1849	13	59–61	167, pp. 401–2
Breage		July 1843	70	9b–10b	
Broadoak	St Mary	29 Jan. 1854	14	58	167, p. 402
Budock	St Budoc	18 Feb. 1858	16	14–15	
Calstock		24 Apr. 1860	16	16–17	167, p. 439
Camborne	St Martin	11 July 1843	70	7b–8b	
Cornelly	St Cornelius	12 Feb. 1858	16	8	
Crantock		4 Feb. 1854	14	54–5	168, p. 6
Crowan	St Crowens	11 Feb. 1870	16	58–9	168, pp. 6–7
Cubert	St Cuthbert	4 Feb. 1854	14	53–4	168, p. 7
Cury		10 Feb. 1870	16	63–4	168, pp. 42–3
Davidstow	St David	7 Feb. 1870	16	66–7	168, pp. 43–4
Duloe	St Cuby	20 Aug. 1862	16	39–40	168, p. 44
Egloshayle		4 Feb. 1850	14	11–12	168, pp. 44–5
Falmouth		7 July 1843	70	8b–9b	
Feock		22 Aug. 1863	16	43–4	168, p. 75
Forrabury	St Symphorian	1 Feb. 1850	14	15–16	168, pp. 75–6
Fowey	St Finbarrus	30 Jan. 1850	13	61–3	168, p. 76

[3] A collected edition of Glynne's notes for Cornwall was produced, *Sir Stephen Glynne's Notes on the Churches of Cornwall*, ed. T. Cann Hughes, reprinted from *Notes & Queries* (Lancaster, privately printed, 1935), but I have only traced two copies, one in the DHC and the other in KK. A similar edition was produced for Devon.

Parish	Dedication (Glynne)	Date of visit	Notebook	Foliation	*Notes & Queries*
Gorran	St Gorran	1 Feb. 1853	14	44	168, p. 112
Grade	St Grade	17 Feb. 1849	13	50–1	168, pp. 112–13
Gulval	St Gulval	July 1843	70	2b	
Gunwalloe	St Wynwallow	10 Feb. 1870	16	64–5	168, pp. 151–2
Gwennap	St Wenep	26 Aug. 1862	16	45–6	168, p. 152
Jacobstow	St James	23 Jan. 1857	14	68–70	
Kenwyn		1843	17	152–3	168, pp. 152–3
Kilkhampton		<1840	17	74–5	168, p. 183
Lamorran	St Moren	12 Feb. 1858	16	8	168, p. 183
Landewednack	St Lantry	17 Feb. 1849	13	49–50	168, pp. 183–4
Landrake	St Peter	28 May 1852	14	28–9	168, p. 184
Lanhydrock	St Hydrock	26 Jan. 1842	17	132–3	168, p. 219
Lanlivery	St Brevita	23 Aug. 1862	16	47–8	168, p. 219
Lanreath		31 Jan. 1854	14	61–2	168, pp. 219-20
Lansallos		30 Jan. 1850	13	64–5	168, p. 220
Lanteglos-by-Fowey		25 Jan. 1842	17	127–9	168, pp. 255–6
Lanteglos-by-Camelford	St Lantry	25 Oct. 1865	16	33–4	168, p. 256
Launcells	St Andrew	21 Jan 1857	14	71–2	168, pp. 256–7
Launceston		<1840	17	76–8	168, p. 257
Lelant	St Uny	July? 1843	70	5b	
Liskeard		1842	17	126–7	168, p. 258
Lostwithiel		1842	17	131–2	168, p. 259
Ludgvan	St Paul	16 Feb. 1858	16	5–6	168, pp. 259–60
Mabe	St Mabe	18 Feb. 1858	16	13	168, p. 295
Madron	St Madern	16 Feb. 1858	16	6–7	168, p. 296
Maker	St Macra	29 May 1852	14	24–5	168, p. 296
Manaccan	St Antonius	17 Feb. 1858	16	2	168, pp. 296–7
Marazion		10 July 1843	70	6b	
Mawgan-in-Meneage		17 Feb. 1858	16	3–4	168, p. 297
Mawgan-in-Pydar		3 Feb. 1854	14	65–6	168, pp. 329–30
Menheniot	St Neot	18 Feb. 1870	16	59–60	
Mevagissey	St Mewa & St Ida	1 Feb. 1853	14	45	168, p. 331

Parish	Dedication (Glynne)	Date of visit	Notebook	Foliation	*Notes & Queries*
Michaelstow	St Michael	31 Jan. 1850	13	66	168, p. 331
Minster	St Metherian	24 Oct. 1865	16	34–5	168, p. 366
Mullion	St Mulleon	17 Feb. 1849	13	53–4	168, pp. 366–7
Mylor	St Melor	19 Feb. 1849	13	54–5	168, p. 367
Newlyn East	St Newlyn	4 Feb. 1854	14	51-52	168, p. 399
Padstow	St Pedrock	3 Feb. 1850	14	7–9	168, pp. 399–400
Paul		8 July 1843	70	1b	
Perranarworthal	St Piran	26 Aug. 1863	16	42–3	168, p. 437
Perranuthnoe	St Peran	16 Feb. 1858	16	4–5	
Phillack	St Felix	6 Feb. 1854	14	56–7	168, pp. 437–8
Poundstock	St Neot	22 Jan. 1857	14	66–7	168, p. 438
Probus	St Probus & St Grace	20 Feb. 1849	14	1–3	168, pp. 438–9
Redruth	St Uny	Aug. 1862	16	15	169, p. 6
Ruan Major		16 Feb. 1849	13	51–2	169, pp. 6–7
Ruan Minor	St Rumon	16 Feb. 1849	13	52–3	169, p. 7
Saltash		28 May 1852	14	26–7	169, p. 7
Saltash	St Stephen	28 June 1852	14	27–8	169, pp. 7–8
Sancreed		7 Feb. 1870	16	55–6	
Sennen	St Senan	14 Feb. 1849	13	48–9	169, pp. 43–4
Sheviock		22 Jan. 1842	17	124–6	
Sithney	St Sithly	11 Feb. 1870	16	57–8	169, pp. 78–9
South Petherwin	St Paternus	11 Feb. 1858	14	72–4	169, pp. 44–5
St Allen		6 Feb. 1854	14	50–1	167, pp. 363–4
St Anthony-in-Meneage		17 Feb. 1858	16	1–2	168, p. 330
St Anthony-in-Roseland		2 Feb. 1853	14	47–8	167, pp. 364–5
St Austell		12 July 1843	17	153–6	167, pp. 365–6
St Blazey		31 Jan. 1853	14	45	167, p. 400
St Breock		4 Feb. 1850	14	5–6	167, p. 402
St Buryan		15 Feb. 1849	13	47–8	167, pp. 438–9
St Cleer		Aug. 1862	16	37–8	
St Clement		5 Feb. 1854	14	55–6	167, p. 439
St Columb Major		4 Feb. 1850	14	3–5	168, pp. 5–6

Parish	Dedication (Glynne)	Date of visit	Notebook	Foliation	*Notes & Queries*
St Enodoc		2 Feb. 1850	14	10–11	168, pp. 74–5
St Erth		6 Feb. 1854	14	57	168, p. 45
St Gennys		23 Jan. 1857	14	67–8	168, pp. 76–7
St Germans		23 Feb. 1849	13	57–9	168, pp. 111–12
St Gluvias		19 Feb. 1849	13	54	168, p. 112
St Ives		11 July 1843	70	3b–5b	
St Just-in-Penwith	St Just	14 Feb. 1849	13	46–7	168, p. 437
St Just-in-Roseland		2 Feb. 1853	14	47	169, p. 6
St Kew		2 Feb. 1854	14	63–4	168, pp. 182–3
St Keyne		Aug. 1862	16	38–9	168, p. 152
St Levan		28 Aug. 1862	16	46–7	168, p. 258
St Mabyn		2 Feb. 1854	14	64–5	168, p. 295
St Martin-by-Looe		23 Feb. 1849	13	65–6	168, pp. 258–9
St Merryn		3 Feb. 1850	14	6–7	168, pp. 330–1
St Mewan		12 July 1843	17	156–7	168, p. 330
St Michael Penkevil		12 Feb. 1858	16	9–10	168, pp. 400–01
St Michael's Mount		10 July 1843	70	6b–7b	
St Minver		2 Feb. 1850	14	9–10	168, p. 366
St Neot		28 Jan. 1854	14	59–60	168, pp. 367–8
St Stephen-by-Launceston		<1840	17	79–80	168, pp. 257–8
St Teath		9 Feb. 1870	16	65–6	169, pp. 79–80
St Thomas-by-Launceston		<1840	17	78–9	168, p. 257
St Veep		1842	17	129–30	169, p. 113
St Winnow		27 Jan. 1854	14	62–3	169, p. 114
Stithians	St Stithian	26 Aug. 1862	16	44–5	169, pp. 44–5
Stratton		<1840	17	75–6	169, p. 45
Talland	St Tallan	30 Jan. 1850	13	63	169, p. 79
Tintagel	St Symphorian	1 Feb. 1850	14	13–14	169, p. 80
Towednack	St Twinnock	9 Feb. 1870	16	56–7	169, pp. 80–1
Tregony	St James	12 Feb. 1858	16	11–12	

Parish	Dedication (Glynne)	Date of visit	Notebook	Foliation	*Notes & Queries*
Trevalga	St Petroc	1 Feb. 1850	14	14–15	169, p. 81
Truro	St Mary	12 July 1843	17	151–2	169, pp. 112–13
Tywardreath	St Andrew	22 Aug. 1862	16	41–2	169, p. 113
Veryan	St Symphoriana	1 Feb. 1853	14	46	169, pp. 113–14
Wendron	St Wendron	1843	70	10b–11b	
Zennor	St Sennar	14 Feb. 1849	13	45	169, pp. 114–15

For the first time for any county, these two sets of antiquarian notes are published here as an ensemble. With those made by the Lysons dating from the first decade of the nineteenth century, and Glynne's around the middle, they provide, jointly, a broad and objective survey of most of the county's churches at a time when they were starting to undergo yet more structural metamorphoses. Originally constructed pre-Reformation,[4] they were stripped of much imagery and liturgical furniture in the latter part of the sixteenth century, butchered further during the Commonwealth, subsequently converted into Georgianised preaching boxes complete with sash windows, box pews, and galleries, then finally restored, and in many cases rebuilt, in the shape of buildings inspired by the Tractarian Gothic revival of the mid to late nineteenth century. As we shall see, the notes record much of the churches' fabric that has since been remodelled or destroyed, by revealing the appearance and functionality of these buildings at the time these antiquaries visited. Moreover, by studying the Lysons brothers' wider correspondence relating to their Cornish endeavour,[5] we can learn even more: as just one example, for instance, we can infer when and by whom the (presumed medieval) glass was ejected from Lezant church, and the window tracery destroyed.[6] Lastly, they complement the same antiquaries' notes for Devon, as well as those made by James Davidson,[7] in their observations on the non-Cornish part of the diocese of Exeter at that time.

The Lysons brothers, *Magna Britannia*, and the Cornish volume

The Lysons family had been long established in Gloucestershire, being fortunate enough to purchase the manor and associated house of Hempsted, near Gloucester,

---

[4] Until recently, Cornish churches had been envisaged as being re-constructed or enlarged during the fifteenth century, yet the results of dendrochronology analyses of (generally) roof timbers suggest that many church building projects were undertaken in the first half of the sixteenth century, extending even into the 1540s. See, for example, the details for Lansallos in the following inventory of parishes.

[5] BL, Add. Mss 9416–20.

[6] Lysons' correspondent, Rev. Charles Mayson D.D., Fellow of Wadham College, Oxford, (rector 1784–1815), had succeeded his father at Lezant, Rev. Peter Mayson (rector 1770–84). Charles Mayson was writing to the Lysons towards the end of his life therefore, recalling alterations in the church made some forty or fifty years previously.

[7] D. and S. Lysons, *Magna Britannia: Being a Concise Topographical Account of the Several Counties of Great Britain; Volume the Sixth, Containing Devonshire*, 2 vols (London, 1822); *James Davidson's East Devon Church Notes*, ed. J. Cobley, DCRS NS 64 (2021).

from the heirs of Robert Atkins, the county's historian, cementing their ownership by commissioning several monumental inscriptions in the church.[8] Consolidating their county position further, they purchased the advowson of Rodmarton, a small parish twenty miles to the south. Daniel was born there (most likely) in 1762,[9] the eldest son of Samuel Lysons (1730–1804), rector of Rodmarton, with Samuel, as the second son, born two years later.[10] They were both educated at Bath grammar school, but while Daniel progressed to Oxford, proceeding to MA in 1785 and to ordination, Samuel opted for the law, entered at the Inner Temple, and practised as a special pleader before being called to the bar in 1798, when he chose the Oxford circuit. Daniel's first position was as assistant curate at Mortlake (1784–9) and Putney (1789–1800), using his time there, and his already well-honed antiquarian interests, to produce *The Environs of London*, 4 vols (London, 1792–6). This was a topographical account of the parishes within a twelve-mile radius of London, containing numerous etchings by Samuel, who, independently, was turning into an artist of some skill.[11] In 1800, Daniel inherited Hempsted Court and a considerable fortune from his uncle Daniel, a noted physician,[12] and on the death of his father succeeded him at Rodmarton, residing in the rectory there until nearly the end of his life. Samuel meanwhile, capitalising on his legal and city contacts, including Horace Walpole and George III and the royal family, ceased practising law on being appointed keeper of the records in the Tower of London;[13] he too had ventured into publishing, focusing on his archaeological work in Gloucestershire.[14] By 1790, both brothers were Fellows of the Society of Antiquaries, and in 1797 also of the Royal Society, in recognition of their antiquarian and archaeological endeavours.

The first few years of the new century were a fulfilling time for both brothers: Daniel, blessed with private means, and doubtless enjoying only light clerical duties; and the well-connected Samuel, capitalising on his legal training and draughtsmanship. The time was, it seemed to them, propitious for the undertaking of a large archaeo-historical venture – an 'extensive' historical project[15] – *Magna*

---

[8] *Historical, Monumental and Genealogical Collections Relative to the County of Gloucester, by Ralph Bigland*, ed. B. Frith, part 2 (Stroud, 1990), 713–15.
[9] *ODNB*, Daniel Lysons (1762–1834), by E. Baigent, available online at: https://doi.org/10.1093/ref:odnb/17296 [accessed August 2023].
[10] *ODNB*, Samuel Lysons (1763–1819), by G. Goodwin, revised B. Frith, available online at: https://doi.org/10.1093/ref:odnb/17298 [accessed August 2023].
[11] L. Fleming, *Memoirs and Select Letters of Samuel Lysons V.P.R.S., V.P.S.A. 1763–1819* (Oxford, 1934), 4–5, lists the drawings he exhibited at the Royal Academy, 1785–1801, which were almost exclusively interior and exterior views of churches and houses. He was coached by Thomas Lawrence RA.
[12] *ODNB*, Daniel Lysons (1727–1800), G. Goodwin, revised C.L. Nutt, available online at: https://doi.org/10.1093/ref:odnb/17295 [accessed August 2023].
[13] Fleming, *Memoirs*, 27–32, recognising the royal patronage that resulted in this appointment.
[14] Such as, *Etchings of Views and Antiquities in the County of Gloucestershire: Hitherto Imperfectly or Never Engraved* (London, 1791); and *An Account of Roman Antiquities Discovered at Woodchester in the County of Gloucester [...]* (London, 1797). The publishers, T. Cadell and W. Davies, in The Strand, also produced *The Environs of London* and were later to be involved with *Magna Britannia*.
[15] That is, that the history of a locality – parish, hundred, county – forms an essential part of the history of England as a whole. It was also the case that the countryside landscape was rapidly changing at that time, making such a study opportune. The Parliamentary enclosures of the eighteenth century, increasing industrialisation, and the concentration of land in estates

Britannia, Being a Concise Topographical Account of the Several Counties of Great Britain. However, despite the enormous legacy of the brothers' working papers bequeathed to the British Museum in 1833, as Jack Simmons relates, they

> tell us nothing about the genesis of the work itself. Doubtless it had been discussed between the brothers in conversation, perhaps for a long time before it was begun; but either nothing was ever put down on the matter in writing, or nothing was preserved. The project suddenly springs out, complete and under way, late in the summer of 1800. Daniel's succession to the Hempsted estate in the previous March [...] must surely have had something to do with that.[16]

It seems just as likely, however, that they were encouraged in this *grand projet* by their eventual publishers, Thomas Cadell (1773–1836) and William Davies (d. 1819), who had efficiently produced Daniel's four-volume *Environs of London* from 1792 to 1796.[17] The Cadell and Davies partnership specialised in publishing historical, archaeological, and topographical works; hence the proposal of a comprehensive county-by-county series of volumes on the lines of the *Environs*, and tapping into the enthusiasm of the local gentry and *noblesse* at seeing their family descents and manorial inheritances put into print, must have had its attractions. Additionally, the publication by Richard Gough in 1780 of *British Topography* identified many counties – particularly among the first few of those to be listed – as having no adequate historico-topographical account, giving them free reign in a comparatively open field. Cornwall, similarly, had no such literary legacy, other than the works of William Borlase, whose areas of study barely overlapped with the Lysons' intentions. Here, as for the first counties they studied, the way was open to forge a new interpretation of its history.[18]

The overall scheme was to produce a number of volumes, each comprising several parts, one per county, as advertised in the first volume, published in 1806:

> Although copious and well-executed Histories of several Counties have been published, and although the *Britannia* of the learned Camden[19] has been univer-

---

combined to alter the physical nature of parishes and their wider topography; see M. Todd, 'From Romanticism to Archaeology: Richard Colt Hoare, Samuel Lysons and Antiquity', in M. Brayshay (ed.), *Topographical Writers in South-West England* (Exeter, 1996), 90–100.

[16] *Magna Britannia Bedfordshire, by Daniel and Samuel Lysons, with a New Introduction by Jack Simmons* (Wakefield, 1978), ix.

[17] Cadell & Davies was a publishing company formally established in London in 1793, and based in The Strand, when the bookseller and publisher Thomas Cadell I (1742–1802) left the business to his son Thomas Cadell II (1773–1836) and the elder Cadell's apprentice William Davies. Cadell & Davies was wound up after Davies's death in 1819, so the last volume of *Magna Britannia* to be published, of Devonshire in 1822, was simply 'Printed for Thomas Cadell'.

[18] See M. Brayshay, 'Introduction: The Development of Topographical Writing in the South West', in Brayshay (ed.), *Topographical Writers*, 1–33, at 12–19.

[19] This refers to William Camden's *Britannia, siue, Florentissimorum regnorum, Angliæ, Scotiæ, Hiberniæ, et insularum adiacentium ex intima antiquitate chorographica descriptio* [*trans., Britannia, that is, A chorographical description of the flourishing kingdoms of England, Scotland, and Ireland, and the islands adjacent, from the earliest antiquity*] (London, 1586). It comprised a county-by-county description of Great Britain and Ireland and combined studies of their landscape, geography, antiquarianism, and history, suggesting how traces of the past and its antiquities could be revealed in the present state of the country. In

sally and justly regarded as an excellent work relating to the kingdom at large; yet, as the former, besides being for the most part very scarce, are moreover so bulky, as to form of themselves a library of no inconsiderable extent; and as the Britannia gives only a general view of each county; it appears to us that there was still room for a work, which should contain an account of each parish, in a compressed form, and arranged in an order convenient for reference.[20]

This initial volume comprised three parts for the counties of Bedfordshire, Berkshire, and Buckinghamshire. Cambridgeshire and Cheshire formed the two parts of the second volume (1810),[21] but thereafter a separate volume was published for each county: Cornwall (1814), Cumberland (1816), Derbyshire (1817), and Devon, itself in two parts (1822). As Sir Joseph Banks, president of the Royal Society (1778–1820), said to the king, the books were such as to add 'dignity to the Kingdom'.[22] They were, however, large, heavy, and cumbersome volumes, contrary to the brothers' intention of producing something that was not 'so bulky as to form of themselves a library'. The large paper editions were even more substantial, not just in paper size[23] and quality, but because they sometimes incorporated supplementary engravings, also published separately by Cadell & Davies as *Britannia Depicta*.[24] Moreover, as their initial advertisement failed to make clear, the promised 'account[s] of each parish' were to form only a part of their endeavour for each county. In addition to the usual antiquarian focus on ecclesiastical and domestic architecture, funeral monuments, dynasties, their heraldry and patterns of manorial descent, they also encompassed many aspects of social and economic history.

Hence, as already standardised for each county so far, the contents of the third volume for Cornwall comprise (v–vi) 'A General History of Cornwall, Etymology, Ancient Inhabitants, Language, and Government, Historical Events', leading into the 'Ecclesiastical Jurisdiction and Division of the County', market and borough towns, fairs, thereafter accounting for its population and their longevity. A section follows entitled the 'Division of Property at the Time of the Domesday Survey', leading into a description of the nobility, gentry, and their seats. Thereafter there is a 'Geographical and Geological Description', its natural history, produce, trades, and ports, all coming before a comprehensive account of 'British and Roman Antiquities', the architecture,

---

1789, Richard Gough (1735–1809), director of the Society of Antiquaries (1781–91), published an enlarged and illustrated edition of *Britannia*, with a second edition in 1806, the year of the Lysons' first publication.

[20] *Magna Britannia, Volume the First, Containing Bedfordshire, Berkshire, and Buckinghamshire [...]* (London, 1806); the quotation is from the page following the dedication.

[21] Cambridgeshire first appeared as a separate part in 1808 but was reissued with Cheshire in 1810 with continuous pagination throughout.

[22] Fleming, *Memoirs*, 32.

[23] Page size of the standard edition, 28 x 21 cm; of the large paper, 34 x 25.5 cm.

[24] *Britannia Depicta: A Series of Views (with Brief Descriptions) of the Most Interesting and Picturesque Objects in Great Britain, Engraved from Drawings by Messrs. Hearne, Farrington, Smith, Turner, Alexander, &c. by William Byrne; The Counties Alphabetically Arranged*, Part I–[VI] (London, 1806–[18]). Specifically for Cornwall, the large paper copy, in addition to the standard thirty-eight pages of illustrations, incorporates another twenty-four from *Britannia Depicta*, of which five are rural views, and the remainder comprising townscapes, with an accompanying short letterpress for each plate.

fixture, and fittings of churches, concluding with 'Ancient Crosses, Well Chapels, Camps and Earthworks, Miscellaneous Antiquities, Customs and Superstitions &c.'

While naïve and unsatisfactory in some ways, and derivative in others, these introductory sections occupy 252 pages of the Cornish volume and are a remarkable distillation of an enormous body of information gleaned from a wide variety of sources – published and unpublished works, a prodigious amount of corre-spondence, and of course their own notes taken in the field.[25] In addition, these 252 pages compare to the 329 pages (58 per cent of the whole), covering the 203 parishes, demonstrating a subtle but continuous shift in focus away from the tradi-tionalist accounts of parishes, to matters of social history, folklore, and the natural environment.[26] It appears that as the series matured and the format of a historical introduction was retained, the brothers were encouraged to say more on and explore these topics further, rather than adhere to the reliable parochial history model. In writing, they seem to have divided the subject matter between them. In an undated letter (late July/early August 1819) from Daniel to John Hawkins,[27] sent soon after Samuel's death,[28] he wrote,

> I must publish Devonshire [...] I have written the parochial accounts & tran-scribed a great part of it for the press and the account of the families. Unfortu-nately my brother had not written any portion of the heads which were in his department – your kind offer with respect to the geology & mineralogy is most acceptable. Mr. R. Smirke[29] will assist with the architecture & possibly Sir R. Hoare[30] may lend me his assistance as to the Roman remains, earthworks &c.[31]

Fieldwork for Magna Britannia – Cornwall

Both brothers appear to have been involved in the fieldwork at the genesis of the overall project, as on 11 August 1800, Daniel recorded in his diary that he 'set off for Bedfordshire', and on 'October 2. Set off on horseback from Putney for the Tour of Berkshire.'[32] Many of the accompanying drawings in the Berkshire volume are signed by Samuel, demonstrating his early participation as well. Their aim was the complete coverage of a county; as they noted in their 'Introduction' to *Derbyshire*

[25] As discussed in their 'Parochial History', *Cornwall*, 1–7.

[26] For example, in *Magna Britannia 1* (Beds., Berks., and Bucks.), the parochial topography occupies 80 per cent of the book; and in volume 2 (Cambs., Cheshire) it is 71 per cent.

[27] Owner of Bignor Park (Sussex) in 1806, a Fellow of the Royal Society and the Geological Society, and much interested in the Roman villa discovered there in 1811, which had been reported on by Samuel.

[28] Samuel died on 29 June 1819, from heart failure, the unrelenting stress of working on *Magna Britannia* thought by many to have exacerbated his symptoms.

[29] [Sir] Robert Smirke (1781–1867), architect, who in 1813 was nominated as one of the three architects attached to the Office of Works and went on to build one of the biggest and most successful architectural practices of the nineteenth century. This contact of Daniel was no lightweight therefore. See H. Colvin, *A Biographical Dictionary of British Architects 1600–1840* (3rd edn, New Haven/London, 1995), 875–81.

[30] Sir Richard Colt Hoare, 2nd Bt (1758–1838), historian of Wiltshire.

[31] F.W. Steer (ed.), *The Letters of John Hawkins and Samuel and Daniel Lysons 1812–1830* (Chichester, 1966), 49.

[32] Fleming, *Memoirs*, 32.

(2): 'We have, as in other counties, visited all the parish churches.' Whether by foot, horse, gig, or carriage, this was no small undertaking in any county, something quantified in Daniel's reflection that between 24 June 1789 and 24 June 1800, while working on the *Environs of London*, he had walked 19,503 miles.[33] Cornwall, clearly, was a county exceptional in its distances and terrain from those already explored, and it is not easy to deduce how they might have achieved their goal, other than a note in the 'Introduction' (6) that 'the church notes, with notices relating to ancient architecture, &c., were collected during personal visits to every parish in the county in 1805, some of which were repeated in 1811'.

Evidence of these expeditions remains in the manuscript accounts pasted into the pages of the volume of 'Sketches, Drawings and Church Notes' for Cornwall and Cumberland, now BL, Add. Ms. 9462. Most of these records are undated and none are signed, but a visit to Perranzabuloe was made on 9 August 1805, a month after the opening of the new church there. Probably on the same trip there were visits to Launceston on 31 July; Boyton, 1 August; Marhamchurch and Otterham, 3 August; Rough Tor, 5 August; St Columb Major, 8 August; St Mawgan-in-Pydar, 10 August; and Lanlivery, 14 August. These notes appear to have been written exclusively by Samuel, frequently embellished by his sketches, in which he economised on time and paper by drawing only the left half, rather than the whole, of window tracery, or a font.[34] However, the Rev. John Whitaker wrote to an unknown correspondent on 22 August 1805, informing them that 'Messrs Lysons were at Bodmin at the beginning of last week.'[35] This confirms that both brothers were in the county at that time, but whether they travelled together, or independently, to visit churches, perhaps meeting every now and then such as at Bodmin, is unclear.

Something of the atmosphere and enthusiasm in which these field trips were undertaken are imparted in a letter of 1807 from Samuel to Daniel, then resident at his rectory in Rodmarton, and, hence, on an expedition to Cornwall unacknowledged in their 'Introduction':

> St. Columb [Monday] June 1st 1807. Dear Brother, After I wrote to you on Friday [29 May] (which I then mistook) for Thursday, I rode to Cotehale, the approach to which is delightfull, thro' a grove of oaks; it is a curious old house certainly of about Hen. 7ths reign I suppose, tho' the old housekeeper wanted to make me believe it was 800 years old. It is filled with old furniture most of which I suspected and was afterwards informed has been picked up at different times & places by the last and the present Lord. I made a drawing of the court

---

[33] Fleming, *Memoirs*, 33; this reckoning therefore suggests an annual total of over 1,700 miles.

[34] This was relatively standard practice at the time. See, for example, the work of John Carter (1748–1817), such as the elevation of the west front of Exeter Cathedral (BL, Add. Ms. 29943, fol. 82), and other drawings, in preparation for his *Plan, Elevations, Sections and Specimens of the Architecture [...] Cathedral Church of Exeter* (London, 1797); or those by Samuel Buck (1696–1779), of houses in Yorkshire (now BL, Lansdowne Ms. 914), for which see *Samuel Buck's Yorkshire Sketchbook*, intro. I. Hall (Wakefield, 1979), 41, 43, 550, 51, 55, and many others. I am grateful to Stuart Blaylock for discussing this with me and pointing me to these references.

[35] KK: RP16/138. Whitaker was rector of Ruan Lanihorne (1777–1808) and a keen historian; the recipient of the letter is not known, but it is deposited in the archive of the Rogers family of Penrose, Helston.

withinside, which will make a good subject for a plate.[36] When at Cotehele, finding that I was only a mile from St. Dominick I proceeded thither & saw the Me-
lyttis Melisifolia or whatever you call it (I forget) on my road.[37] At St. Dominick
I met with a very obliging man in the Rector Mr. Clarke[38] who was just going to
dinner & pressed me to stay, he gave me some Cachagee Cyder[39] (made I think
he said at his father's in Somersetshire) the finest I have tasted – and some very
capital Dufflin Cyder made at Calstock which is a noted place for it, the Dufflin
is a sort of small russet. On my return to Callington in the evening I took St. Mel-
lion & Pillaton. In Callington Church I found an alabaster Monument with the
effigies of a Knight of the Garter about the time as I should suppose of Edward
4 or the beginning of Henry 7. The sexton woman told me it was a Lord Roos.

Sat. 5, Morning.[40] I rode by way of Southill, Linkinhorn, Stoke [Climsland]
& Lezant, to Launceston, are without a good deal of note; the next morning I
did what I wanted ^to my diary^ from under a doorway, & having lost a day,
did not know that it was Sunday 'till I heard the bells go for Church! There are
200 French Officers prisoners at Launceston, some of whom were at Church.
They made a curious appearance, some of them with great coats with Capes 2
feet deep – to cover over their hats by way of [a] hood. In the afternoon I rode
to Bodmin to a late dinner. This morning [Monday, 8 August] I called on Mr.
Gilbert[41] who was very civil as was also Mr. Wallis[42] who will send me a very
compleat list of the Clergy with those who are resident marked, and the post
towns. He is registrar or something or other – said he was just returned from the
visitation with the Archdeacon. I have been at Rialton & took notes of the house
& a copy of the ancient inscription which appears to me to be HONEMIM[ORUS]
TRIBUNUS.[43] It is more legible than any one I have seen in Cornwall. I called

---

[36] Published as *Cornwall*, pl. opp. ccxliv. No preparatory sketch for this plate appears to have
survived.

[37] In their introduction (cxcix), Lysons mention that 'the *melittis grandiflora*, [grows]
between Cotehele and St. Dominic', which is presumably the species name that Samuel was
endeavouring to recall. This is still a recognised name for the plant, more commonly known
as 'Bastard Balm', although the Royal Botanic Gardens at Kew have it more precisely categorised as *Melittis melissophyllum subsp. Melissophyllum*. The species name (rather than the
genus name) here relates closely to Samuel's attempt, with -phyllum and -folia approximately
synonymous.

[38] Rev. John Clarke, rector (1803–35).

[39] The Cachagee/Coccagee is regarded as one of the oldest and best of cider apples, originating in Ireland, but which, *c.* 1710, was taken to Somerset and promoted in the area around
Minehead as being suitable for cider. Thereafter it was commonly planted in the west of
England. See R. Hogg, *The Apple and Its Varieties: Being a History and Description of
the Varieties of Apples Cultivated in the Gardens and Orchards of Great Britain* (London,
1859), 57.

[40] This would in fact be Saturday, 6 August.

[41] Davies Gilbert (1767–1839), scientific administrator, applied mathematician, and historian,
MP for Bodmin (1806–32).

[42] John Wallis (1759–1842), solicitor, mayor of Bodmin seven times, registrar of the archdea-
conry court (1795–1842), town clerk of Bodmin (1798–1830).

[43] This stone was at Rialton Barton, but in 1991 it was moved to the Royal Cornwall Museum,
Truro. See Lysons, *Cornwall*, ccxxiii, for the stone, sketched in BL, Add. Ms. 9462, fol. 7v.;
for a description, see E. Oshaka, *Corpus of Early Christian Inscribed Stones of South-west
Britain* (London, 1993), 220–3. For Rialton, see *Cornwall*, ccxliv.

with Mr. Gilbert this morning on his sister Mrs. Semple, who now lives with
him at Bodmin.
St. Austell, 12 o'clock Tuesday [9 August]. I fear it is set in for a wet day
and that I shall be able to do no more than reach Menabilly,[44] in which case I
cannot expect to finish my work at Fowey, & get further than Lostwithiel or
Liskeard tomorrow, and shall probably find the 8 remaining churches will take
me two days, and if so I should hardly get to Dartington before Sunday morning,
as there is also a Devonshire Church or two near the Tamar which it would be
quite out of my way to take at any other time. There is one where the Rector is
a Mr. Hobart (of the 'N' family) whom I saw for a few minutes at Mr. Clarke's
at St. Dominick. I shall finish as I go, tho' I should be delayed for a day or two
[...] My road today lay by way of ^St.^ Roach & over Henborough Down, from
the top of which is the most extensive view in Cornwall. There is a beacon with
a soldier constantly to guard it. I don't intend going round the sea coast by West
Looe as I had intended, since I find I have less time to spare than I expected, & it
would delay me a good deal. With much love I remain your affectionate Brother,
S. Lysons.[45]

The frank and gossipy nature of this fraternal correspondence – the 'taking' of
churches together with a wide variety of other observations – provides an insight
into the difficulties, yet opportunities, of a tour in the south of the county. For
example, the Saturday started at Callington, where presumably he had lodged, via
several small and remote parishes, ending up at Launceston, a total of around twenty
miles over deeply rural terrain. This compares not unreasonably with the excursions
of Rev. J.H. Mason, the rural dean of Trigg Major, where in 1808 he once rode
twenty-six miles in a single day, as well as meeting the wardens and incumbents at
nine churches.[46] All these journeys, too, were undertaken on roads described in 1809
as 'very narrow, crooked, and dirty; continually up and down',[47] although Samuel
noted the road from Bodmin to Altarnun was 'not very hilly [...] with some pretty
scenery', and around Temple Moor he travelled on an 'excellent road of gravel
formed of decomposed moor stone'.[48]
Yet how Samuel, as a stranger, navigated these minor roads, is open to question.
The mail coach routes, turnpike and carriage roads were well recognised and receive

[44] Presumably hosted by Philip Rashleigh (1729–1811), the mineralogist and antiquary; the
Lysons later acknowledge assistance from his brother Charles Rashleigh (1747–1823).
[45] BL, Add. Ms. 9418, fols 353r.–354r.
[46] Mason was vicar of Treneglos and Warbstow (1804–57), and when on his duties as rural
dean recorded that between 22 September and 8 October 1808, he covered a total of 151 miles,
from Morwenstow in the north to Davidstow in the south, KK: P4/2/43. Journeys of twenty
to thirty miles were undertaken not uncommonly by churchwardens in the sixteenth century
and later, travelling to visitations and church courts, for instance, but they would have ridden
directly to their destination rather than touring the countryside; see J. Mattingly, 'Travel as
Duty: Some Tudor Churchwardens in the West Country', in C.M. Barron and M. Carlin (eds),
Medieval Travel: Proceedings of the 2021 Harlaxton Symposium (Donington, 2023), 222–32.
[47] T. Gray (ed.), *Cornwall. The Travellers' Tales, Volume 1* (Exeter, 2000), 84, from Louis
Simond's *Journal of a Tour and Residence in Great Britain [...]* (Edinburgh, 1815).
[48] BL, Add. Ms. 9462, fol. 60r. This is also confirmed by Rev. Swete a decade or so earlier; 'A
Tour in Cornwall in 1780 by the Rev. John Swete M.A.', ed. P.A.S. Pool, *JRIC* NS 6.3 (1971),
185–219, at 194.

three full pages of coverage in *Cornwall* (cxci–cxciii), albeit, perhaps ruefully, the account concludes with 'The cross-roads are not much travelled.' In 1789, John Cary had produced a new set of county maps to illustrate Richard Gough's translation of Camden's *Britannia*, and the Cornish map is crammed with intricate detail about villages, hamlets, and even farmsteads.[49] The Lysons brothers would have been well aware of this publication and the map for Cornwall, and it may have assisted Samuel in planning his journeys, together with information gleaned from the inhabitants of the villages he passed through. Another cartographic aid would have been *A New and Accurate Map of the County of Cornwall from an Actual Survey*, by Thomas Martyn (1748), either in its one-inch to one-mile scale, perhaps as separate sheets when on the road, or in its reduced format published in 1784.[50] When Francis Rodd of North Hill wrote to Daniel on 7 March 1813, he sketched a shield bearing 'the arms of Wadge as described on Martin's map of Cornwall', so clearly he expected Lysons to be aware of this source.[51]

Circulation of the Parochial Queries, and subsequent correspondence

Samuel mentions in his letter John Wallis's intention to send Daniel a 'very compleat list' of clergy, which they required to start circulating, county-wide, a two-page questionnaire, usually addressed to a parochial incumbent, and/or a gentleman landowner, which requested answers to enquiries about the parish, landowners, and manorial holdings. This was an investigative mechanism adopted early on for the first counties of *Magna Britannia*[52] and may well have been inspired by the method employed by Rev. Jeremiah Milles, dean of Exeter, in his research into the history of Devon.[53] These documents were individually written to start with, but later, as the format proved successful, they were printed on foolscap sheets,[54] leaving space in which the responses were to be entered; an encouragement was that they could be returned to Daniel at Rodmarton post-free.[55] By the time the questionnaires were

---

[49] *Britannia, or, A Chorographical Description of the Flourishing Kingdoms of England, Scotland, and Ireland, and the Islands Adjacent, from the Earliest Antiquity/by William Camden; Translated from the Edition Published by the Author in MDCVII; Enlarged by the Latest Discoveries, by Richard Gough [...]*, 3 vols (London, 1789). Specifically for the maps see R.C.E. Quixley, *Antique Maps of Cornwall and the Isles of Scilly*, 2nd edn expanded by J.M.E. Quixley (Penzance, 2018), 138–41.

[50] Quixley, *Antique Maps*, 118–21. It is also listed by R. Gough, *British Topography*, 2 vols (London, 1780), i, 276.

[51] BL, Add. Ms. 9419, fol. 332r. The 146 shields of arms of the subscribers appeared only on the original 1748 publication, to which Rodd was a subscriber.

[52] *Magna Britannia Bedfordshire [...] Simmons*, x.

[53] Jeremiah Milles (1714–84) circulated his 'Parochial returns' among Devonshire parishes, reaping rewards in the replies to a long and varied list of printed questions. Milles was president of the Society of Antiquaries (1769–84), and although his term of office did not directly coincide with the Lysons' Fellowships, they must have been aware of his reputation, research, and methodology, duly promoted by Richard Gough; see Gough, *British Topography*, i, 301; and *ODNB*, Jeremiah Milles (1714–84), by P.W. Thomas, available online at: https://doi.org/10.1093/ref:odnb/18752 [accessed October 2023].

[54] By Strahan and Preston, Printers Street, London.

[55] This was a concession engineered for the brothers by Francis Freeling (1764–1836), secretary to the Post Office, who was a bibliophile and Fellow of the Society of Antiquaries; *Magna Britannia Bedfordshire [...] Simmons*, x.

circulated in Cornwall in 1807, additional queries were hand-written on the printed sheets, sometimes specific to an individual parish. Perhaps this was a sign that Daniel was already champing at the bit to get started on the county and tailoring his enquiries following his 1805 expedition.

In a letter (unattributed but likely to Rev. Richard Gerveys Grylls (1758–1841), rector of Helston) of 17 August 1807, Daniel wrote:

> We return ourselves very much obliged to you for your kind offer of procuring information for us in answer to our Queries of the parishes with which you are involved. Our papers are prepared for all the parishes in the County but not having received as yet a corrected list of Clergy & Parishes with the post towns of each, which Mr. Wallis has been so good as to promise us – those only are yet sent out which we knew properly how to address […] Our Queries we hope will not in general be deemed very troublesome and have endeavoured to make them as little as possible, while collecting whatever we could obtain from ancient public records & personal observations.[56]

Wallis evidently supplied the list, and the questionnaires were duly despatched. A typical example is that for Illogan, which introduced,

> The Revd. Daniel Lysons, and Mr Samuel Lysons, being engaged in the publication of a work entitled 'Magna Britannia,' in which they propose to give a short account of every parish in each county, will be very much obliged to *Mr Basset, or the resident Minister*, if he will have the goodness to favour them with answers to the following queries. I. The distance and bearing of *St. Illogan* from the two nearest market towns? II. What are the principal Villages in the parish? III. Are there any, and what Gentlemen's seats in the parish? IV. What ancient seats of Gentry or Nobility, in a state of decay, or occupied as farm houses? *Qu. as to the forms or any ancient families becoming extinct, or if extinct only in the male line; by what families now are principal.* V. What Manors are there in the parish? who are the present Proprietors? and through what Families have they passed of late years, as far as can be ascertained with certainty? *Qu. whether Sir John St Aubyn's Manor of Treloweth is in St Illogan parish?*[57] VI. Are there any Alms-houses, or endowed Schools in the parish? VII. Are there any Chapels, or sites of decayed Chapels, in the parish?[58] (Figs 1a/b)

The correspondent who completed and returned this questionnaire was the curate, Rev. J.J. Keigwin, who followed up with a letter of 22 June 1808:

---

[56] BL, Add. Ms. 9417, fol. 229r. The letter was written only a few days after he must have received Samuel's, so it seems rather precipitate to have expected the list from John Wallis in the intervening period.

[57] The written response was 'The Estate of Treloweth in this Parish belongs to Honble. Mr. Agar and not Sir Jno. St Aubyn; he came to it by marriage of Miss Hunt, the niece of the late Mr. Hunt of Landhitherock [Lanhydrock] in this County.' This was the Hon. Charles Begenal Agar (1769–1811), who on his marriage in 1804 with the sole heiress and representative of her great-uncle Henry Robartes, 3rd earl of Radnor, retired from legal practice in London to manage the Cornish estates.

[58] BL, Add. Ms. 9418, fols 184r.–v. The words italicised have been written in.

Mr. Wallis, who handed me these two letters containing certain Queres respecting the Manore & families in the two parishes of Illogan and Camborne, desired
me to answer them & annex the Answers to the Queres; which I have done to
the best of my Information – and I believe it will be found pretty correct: should
there be any more information in my power to afford you in your arduous work,
respecting these Parishes, I shall be glad to give it to you. The authors that have
written on the antiquities of Cornwall are Borlase, Carew, Hals,[59] part of whose
parochial History was printed alphabetically as far as the letter I – the rest is in
manuscript I believe in the possession of Mr. Rose Price, Keneggy near Penzance, Cornwall, & would be of great use to you, could it be obtained. Tonkin's
M.S. which is in the possession of Lord de Dunstanville, is a work of superior &
more useful merit to the former: as it does not deal so much in idle scandalous
stories, as the former.[60]

He concludes,

Would any one of you Gentlemen have the goodness to give ^me^ the inscription that is on the font, which formerly belonged to Camborne Church, & is now,
in the plantation near the pond at Tehidy. Mr. Jenkins of Treworgy told me one
of you copied the Inscription in his presence.[61]

Clearly, if the questionnaire had been delivered to 'Mr Basset',[62] he delegated the
duty of responding to John Wallis, the registrar, who in turn tasked Keigwin to
answer the questions for both Camborne and Illogan ('these two letters'), the process
taking many months.

Yet the spirit of the correspondence is typical of the manner in which the
questionnaires were digested; as the Lysons acknowledge in their 'Introduction'
(6–7), they were willingly assisted by many interested parties. This assistance
took several forms. First, the printed questionnaire, or an awareness of it, became

---

[59] Richard Carew (1555–1620), was an Elizabethan antiquary and member of a prominent
gentry family at Antony. His *Survey of Cornwall* (London, 1601) was only the second history
of an English county to be published. It was republished in 1811 in a greatly expanded edition
by Lord de Dunstanville, Keigwin's ultimate patron. William Borlase (1696–1772), rector
of Ludgvan (1722–72), was an antiquary, naturalist, and geologist, publishing three major
works on the antiquities and natural history of the county and the Isles of Scilly. William Hals
(1655–1737?), a gentleman antiquary, devoted much of his life to the preparation of a history
of Cornwall, but as Keigwin's letter relates, only a portion was published *c.* 1750 (parishes
A–Helston). His manuscript (now BL, Add. Ms. 29762) was incorporated into the works of
Cornish historians in the nineteenth century. See J. Walker, 'Cornwall', in C.R.J. Currie and
C.P. Lewis (eds), *English County Histories: A Guide* (Stroud, 1994), 85–90. For Hals, see J.
Whetter, *Cornish People in the 18th Century* (Gorran, 2000), 1–15.
[60] The contribution of Thomas Tonkin (1678–1741/2) to the study of Cornish history is often
underrated, as his work remains in a fragmentary state, in manuscript, although after his death
his material was used by several authors, such as William Borlase, Lord de Dunstanville, and
Davies Gilbert; see H.L. Douch, 'Thomas Tonkin: An Appreciation of a Neglected Historian',
JRIC NS 4.2 (1962), 145–80.
[61] BL, Add. Ms. 9418, fol. 185r. Samuel made three sketches of the font at Tehidy, BL, Add.
Ms. 9462, fols 23v., 24r.
[62] Sir Francis Basset, 1st Bt (1757–1835), of Tehidy, Illogan, retired from Parliament in 1796
(MP for Penryn 1780–96) and thereafter devoted himself to agricultural and antiquarian
interests on his considerable estates.

St. Illogan R.

(Deanery of Penwith)

The Rev^d. DANIEL LYSONS, and Mr. SAMUEL LYSONS, being engaged in the publication of a work entitled " MAGNA BRITANNIA," in which they propose to give a short account of every parish in each county, will be very much obliged to *Mr. Basset or the resident Agent* if he will have the goodness to favour them with answers to the following queries.

I. THE distance and bearings of *St. Illogan* from the two nearest market towns? *Two Miles from Redruth to Truro 10 Miles the former lies south east the latter east from Illogan; from the former North west from the latter west which is the Post Town? Redruth*

II. What are the principal Villages in the parish?
Pool & Portreath or Bassets Cove

III. Are there any, and what Gentlemen's seats in the parish?
Tehidy Park – The seat of Lord de Dunstanville

IV. What ancient seats of Gentry or Nobility, in a state of decay, or occupied as farm houses.
N.B. Names of the Chief Gentry Nanze the seat formerly of the Nanzes who are now extinct & had occupied by Hugh Phillips Farmer In as to the freehold of de Dunstanvilles. The times of any ancient families becoming extinct or if extinct only in the male line or what families now represented. The time of the Nanze extinction not Known — what became of the Ascendants if any.

V. What Manors are there in the parish? who are the present Proprietors?

Nancekute
Nancekute

prietors? and through what Families have they paffed of late years, as far as can be afcertained with certainty? *The manors in this Parish are Iskedy & Nancekute, both belonging to L.? de Dunstanville; the latter came by purchase of the Rodd family of Devonshire into the Rodd Family, about 60 or 70 years ago* ✕ *Rodd*

The Eftate of ... in this Parish belongs to Hon.ble M.r Agar ✕

VI. Are there any Alms-houfes, or endowed Schools in the parifh? *One Alms House — for four widows or old women — endowed by the Hon.ble Mifs Baffet — The Daught.r of L.d de Dunftanville — There is no endowed school in the Parish — There is one at Pool ... has a benefaction from L.d De Dunftanville*

VII. Are there any Chapels, or fites of decayed Chapels, in the parifh? *None.—*
A new chapel now in building by L.d de Dunftanville to be endowed by him, & to be opened ... Who is Patron of the Rectory? There are some Meeting Houses belonging to the Wesleian Methodists ... Lord de Dunftanville in this Parish—

Mr. Baffett is requefted to addrefs The Rev. Mr. LYSONS, under cover to FRANCIS FREELING Efq. General Poft-Office.

✕ *And not S.r Jno. St. Aubyn — he came to it by marriage of Mifs Hunt — The Niece of the late M.r Hunt of Lanhidrock in this County.*

common currency within the networks of gentry communication. Francis Vyvyan Iago (Arundell), rector of Landulph (1805–46), an archaeologist of note and Fellow of the Society of Antiquaries,[63] wrote to Daniel, 'Mr. Carew, whom I saw a day or two since, asked me if your Queries on Antony, Sheviock & the adjoining Parishes had been satisfactorily answered – if not, and you would mention the deficiencies to me, he would use his best endeavours to assist in supplying them.'[64] John Austen, of Place, Fowey, commented to Daniel,

> I was right in my conjecture about Mr. William Rashleigh of Menabilly having a number of valuable papers – he found them just before he went to Town – but had no time to copy them for you, which I lamented much, as I think the correspondence he has about the time of the Rebellion, would have thrown much light on the Cornish politics of the day.[65]

Secondly, ecclesiastical links were also important, not least as the Queries were addressed to the parish incumbent. Assistance was offered at the outset by John Fisher, bishop of Exeter (1803–7), suggesting worthwhile clerical and other contacts on their tours of the county:

> Archdeacon Moore[66] upon his Visitation, – & I upon mine, have prepared the Clergy to expect you, & you will find them ready to give you every assistance in their power. At Bodmin I wish you to apply to Mr. Gilbert the Clergyman:[67] he will not only give you all the Information you may want himself, but he will point out to you those Gentlemen from whom you may receive assistance. If you go Southward from Bodmin to Lostwithiel you will meet with a valuable Clergyman at St. Winnow, Mr. Walker[68] – at St. Austell you ^will^ inquire for Charles Rashleigh Esq. at Duport.[69] Between Grampound & Tregony you will meet with great assistance from F. Gregor Esq., the Member of the County:[70] not far from him lives Mr. Whitaker who has written many things on the history and antiquities of Cornwall.[71] At Truro you will see the Minister of the Place Mr. Carlyon,[72] and about 3 miles from Truro L. Gwatkin Esq.[73] At Penryn near

---

[63] ODNB, Francis Vyvyan Jago Arundell (1780–1846), by W.P. Courtney, rev. C. North, available online at: https://doi.org/10.1093/ref:odnb/715 [accessed January 2024]. He assumed the name 'Arundell' in 1815.

[64] BL, Add. Ms. 9418, fol. 261r., dated 12 August 1812, so well over four years since the Queries were originally circulated.

[65] BL, Add. Ms. 9416, fol. 44v., dated 7 February 1813.

[66] Rev. George Moore, archdeacon of Cornwall (1788–1807).

[67] This individual is difficult to identify; possibly Rev. Thomas Gilbert, vicar of Constantine (1774–1817) and a prebendary of Exeter (1800–15) is intended? The incumbent at the time of the bishop's letter was the Rev. John Pomeroy (1778–1813).

[68] Rev. Robert Walker, vicar of St Winnow (1781–1834).

[69] Charles Rashleigh (1747–1823) was an entrepreneur who built Duporth Manor, half a mile inland from his later coastal developments at what is now Charlestown.

[70] Francis Gregor (1760–1815), MP for the county of Cornwall (1790–1806), of Trewarthenick, in Tregony.

[71] Rev. John Whitaker, rector of Ruan Lanihorne (1777–1808).

[72] Rev. Thomas Carlyon, rector of St Mary's Truro (1802–26).

[73] Robert Lovell Gwatkin (1757–1843), of Killiow, Kea.

Falmouth I wish you to inquire for Mr. Canon Howel of Gluvius:[74] he will assist you much. At Helston Mr. Grylls[75] a Clergyman will be very useful to you. At Marazion inquire for Mr. Hutchens of St. Hilary[76]: at Penzance, Mr. Borlase of Castle Horneck.[77] On the Northern Coast at Camborne you will be assisted by Stackhouse Esq. of Pendarvis,[78] at Redruth Mr. Rogers the Clergyman will assist you.[79] At Helston you will hear of Mr. Polwhele who has promised me to assist you – he is at this time engaged in a History of Cornwall.[80]

These gentlemen are all I know personally. They will, I am sure, assist you to the best of their knowledge. Should I not have left Exeter before your return I shall be most happy to wait upon you & your Brother.[81]

This list was a veritable *Who's Who* in the county at that time, and of course, with episcopal invitations thus issued, the brothers would surely have been guaranteed a welcome in many parts of the county. In like manner, Rev. William Short, archdeacon of Cornwall (1807–28), wrote that he would be

extremely happy to be instrumental in obtaining any information you are in want of, by dispersing your papers at the next visitation, and recommending your work to the attention of the clergy. My visitation commences on the eighth of May in Launceston. If therefore you can forward your papers before that time to Mr. Wallis at Bodmin, he will arrange them in such a way that the clergy may obtain them without difficulty or expense.[82]

Similarly involved with the clergy on the Lizard, Rev. Grylls policed their responses, highlighting some of the pitfalls of this kind of circular questionnaire. Writing as late as 1812, he informed Daniel that

---

[74] Rev. John Howell (d. 1824), vicar of Gorran (1796–1824), curate of Penryn (1796).

[75] Rev. Richard Gerveys Grylls (d. 1841), curate of Helston, vicar of Breage, Cury, Germoe, and Gunwalloe from 1809, and vicar of Luxulyan (1813–52).

[76] Rev. Malachi Hitchins, vicar of St Hilary (1775–1809).

[77] Rev. William Borlase (1741–1812), vicar of Madron and Zennor, nephew of William Borlase the antiquary.

[78] This may be intended to be John Stackhouse (1741–1819), naturalist, although his funeral monument in Camborne church records he moved to Bath in 1804, so probably before the date of this letter. Pendarves was thereafter occupied by Edward William Stackhouse (1775–1853), MP for Lostwithiel (1826–53).

[79] Rev. Hugh Rogers (1780–1858), rector of Redruth until 1816, and thereafter of Camborne (1816–58).

[80] Rev. Richard Polwhele (1760–1838), poet, topographer, theologian, and literary chronicler, published a *History of Cornwall* in seven volumes (1803–8). He adopted a literary and cultural focus rather than a more traditional antiquarian approach, yet the Lysons' work might have been seen as a serious competitor in this genre.

[81] BL, Add. Ms. 9417, fols 127r.–128v. The letter is undated, but Fisher was translated to Salisbury in 1807, and Francis Gregor resigned from Parliament in 1806, so the letter must relate to the Lysons' initial tour in the county in 1805. Many of the individuals mentioned corresponded with Daniel during his preparation for publication of the volume.

[82] BL, Add. Ms. 9419, fol. 414r., undated.

Mr. Wills[83] accidentally mislaid your Queries, but on the presumption of you having seen his Curate, Mr. Trevethan, [and] from him obtained the required Information, he was unwilling to trouble you by asking for them again. If you will, however, now send them he will answer them as well as he can both at Wendron and Helston. Mr. Stephens, Rector of Landewednack & Ruan Major,[84] writes me, that he sent his Answers to you to the General Post Office according to your Request. But that if you will forward the Queries to him again under a Frank, he will reply to them immediately. Mr. Willcock, Curate of Mullyon, & who also officiates at Grade, will most readily answer the Queries on receiving them.[85] I have not yet heard from Mr. Whitehead, Curate of St. Keverne,[86] but I have no doubt of his ready compliance here.[87]

Lastly, there were numerous individuals who took immense pains on behalf of the brothers, almost always responding to a flurry of letters from Daniel, who capitalised (perhaps unwittingly? – certainly unashamedly) on their good nature, to answer a range of queries that mined their expertise. Francis Basset, FRS, 1st Lord de Dunstanville, was a frequent correspondent offering much information not just on dynastic and manorial matters but on the mining industry as well.[88] John Austen, of Place, Fowey, having inherited the Treffry estates, was a prolific source of antiquarian and genealogical information, with the contents of his letters – often seven or eight sides of paper crammed with writing – accompanied by laboriously drawn-out pedigrees, as well as a plan of Fowey harbour in 1812.[89] While Richard Carew at Antony was not quite so helpful,[90] John Wallis, registrar at Bodmin, wrote nearly a hundred letters, in addition to doing whatever he could to act as the clearing house for the clergy's responses to the Queries.[91] Richard Polwhele also assisted, but one senses a degree of reticence in his correspondence, perhaps surmising that the Lysons were attempting to republish his own work. There were, however, other constraints upon his co-operation, as although he wanted a copy of *Cornwall* on publication, he was able only to offer some of his own publications in exchange, because 'my family of 13 children are in the way of all such purchases'.[92]

As well as maintaining a high frequency of correspondence with Daniel, many of these gentlemen-antiquary-clergymen went to considerable personal lengths to assist. John Rogers of Mawnan visited Mullion church and 'ascertained the date of the building. Over one of the arches [...] within the chancel is the following

[83] Rev. Thomas Wills, vicar of Wendron and Helston (1784–1837).
[84] Rev. John Nichols Stevens, rector of Landewednack and Ruan Major (1799–1822).
[85] Rev. William Wilcock, curate of Mullion (1810–16), Grade, and Ruan Minor (1813–16).
[86] Rev William Whitehead, curate of Grade and Ruan Minor in 1803.
[87] BL, Add. Ms. 9417, fol. 234r., dated 4 April 1812. As this letter was written some five years after the initial circulation of the Queries, it invites speculation as to the initial overall response, and how many parishes had to be chased up, albeit something beyond the scope of this essay.
[88] BL, Add. Ms. 9417, fols 11–97.
[89] BL, Add. Ms. 9416, fols 17–78, the plan of the harbour at fol. 28r.
[90] BL, Add. Ms. 9416, fols 234–85.
[91] BL, Add. Ms. 9420, fols 180–372.
[92] BL, Add. Ms. 9419, fol. 218r., dated 25 August 1814, post-publication of *Cornwall*.

inscription', and he continued with a transcript, a description of the woodwork, glass, and a painted figure on the chancel screen. He concluded by reporting: 'Over an arch in the south part of the chancel is another inscription, which I could not at once decipher. If upon a second visit I succeed [...] I will send you a copy.'[93] Sure enough, a month later, Rogers sent a neatly drawn facsimile of the two inscriptions: 'They are cut in relief in oak, & upon scraping off some of the whitewash I found the first of them had originally been gilt.'[94] Rev. W.L. Morgan of Lewannick replied to Daniel:

> I examined the Register of this Parish for the name Lower but could nowhere find it. I then went to South Petherwyn and examined that Register but could not there succeed. I then went to North Hill and in the Church-yard I found a small headstone erected to the memory of Alexander Lower of the parish.[95]

Rev. C. Cardew of St Erme had 'sent to St. Ives for the Corporation Seal, but received no answer till last evening. I now inclose it.'[96] And after several years of correspondence, even the industrious John Austen of Place concluded that recording all the heraldry in the church of Lanteglos-by-Fowey was a step too far: 'In fact [...] I found that unless I took up my abode in the Church for a week, with sponge, washkit and soap, it would be impossible for me to copy these Arms.'[97]

Not everyone was so enthusiastic or co-operative, however. In 1808, Rev. Francis Vyvyan Iago sent them

> a correct list of the Parishes in the Deanery of East, the names of the Incumbents & the officiating Clergymen. I cannot positively point out to you who are, & who are not likely to attend to your Queries, but am afraid the number of persons who will answer them satisfactorily will be very few. Those I have marked appear to be the most likely.[98]

In this manner, an undated and unsigned response stated: 'From the short period of time which has elapsed since Mr. Kingdon became acquainted with the parishes of South Petherwin & Trewen, he must beg leave to decline answering Messrs. Lysons queries for the moment.'[99] The curate at Lanhydrock replied: 'I must request that you will not impune to intentional Rudeness or Neglect my having taken no Notice of your letter before.'[100] And although the curate at Landrake was clearly more enthused, 'I should have answered your Queries sooner but have been wanting

---

[93] BL, Add. Ms. 9419, fols 353–4, dated 21 December 1809. The round trip from Mawnan to Mullion is around twenty-five miles, duly undertaken in the winter.

[94] BL, Add. Ms. 9419, fol. 355r., dated 24 January 1810.

[95] BL, Add. Ms. 9419, fol. 91r., dated 15 February 1813.

[96] BL, Add. Ms. 9416, fol. 210r., dated 12 May 1813.

[97] BL, Add. Ms. 9416, fol. 65v., dated 8 May 1814.

[98] BL, Add. Ms. 9418, fols 10–11. Of the twenty-six parishes listed, eleven were served by curates with non-resident incumbents, and only six of the clerics were thought 'likely' by Arundell to respond.

[99] BL, Add. Ms. 9418, fol. 170r.

[100] BL, Add. Ms. 9419, fol. 54r., dated 26 August 1807, so only a very few days after the circulation of the Queries.

to obtain fuller information respecting the Manor of Landrake from the Steward. Unfortunately, however, he declines giving any.'[101]

Organisation of the information received into a publishable format

The chronology of the correspondence is signal in revealing how the Lysons managed their research. Knowing that they toured the county in 1805, then Samuel by himself in 1807, these visits took place prior to the circulation of the Queries – which stimulated a flurry of responses in 1807/8 as might be expected. Thereafter, there was very little exchange of letters until 1811/12. Presumably this lean period was when the focus was on the publication of *Cambridgeshire* (1808) and *Cheshire* (1810), but with this leap-frogging of research and the consolidation thereof for different counties, so the momentum for Cornwall was lost. There were other distractions as well. In 1811, Daniel wrote to Iago: 'The republication of "The Environs of London" has engaged my time very much more than I expected.' However, he goes on, 'Mean time I have been getting on with Cornwall & have drawn up the account of the first fifteen parishes taken alphabetically from Advent to Breage inclusive, including of course St. Austell and Bodmin.'[102] What appears to have taken place at this time was a thorough re-assessment of the material the brothers had by then accumulated, identifying gaps in their coverage and knowledge. To reinvigorate the project, and allied to Samuel's final visit to the county in 1811, an advertisement was placed in *The Cornwall Gazette*.[103] Headed 'Parochial Account of Cornwall', it continues:

> The Rev. Daniel Lysons and Mr S. Lysons, after having experienced some unexpected delays in the progress of their work entitled *Magna Britannia*,[104] express their thanks to the greater part of the Clergy of this county, for communications relating to their respective parishes, and they earnestly request answers from the incumbents, or officiating Curates of those parishes (about forty in number) from which no communications have as yet been received. If the queries which were circulated have been mislaid, or an intimation to that effect, they will be renewed. Mr. D. and Mr. S. Lysons take the liberty of requesting, that such Gentlemen, possessed of manorial property, as wish to see the account of their several manors correctly stated, will have the goodness to favour them with a brief statement of their descent for the last hundred or hundred and fifty years.

However, the editor of the newspaper, Richard Taunton, reported that the advertisement

---

[101] BL, Add. Ms. 9418, fol. 43r., dated 17 November 1807.

[102] KK: X94/1, dated 6 February 1811.

[103] *The Cornwall Gazette*, 13 April 1811, 1, col. 6.

[104] Immediately following the title page for *Cheshire*, an advertisement states: 'Having found our account of Cheshire, unavoidably extends to a much greater length than we expected, we have been obliged, contrary to our original intention, to close our second volume without proceeding further than that county.' There is already, in 1810, the unmistakable sense that the work was taking far longer than anticipated, and that the brothers' obsessive thoroughness, not least in these first counties for which no histories had previously appeared, was slowly but unrelentingly choking the production processes.

has produced only two applications – the first from the Revd. Jeremiah Collins, curate of Ladock near Truro, and the other from the Rev. W.A. Morgan, Vicar of Lewannick and Curate of Stratton [...] The first is anxious to receive another of the list of printed Queries, and the second says 'that no Queries from you ever came to his hands, or undoubtedly he would have answered them'.[105]

But there were, meanwhile, correspondents who wrote to the brothers direct. One E. Angove responded, 'In consequence of an advertisement in the Cornwall Gazette' and annexed his letter with an account of the descent of the manor and barton of Trengoffe, Warleggan, later incorporated into the published text.[106]

By such means, Daniel regained his focus on Cornwall. For example, Rev. Ralph Baron, vicar of St Breward, had responded to the Queries in 1808 with a three-page reply, concluding: 'These are all the particulars that I recollect respecting this Parish.'[107] He wrote again, but not until 11 April 1811, some three years after the initial contact, in answer to Daniel's new 'Enquiry respecting St. Breward.'[108] Similarly, Rev. Thomas Trevenna Hamlyn, curate of St Ervan, wrote at length about St Ervan and St Eval parishes in July 1808,[109] resuming the correspondence only in 1812, 'in answer to your Queries [...] I am sorry that after my utmost researches (which have not been opposed) it is not more important',[110] albeit, several more letters from Hamlyn followed, imparting ever more intricate detail, the last dated 6 March 1813.[111]

The dizzying exchange of correspondence, the large number of respondents, and the lengthy nature of their replies produced an enormous mass of letters. This presented Daniel with not just a huge quantity of physical material – the documents containing pedigrees, tricked shields,[112] transcripts of inscriptions, accounts of manorial descents, and so on – but equally, a colossal amount of information was now entirely at his disposal. The Cornish correspondence today occupies five large volumes, each containing three to four hundred folios; that for Cumberland, an equally remote county where they similarly relied on the resident clergy and gentry for particulars, takes up only two. The number of letters from Devonshire correspondents matches those of Cornwall, at five volumes again, but they relate to a county with more than twice the number of parishes (471 compared to 203), eventually published in an edition of 936 pages, half as much again as Cornwall. And all this was in addition to the considerable amount of literature on the county they consulted, as acknowledged in their 'Introduction' (*Cornwall*, 1–7). Comparisons with Cambridgeshire (two volumes of correspondence, two

---

[105] BL, Add. Ms. 9420, fol. 1r., dated 3 May 1811, three weeks after the advertisement appeared. He added that the advertisement had appeared only once, 'as Lord de Dunstanville did not inform me it was to be repeated'. Presumably de Dunstanville acted as the brothers' agent here.

[106] BL, Add. Ms. 9416, fols 1–2, dated 26 May 1811.

[107] BL, Add. Ms. 9416, fols 100–1.

[108] BL, Add. Ms. 9416, fol. 102r.

[109] BL, Add. Ms. 9417, fols 299–300.

[110] BL, Add. Ms. 9417, fol. 301r.

[111] BL, Add. Ms. 9417, fol. 306r.

[112] That is, shields drawn in outline with the charges sketched in, and the tinctures noted by abbreviations.

pages of bibliography),[113] and Cheshire (two volumes of correspondence, four pages of bibliography),[114] make it even clearer that the mass of data collected for Cornwall was more than double that acquired for any county they had previously studied. What is also explicit is how very little of the entire repertoire of information was eventually published. For all the precision and effort their correspondents demonstrated – the inscriptions at Mullion church never appeared in print, and the records of Lanteglos-by-Fowey, Hall, and Place, so painstakingly communicated by John Austen, were summarised in a few lines only – perhaps more than 90 per cent of it remains in manuscript.

The load of assimilating these data fell to Daniel, who was blessed not only with the material prosperity enabling his devotion to the task, but equally with an incisive, analytical mind. He was fully capable of maintaining an ongoing currency of the queries he raised with innumerable correspondents simultaneously, and able to filter phenomenal quantities of information, brutally to summarise and organise it into a publishable form. Cornwall was his greatest challenge yet, however, and it took its toll on his health. On 13 March 1813, he wrote to Iago from Bath: 'I have just arrived at this place, where I am ordered to lay aside my work for a month, having made myself quite ill by working too hard. I cannot however wholly lay it aside.'[115] Two months later, Rev. Cardew wrote: 'I am sorry to find that your health has suffered by your intense application. And tho' the public understandably wish you to proceed with, &, if possible, to complete your present immense work, yet surely neither your life, nor health ought to be sacrificed to their wish.'[116]

By January 1814, however, he was busy preparing the final manuscript for the printers, although this was achieved only after two years' piecemeal preparation of the parochial accounts. On 14 August 1812, he wrote from Hempsted Court to Iago: 'We stay at home this summer in hopes of getting the Parochial account of Cornwall off our hands. We are proceeded a considerable way in letter "L".'[117] He was his own worst enemy, however, as instead of being content with the texts so far prepared, he continued: 'In giving the last look over some of the earlier parishes preparatory to their going to press, I observe one or two of my original queries still remaining.' Later that month, he updated Iago:

> We are now getting in just forwardness if we could get together our Desideratum of Information. The whole of the sheets of the parochial account is now in Paper, blanks being left to supply the deficiencies of Information. We have never had any answer from St Neots, Southill or Stephens Saltash.[118]

Six months later, he told Iago: 'I have just finished transcribe [sic] the head of Cornish families which will be soon wanted for the press';[119] and a month later, he

---

[113] BL, Add. Mss 9412–13; the bibliography is *Cambridgeshire*, 76–8.
[114] BL, Add. Mss 9414–15; the bibliography is *Cheshire*, 465–9.
[115] KK: X94/1.
[116] BL, Add. Ms. 9416, fol. 210r., dated 12 May 1813. The phrase 'your present immense work' related to the entire *Magna Britannia* project rather than just the publication of Cornwall.
[117] KK: X94/1.
[118] KK: X94/1, dated 29 August [1812].
[119] KK: X94/1, dated 1 February 1813.

lamented: 'The printers are hunting me.'[120] By the start of 1814, the text was slowly being finalised, although Daniel was still intent on receiving answers to queries up to the publisher's deadline. In January 1814, for instance, he wrote to Thomas Carlyon, 'I have just been transcribing Probus for the press & shall be most obliged to you for an answer to a couple of queries which I omitted to send.' He concludes, understandably: 'You will much oblige me by an early answer.'[121] A detailed response was duly despatched on 8 February, the information on both matters heavily condensed by Daniel into half a dozen lines of print.[122] Instances such as these – and there are many – suggest that there were numerous last-minute changes, and/or filling the 'blanks' that had been left in the parochial accounts.

The myriad aspects of the county's wider history – its topography, history, architecture, and landscape – probably contributed by Samuel, were most likely completed well before 1814 and much less influenced by correspondents. That said, Samuel wrote to Iago in 1813 that 'having heard from my brother that you were going to Launceston about this time [...] If you should be there and could conveniently manage to make a sketch of the exact form of the arches of the doorways in the Keep of the Castle, in outline, I should be greatly obliged.'[123] Yet Daniel's obsession with the minutiae of all and every aspect of the family, manorial, and parochial histories, particularly those he considered weak, ensured that the very latest nuggets of information were eventually collected, whether or not they were published.

Publication of Magna Britannia – Cornwall *and the aftermath*

The work finally appeared in early August 1814, as Daniel wrote to Iago: 'I am just released from town having seen our Cornish volume fairly launched. We presented it to her Majesty & had a very agreeable audience.'[124] An advertisement was placed in *The Cornwall Gazette*: 'Lysons's Magna Britannia. Cornwall. This day is published, handsomely printed in 4to. with numerous Engravings, of Views, Antiquities, &c., price £3.15s. in boards. A few Copies on Imperial paper, with Proof Impressions, price £6.6s. in boards.'[125] The insertion also publicised 'Twenty-four views in Cornwall, of Britannia Depicta; a series of Views of the most interesting and picturesque objects in Great Britain, engraved from drawings, by J. Faringdon, R.A. Price £3.15s.' And attention was drawn to the continuing availability of 'The Two First Volumes of Magna Britannia' containing the 'Counties of Bedfordshire, Berks, Bucks, Cambridgeshire and Cheshire [...] Also

[120] KK: X94/1, dated 4 March 1813.
[121] BL, Add. Ms. 9416, fol. 302r. The queries related to the founding of the school at Probus, and Treverne in the parish.
[122] BL, Add. Ms. 9416, fols 304–5.
[123] KK: X94/1, dated 23 March 1813. If Iago responded, his sketch does not survive, and the detailed plans of the castle and section of the building, with Samuel's description, acknowledge only Lieutenant-Colonel Mudge (*Cornwall*, ccxxxviii–ix, and pls between).
[124] KK: X94/1, dated 8 August 1814. Samuel was a particular favourite of the queen and Princess Elizabeth; see Fleming, *Memoirs*, 17–20.
[125] *The Cornwall Gazette*, 20 August 1814, 3, col. 4. The price for *Cornwall* compares to £3.3s. for *Cheshire*, and although the Cornish volume is physically larger, it is only slightly so, suggesting the increase of 12s. manifests either higher production costs or a need to maximise returns on the publisher's investment.

the First, Second, and Third Parts, of Britannia Depicta; containing Views in the same Counties.' The advertisement concludes with 'The Account of Cumberland is in the Press, and will be published early in the next year.' There is a strong sense of setting the publication of *Cornwall* within the framework of the entire *Magna Britannia/Britannia Depicta* enterprises by publicising what they had already achieved, albeit in a newspaper with probably little circulation out of county. Also, with Cumberland promised shortly thereafter, the publishers were doubtless acting in self-justification, that this massive project was actively in progress, with one county being efficiently rolled out after another.

There was extended and favourable editorial comment in the *Gazette*:

> It is a large quarto, containing 670 pages, closely printed, and accompanied with 43 plates of views and antiquities, for the most part etched by Elizabeth and Letitia Byrne, from drawings, chiefly from the pencil of J. Faringdon, R.A. The work is said to excel every prior publication on the subject, and as the greater part of it consists of a *Parochial History*, it must be interesting to almost every Cornishman. There is indeed, but one history of the kind, and that an extremely scarce and imperfect one,[126] viz. Hals's, ten numbers of which containing an account of 72 Parishes, from Advent to Helston inclusive, were published about the year 1750.[127]

The general approval with which the book was greeted can be summarised by the contents of a letter to *The Cornwall Gazette* by 'A', who concluded that 'future writers will, no doubt, do justice to Messrs. Lysons' Cornwall, by acknowledging its merits, as they cannot fail to build on its plan, and make frequent use of its materials'.[128] Many of Lysons' correspondents were equally laudatory – but were equally forthcoming in providing corrections and amendments. The response of Rev. Cardew of St Erme, an assiduous collector of information for the brothers, is not untypical. He lists three pages of corrections but also commented that he had read the book 'with much satisfaction, & beg to return my best thanks for the entertainment which I have received from it. That I have discovered some errors is not to be wondered at. But few of them are of much importance.'[129] There were, however, a few individuals who were less generous. Rev. William-Augustus Morgon, of Lewannick, was the most vocal, from the start writing not only to Richard Taunton (of the *Gazette*) in Truro, highlighting errors and making corrections,[130] but directly to Daniel as well: 'You and your Brother have made some very great errors in your History of Cornwall', commenting thereafter on a few parishes in his purlieu.[131]

[126] As Daniel wrote to Francis Vyvyan Iago, 'Hals's Cornwall is extremely rare. I scarcely think that there is more than one copy of it in London, except that which my brother bought'; KK: X94/1, dated 6 February 1811.

[127] *The Cornwall Gazette*, 27 August 1814, 3, col. 1, presumably written by Richard Taunton. The absence of Polwhele's *History of Cornwall* being mentioned as a comparator speaks volumes as to how its unorthodox format and subject matter might have been cautiously received at that time.

[128] *The Cornwall Gazette*, 15 October 1814, 4, col. 1.

[129] BL, Add. Ms. 9416, fols 227–8, dated 29 December 1814.

[130] BL, Add. Ms. 9419, fols 102–3.

[131] BL, Add. Ms. 9419, fol. 104r., dated 20 August 1814. Paradoxically, prior to publication, Morgon had answered several of Daniel's enquiries and expressed an enthusiasm for the

This was followed a week later by: 'The following errors I am sorry to find in your History of Cornwall and you are at liberty to say that you had this information in a note from me'; there were seven enumerated points and additional comments on the content of individual pages of *Cornwall*.[132] Daniel responded testily on 2 September:

> This day's post has forwarded to my brother [...] your letter of the 20th [...] I shall take the answering of it upon myself since as the whole of the Parochial History was written by me I am the man competent to make observations upon it [...] I rather wonder that as I was your only correspondent, you should have troubled him at all on the subject. Your letter to me, I must say, struck me as commencing rather abruptly – that to my Brother appears more so & tho I dare say you might not intend the uncivil, [it] scarcely bears the appearance of civility. The first very great error which you charge us with in your letter to him is that Tregeare, which we call so, is not a Barton. I have already observed upon this & think that a Cornish Jury, according to the different acceptation of a barton might find some difficulty in deciding whether it is any error or not.[133]

The correspondence eventually fizzled out, but such comments clearly rankled, and stimulated the brothers to act, writing an open letter not to the Truro-based *Cornwall Gazette* but to the editor of the *Exeter Flying Post*, a newspaper with a much wider geographical distribution:

> Since the publication of the third volumes of our work, entitled Magna Britannia, containing the account of Cornwall, we have received several communications by letter, of corrections; some of which, upon examination, appear to have been errors of the press, which had been overlooked; few of them are important; and with respect to the greater part, we are borne out by the authority of our informants.
>
> That our correspondents were all equally desirous of giving correct information we have no doubt, yet, from misconception or inadvertency, it appears that in some instances we have been mis-informed.
>
> Every liberal minded person who peruses our volume will, we flatter ourselves, readily admit that we have spared no pains to ascertain the truth; and every practicable method was adopted previously to its publication, to procure corrections of those errors, which are inseparable from such work. As we propose, 'ere long, to publish an additional list of corrections, which will be delivered *gratis* to all those who may already have purchased the volume [...] we shall be much obliged to those who may have observed any errors in our Cornish volume, if they will have the goodness to favour us with corrections of them.[134]

Following this plea, 'Further Additions & Corrections' appeared on 1 May 1815, the pagination (363–81) running continuously. Such additional sections had already been issued for the counties previously published. For example, two versions were incorporated into the re-issue of *Bedfordshire, Berkshire and Buckinghamshire*

project.

[132] BL, Add. Ms. 9419, fols 108–9, dated 27 August 1814.
[133] BL, Add. Ms. 9419, fol. 106r., the draft of Daniel's response to Morgon. Morgon's letter to Samuel has not been found.
[134] *Exeter Flying Post*, 24 November 1814, 3, col. 1.

in 1813, this prodigious endeavour coming at a time when work on Cornwall was in full swing, and correspondence with the clergy and gentry of Cumberland and Derbyshire starting to become more engaging.[135]

The overall mental and physical grind entailed in the publication of *Cornwall*, and the frustration inherent in dealing with the later corrections and amendments – all the while upholding a focus on the wider *Magna Britannia* project – should not be underestimated. It is hardly surprising that the health of both brothers suffered during this time. It had been a protracted task, starting with a field trip in 1805, another in 1807, the despatch of the Queries the same year and dealing with and chasing up the responses, a last field trip in 1811, the preparation of the 'Parochial History' from 1812 onwards, culminating in a perpetual stormy sea of corrections, revisions, and additions – together with work proceeding on other counties – all of which Daniel had to distil into a succinct, publishable volume.[136]

Lysons' Church Notes for Cornwall

Fundamental to the 'Parochial History' were the 'Church Notes', transcribed in this volume, and made primarily by Samuel, writing for the most part on the poor-quality paper pages of a series of small, portable notebooks. This was a technique that had, perhaps of necessity, evolved in their explorations, as for the first three counties investigated there were no notes at all like this;[137] yet for Cambridgeshire and Cheshire, sheets of notebook paper start to appear.[138] The notes for Cornwall contain an enormous amount of information on the buildings and their contents, recorded in both text and numerous sketches of variable quality, yet their extent and variety seem slightly eclectic. Several churches with notable architectural features are described only briefly: Breage, for instance, has no mention of the magnificent west tower. Other entries, however, comprise lengthy expositions on the architecture, fixtures, fittings, and the monumental landscape, the descriptions frequently extending into accounts of buildings and topographical features in the parochial hinterlands. At St Ive, for instance, having transcribed a late sixteenth-century monumental inscription in the church to Blanch and John Wrey, Samuel notes: 'The seat of the Wreys was fitted up as a farm.' The differences in detail are curious therefore, particularly as he appears to have used a standard method of church recording. Yet when, years later, the notebooks

---

[135] BL, Add. Mss 9421–2 (Cumberland correspondence); 9423–5 (Derbyshire correspondence).
[136] He must have become accustomed to working like this, or perhaps it was his favoured method of research, as correspondence relating to *The Environs of London* similarly fills six volumes (BL, Add. Mss 9431–6), as well as his miscellaneous collections for publication, which fill seven large folio volumes (BL, Add. Mss 9451–7).
[137] BL, Add. Ms. 9460, a large folio volume, is entitled 'Lysons' Topographical Collections: Bedfordshire, Berkshire & Buckinghamshire; Sketches and Church Notes'. It comprises a miscellany of sketches, with accomplished pen and ink drawings, some with coloured washes, of stained glass, architectural interiors and exteriors, funeral monuments, and fixtures such as fonts and woodwork. Coverage is patchy, and there are no written notes of visits to churches, with just the occasional thought on the architectural setting. It suggests, perhaps, that Daniel, on his fieldwork – as we know, he set off in 1800 into Bedfordshire and Berkshire – made few, if any, notes, or if he did, he did not preserve them.
[138] BL, Add. Ms. 9461, a large folio volume entitled 'Church Notes & Sketches for Cambridgeshire & Cheshire'. There are numerous vignettes and full-page drawings, but most of the text notes are on sheets of paper around 11–13 cm wide and up to 21 cm in length, larger than those of the Cornish notes, as will be discussed.

were physically dissected and adapted for publication, information about any singular features was incorporated into the introductory sections – by Samuel – and any monumental heritage relating commemorated families to landholdings incorporated into the parochial histories – by Daniel. Hence, a 'standard' Cornish Perpendicular church rarely featured in the history of a parish, its unremarkable form contributing virtually nothing to the construction of what the Lysons considered sufficiently notable to publish.[139]

Samuel's method on a church visit was, very briefly, to record a church's groundplan – nave, aisles, transepts, chancel, tower etc. – followed by the internal architecture, continually logged as 'obtuse arches, clustered pillars'. This was a shorthand notation for the highly repetitive late Perpendicular Cornish church interior, describing the use of attached shafts in the main axes and four hollows in the diagonals of the piers, forming depressed, or three-centred arches of the arcades.[140] He was, however, as in previous counties, limited in his ability to understand and articulate the architectural development of the Cornish church, as a reliable textbook devoted to architectural analysis and descriptive vocabulary had yet to appear.[141] Hence, in his section on 'Ancient Church Architecture' (ccxxviii–ccxxxi), Samuel still retained the style categorisation he had adopted in 1806 for the inaugural commentary for *Bedfordshire*. Hence, 'the general name of *Saxon*, that being the appellation by which it is best understood, and not having hitherto discovered any difference sufficiently striking to constitute a distinct style', was employed to describe a semi-circular arch, citing in the process numerous examples drawn – literally – from his notes.[142] Going on,

> we have also in conformity to general usage, called that style, of which the pointed arch is the leading feature, Gothic; as, however inappropriate to the term may be if we regard its etymology, it is in our opinion better to employ it, sanctioned as it is by common use, than to adopt either of those which have been proposed in its stead, and which are not so generally understood.[143]

---

[139] The fact that much material in the fieldwork notes was never published was clearly acceptable to Samuel. He continued with the same energy and recording technique in Devon (BL, Add. Ms. 9464), among the last of the counties he toured, and at which time he would have been thoroughly conversant with the selective editorial policy of his brother.

[140] See Beacham and Pevsner, *Cornwall*, 30.

[141] This was to be T. Rickman, *An Attempt to Discriminate the Styles of English Architecture, from the Conquest to the Reformation* (London, 1817). Prior to the publication of that study, there were attempts by various antiquaries to categorise architectural styles, notably in F. Grose's *Antiquities of England and Wales*, 8 vols (new edn, London, [1809]), which contains a section entitled 'Architecture', i, 107–27.

[142] *Bedfordshire*, ix. In *Cornwall*, the doorways at Cury, Kilkhampton, and Morwenstow, with those of the south porch and aisle at St Mary's Launceston, were worked up into published plates from his initial sketches.

[143] *Bedfordshire*, ix. The last comment may well be a dig at the efforts and publications of John Carter, draughtsman to the Society of Antiquaries of London (1795–1817?), at a time when Samuel was the director (1798–1809). The two men were opposed to each other on many matters, and Carter's crowning achievement, *The Ancient Architecture of England*, 2 vols in 1 (London, 1795–1807), in which he attempted a definitive architectural classification, would have been anathema to Samuel. See J.M. Crook, *John Carter and the Mind of the Gothic Revival* (London, 1995), 41–3; and R. Sweet, 'The Incorporated Society and Its Public Role', in S. Pearce (ed.), *Visions of Antiquity: The Society of Antiquaries of London 1707–2007*, *Archaeologia* III (London, 2007), 74–97, at 88–90.

The architectural descriptions employed in *Derbyshire*, probably the last written by Samuel, were equally structured in terms almost identical to those used in *Bedfordshire*, published some ten years earlier.

This descriptive conservatism also points, perhaps, to a desire for upholding a conformity of nomenclature throughout the larger project of *Magna Britannia*, as one county followed another. Perhaps too, it manifests an indifference – possibly even an antagonism – to initiatives in architectural descriptions. Until Thomas Rickman's *Attempt* appeared, studies tended to illustrate churches *en masse* as models of the features being analysed, whereas Samuel viewed each church individually, as the cornerstone of the parish, and of course as the functional repository for funeral monuments and the genealogical information they discoursed.[144]

Following this architectural account in *Cornwall* are the customary sections on 'Ancient Painted Glass' and 'Rood-lofts, Screens, &c.' Many examples are mentioned, but only briefly, and there is a sense of opportunities lost. For instance, Samuel's account of the imagery in the St Neots' glass is heavily contracted from the comprehensive details he recorded in his notes; and his description of the east window at St Winnow, 'nearly filled with painted glass', occupies a mere two and a half lines of text. However, while the series of 'Bodmin-style' Norman fonts, with later categories, are also just briefly identified, eleven examples are illustrated from his drawings, the published versions beautifully worked up from smaller, preparatory sketches. 'Ancient Crosses' and 'Well-Chapels' are separately considered, but despite their sculptural magnificence, only five are pictured. Similarly, the proficient drawing in his notes of the 'Holy Chair' at Germoe,[145] styled 'Saxon' (ccxxxix), and which included a plan and dimensions, was never published, despite its unique character. Clearly, Samuel faced difficulties in interpreting – and often sketching – religious figural imagery. We see this not only in his accounts of the glass, for example, but in the way he interpreted the (relatively clear) carving of the Annunciation in the head of the lantern cross at St Mawgan, construing it as a king and queen with a serpent (ccxlv). Similarly, the Agnus Dei sculpted on a Norman tympanum at St Michael Caerhayes was described and sketched as a man on horseback (ccxxviii). In mitigation, we do not know how straightforward it was to view these artefacts, in churches that were frequently in poor condition, quite often dark, full of high pews, and with interiors whitewashed over to disguise the dirt, damp, and mould, simultaneously obscuring finer

---

[144] R. Sweet, *Antiquaries: The Discovery of the Past in Eighteenth-Century Britain* (London, 2004), 264–7. For example, Grose's *Antiquities of England and Wales* (fn. 141) illustrated hundreds of churches but generally failed to classify coherently their architectural styles. However, Rickman was a Quaker, and it has been argued that his dissociation from the Church of England enabled him to detach himself from contemporary debate about the origins and meaning of 'Gothic', because of its association with the barbarity of 'Goths' and Sir Christopher Wren's theory of its origins in Islamic architecture. Rickman's taxonomy of architectural styles was, therefore, both original and grounded in observation rather than perpetuating academic introspection. For Rickman, see Colvin, *Biographical Dictionary of British Architects*, 812–17; and for observations on the meaning of 'Gothic' at that time, see K. Clark, *The Gothic Revival: An Essay in the History of Taste* (New York, 1929), 4–9, 86–97; P. Frankl, *Gothic Architecture* (Harmondsworth, 1962), 217–20; and G. Henderson, *Gothic*, 179–200.

[145] BL, Add. Ms. 9462, fol. 34r.

sculptured detail.[146] In Cornwall, Samuel employed his artistic abilities instead to record architectural features, such as fonts, piscinae, window tracery, corbels, and pillar bases. For some reason, no Cornish stained glass is illustrated, despite the inclusion of several plates of glass in other *Magna Britannia* volumes. It is curious that the arrangement of the donor figures in the St Neot glass resembles that in the window at Siddington (Gloucestershire), which he had first published nearly two decades earlier, so the depiction of such secular imagery – albeit in two dimensions only – was within his capabilities.[147] It appears that as time went on and, perhaps, the pressures of publication increased, he restricted his sketching to features more easily delineated within the technical limits of his vocabulary. One might not unfairly conjecture, perhaps, that despite his tuition from John Faringdon R.A., his artistic abilities lay more as a draughtsman than as a portraitist.

As for stained glass, so for funeral monuments, the discussion of which in *Cornwall* occupies fewer than three pages of text, and none are pictured. However, in *Cambridgeshire*, a similar study extends over eleven pages (61–71) with ten illustrations, some large format, and in *Cheshire* it is nine pages long with six illustrations (444–52); even in *Cumberland*, not a county renowned for its monumental heritage, there are five pages of descriptions with four plates (cxciv–cxcviii). And unlike the Cornish sections on crosses, and wells, for which references to Borlase's and others' publications are cited, there is just a single footnote for the entire topic of monuments, so the reader remains undirected elsewhere for additional information. In fairness, earlier authors (like Borlase) also make little of the late medieval commemorative material in the county, yet Richard Gough (1735–1809) had, twenty years previously, published his enormous and sumptuously illustrated work entitled *Sepulchral Monuments in Great Britain, Applied to Illustrate the History of Families, Manners, Habits and Arts at the Different Periods from the Norman Conquest to the Seventeenth Century* (London, 1786–96). At that time, moreover, he was the director of the Society of Antiquaries, to which, as we know, Samuel was elected Fellow in 1786. Under Gough's influence, the 'emotional impulse' provided by the French Revolution – and the later wars – ensured the attention of the Antiquaries was focused by a number of papers on medieval architecture and sepulchral monuments, shifting the emphasis away from the traditional scrutiny of the heraldry and inscriptions to the study of forms and effigies.[148] It is inescapable that Samuel

---

[146] There is also an inference in the widely sanctioned encouragement of whitewash, that apart from its practical uses, it perpetuated a practice that originated post-Reformation and was reinforced during the Commonwealth, in a determination to eliminate images irretrievably. This was, of course, exactly contradictory to the aims of Lysons to record such things. See V. George, *Whitewash and the New Aesthetic of the Protestant Reformation* (London, 2012), 158–89. It was a requirement of Bishop Carey (1820–30) that the interior of a church should be 'well plaistered and whitened within', see *The Diocese of Exeter in 1821: Bishop Carey's Replies to Queries before Visitation; Volume I; Cornwall*, ed. M. Cook, DCRS NS 3 (1958), xiv.

[147] [S. Lysons], *Etchings of Views and Antiquities in the County of Gloucestershire: Hitherto Imperfectly or Never Engraved* (London, 1791 and later), pl. XXXIX [published 1792]; and a more sophisticated drawing still was made in 1801 and published in his *A Collection of Gloucestershire Antiquities* (London, 1803), pl. XIII.

[148] See S.F. Badham, 'Richard Gough and the Flowering of Romantic Antiquarianism', *Church Monuments* 2 (1987), 32–43.

would have received an excellent grounding in the subject, but the focus on heraldry and text persisted in Cornwall.[149] For example, the noteworthy effigies at Mawgan-in-Meneage, Sheviock, and Stratton are all briefly described, but Samuel made only simple, outline sketches of the figures, none of which would have been suitable for publication (Fig. 2).

The splendid tomb of Sir John Colshull (d. 1483) at Duloe was described as 'under an arch [...] richly ornamented with vine leaves and grapes' (ccxxxvi); and that of Lord Willoughby de Broke (d. 1502) at Callington was 'much enriched with Gothic tracery' (ccxxxvi); yet they remained unsketched. The brasses to Margery Arundell (d. 1400) at East Antony, and Nicholas Assheton (d. 1476) at Callington, are of equal magnificence to those drawn and subsequently published in earlier volumes, yet Samuel drew just a mere caricature of Margery's headdress (Add. Ms. 9462, fol. 19r.).

It is difficult to suggest why this comparative inattention to church monuments might have been. Admittedly there is nothing in the county to rival the de Luda tomb at Ely cathedral (*Cambridgeshire*, 62), but the Colshull and de Broke effigies are very fine and impressive artefacts, and their tombchests are geometric compositions bristling with heraldry – the sort of structures that one might think would appeal to Samuel's pencil. Equally, in *Cumberland*, the brass of William Stapleton (d. 1458) at Edenhall, remarkable for its heraldic costume but otherwise of mediocre quality, is illustrated in large format (cxcvii); but that far more prestigious example to Thomas Mohun (*c.* 1440) at Lanteglos-by-Fowey, notably set within its canopied, heraldic tomb recess, remained virtually unacknowledged.[150] Perhaps, too, the remarkable effigial tomb to Bishop Vyvyan (d. 1533) at Bodmin was afforded scant attention because it was not sculpted in the artistic style that he cared for (or understood?); but it is bizarre that in Cornwall he drew so little of this material compared to other counties.

Was it a matter of speed, and he felt he did not have time? – although as we have seen, after a cider-fuelled dinner, he enjoyed a leisurely spell at Callington, content to puzzle out the inscription on Assheton's brass rather than drawing it. Or was it also that the publication date of *Cornwall* appears constantly to slip, so using specialist artists such as Frederick Nash (1782–1856), employed for *Cambridgeshire*, or Charles Stothard (1786–1821), whose expertise lay in painting tomb monuments and stained glass, would have been a process too rushed, or was not allowable as a publication expense?[151] And of course, for funeral monuments and brasses, as for sculpture: there was no adequate vocabulary to call upon for help in interpretation – although when faced with the Eliot monument by

[149] J. Evans, *A History of the Society of Antiquaries* (Oxford, 1956), 205. Samuel even gave a paper himself on the tombs in Tewkesbury Abbey, in 1801, *Archaeologia* 14, 143.

[150] This despite a vignette of it incorporated into a letter from the (almost) indefatigable John Austen of Place, BL, Add. Ms. 9416, fol. 66r., dated 8 May 1814.

[151] See *Magna Britannia Bedfordshire [...]* Jack Simmons, xxi–xxii, whose analysis of the illustrations reveals that while most, if not all, of the plates for the earlier counties incorporated drawings by Samuel, for *Cumberland* it was down to one-third, and for *Devonshire* only two out of twenty-two were his. For Cornwall, sixteen of the thirty-four attributable plates are by Samuel, the others being landscapes by his tutor John Faringdon, or the *Britannia Depicta*. See also J. Marchand, 'The Illustrations in the Magna Britannia: The Contribution of Charles Alfred Stothard (1786–1821)', in Brayshay (ed.), *Topographical Writers*, 101–4.

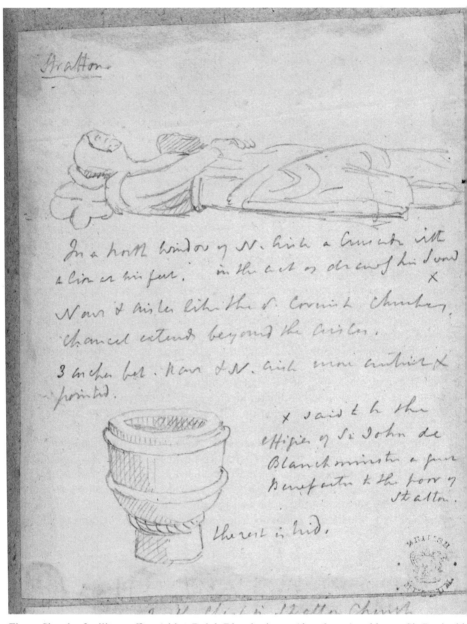

Fig. 2. Sketch of military effigy (either Ralph Blanchminster (d. 1267x77) or his son Sir Reginald (d. 1277x83)), Stratton church; © British Library Board, Add. Ms. 9462, fol. 56r.

Rysbrack at St Germans, and the equally fine Pyper monument at St Mary's Launceston, Samuel let his guard slip sufficiently to pronounce them 'splendid'. Yet we need to look past the monuments' aesthetics to consider the reasons why the Lysons considered them at all; indeed, Samuel noted myriad inscriptions and heraldry but almost exclusively for the genealogical and heraldic data they discoursed. Despite, as Nigel Saul has highlighted, 'a remarkable scarcity of tombs and brasses from the pre-Reformation period' in the county,[152] the notes are in fact crammed full of monumental information, but – for Cornwall – so very few of these artefacts were considered in further detail. For example, one of the most coherent series of monumental commissions was the large number of brasses to the St Aubyn family at Crowan, dating from *c.* 1420 to 1626, yet their inscriptions and heraldry were, by the early nineteenth century, so mutilated as to render identification difficult. In consequence, Samuel noted simply 'brasses on slabs' (Add. Ms. 9462, fol. 27r.), not realising that the evidence of a once grand dynastic heritage lay in front of him; and there must have been other instances when his interpretative incapacity meant he glossed over monuments rather than recording them in their entirety.

Consolidation of the Church Notes

Samuel's distillation of his church notes occupies around ten pages of the 'Introduction', and for the first time the entire section is paginated in lower-case Roman numerals compared to the earlier volumes, which use Arabic numerals throughout.[153] His notes were also scrutinised by Daniel, so he could incorporate information on the churches, and, principally, the monuments they contained, in his 'Parochial History', as we have seen. One can only hypothesise how he managed this demanding task, as the entries on each church vary considerably in length, and, hence, on the amount of paper they occupy. Some are of one to two lines only, suggesting more than one church was recorded on a notebook page, whereas others extend over several separate sheets. Moreover, they would have been compiled in a geographically haphazard order, something complicated further by the three separate visits to the county.

At some point, therefore, entries for individual churches were identified and separated from others on the same sheet, put into alphabetical order, and pasted on to large folio sheets. Those for Cornwall were combined with those for Cumberland to form a large, half-leather bound volume (the size of the folios is 51 x 31 cm), which Daniel presented to the British Museum in 1833, shortly before his death, as part of his working archive. Catalogued as Additional Manuscript 9462, and without a title page, it comprises:

---

[152] N. Saul, 'Why Are There So Few pre-Reformation Monuments in Cornwall?', in C. Steer (ed.), *The Monuments Man: Essays in Honour of Jerome Bertram* (Donington, 2020), 150–70, at 150. The causes were several: losses incurred during the widespread and large-scale church rebuilding programmes of the late fifteenth century; there was also no tradition of effigial sculpture in the county, something predicated by the intractability of finely working granite; and also because of the absence of a resident higher nobility, leaving monumental commissions to the knightly and squirearchical landowners.

[153] This was something presumably facilitated by the appearance of *Cornwall* as a separate county volume, without, for instance, the requirement for continuous numbering from the start of *Cambridgeshire* to the end of *Cheshire*.

Fol. 1	map of Cornwall by Thomas Martyn (1784), with geological areas identified.[154]
Fol. 2	map of Cornwall, J. Gibson *sculpsit* [1762].[155]
Fols 2v.–3r.	map of the entrances to Fowey and Falmouth harbours.[156]
Fol. 3v.	map of the area between Looe and Fowey, including Lerryn and Pelynt.
Fol. 4	map of Cornwall divided into hundreds, C. Smith, 6 January 1804.[157]
Fol. 5	map of Cornwall, western portion, by Thomas Martyn (1784).
Fol. 6	map of Cornwall, eastern position, by Thomas Martyn (1784).
Fol. 7r.–v.	drawings of standing and inscribed stones, including at the top of the recto a sketch of the Ignioc Stone acting as a gatepost to the vicarage garden;[158] three inscribed stones were later published (pl. between cxx and cxxi).
Fol. 8r.	reproduction of the original sketch of a gold *lunula*[159] (later published as the pl. opp. ccxxi); a note explains: 'This drawing was transferred from the Department of Antiquities 26 November 1841. It accompanied the letter of Mr. Trafford Leigh in which he offered to sell the Ingot to the Trustees.'
Fol. 8r.	sketch of inscribed stone.
Fol. 8v.	sketch of gold *lunula* (as for fol. 8r.).
Fol. 9r.–v.	written account of a meeting of the Society of Antiquaries, 20 February 1783, discussing the finding and meaning of the *lunula*.[160]
Fol. 10	coloured drawing as a plan of 'Castle an Danis, Ludgvan, Mounts Bay, Cornwall', with two sections, one with dimensions; scale of one inch to about sixty-five feet (ccxxxviii).
Fols 11–11*	coloured drawings as a plan and elevation of Launceston Castle keep (pl. between ccxxxviii and xl).
Fol. 12r.	sketch 'Keep of the Castle, South Side', headed 'Launceston July 30 1805'; two plans of the keep, one with dimensions.

[154] Quixley, *Antique Maps*, 12, see fn. 50.

[155] Quixley, *Antique Maps*, 126–7.

[156] These plans were redrawn from charts in BL, Ms. Cotton, Augustus I, i, fols 36–8 (1539–40).

[157] Quixley, *Antique Maps*, 164–5.

[158] A. Preston-Jones, A. Langdon, and E. Oshaka, *Ancient and High Crosses of Cornwall* (Exeter, 2021), 90–1.

[159] This refers to a specific kind of archaeological solid collar or necklace, made in the form of a crescent, dating from the Bronze Age or later.

[160] See *Archaeologia* 2, 36; and the 'Minute Book of the Society of Antiquaries' 18, 347–50, Society of Antiquaries Library: SAL/02/018/040.

Fol. 12v.   drawing of the south side of 'Trefry Castle [Place], Fowey',
             dated 22 May 1753.[161]

Fol. 13r.   plans with dimensions of 'The ancient site of a house',
             Binnamy, and 'Plan of the Chapel at "Wallsborow"'; initials
             'W.I.' [Wrey I'ans].[162]

Fol. 14   'These rough Sketches of all the ancient Military Works
             in the Hundred of Stratton contain measures thereof', at
             Kilkhampton, Launcells, Stratton, Week St Mary, Whitstone,
             dated April 1813, 'For Samuel Lysons', from Wrey I'Ans.

Fols 15v.–16r. plan of Stratton hundred with geographical features marked,
             together with '"Burrows" (Places of Burial) in the above
             Hundred [...], "Castles" & "Camps" & or Fortifications
             (colord red)', 'hastily (& incorrectly) copied by W[rey]
             I['Ans] [...] For Samuel Lysons Esq.'

Fol. 17   'a few general Remarks on the Fortifications in the Hundred
             of Stratton, Cornwall, submitted to Mr Lysons by Wrey I'Ans
             [...] Whitstone House, Stratton, Cornwall, 25th April 1813'.

Fol. 18r.   plan of Golden Camp; and a pasted-in sheet of blue paper
             with text entitled 'The content of Golden Camp [...] The
             content of Carvossa Camp', unattributed.

Fol. 18v.   plan of the turnpike road from Truro to St Austell going
             around the mound; plans of Castle An Dinas and Warbstow
             Burrows (pl. opp. ccxlix).

The church notes commence on fol. 19r. with those for Antony, supplemented by
short descriptions of some of the Carew portraits at Antony House. There are usually
eight to ten entries for churches dissected from the notebooks and neatly pasted in
two columns on the rectos of the folios (Fig. 3).

The size of the sheets of notes varies considerably, but all are around 11 cms
in width and extend up to 17–18 cm in length, although some, bearing only a few
lines of text, are only 1–2 cm in length. Such sheets in their entirety accommodate
sketches of architectural or other features; for example, the drawing of Chun
Cromlech (pl. opp. ccxix) on fol. 24v., and some of the notes on Bodmin church
on fol. 21r. likewise. Many records of archaeological sites and artefacts are interspersed in the agglomeration of church notes at the appropriate alphabetical point;
for example, Chapel Carn Brea, Chun Cromlech, and The Cheesewring are all found
among the notes for parishes beginning with 'C'. Drawings of crosses are also
added, and separately bound in are rubbings of the relief inscriptions from the south
aisle of Bodmin church (fol. 21*), in several strips folded to fit, and the 'Loveybond'

[161] Presumably taken from Borlase's collections (*Cornwall*, ccxlii); the embattled tower to the
left of the façade no longer exists.
[162] Col. Wrey I'Ans (1738–1816), of Whitstone House, was lieutenant-colonel commandant of
the Cornwall Provisional Cavalry, JP for Devon and Cornwall, and possessed a natural interest
in the remains of the military fortifications in his native hundred of Stratton. His efforts are
cited and acknowledged (*Cornwall*, ccxlvii).

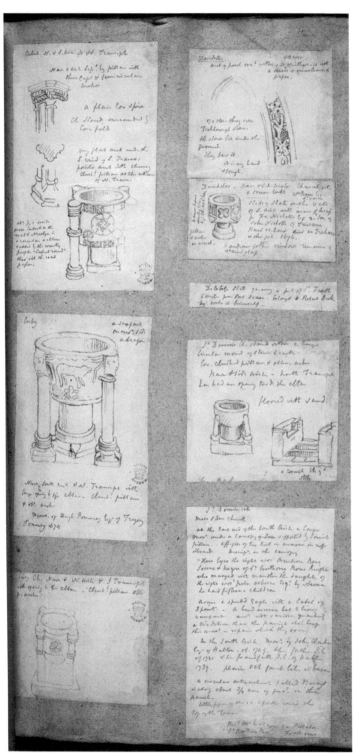

Fig. 3. View of arrangement of a folio page; © British Library Board, Add. Ms. 9462, fol. 29r.

inscription at Egloshayle (fol. 30v.). Other drawings, frequently of fonts and window tracery, are pasted in, chiefly on the versos. The appearance is that of an elaborate and ordered scrap book, in which any and every piece of information on the county gleaned by Samuel was preserved.

The notes finish at fol. 59r. with the account of Zennor church; there are observations on the countryside and various customs encountered, such as sanding roads, on a single sheet on fol. 59v. Fol. 60r. bears nine separate sheets of paper with impressions of the scenery and people – 'The poor people seem to do very well here, they have generally pigs & goats & sometimes a cow or two' – and a sketch of a ditched camp. Fol. 61r. bears a sheet of tracing paper with drawings of six fonts (published as pl. opp. ccxxxiii).

At fol. 62, the start of the county of Cumberland is denoted by a county map; from there to fol. 124 there are many drawings of inscribed stones and Roman inscriptions/ antiquities; fol. 125 is headed 'Cumberland. Sketches & Measurements by Richard Smirke &c.',[163] followed by elevations and plans of Carlisle Cathedral from fols 126 to 133; fol. 134 carries sketches of part of the nave of Lanercost Priory Church; and fols 135–76 are the church notes for Cumberland, with rough pencil notes on sheets or part sheets of paper, as for Cornwall.

Equally integral to the publication of *Cornwall*, and the ultimate writing-up for the press of the introductory sections and the 'Parochial History', are two other 'scrap book' volumes prepared, presumably, by Daniel, now BL, Add. Mss 9444, 9445. The former is entitled 'Historical Notices' and comprises 435 folios (41 x 28 cm page size), crammed with manuscript notes on rectos and versos, interspersed with numerous cuttings of all shapes and sizes of paper, including newspaper articles and letters. It is divided into many sections, roughly coinciding with those of the 'Introduction' to Cornwall, such that at fol. 4 there are notes on the Duchy; fol. 11 – 'Ecclesiastical Divisions, Lists of Parishes'; fol. 28 – 'Monasteries – Saints'; fol. 35 – 'Market & Boroughs Towns', and so on. There are large sections devoted to manorial history and Cornish families, but there is nothing relating to the 'Ancient Church Architecture' and the topics that follow in the published book. One might presume that Samuel's preparatory papers for these sections do not survive, that is, either he never sent them to Daniel for his retention, or he despatched them direct to the publisher. The volume concludes with a list of corrections (fols 314–5), followed by around one hundred folios of 'Sundry Queries, Memoranda &c.', used by Daniel to extract all he could out of the supplementary data received post-publication. Fols 416–22 comprise 'Corrections', and fols 423–35 'Errata & additions for an Appendix'. The end of this volume seems to have acted as a kind of clearing house of information after *Cornwall* had appeared, facilitating the arrangement of the haphazard responses received, in order to create what would be the final (second) appendix.

Add. Ms. 9445 is a similar, but thankfully lesser, volume, both in its length (302 folios) and size (37.5 x 24.5 cm), entitled 'Parochial History'. The format is much the same, with notes, cuttings, letters, and sketches, all arranged in alphabetical order of parishes, from Advent (fol. 1) to Zennor (fol. 302) (Fig. 4).

---

[163] This was Richard Smirke (1778–1815), brother of the architect Daniel was considering employing for the completion of the Devon volume in 1819, after Samuel's death; see fn. 29.

Interspersed within these myriad data are notes on several churches not visited (or not accounted for) by Samuel in Add. Ms. 9462. Hence, details of Advent church appear here, with a sketch of the font, made on the usual paper and pasted on to the folio; and there are many more, with rudimentary drawings of (almost exclusively) fonts, and transcripts of monumental inscriptions, together with copies of inscriptions apparently duplicated from Samuel's own notes. The authorship of this volume is open to question, but it almost certainly contains those records made first-hand by Daniel on his tour of the county in 1805 (and perhaps later?). There is an obvious difference between the two sets of notes: Samuel's are almost exclusively in pencil, in some cases very faint, whereas those in this volume have the lines inked in over the pencil, the original outlines in many cases still clearly detectable (Fig. 5).

From the contents of this volume, one can begin to understand how Daniel made sense of it all, parish by parish, whether using his own or his brother's notes, incorporating information gleaned from Borlase, Hals, and Tonkin (usually written in ink directly on to the folios) and assimilating correspondence on the descent of manors and advowsons, families and their estates, all underpinned by the dynastic histories he could deduce from heraldry and inscriptions inside each church.

The genesis of the volumes that include the church notes transcribed here is open to question, however. Daniel presented sixty-three volumes of his working papers to the British Museum in 1833, and allowing for differences in format, they are uniformly bound in half leather with raised bands on the spines, and neatly labelled.[164] This suggests that the binding was commissioned not long before he donated the collections – which in turn leads one to ask how he managed the mass of papers before then. To retain any semblance of order without having them bound must have been challenging, so perhaps the volumes were created piecemeal, as county followed county, bound in utilitarian boards, and were then more prestigiously rebound for formal presentation in the 1830s.[165] Whatever the case, the church notes, *per se*, form only a very small part of the published work, although clearly the evidential heritage content of each building underpinned much of the 'Parochial History'. Why else, it might be asked, did the Lysons themselves attach such importance, as they continually stress, to visiting and recording every church in a county, when the bulk of the contents of the *Magna Britannia* volumes was derived from other sources? Did they, like Sir Stephen Glynne, quite simply, enjoy touring the countryside 'taking' churches? Yet that said, in virtually all other aspects of their industry – passion, even – for their

---

[164] The field notebooks that survive, BL, Add. Mss 9465–71, are excluded from this observation, as they are in oblong octavo format, scruffier, and contain church notes for Cambridgeshire, Cheshire, Devonshire, and Middlesex. Analysing their contents, one can speculate further on the brothers' working methods of church recording. For example, for Devonshire (Add. Ms. 9469, fol. 78r.) there are notes for Ilsington church, 'Clustered columns, flat arches', which are not repeated in the formalised Devonshire volume of 'Church Notes' (Add. Ms. 9464, fol. 43r.), yet both record (with slight variations) the monumental effigy of a lady, and in the 'Church Notes' the figure is sketched. Two visits were apparently made to Ilsington, perhaps one by each brother, or maybe both were by Samuel (the writing is difficult to attribute to either brother)? It is also curious that the contents of these field notebooks were not dissected and pasted into the formalised 'Church Notes', or at the least, copied from one to the other.

[165] There are no binders' labels found in the volumes examined to provide an attribution.

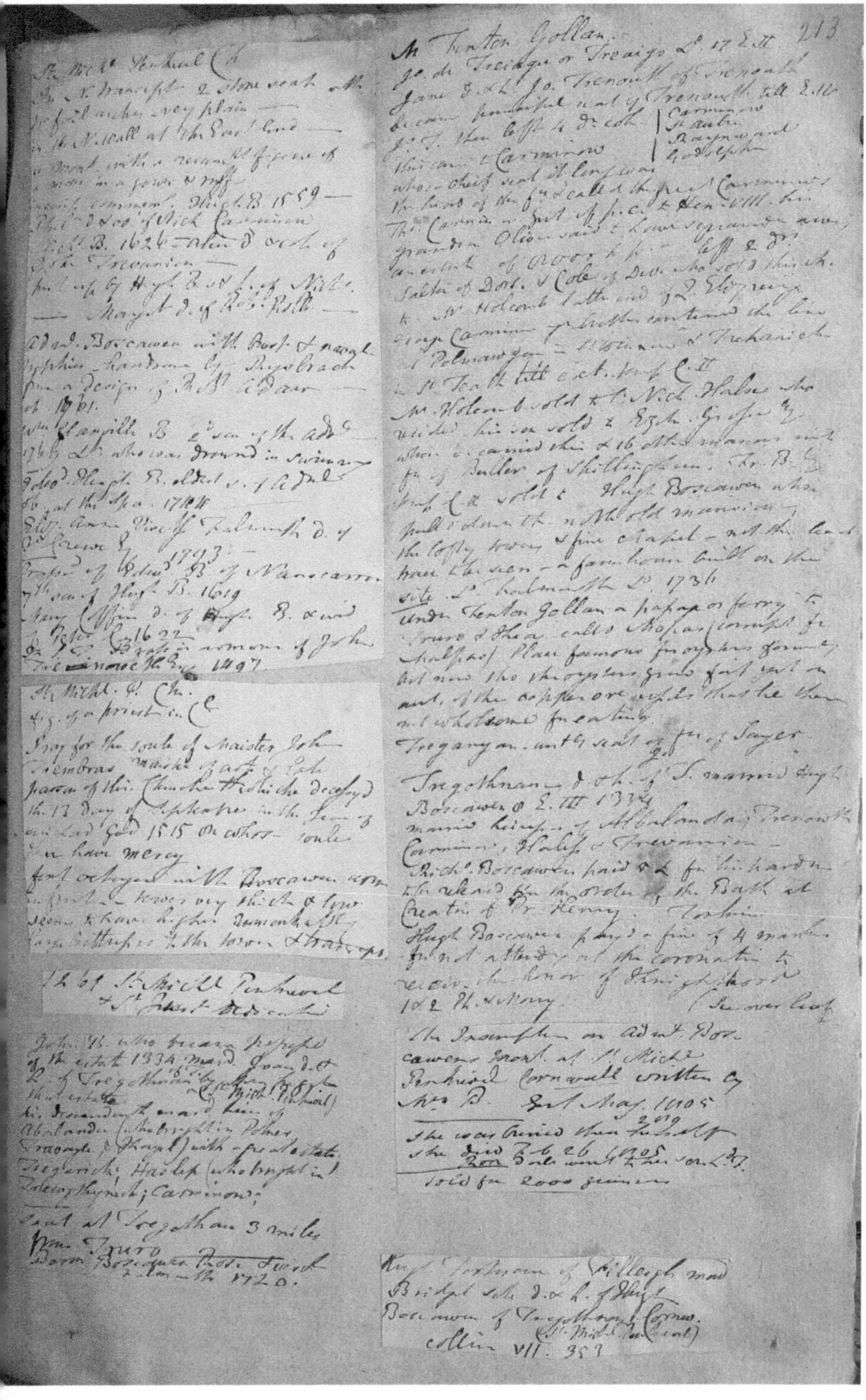

g. 4. View of arrangement of a folio page; from the British Library Archive, Add. Ms. 9445, l. 213r.

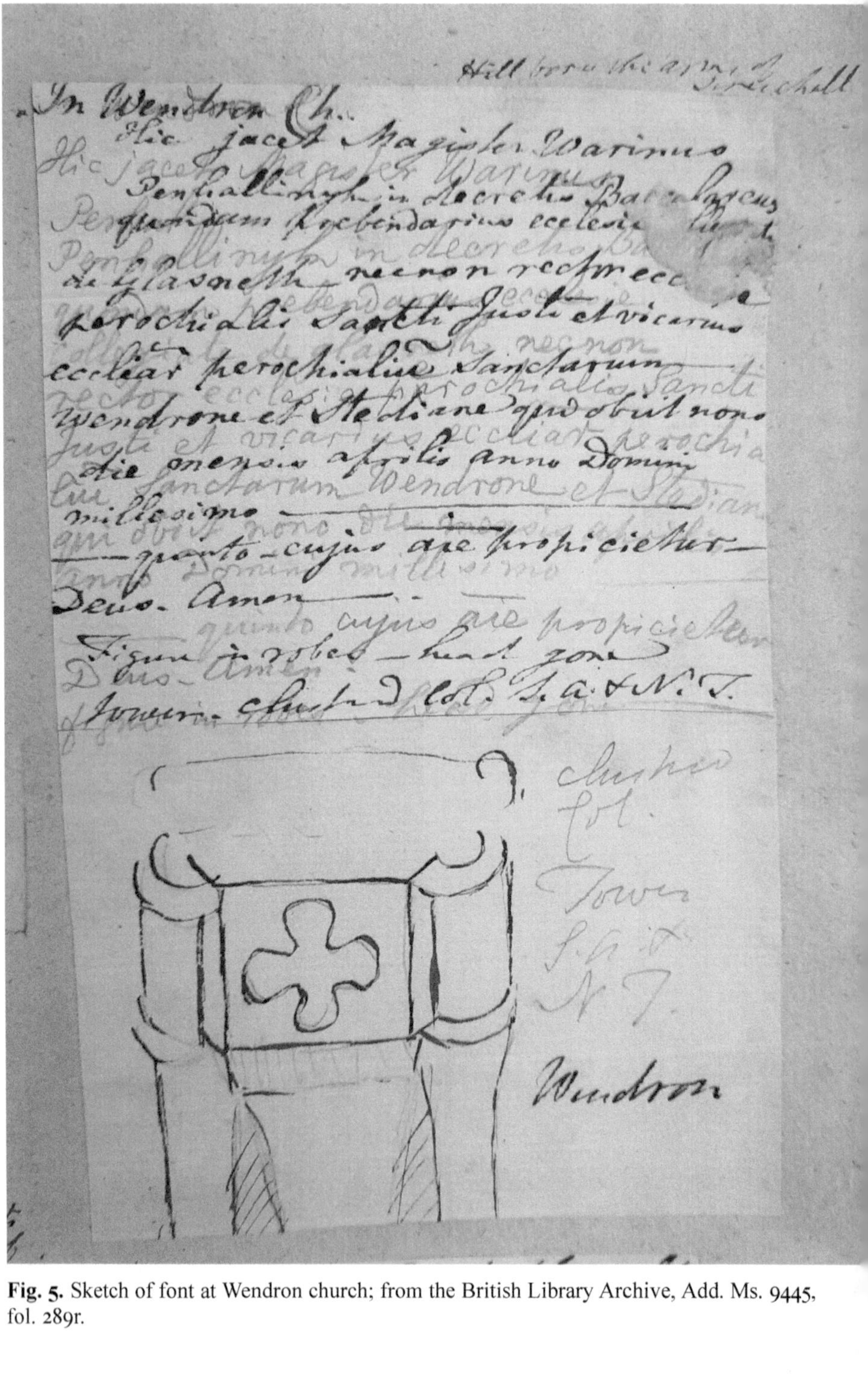

Fig. 5. Sketch of font at Wendron church; from the British Library Archive, Add. Ms. 9445, fol. 289r.

edification of something on the scale of *Magna Britannia*, the contrasts between the Lysons and Glynne are acute.

Sir Stephen Glynne, 9th Bt, of Hawarden (Clwyd)

Sir Stephen, like the Lysons, was a pioneer recorder – although almost exclusively of religious buildings, as domestic houses or other secular establishments were rarely documented. His expeditions and notes were made purely for his own enjoyment, with no consideration of the kind of publication that so enervated, yet stressed, the Lysons. Instead, he accumulated a vast quantity of information as first-hand observations on approximately 5,500 churches, principally in England and Wales.[166] These are contained within a series of 107 notebooks, in which he ordered the notes topographically rather than chronologically, the visits ranging in date from *c.* 1825 to his death in 1874.[167] They reside among the Glynne-Gladstone manuscripts at Gladstone's Library, Hawarden, together with much family correspondence, and financial and estate papers.[168] However, some of Glynne's pocket notebooks and diaries relating to his tours found their way into the NLW, Aberystwyth;[169] these otherwise little-explored personalia provide a unique insight into his working methods – something we can only surmise with the Lysons' – and neatly complement the church notes he made on his journeys throughout Cornwall.

A brief biography

It will be useful to the reader of Glynne's Cornish church notes to understand the character of their compiler, and how a childhood interest in church buildings and music matured into a passion that contributed to his near bankruptcy. Stephen Richard Glynne was born on 22 September 1807, the eldest son of Sir Stephen Glynne, 8th Bt, and Mary his wife, second daughter of Richard, 2nd Baron Braybrooke, of Audley End (Essex). The founder of the baronetcy was Sir John Glynne (1602–66), an enterprising (and fortunate) lawyer, who served both the Commonwealth and then Charles II. He purchased the Hawarden estates in 1653, and thereafter, by the not unusual combination of advantageous marriages and land management, the family estates expanded. The hall was rebuilt by Stephen's father, who introduced turrets and crenelations to justify the title 'Hawarden Castle', but otherwise, generations of Glynnes appeared to enjoy the conventional life of a country squirearchical family.

---

[166] The total is difficult to estimate with complete accuracy; see D. Parsons (ed.), *Sir Stephen Glynne's Sussex Church Notes*, Sussex Record Society 101 (Lewes, 2021), xvii, for the most recent assessment.

[167] See L. Butler, 'Sir Stephen Glynne: A Pioneer Church Recorder', *Church Archaeology* 17 (2013), 93–105.

[168] Catalogued in *Handlist of the Glynne-Gladstone Mss in St Deiniol's Library, Hawarden*, compiled by C.J. Williams, List & Index Society Special Series 24 (1990). Until 2018, the archive was administered by the Flintshire Record Office, but it is now under the management of Gladstone's Library.

[169] They are among a large number of documents relating to the Glynne of Hawarden estate, deposited by Henry Neville, 1st Baron Gladstone of Hawarden, in 1935. He was the third son of W.E. Gladstone and his wife Catherine Glynne, sister of Sir Stephen, and dying without issue, the barony became extinct.

This harmonious existence was disrupted in 1815 by the premature death of the 8th baronet, leaving Stephen, aged eight, to inherit the title and estates. Unlike his father and other close family members, he was precocious, quiet, and reserved, finding pleasures in intellectual pursuits rather than riding with the hounds;[170] moreover, he possessed a remarkably retentive memory. As W.E. Gladstone – a consummate politician acquainted with many leading intellectuals – recalled, 'his memory was, on the whole, decidedly the most remarkable known to me of the generation and country'.[171] Early on, he was developing an enthusiasm for church architecture and music, interests cultivated further at Eton, where he was considered the cleverest boy there.[172] At the age of thirteen, he thought nothing of riding twenty miles or so in search of churches to explore, clearly manifesting an already refined appreciation of their architectural features. Something of this passion is found in letters to his widowed young mother, written on a trip to the south of England in September 1825:

> We came first to Romsey where there is an immensely large & highly curious ancient Church, mostly of Norman work, & quite a Cathedral to all appearance [...] The Cathedral [Winchester] is now in a state particularly favourable for seeing it to advantage, it having undergone very just & excellent repairs & improvements for the last 5 years, which are just finished[173] [...] The Monumental Chapels are richer than perhaps any in England, & have been kept up beautifully, & of late very much smartened up.[174]

Nine months later, he reported from Rouen (France):

> The Cathedral is beyond anything rich and magnificent, both interior & exterior [...] There is another church [Saint-Ouen] very nearly equal in extent & beauty to the Cathedral and much better in situation, as it stands partly open. All the churches are very rich and contain some painted glass far superior in brilliance & richness to any I ever saw, & it is in very fine preservation.[175]

Unsurprisingly, perhaps, he did not thrive at Christ Church, Oxford; where was the motivation to succeed when he already enjoyed an annual income of £9,320 from the Hawarden estates? It was there, however, that he first met his future

---

[170] A.G. Vesey, 'Sir Stephen Glynne, 1807–74', *Journal of the Flintshire Historical Society* 30 (1981–2), 151–70, at 152 fn. 6, suggests he may have inherited this character from his mother's family, with his great uncle, Thomas Grenville (1755–1846), notably encouraging his love of books.

[171] *ODNB*, Sir Stephen Richard Glynne, 9th Bt (1807–74), by A.G. Veysey, available online at: https://doi.org/10.1093/ref:odnb/10844 [accessed August 2020].

[172] Veysey, 'Sir Stephen Glynne', 153.

[173] A series of repairs was carried out in the cathedral in the first two decades of the nineteenth century; see P. Barrett, 'Georgian and Victorian Restorations and Repairs, 1775–1900', in J. Crook (ed.), *Winchester Cathedral: Nine Hundred Years 1093–1993* (Chichester, 1993), 315–28, at 317–20. That Glynne, just turned eighteen years old, recognised the changes for what they were, is a reflection on the then extent of his architectural and ecclesiastical knowledge.

[174] GL, Glynne/Gladstone Mss 14, letter of 29 September 1825.

[175] GL, Glynne/Gladstone Mss 25, letter of 19 June 1826.

brother-in-law William Ewart Gladstone (1809–98)[176] and counted Sir Thomas Dyke Acland (1809–98)[177] among his friends. He graduated in 1828, but rather than going home and assuming control of his estates, he shirked his immediate responsibilities and continued his foreign travels: 'The Cathedral [Amiens] looks quite stupendous in point of height & general content [...] I am looking forward to the rich treat of examining it tomorrow together with 9 other fine large Churches which this City contains.'[178] This combination of a singular – in being both unusual, and also a solitary occupation – obsession with ecclesiastical architecture, and his 'peculiarly quiet and retiring disposition',[179] made him uninterested and ineffectual (perhaps intentionally so?) in fulfilling the various roles in local society expected of him as a baronet and landowner. A visitor to Hawarden at that time noted:

> Sir Stephen [...] [was] [...] very glad to escape the hunting party; he is [...] pretty, small, shy, kind, gentle-looking [...] His study and pursuit is Antiquity and Cathedrals; there are only two in England that he has not seen, and that so thoroughly as to know all their details by heart. He has made a good collection of topographical works and seemed very happy to find anybody who cared about them and liked to be shown the fine prints. My friend, Rickman's *Architecture* lay upon the table interleaved with observations of his own. He never rides or shoots or dances, or likes any young man's pursuit, so that he keeps aloof in his own home except just the going in to dinner. He seems amiable and much respected and loved by his own people – 'such a good young gentleman'.[180]

Despite his election as an MP from 1832 to 1837 for Flint Boroughs, and from 1837 to 1847 for Flintshire, he had little interest in politics; he was frequently absent, and never spoke in the House.[181] And although for many years lord lieutenant for Flintshire, a role perhaps more to his liking than subordinate duties, his social apathy unhappily extended to the management of his estates, which eventually became so indebted they had to be taken in hand by his brother-in-law

---

[176] At the London home of his friend and then fellow-Conservative MP James Milnes Gaskell (1810–73), who had shadowed Glynne's and Gladstone's educational path through Eton and Christ Church, Gladstone met Catherine Glynne, Sir Stephen's sister. Their marriage took place on 25 July 1839 and was a joint wedding shared with Catherine's sister Mary Glynne and her husband-to-be, George Lyttelton (1817–76), who had just succeeded his father as 4th Baron Lyttelton.

[177] As the 11th Bt, he succeeded his father, Sir Thomas Dyke Acland 10th Bt, only in 1871, but in 1837 he was MP for Somerset West, where the family had estates, so would have maintained a Westminster link with Glynne.

[178] GL, Glynne/Gladstone Mss 25, letter of 18 March 1829.

[179] 'Obituary', *Archaeologia Cambrensis* 5, 4th series (July 1874), 249.

[180] G. Battiscombe, *Mrs Gladstone: The Portrait of a Marriage* (London, 1956), 17–18. Clearly, too, Rickman's *An Attempt to Discriminate the Styles of English Architecture*, is revealed as a formative influence on how Glynne's analytical acumen developed in an understanding of architectural principles.

[181] Veysey, 'Sir Stephen Glynne', 155; for his political career, in which 'he repeatedly professed his support for reform, retrenchment, protection and the abolition of sinecures', views unsurprising, considering his character, see: https://www.historyofparliamentonline.org/volume/1820-1832/member/glynne-sir-stephen-1807-1874 [accessed June 2022].

Gladstone: he closed Hawarden Castle in 1848, sold off some of the property, and placed Glynne himself on an annual allowance of just £700. There is an evident contrast between the lack of attention Glynne paid to the financial catastrophe that was about to disrupt his lifestyle and the much greater importance he attached to his election as the first president of the Cambrian Archaeological Society from 1847 to 1849, 'an office which he filled to much advantage'[182] in that society's infancy. His financial purgatory, was, however, relieved somewhat in 1853 when Gladstone and his sister went to live at Hawarden. He was useful to Gladstone for his opinions on church matters, particularly the suitability of individuals for appointments and preferments, views no doubt honed during his role as the lord lieutenant. All the time, Glynne continued travelling at home and abroad, keeping detailed notes and an informed commentary on all he saw, with some years naturally more fruitful than others. For example, there was a 'high' in 1842 when he recorded 161 churches, and a low of seventy-five in 1848 – perhaps resulting from his change in circumstances in that year. Yet during the 1850s he averaged around 104 churches visited per year, increasing to 120 during the 1860s. Even in the 1870s, when he was in his sixties, Glynne showed few signs of slowing down, with 129 churches noted in 1870, although by 1873 the total was down to eighty-eight as, perhaps, the strain of incessant travelling started to impact upon his health.[183]

Glynne collapsed and died in London, suddenly, on 17 June 1874, aged sixty-six, his body later transported to Hawarden church for burial. He is commemorated there by a very fine effigy of white marble by Matthew Noble (1817–76), set on a raised tombchest with blind arcading on its front, within a low arched recess in the Whitley chancel, bearing the inscription: 'Stephen Richard Glynne Bart. Lord Lieutenant of the County of Flint, Born the 22nd day of September A.D. 1807, died the 17th day of June A.D. 1874'[184] (Frontispiece). As A.G. Veysey concludes:

> Reserved but affable, modest and unassuming, he disliked fuss and controver-
> sies [...] [and] [...] had little inclination or the attributes required to be an ef-
> ficient landowner and leader of local society. However, after reading his many
> travel journals, diaries and the massive collection of church notes he left behind,
> one cannot but admire and be grateful for the energy and determination of a Vic-
> torian antiquarian whose researches and life work are of lasting value.[185]

[182] 'Obituary'.
[183] These figures are taken from the *Index to the Church Notes of Sir Stephen Glynne in St Deiniol's Library, Hawarden*, Clwyd Record Office (1977) and, for visits post-1840, would appear to be accurate estimates.
[184] See Roscoe *et al.*, *Dictionary*, 890. The tomb recess was designed by John Douglas (1830–1911); see E. Hubbard, *The Buildings of Wales: Clwyd (Denbighshire and Flintshire)* (London, 1994 edn), 73–7, 367.
[185] Veysey, 'Sir Stephen Glynne', 167.

Glynne's working methods and his expeditions to Cornwall

Three years after Glynne's death, his nephew (and heir) W.H. Gladstone saw fit to publish the church notes for Kent, which covered some 312 churches.[186] His 'Preface' sheds some light on his uncle's work, his tours, and how the information assimilated on these personal visits was later formally written up into the extended series of notebooks that are preserved today:

> The Kentish Notes were commenced in 1829, and a considerable portion of the work was done prior to 1840, including all those descriptions to which no date is prefixed: the remainder was carried on year by year without intermission, a certain number of weeks or months being regularly allotted to it [...] The labour of accumulating such a mass of details as are here given may be readily conceived, but it was, in the truest sense, a labour of love, and the very act of exploring the county to its furthest recesses, and acquiring all sorts of local information by the way, was a process thoroughly congenial to the author. It mattered little to what extent successive modifications had interfered with the original design of the church under examination; Sir Stephen Glynne would at once, as if by instinct, read its architectural history, and a very short time usually sufficed for the jotting down of brief memoranda respecting the fabric and its appurtenances, to be afterwards drawn up into the full but compendious form in which they are here presented [...] His memory, too, was marvellous. The details of the 5,530 churches he has described were not merely committed to paper, but were continually carried in his head, so that he could at any moment give off-hand a clear and accurate account of any one of them.[187]

Two sources of information about Glynne's expeditions to Cornwall survive, in addition to the volumes of church notes themselves. The first comprises four small notebooks, which contain his original observations in the field (as identified above by Gladstone),[188] one of which, NLW, Glynne of Hawarden Ms. 185, is a hard-backed, unpaginated 'Memorandum Book' (10.5 x 6.4 cm), which retains the original short, thin pencil secured in a side pocket. It is filled with rough notes and sketches, sometimes extremely faint, of architectural features of churches in Kent, Sussex, and north-west Devon, and also includes his first-hand impressions of five churches in north-east Cornwall, recorded in January 1857: Jacobstow, Launcells, Poundstock, St Gennys, and Stratton.[189] Because of the rare survival of this material, these Cornish entries have been transcribed here as supplementary to the 'full but compendious form' of the formalised notes for each building, so one can identify the

---

[186] Sir S.R. Glynne, *Notes on the Churches of Kent*, ed. W.H. Gladstone (London, 1877).
[187] Glynne, *Churches of Kent*, iv–v.
[188] NLW, Glynne of Hawarden Mss 185–88, 'Four Note Books Kept by Sir S.R. Glynne (the 9th Baronet) for Lists and Notes of Churches'. Ms. 186 contains lists of churches in dioceses, and some of those visited in day date order, including some in Cornwall. The haphazard nature of the churches listed is difficult to construe, other than perhaps Glynne was trying to see if he had visited a church on every day of a year, albeit in different years. Ms. 187 contains a detailed tabulation of the dimensions of cathedrals. Ms. 188 is an odd compilation of drawings, memoranda, and lists of churches abroad.
[189] Parsons (ed.), *Sussex*, xvii, suggests the notes for Sussex and Kent were made in 1850.

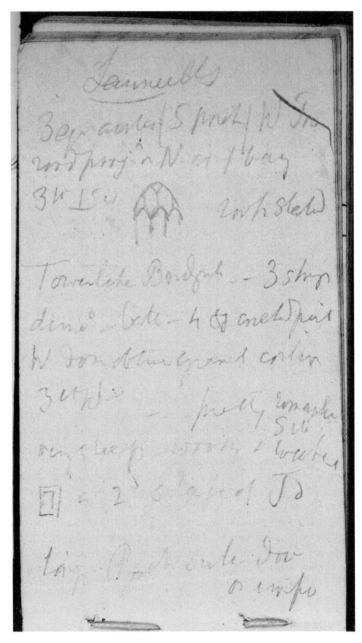

Fig. 6. Page from field notebook of Sir Stephen Glynne (1857) for Launcells; © Sir Charles Gladstone, 8th Bt, image supplied by Llyfrgell Genedlaethol Cymru/National Library of Wales, Glynne of Hawarden Ms. 185.

extent to which the notes compiled later on were based on the earlier written record and how much derived from memory (Fig. 6).[190]

Some of the pages are struck through with ink, presumably signifying that they had been transcribed; one might surmise that because so few of these notebooks have come down to us, they were small and simply disposed of once they had served their purpose.

The second source is a series of twenty-one small pocket diaries, one per year, in which Glynne recorded information about his tours around the country.[191] The earliest of these is for 1825, and thereafter there is a broken series from 1840 to 1874, albeit with sixteen years – including some when he visited Cornwall – missing. It is valuable to quote at length from these diaries to include all the entries relating to Cornwall. Not only do they clarify how he physically toured the county using a variety of transport, but equally to look upon them as testament to the sheer indefatigability of the man. After all, he recorded that he walked twenty-one miles on the exposed north coast in early February, in 'fog, wind, rain & mist': it was not something for the fainthearted:

NLW, Glynne of Hawarden Ms. 37, pocket diary, labelled 'Tilt's Pocket Alma-nack, 1842'. January 10 – by Bristol to Powderham. 12 – Party at dinner. 13 – In Exeter Cathedral, afternoon very fine, party at dinner. 16 – Powderham church, Cofton chapel. 17 – fine, rode to Whiteway & Ashton.[192] 18 – rode to Mamhead. Damp. 19 – fine, rode to Christow, &c. 20 – rode to Newton & Kenn, Kenton. G. Fortescue came.[193] 21 – damp & cold, party at dinner & Charades evening. 22 – all party dispersed, went by coach to Devonport, then posted to Boconnoc, arrived at ½ past 7. Saw Sheviock Church. Sundry Fortescues just arrived, rainy. 23 – stormy with sun. Boconnoc Church in afternoon. 24 – very wet, rainy at Boconnoc. 25 – very fine & bright, beautiful, to Fowey harbour & Lanteglos church. 26 – rode to Lanhydrock, windy. 27 – left Boconnoc by mail to Exeter, bright & showery.

NLW, Glynne of Hawarden Ms. 38, pocket diary, 'Peacock's Historical Almanack 1843'. July 5 – extremely hot, much engaged with packing &c. all day, evening party lively [illegible]. 6 – set off early to Southampton thence by steamer at 3 to Falmouth. Day rather cloudy & heavy rain at an early hour, passage rather rough. 7 – Plymouth at 5am, Falmouth 3pm, day fine, lovely afternoon, the sea blue as Mediterranean. 8 – showery, coach to Helston, gig

---

[190] A set of church notes made on a loose sheet tucked into vol. 88 of the Church Notes for Yorkshire is transcribed by Butler (ed.), *Yorkshire*, 44, again revealing the brevity of the field notes compared to the comprehensive written account.

[191] NLW, Glynne of Hawarden Mss 34–54, 'Memorandum Books of Sir Stephen Richard Glynne, 9th Bart.'

[192] Whiteway House, Chudleigh, the residence of Montagu Edmund Newcombe Parker (1807–58), MP for South Devon (1835–41), and a Westminster contemporary of Glynne.

[193] George Matthew Fortescue (1791–1877), who settled at Boconnoc after his marriage in 1833 to Lady Louisa Ryder, daughter of the earl of Harrowby. Although the Boconnoc estates were still owned by Fortescue's aunt, Lady Grenville (1772–1864), who in turn had inherited them on the death of her brother, 2nd Baron Camelford, in 1804, he effectively managed the estates until he inherited them on Lady Grenville's death. See C. Lorigan, *Boconnoc: The History of a Cornish Estate* (Stroud, 2017), 85–9.

to Penzance – at Vicarage,[194] evening fine, walk to Paul. 9 – service morning & evening St Mary, Penzance; afternoon St Paul.[195] Very excellent music & all in high style. Fine day, but not very warm. Lovely walk. 10 – glorious day, bright & clearest sky with fresh breeze. Left Penzance, walked round by St Michael's Mount, Marazion, to St Ives, where arrived at 6. Sea rough & rough passage back from the Mount. 11 – Cold morning & cloudy till 3. Left St Ives, waited some time at Camborne & dined, coach passed without stopping, very fine after 2 (pm) but not warm. Slept at Truro. 12 – very fine brilliant morning & warm & bright through the day, by coach to St Austell, thence to the [illegible] & by gig to Tor Point where arrived at midnight & slept. 13 – less bright but warm: at Plymouth.

NLW, Glynne of Hawarden Ms. 43, 'The Gem or Useful Pocket Book adapted for the Youth of Both Sexes 1849'. February 12 – Very fine & rather frosty. Went to Bristol to Church, Morning & to the Cathedral afternoon.[196] At 10 embarked by steamer for St Ives. 13 Tuesday – Very fine day, excellent passage, uncommonly still. Reached St Ives at 4, walked to Zennor, slept there. 14 Wednesday – Most beautiful bright day. Walked by S. Just to Sennen. Slept at the Last Inn in England. 15 Thursday – Less bright, weather damp feeling, explored the Lands End, walked to Penzance. 16 Friday – Not much sun. Went by Van[197] to Helston then walked to Cadgwith on the Lizard, afternoon most lovely. 17 Saturday – Glorious day, bright, clear & warm, walked round the Lizard to Helston. 18 Sunday – Bright morning, afternoon less so & cool; at Helston Church morning & evening. 19 Monday – Not bright; went in van to Penrhyn, walked thence to Mylor & dined. Close afternoon & rain afterwards, slept at Truro. 20 Tuesday – Very rainy & high wind, travelled strait to Bodmin & staid there. Ash Wednesday 21 – Dull morning, afternoon very wet & close. At Bodmin Church in morning, went afternoon to Liskeard. 22 Thursday – Threatening morning, turned out very fine. Walked from Liskeard to Looe, thence to St Germans. 23 Friday – Extremely fine & bright. Walked to Plymouth. St Mathias 24 Saturday – Rainy & dull. Went to Exeter, at morning & afternoon services in Cathedral, reached Bristol at night.[198]

---

[194] The curate in residence was Rev. Edward Shuttleworth (1806–83), appointed in March 1840, moving to Egloshayle in 1849. This may have been a visit by invitation, as Shuttleworth was an enthusiast of church music, publishing several articles and musical scores, and would have been someone with whom Glynne could enthusiastically have conversed; see G.C. Boase and W.P. Courtney, *Bibliotheca Cornubiensis: A Catalogue of the Writings, Both Manuscript and Printed, of Cornishmen, and of Works Relating to the County of Cornwall [...]*, 3 vols (London, 1874–82), ii, 649.

[195] Presumably St Paul's church, Penzance, which in 1843 would have just been completed. It was built by Rev. Henry Batten, the previous curate of St Mary's, and was intended as a proprietary chapel for use by supporters of the Oxford Movement. As such, therefore, Glynne would have appreciated the cruciform plan, the high-pointed arch-braced roof, and the large lancet windows with slender, elegant shafts; see Beacham and Pevsner, *Cornwall*, 427.

[196] In this diary, the entry for each day is demarcated by a line drawn under it, adding clarity.

[197] The *OED* describes this as meaning in 1829, 'A covered vehicle chiefly employed for the conveyance of goods, usually resembling a large wooden box with arched roof and opening from behind, but varying in size and form.' Clearly, this was a far from luxurious means of transport, yet it served its purpose in carrying Glynne from Penzance to Helston quickly enough that he had time to walk twelve miles to Cadgwith in the afternoon.

[198] After three nights at Bristol on 27 February, he went back to London.

NLW, Glynne of Hawarden Ms. 44, 'The Bijou or Ladies Companion for 1850'. 27 January Septuajesima at Bangor Cathedral, morning & afternoon. Frosty & very cold and no sunshine, at 8 by train to Birmingham. 28 – Rainy morning & rather chill. Went by train to Bristol, dined there & thence to Exeter, mild afternoon & damp. 29 –very mild & damp. Went by train to Plymouth & by Van to Looe. Much rain. 30 – Foggy, but scarcely any rain. Walked to Fowey from Looe. Views impaired by mist, dined at Fowey & went in Van to Bodmin. 31 – Bad day, very much rain. Walked to Camelford & did not proceed further because of the rain. February 1 – A very bad day, fog, wind, rain & mist, but not very mild. Walked 21 miles by Boscastle, Tintagell & Endellion & stopped at St Minver.[199] 2 – better day & no rain, but windy, mild air, got to Padstow early. 3 – Sexagesima, very fine & bright. Strong south west wind, at morning & evening church, at night drove to St Columb. 4 – a very bright morning & fine until 4 when heavy rain came on in occasional showers. Walked to Wadebridge & passed the night there. 5 – travelled by Omnibus[200] from Wadebridge to Plymouth, 12 hours; fine morning early but afterwards very rainy. 6 – very windy night, quite a gale. Cold day, much wind & showers, very unpleasant. Went from Plymouth to Bristol by train.

NLW, Glynne of Hawarden Ms. 45, 'The Commercial Pocket Book for 1853'. January 28 – travelled via Bristol to Exeter, a cold day. 29 – dry & fine, but sunless, went by rail to Plympton then walked to Yealhampton & Noss [Mayo] to Plymouth. 30 – Sexagesima, raw & much rain. Morning at St Andrews & evening St James. Slept at Devon Port. 31 – very lovely day. Frosty morning then bright sun. By Bus to St Blazy & walked to Mevagissey. February 1 – Fine early: afterwards cloudy but dry until night when it rained hard. Walked to St Mawes. 2 – bad morning, fine afternoon. Walked by Flushing to Truro, at night damp & rain. 3 – horrid day, incessant rain & very cold. Went by bus to Plymouth. 4 – very cold & snow in morning, afterwards rain but wintry, went by Torquay to Exeter.

NLW, Glynne of Hawarden Ms. 48, 'Renshaw's Gentleman's Pocket Book for 1858', February 8 – Very fine bright day. Went by train to Exeter, at afternoon service in Cathedral. 9 – Horrid rain till 2. Went by Crediton to Bere; thence walked to Sticklepath. Mild. 10 – Walked to Bridestowe, nearly blown away by cutting high wind. Reached Launceston in 'Bus. Very cold & high wind. 11 – Fine & sunny. Went by coach to Truro. Much milder towards evening. 12 – at Truro. Dull mild day, Walked to Tregothnan & Tregony & back by Coach. <On facing page: On this day lost my Pocket book containing a [illegible] &c., probably dropt out of great coat pocket, & bought this book & continue diary.> 13 – Dull & fair, drove to Perranzabuloe. In evening by rail to Penzance. Sunday 14 – at Penzance. Cloudy & showery, no vicar pm, much fog. At St Mary's Church morning. 15 – Bad day, with much snow storm, but snow did not lie, drove to Logan & Tol Pedr Penarth. 16 – Lovely day, frosty, very bright, walked to Madron, Ludgvan & Marazion, thence to Helston. Ash Wednesday 17 – at Helston. Cold day, at Church morning

---

[199] Curiously, no notes survive, either as field observations or written-up accounts, for the church of St Endellion.
[200] The *OED* describes this as 'a four-wheeled public vehicle for carrying passengers, usually covered, and frequently with seats on the roof as well as inside, plying on a fixed route', and at this period pulled by horses.

& afternoon, drove to Manaccan etc. 18 – Very fine but high wind & cold. Went
by 'Bus to Falmouth, walked to Mabe. At Church at 4. 19 – Cold wind, went by
mail to Plymouth, arrived at 6pm. 20 – Less cold. Went by train to Exeter thence
to Bristol & Bath.

What is apparent from these diaries is how Glynne dipped in and out of Cornwall,
as he did in other counties (Maps 1, 2 and 3).[201]

He usually travelled from Bristol to Exeter when the rail connection was fully
operational by 1844, then to Plymouth, connected in 1849. Twice he boarded a
steam packet, once from Bristol to St Ives,[202] and once from Southampton to
Falmouth.[203] On the return trip, he usually headed to Bristol, whence he could go to
London, or north via Birmingham. Clearly, Cornwall was a particular destination
in itself, rather than a county only to be explored following a tour of Devon; in
1850, for instance, he left Bangor on 27 January, reached Exeter on the 28th, and
was in Looe the following day! His Cornish itineraries could be ferocious, often
undertaken in the winter months. He thought little of walking fifteen to twenty
miles in a day (and in winter these would be short days), let alone tackling the
steep gradients involved in places – out of Boscastle to Tintagel, for example, in
February 1850 – in addition to making notes in dark, cold, damp churches and
carrying his journey's essentials with him. Glynne evidently used many inns but
never commented on their facilities or welcome.[204] When staying at Powderham
Castle or Boconnoc House, he was happy enough to use horses from their stables
to ride to churches and houses in the vicinity, but he rarely seems to have borrowed
a horse from an inn to explore roundabout, perhaps because he wished to move
on and spend the following night elsewhere. He also used gigs, on one occasion
in February 1858, when, perhaps forced by fog and snow, he abandoned church
visits for the day and was driven instead to Logan rock and the headland Tol-Pedn-
Penwith close by. Yet the day after, 'a lovely day', he walked nearly twenty miles,
from Penzance to Madron, and then via Marazion and Ludgvan, to Helston, where
he stayed the night.

It is salutary for us to take a step back from a scrutiny of Glynne's church notes,
to consider this most unusual man therefore, trekking through the muddy Cornish
lanes in all weathers and benefitting from what protection he could get from the
impenetrable hedges to either side. He must have cut a solitary, lonely figure on
his travels, wrapped up in his great coat, probably eschewing any casual company,
and using inns merely as places of rest and recuperation, rather than as a means of
social intercourse, and a potential source of local history. His personal, and highly

---

[201] As identified particularly by Butler (ed.), *Yorkshire*, 6–8; and Parsons (ed.), *Sussex*, xxi–
xxv, maps I–V.

[202] These ships were operated by the Hayle Steamship Company (renamed the Hayle & Bristol
Steam Packet Company in 1848), with three sailings a week and the price of a cabin at one
guinea; see an advertisement for the company in the *RCG*, 31 January 1840, 3.

[203] There were several steamer services between Southampton, Bristol, Liverpool, and Ireland,
which used to call in at Plymouth and Falmouth en route; see R. Fenton, 'Cornish Steam Ships
and Owners: The View from England', *TROZE: The Online Journal of the National Maritime
Museum Cornwall* 1.3 (March 2009), 3–21, available online at: https://nmmc.co.uk/collection/
troze/ [accessed August 2023].

[204] For which see the account by Rev. Swete: 'A Tour in Cornwall in 1780 by the Rev. John
Swete M.A.', ed. P.A.S. Pool, *JRIC* NS 6.3 (1971), 185–219.

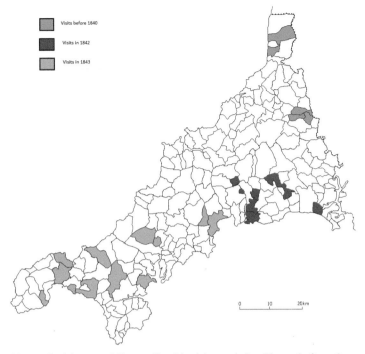

Map 1. Parish map of Cornwall, with visits made by Glynne before 1840, and in 1842–3.

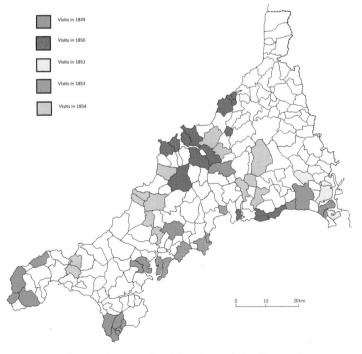

Map 2. Parish map of Cornwall, with visits made by Glynne 1849–54.

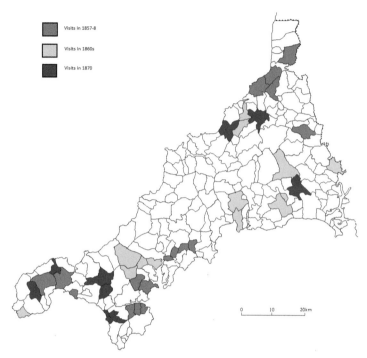

Visits in 1857-8

Visits in 1860s

Visits in 1870

0   10   20km

Map 3. Parish map of Cornwall, with visit made by Glynne 1857–70.

individual pleasure, arose from the 'discovery' of another church: one more building architecturally scrutinised, briefly recorded, and duly memorised, each to be written up in his series of notebooks when the opportunity arose. One senses something of his character in his diary description of a few days spent in London after his visit to Cornwall in 1850:

> February 7 – reached London train at 11. Went to Education meeting, Willis's Rooms, very unpleasant showery day, dined with Courtenay, met Lord & Lady Devon. 8 – fair day, in London, walking, paying bills &c., at Vespers at St Pauls, dined with W.E. G[ladstone]. 9 – windy, close and threatening rain – walked about doing chores.[205]

Despite this intimate circle of friends, the personal frustration of activities other than visiting churches is clear to see.

Glynne's first dated tour to Cornwall was in 1842, but he had earlier strayed over the border during a brief foray in west Devon, recording the churches at Kilkhampton, Stratton, and Launceston in the late 1830s. On the 1842 expedition, of six nights only, he took advantage of the hospitality of the Courtenays at Powderham – although what *would* he have made of the charades evening? – before leaving for Devonport

---

[205] NLW, Glynne of Hawarden Ms. 44. Willis's Rooms was a set of assembly rooms in St James, London, popular with politicians for meetings and other activities. 'Lord & Lady Devon' would have been William Courtenay, 10th earl (1777–1859) and his second wife; his son, William Courtenay (Lord Courtenay) (1807–88), was a contemporary of Glynne at Christ Church, Oxford.

by coach, crossing the Tamar, and arriving with members of the Fortescue family at Boconnoc. Once there, he did not venture far, hindered by poor weather, visiting only seven churches, before returning direct to Exeter by mail coach. In contrast, that autumn, he spent over three weeks in Devon based at Powderham Castle and Killerton House,[206] recording many churches in those areas, before abruptly taking off to Clovelly to explore the north coast.[207] He remained only a week in Cornwall in the summer of 1843, in the main exploring Penwith, and he did not return to the county until February 1849. On that expedition, he stayed slightly longer, to see more churches in Penwith before travelling on to The Lizard, then going east to Falmouth, Bodmin, and Liskeard. During another six-day tour in January/February 1850, he recorded fourteen churches, travelling from Talland, Lansallos, and Fowey on the south coast, to visit a string of parishes in the north, from Tintagel to St Columb Major to Wadebridge, whence he took a very slow 'Omnibus' back to Plymouth. Bizarrely, in the January/February of 1853 he paid a visit to six churches on the south coast over three days, having lodged initially at Devonport, yet it appears he travelled from Birmingham to Bristol to Exeter to Plymouth specifically to make that trip.

One of Glynne's more extended stays in the county was from the 27 January to 6 February 1854, with another fourteen churches visited, commencing at St Winnow and 'Broadoak' [Braddock] – it is likely he was at Boconnoc again[208] – before travelling to the north coast and proceeding westwards to St Erth and Phillack, perhaps catching the steamer from Hayle or St Ives back to Bristol.[209] In February 1858, he spent nine days in Cornwall, starting at South Petherwin before settling into an exploration of The Roseland, where he was upset by the loss of his notebook on the route from Tregony to Truro. That day, he recorded the churches of Cornelly, Lamorran, St Michael Penkevil, and Tregony, so if losing his notebook robbed him of his *aide-mémoire*, it did not in any way appear to render his later accounts of these buildings deficient. He stayed for three nights at Penzance, exploring more of Penwith, itemising his expenses there:

Penzance bill £1 12s. 0d.
Driver 5s. 0d.
Churches 2s. 6d.
Marazion 3s. 10d.
Omnibus 1s. 0d.
Stamps 1s. 0d.
Logan Rocke 1s. 8d.
Letter 0s. 8d.

---

[206] Glynne was a good friend of Sir Thomas Dyke Acland, 11th Bt (1809–98), a contemporary at Christ Church, MP (1837–47), and eventual owner of the Killerton estates in east Devon.
[207] NLW, Glynne of Hawarden Ms. 37, 17 November: 'At Clovelly, fine & warm with wind & some cloud. Good rocks & coastal scenery.'
[208] The Boconnoc estates were owned by Anne (1772–1864), the wife of William Wyndham, Lord Grenville (1759–1834), and the aunt of George Matthew Fortescue, who resided there and entertained Glynne. William was the younger brother of Thomas Grenville, Glynne's great uncle through his mother's side, so Anne Wyndham, Lady Grenville, was Glynne's great aunt by marriage.
[209] No diary survives for this journey.

These amounts are self-explanatory, with, presumably, the sum expended at the Logan Rock paid to a guide who would have made the stone move,[210] and the half-crown to churches as gratuities to sextons. Glynne's final visit to the county was not until twelve years later, in 1870, when he was sixty-two years of age.[211] The itinerary reveals an interest in, and possibly targeted visits to, churches on the Lizard peninsula, the north coast, and the Roseland peninsula, perhaps based on his by now acquired knowledge of reliable inns and means of transport around the region; the churches of Penwith also appeared to uphold a particular fascination for him, one maybe reignited by the publication in 1865 of Blight's *Churches of West Cornwall*.

It is evident from these tours that he much preferred 'flying about'[212] the county, and noting churches on the move, to settling in a region with the intent of visiting all the parishes in the vicinity, as a kind of saturation coverage. Yet despite this, it is hard to explain the isolation of two churches, not far from Truro, visited in 1863, and two on the north coast in 1865; it is possible that others were recorded on those occasions, of which we know nothing – and of course one should not presume that on every day when on tours around the country, he took in churches.[213] However, in 1870 he records that he was at Davidstow near Camelford on 7 February, at Sancreed near St Ives the same day, on the 9th he was still in Penwith at Towednack, before apparently travelling fifty miles back east to St Teath that same day. His memory must be at fault here, with St Teath and Davidstow presumably recorded together (7th), thereafter going west on the carriage road to Redruth, Hayle, or Penzance, ending up at Sancreed and Towednack. After passing a couple of days on The Lizard, probably based in Helston, he finished at Crowan and Sithney churches on 11 February, before travelling east, the last church he noted in Cornwall being Menheniot on the 18th. One can only surmise how he spent the week between these last Cornish visits. He could, of course, have stayed for an unrecorded time at Boconnoc before travelling by rail to Plymouth, perhaps disembarking at Menheniot station (opened in 1859) – the church spire is clearly visible from the line – to note his last 'fair specimen of a Cornish Church'.[214]

---

[210] This geological feature, or 'Lodging Rock', comprised a large boulder that was so shaped that even gentle pressure could cause it to move, or 'lodge'. However, in 1824, the rock was removed – just to prove a point – and was thereafter replaced, but without having the same facility of movement. A strongman guide was often employed to move the rock thereafter; see D. Gilbert, *The Parochial History of Cornwall: Founded on the Manuscript Histories of Mr. Hals and Mr. Tonkin, with Additions and Various Appendices*, 4 vols (London, 1838), iii, 30–2.

[211] No diary survives for 1870.

[212] Veysey, 'Sir Stephen Glynne', 162.

[213] No diaries survive for these years.

[214] As David Parsons also speculates on Glynne in Sussex: 'The single [church] visits [...] are intriguing. Why travel, even from the family home in London, just to visit one church? Maybe these represent an opportunity to pick up a church *en route* to somewhere else. In the case of Barnham, on 13 November 1867, the only visit between the end of 1863 and 1868, it might have been a railway journey; Barnham is a junction and its station had been opened the previous year – was Glynne changing trains and with time on his hands decided to look at the parish church?', *Sussex*, xxiv. The comparative isolation of the two Cornish churches recorded in both 1863 and 1865 remains puzzling, however, even more so as the remote and tiny church of Trentishoe on the north Devon coast was visited on 20 October 1865, without any others recorded, five days before he was in Cornwall.

Glynne's coverage of the churches in this most remote of counties is impressive. He visited 120 or nearly 60 per cent of the total,[215] which compares not unfavourably with other counties; for example, in Derbyshire it is 78 per cent, Durham 46 per cent, Herefordshire 68 per cent, Nottinghamshire 60 per cent, and so on.[216] Additionally, most of the significant churches in the county were visited, although there were some exceptions on Bodmin Moor, such as Altarnun, Blisland, and Cardinham, which were perhaps too difficult to travel to in his favoured winter months.[217] Another exception is St Endellion, although as previously noted, he walked to it in 1850. Was it shut, perhaps – this was 1 February, and it was a vile winter's day – which also invites the question of how many other churches did he try to visit, which went unrecorded either in his diaries or his notebooks, because he was denied access?

Table 2. Parishes visited by Glynne, listed in chronological order and identified by his diary entries.

Parish	Dedication	Date of visit	Diary entry
Kilkhampton		<1840	
Stratton		<1840	
Launceston		<1840	
St Thomas-by-Launceston		<1840	
St Stephen-by-Launceston		<1840	
Sheviock		1842	NLW, Glynne 37
Liskeard		1842	
Lanteglos-by-Fowey		1842	NLW, Glynne 37
St Veep		1842	
Boconnoc		1842	NLW, Glynne 37
Lostwithiel		1842	
Lanhydrock	St Hydrock	1842	NLW, Glynne 37
Truro	St Mary	1843	
Kenwyn		1843	
St Austell		1843	NLW, Glynne 38
St Mewan		1843	
Paul		1843	NLW, Glynne 38
Gulval	St Gulval	July 1843	

[215] He recorded 121 churches, to include St Michael's Mount. St Catherine's Whitstone is the Devon parish, not the Cornish one, despite being indexed by Gladstone's Library as in Cornwall.

[216] Butler, 'Sir Stephen Glynne', 103, tabulates Glynne's coverage. However, he uses the published accounts of churches, noting only ninety-three churches for Cornwall, using the incomplete *Notes & Queries* series for his calculation.

[217] Of his fourteen expeditions to Cornwall for which we know the dates, eight took place in January/February.

Parish	Dedication	Date of visit	Diary entry
St Ives		1843	NLW, Glynne 38
Lelant	St Uny	1843	
Marazion		1843	NLW, Glynne 38
St Michael's Mount		1843	NLW, Glynne 38
Camborne	St Martin	1843	NLW, Glynne 38
Falmouth		1843	NLW, Glynne 38
Breage		July 1843	
Wendron	St Wendron	1843	
Zennor	St Sennar	14 Feb. 1849	NLW, Glynne 43
St Just-in-Penwith	St Just	14 Feb. 1849	NLW, Glynne 43
Sennen	St Senan	14 Feb. 1849	NLW, Glynne 43
St Buryan		15 Feb. 1849	
Ruan Major		16 Feb. 1849	
Ruan Minor	St Rumon	16 Feb. 1849	
Landewednack	St Lantry	17 Feb. 1849	
Grade	St Grade	17 Feb. 1849	
Mullion	St Mulleon	17 Feb. 1849	
St Gluvias		19 Feb. 1849	NLW, Glynne 43
Mylor	St Melor	19 Feb. 1849	NLW, Glynne 43
Probus	St Probus & St Grace	20 Feb. 1849	
Bodmin	St Petroc	21 Feb. 1849	NLW, Glynne 43
Antony	St Anthony & St John	23 Feb. 1849	
Antony	St John	23 Feb. 1849	
St Germans		23 Feb. 1849	NLW, Glynne 43
St Martin-by-Looe		23 Feb. 1849	NLW, Glynne 43
Fowey	St Finbarrus	30 Jan. 1850	NLW, Glynne 44
Talland	St Tallan	30 Jan. 1850	
Lansallos		30 Jan. 1850	
Michaelstow	St Michael	31 Jan. 1850	
Tintagel	St Symphorian	1 Feb. 1850	NLW, Glynne 44
Trevalga	St Petroc	1 Feb. 1850	
Forrabury	St Symphorian	1 Feb. 1850	
St Minver		2 Feb. 1850	NLW, Glynne 44
St Enodoc		2 Feb. 1850	
St Merryn		3 Feb. 1850	
Padstow	St Pedrock	3 Feb. 1850	NLW, Glynne 44

Parish	Dedication	Date of visit	Diary entry
Egloshayle		4 Feb. 1850	
St Columb Major		4 Feb. 1850	NLW, Glynne 44
St Breock		4 Feb. 1850	NLW, Glynne 44
Maker	St Macra	29 May 1852	
Saltash		28 May 1852	
Landrake	St Peter	28 May 1852	
Saltash	St Stephen	28 June 1852	
St Blazey		31 Jan. 1853	NLW, Glynne 45
Gorran	St Gorran	1 Feb. 1853	
Mevagissey	St Mewa & St Ida	1 Feb. 1853	NLW, Glynne 45
Veryan	St Symphoriana	1 Feb. 1853	
St Just-in-Roseland		2 Feb. 1853	
St Anthony-in-Roseland		2 Feb. 1853	
St Winnow		27 Jan. 1854	
St Neot		28 Jan. 1854	
Broadoak	St Mary	29 Jan. 1854	
Lanreath		31 Jan. 1854	
St Kew		2 Feb. 1854	
St Mabyn		2 Feb. 1854	
Mawgan-in-Pydar		3 Feb. 1854	
Newlyn East	St Newlyn	4 Feb. 1854	
Cubert	St Cuthbert	4 Feb. 1854	
Crantock		4 Feb. 1854	
St Clement		5 Feb. 1854	
St Allen		6 Feb. 1854	
Phillack	St Felix	6 Feb. 1854	
St Erth		6 Feb. 1854	
Launcells	St Andrew	21 Jan. 1857	
Poundstock	St Neot	22 Jan. 1857	
St Gennys		23 Jan. 1857	
Jacobstow	St James	23 Jan. 1857	
South Petherwin	St Paternus	11 Feb. 1858	
St Michael Penkevil		12 Feb. 1858	
Cornelly	St Cornelius	12 Feb. 1858	
Lamorran	St Moren	12 Feb. 1858	
Tregony	St James	12 Feb. 1858	NLW, Glynne 48

Parish	Dedication	Date of visit	Diary entry
Perranuthnoe	St Peran	16 Feb. 1858	
Ludgvan	St Paul	16 Feb. 1858	NLW, Glynne 48
Madron	St Madern	16 Feb. 1858	NLW, Glynne 48
St Anthony-in-Meneage		17 Feb. 1858	
Manaccan	St Antonius	17 Feb. 1858	NLW, Glynne 48
Mawgan-in-Meneage		17 Feb. 1858	
Mabe	St Mabe	18 Feb. 1858	NLW, Glynne 48
Budock	St Budoc	18 Feb. 1858	
Calstock		24 Apr. 1860	
Redruth	St Uny	Aug. 1862	
St Cleer		Aug. 1862	
St Keyne		Aug. 1862	
Duloe	St Cuby	20 Aug. 1862	
Tywardreath	St Andrew	22 Aug. 1862	
Lanlivery	St Brevita	23 Aug. 1862	
Stithians	St Stithian	26 Aug. 1862	
Gwennap	St Wenep	26 Aug. 1862	
St Levan		28 Aug. 1862	
Feock		22 Aug. 1863	
Perranarworthal	St Piran	26 Aug. 1863	
Minster	St Metherian	24 Oct. 1865	
Lanteglos-by-Camelford	St Lantry	25 Oct. 1865	
Sancreed		7 Feb. 1870	
Davidstow	St David	7 Feb. 1870	
St Teath		9 Feb. 1870	
Towednack	St Twinnock	9 Feb. 1870	
Cury		10 Feb. 1870	
Gunwalloe	St Wynwallow	10 Feb. 1870	
Sithney	St Sithly	11 Feb. 1870	
Crowan	St Crowena	11 Feb. 1870	
Menheniot	St Neot	18 Feb. 1870	

From the accompanying table (Table 2), it is clear that many parishes visited by Glynne were not mentioned individually in his diaries. The tabulated chronology is therefore based on the dates of his notes (which as we have seen are sometimes incorrect), or a close geographical proximity to those he mentions; yet it is the churches he did not record that are intriguing. For example, after attending Bodmin church on the morning of Ash Wednesday, 21 February 1849, he ventured forth in the afternoon to Liskeard, but there are no notes of any churches visited, despite several being within easy walking/riding distance. The following day, which 'turned out very fine', he journeyed from Liskeard to Looe, a mere eight miles or so of relatively easy going, the route taking him very close to St Keyne and Morval, yet no churches were recorded that day. Similarly, we know he stayed overnight in Bodmin on 30 January 1850, the day after, despite 'very much rain', walking to Camelford and recording Michaelstow *en route* – not mentioned in his diary but dated in the church notes. Yet he would also have passed very close to Helland, St Breward, and St Tudy; again, on a foul, wet winter's day, were they closed, or did he simply lose heart?

Such hypotheses are interesting, but in the absence of what David Parsons terms a 'Master Plan' of visits,[218] other than his apparent partiality to the churches and scenery of Penwith, we are none the wiser about why he singled out the churches he did. Comfortable accommodation would have been open to him for the asking at Boconnoc, as we have seen, yet he appears to have stayed there infrequently, as even for the years for which his diaries have not survived, there is no geographical link to the districts visited and Boconnoc. He also visited Tregothnan but does not appear to have received any hospitality there.[219] One might hazard that his peculiar solitariness or personality was such that he preferred the anonymity of country inns rather than the conviviality – and charades – involved in country house living. Also, as we have some data on both his itineraries and the extent of his field notes, it is equally speculative to discuss how these rough notes were transformed into ordered, polished, written accounts. Some have suggested that Glynne wrote them up very soon after his visits,[220] whereas others have proposed that a longish interval was more likely.[221] Considering the sheer practicalities of the former, he would have had to have transported suitable writing materials with him, including the selected, formalised notebooks relevant to his tours, and also to have enjoyed appropriate accommodation and furniture, perhaps not always available in a country inn.[222] It seems more likely that he spent time when settled – at Hawarden among his books, or in London – writing up observations from his field notes and diaries, combining them with his recollections, to produce objective, fluidly written, coherent accounts of individual church buildings. Did his obsession for recording the weather conditions on his tours also assist in taking him back in his memory to a specific church, as it still can do for us?

Consider, therefore, his departure from Cornwall on 12 July 1843 'by gig to Tor Point where arrived at midnight & slept'; or on 5 February 1850, a day marked by twelve hours spent in an omnibus to Plymouth, an overnight stay there 'very

[218] Parsons (ed.), *Sussex*, xxv.
[219] However, at that time Tregothnan was the home of Evelyn Boscawen, 6th Viscount Falmouth (1819–89), who bred racehorses at Mereworth Castle (Kent) and was frequently absent from his Cornish house.
[220] Butler (ed.), *Yorkshire*, 24–5, note 39; M. McGarvie (ed.), *Sir Stephen Glynne's Church Notes for Somerset*, Somerset Record Society 82 (Taunton, 1994), xvi–xxi.
[221] D.C. Cox (ed.), *Sir Stephen Glynne's Church Notes for Shropshire*, Shropshire Record Series 1 (Keele, 1997), xi–xvii; Parsons (ed.), *Sussex*, xviii–xx.
[222] It is salutary to consider the dedication of Nikolaus Pevsner's *Yorkshire: The North Riding* (London, 1966) – a century after Glynne – which was 'To those publicans and hoteliers of England who provide me with a table in my bedroom to scribble on.' I am indebted to Stuart Blaylock for this charming reference.

windy night, quite a gale', followed by a 'very unpleasant' journey from Plymouth to Bristol: these are far from propitious circumstances in which to concentrate on writing up notes. There is also some evidence of delays in composing his accounts. For example, in a run of descriptions of churches in Devon visited in 1857 (GL, Glynne Notebook 14, fols 70–89), South Petherwin, visited in 1858, interrupts the sequence, occupying fols 72–4. This suggests that the Devon churches were written up after the visit to South Petherwin of a year later, as there is no break in the foliation, or gaps left on the pages. In addition, if Glynne's memory was as forensically accurate as generally recognised, would it have made much difference if he wrote up the notes soon after the visits or following a year or two – or, as in the case of two churches in Sussex, after an interval of nearly thirty years?[223] We can see from the surviving field notes for four Cornish churches that they contained sufficient information to underpin the composition of a detailed account of the building, so that his recollections – whenever they might have been called upon – simply helped to create a coherent and ordered report.[224]

One can also speculate on the literature Glynne may have studied before undertaking his tours; when his single-minded purpose was to travel to Cornwall, for instance, on his steamship journeys direct to Falmouth and St Ives, one might imagine that he had made reasonable topographical and antiquarian preparation beforehand. He must, surely, have been aware, like the Lysons brothers before him, of the Cornwall section of Gough's *British Topography*, and the information contained in Borlase's *Antiquities Historical and Monumental of the County of Cornwall*, about archaeological and landscape features, particularly in Penwith. We know he consulted the Lysons' work as he makes occasional acknowledgement, relating to the font at Bodmin, for instance. Yet he does not use their architectural style nomenclature, and his descriptions of the churches at Egloshayle and Padstow make little recognition of the features the Lysons illustrate. The only topographical work with comprehensive coverage of individual church buildings at the time was C.S. Gilbert's *Historical Survey*, but despite the sponsorship of engravings of their seats by the county's gentry, it was a work rather poorly received,[225] and the descriptions of churches were based more on whimsical romance rather than architectural accuracy. Whether Glynne knew of the work is impossible to say, but it would certainly have been in the library at Boconnoc, as it contained a lengthy description of the house, and an engraving sponsored by 'Lord & Lady Grenville [...] as an encouragement of this Work.'[226]

Glynne would also have benefitted from a network of correspondents to encourage and guide him. His second expedition to Cornwall in 1842 may have been stimulated by a letter from J.L. Parker, of 24 Hill Street, Berkeley Square:

---

[223] Parsons (ed.), *Sussex*, xviii.
[224] Notes for the fifth Cornish church recorded in this series, Stratton, were much shorter than for the others, as he had already visited the parish before 1840; these field notes were supplementary therefore, and simply confirmed what he had already noted.
[225] John Austen of Place wrote to Daniel Lysons on 8 May 1814, commenting: 'There is a man called Gilbert now writing a History of Cornwall – he shewed me his work, which is incorrect'; BL, Add. Ms. 9416, fol. 66v.
[226] C.S. Gilbert, *An Historical Survey of the County of Cornwall, to Which Is Added a Complete Heraldry of the Same; With Numerous Engravings*, 2 vols (Plymouth Dock, 1817–20), ii, 908–12.

[I] find you are visiting Devon where I hope you find the mild climate agrees with you. In some parts you will find much to interest you, particularly up the Tamar – and by no means miss visiting Cothele, Lord Mount Edgcumbe [...] should you extend your trip into Cornwall, you will see Boconnoc, of course, & if so, pray go to Lostwithiel & down to Fowey – but first introduce yourself with my compliments to Mr Hext at Restormel Castle, a most hearty liberal Gentleman, & very intelligent & agreeable person, & Mrs Hext, a Liverpool lady, Miss Stainforth.[227] He can shew you many interesting things in that neighbourhood.[228]

In 1862 Glynne was in correspondence with John J.G. Fuller,[229] of Camelford, who wrote to him settling on a price of £1 for twenty-two sketches of various antiquities in the Cornish countryside, as well as offering a few hints on visiting churches:

Lewnewth is about to be handed over to some country masons, to restore it – or more probably spoil what is really good [...] Minster is entirely surrounded and embedded by trees, the entrance is at the 2 stone uprights on jams, under the overhanging boughs of the twisted trees, & in the summer highly picturesque. Tintagel church from the N.E. corner shews most of the early windows on that side, differing entirely from those on the other side of the building. From the depression of the roof & other corroborative remains, the tower has evidently been in the centre of the building – the slab and cross now lying in a corner of the Chancel, was I believe discovered by the present Vicar Rev. R.B. Kinsman[230] (a good Antiquarian & Artist) among some rubbish during the restoration [...] on the N. side of the church in the ~~church~~ Porch is a door way similar to the one at S. Juliott.[231]

Was it this letter that inspired Glynne's visit to Minster (1865), and his repeat visit to Tintagel (1870), when he noted the cross slab identified by Fuller? As an alternative approach, perhaps aiming more to entice Glynne to visit her than imparting antiquarian information, Charlotte Neville Grenville, Glynne's aunt (1789–1877), wrote:

At Hayes there is one of the most restored churches, with a very curious antient appendage now used as a vestry room; and at Keston if you wish to see it, a specimen of a Church as it has been left as it were in that darkest of ages, the eighteenth century.[232]

Similarly, on 9 May 1856, Lady Charlotte Proby (1788–1860) wrote from Elton Hall, Huntingdonshire, 'I shall be delighted to see you on Tuesday 22nd for as many days

---

[227] John Hext (1766–1838) married in Liverpool Elizabeth, daughter of Thomas Stainforth; he died at Restormel.
[228] GL, Glynne Gladstone Ms. 27, letter dated 14 February; there is no year date given, but it must have been before Hext's death.
[229] John James Gibson Fuller (b. 1804), a sketch artist in Devon and Cornwall for various publications.
[230] Rev. Richard Byrn Kinsman (1811–94), vicar of Tintagel (1851–94), where he is buried.
[231] Loose letter tucked into GL, Glynne notebooks 14.
[232] GL, Glynne Gladstone Ms. 27, letter dated 17 February. Keston was visited in 1832, but there is no record of a visit to Hayes.

as I and my Churches can tempt you to stay.'[233] While such recommendations may indeed have appealed to Glynne, overall it is the apparent lack of planning, and an impetuousness, as far as we can perceive today, that is so characteristic of his expeditions.

Glynne's Church Notebooks

The Cornish church notes are contained within four volumes of the complete series of 107 notebooks. They are described here not in numerical order, something determined after Glynne's death, but in the chronological order of the notes they contain. The dates of the visits have been verified from Glynne's own 'Index Volume' (vol. 107).

Volume 17 is a half-leather bound book with green covers (24 x 19 cm), comprising ninety-one folios numbered 67–157, labelled 'Devon & Cornwall' inside the front cover, and with a place-name index inside the back cover. It commences at fol. 67 with notes on Great Torrington (Devon), with entries for the five Cornish churches visited before 1840 occupying a block (fols 74–80), between Hartland (fols 72–3) and Bridestowe and Mamhead (fols 80–1). Later in the volume are notes of the seven churches visited when Glynne stayed at Boconnoc in 1842, Sheviock (fols 124–6) to Lanhydrock (fols 132–3), sandwiched between Tavistock (fol. 123) and Hatherleigh (fols 133–4). The volume concludes with notes for four churches visited on 12 July 1843, which was the last day of his five-day tour in the county, from Truro St Mary (fol. 151) to St Mewan (fols 156–7), the final entry being for Plymstock (fol. 157). The writing is clear and flowing, easily legible, with a pronounced forward slope, and on the rectos only, with few corrections or additions on the versos, although there are some insertions between the lines accommodating afterthoughts. One peculiarity is that the writing style of the notes for Lostwithiel and Lanhydrock changes abruptly to a more vertical script, using a finer nib, before returning to normal for Hatherleigh. On fol. 131v., there is a very finely drawn sketch of the top of the spire of Lostwithiel church: was that the reason for the change in implement (Fig. 7)?

Volume 70 is a leather bound, soft cover notebook (24.5 x 19.5 cm) comprising forty-four folios numbered 1B–43B.[234] Inside the front cover is 'South Wales & Monmouthshire', which is also how the volume is listed in the Gladstone's Library Index to the notes. Inside the rear cover, and inverted, it is labelled 'Diocese of Exeter'. Fol. 0 is entitled 'List of Churches in Exeter Diocese herein noted'. The volume proper commences with notes on Paul (fol. 1B) proceeding to Wendron (fols 10B–11B) for the Cornish churches visited in July 1843. The rest of the book accommodates notes for churches in Devon all visited in 1845. Again, the writing is flowing and clearly legible, on the rectos, with only a few additions on the versos, or corrections to the main text. The exceptions are the accounts of the Cornish churches in Penwith, which Glynne liberally supplemented on the facing versos with information extracted (and acknowledged) from Blight's *West Cornwall*, or from revisits, themselves perhaps, as has been suggested, stimulated by Blight's architectural reading of a particular building. The script of these additions is typical of Glynne's

---

[233] GL, Glynne Gladstone Ms. 27. Whether Glynne accepted this invitation is impossible to say, although there is no record of any churches visited in the vicinity around that time.
[234] Each of the inked-in folio numbers has a lightly pencilled 'B' under it, hence the numeration here, although the reason is not clear.

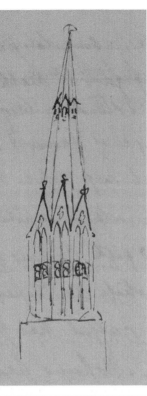

Fig. 7. Sketch of Lostwithiel church spire; image courtesy of Gladstone's Library, Hawarden, Wales, reproduced with kind permission of the Gladstone Estate, Hawarden, Wales, Glynne Notebooks 17, fol. 131v.

Fig. 8. Amended account of Wendron; image courtesy of Gladstone's Library, Hawarden, Wales, reproduced with kind permission of the Gladstone Estate, Hawarden, Wales, Glynne Notebooks 70, fol. 9Bv.

Chancel is long & is the oldest portion – On the S. near its extremity is a small
ing (as at Mullion) only arched – that eastward of it wider, but less high
the N wall of the Chancel near the altar steps is a segmental recess
probably an Easter Sepulchre –
N side is a single lancet trefoil headed.
E window is early Dec^d – of 3 lights without tracery –
N. wall of the Chancel has a plinth extending from the junction
Transept, probably added for strengthening the wall.
there is the rood staircase in the angle at the junction of the Transept
The E window of the Transept is a pretty Dec^d one –

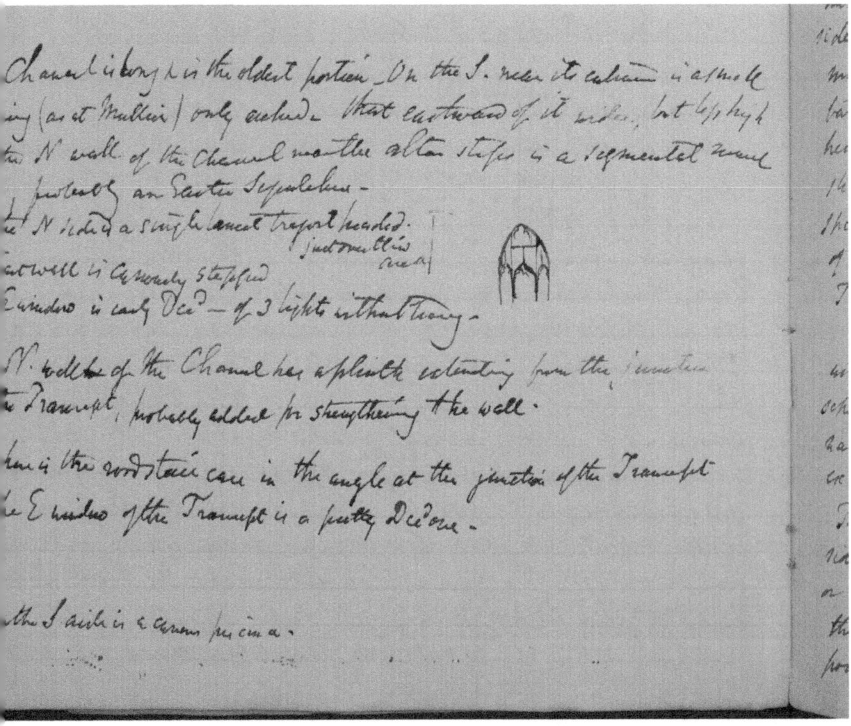

later handwriting: irregular line spacing, poorly defined letter forms, generally implying a 'hurried' manner (Fig. 8). Tucked into the volume is an undated offprint from *The Ecclesiologist* 10 (1850), 356, relating to Lelant and St Ives, although Glynne adds nothing to his own notes from its contents.

Volume 13 is the same format as volume 17 and comprises sixty-six folios numbered 1–66. The inside front cover is labelled 'Diocese of Exeter – Counties of Devon & Cornwall'; inside the back cover is an index of place names. Most of the entries are written in black ink, but there are occasional entries in blue. This is the sister volume to 17, the pagination of which starts at 67, yet the churches described here were visited later, from 1845 to 1850; the reason for the mismatch is unclear. It commences with Holne (fol. 1) to Beer (fols 44–5), and concludes with a series of twenty Cornish churches, starting with Zennor (fol. 45) visited on 14 February 1849, and ending with Michaelstow (fol. 66), visited on 31 January 1850. This church is one of a group of four (of the fourteen churches accounted for on that 1850 tour), in the middle of which is the description of St Martin-by-Looe, visited in 1849, again suggesting that Glynne wrote up his notes in batches when convenient, rather than as soon as possible after the visits. By now, his handwriting is starting to become less precise, but with few corrections or additions, and the accounts remain fluent and comprehensive, even when of extended length – such as that of Fowey (fols 61–3).

Volume 14 is a half-leather bound notebook, with red covers (24 x 19 cm) and a missing spine, comprising ninety folios, with 'Diocese of Exeter' inside the front cover. It starts with Probus (fol. 1), visited in 1849; if strict chronological order of his notes had interested Glynne, he could have inserted this account in volume 13 in place of one or more of the churches visited in 1850 in that volume. Thereafter there are notes for the remainder of the 1850 Cornish churches (fols 1–16), followed by those in Devon for 1851 and 1852 (fols 16–24). In May 1852, he was in south-east Cornwall (fols 24–9), the accounts of the four churches there interrupted by Egg Buckland and Stoke Damerell (Devon). He visited Gorran and five other parishes in 1853 (fols 44–8), and a year later, resulting from a tour in January/February 1854, a total of fourteen Cornish churches are written up, starting with St Allen (fol. 50) and finishing with St Winnow (fol. 63). A final section (fols 66–72) records visits to the north-east of the county in January 1857, then South Petherwin in 1858 (fols 72–4), ending with a few Devon parishes recorded in 1861–2. The chronology of the volume extends from 1849 to 1862 therefore, roughly alternating Cornish and Devon churches, and proceeding in roughly chronological order. The entries are written almost exclusively on the rectos with only a few supplementary notes on the facing versos, although the handwriting demonstrates a mild deterioration during the book's progression, as might be expected: he was forty-two years old at the start, fifty-five by the time it was completed.

Volume 16 is a half-leather bound notebook with green covers (24 x 19 cm), spine missing, comprising sixty-six folios, matching volume 13 therefore, with 'Diocese of Exeter' on the title page.[235] Inside the back cover is a place names index. It starts (fols 1–16) with a batch of notes on Cornish churches, with a considerable amount of extra material, including comments and sketches, on the versos facing fols 1–5, taken in the main from Blight's *West Cornwall*. It is odd, however, that even though

---

[235] Volume 15 is devoted entirely to Devon churches, visited in 1826 and before 1840, recording Glynne's earliest visits to the diocese.

Blight described Lelant and Madron churches (fols 5–7), recording features that Glynne made nothing of, that he added no further details. This collection of Cornish notes finishes with Calstock (fols 16–17), visited in 1860, when he was at Lamerton, Kelly and other Devon churches not far off. The notes for Redruth, made in August 1862, were inserted on to fol. 15, in an obvious gap between finishing Budock and starting Calstock. Devon churches recorded between 1860 and 1864 fill the following pages (17–36), with Lanteglos-by-Camelford and Minster (fols 33–5) interrupting the sequence, even though they were not explored until 1865. Strangely, too, a second group of Cornish churches recorded in 1862–3 follows (fols 37–48), before returning to Devon. The book ends with notes of nine Cornish churches made in February 1870 (fols 55–66) with Buckfastleigh inserted into this series, and the account for Davidstow running on to the terminal verso. Glynne's writing continues slowly to deteriorate, and as can be seen from the above description, the chronological and topographical arrangements are increasingly haphazard.

Volume 64 is a notebook with marbled covers, in fragile condition, with the spine missing (20 x 16.5 cm). The cover is labelled 'Churches Classified according to Architecture', whereas inside the front cover is 'Church Notes. Monumental Inscriptions &c.' The first three pages (it is unpaginated) are taken up with transcripts of monumental inscriptions and comments on funerary monuments in Lanteglos-by-Fowey, Stratton, Launceston, and Sheviock. This book is paired with volume 65, in which Glynne attempted to categorise the features of the churches he had seen. Examples of this analytical industry, found in volume 64 in the pages after the inscriptions, are 'Rectilinear Windows', listing churches with fifteen decreasing to five lights; 'Churches in which there is a combination of Early English & Decorated'; 'Early English – wholly or with very little of any other style'; and so on. Presumably his interest in these investigations swiftly took over from the transcribing of inscriptions, although it is unclear why.

The entire series of 107 notebooks encompassing counties and dioceses is generally arranged in alphabetical order, starting with volumes 1 and 2 for Bedfordshire and Huntingdonshire, until 59, which covers Wiltshire, Hampshire, and the South Downs. Regions of Wales are found in 66–71, but from 72–106 a variety of counties is covered, ranging from Gloucestershire and Herefordshire to Sussex to Yorkshire. However, they are numbered now, and grouping volume 70 as integral to volumes 13–17, the notes for the churches of the Exeter diocese form a cohesive group of six notebooks. Also, as the above analysis suggests, in the main, groups of churches visited on a particular tour were recorded serially in a single volume (with the occasional chronological *non sequitur*), whether or not they encompassed one or both counties together. This retained the concept of covering a specific region, such that whenever Glynne transferred his sometimes quite disordered field notes into his formalised notebooks, he was careful to conserve a sense of local connections between the churches of a county or diocese.[236] Hence, the growing archive of descriptions of Cornish churches must have been intermittently consulted and appreciated by Glynne, such that he began to recognise the stamp of the buildings' shape, local architectural style, and general features for what they were, rather than, ecclesiologically, what he might have wanted them to be.

---

[236] This might seem unremarkable, but for some counties the field notes comprise disorganised scraps of paper; for example, for several churches in the vicinity of Okehampton, notes on a tour of 1845 were made on sheets of black-edged funeral notepaper, now tucked into volume 16.

Glynne's architectural and ecclesiological views

Glynne's descriptions of churches follow a general pattern. First there is an account of the exterior of the building to establish its plan, noting the shape of windows and doorways, with special attention paid to the tower and belfry windows. A description of the interior follows, with the architectural features of the nave, arcades, and transepts all noted, before proceeding eastwards into the chancel and any associated chapels. Numbers of window lights and tracery patterns are scrupulously recorded, as are differences between the roof structures of the various parts of the church, and particular features such as a piscina, sedilia, squint, and the roodloft stairs. Fixtures and fittings follow, encompassing woodwork such as bench ends, the pulpit and screen, and medieval glass, but they receive only brief attention, although the font is usually described in detail. Tomb monuments and brasses are also noted, sometimes with the inscriptions transcribed, and the account usually closes with a commentary on the setting of the building in the landscape.

Unlike in other counties, where Glynne's notes start in the 1820s and 1830s, the earliest notes for Cornwall were compiled, as we have seen, a short time before 1840. In the descriptions of these five churches, he uses 'Rectilinear' for the 'Perpendicular' style, and, like Samuel Lysons, with his shorthand notation of 'clustered pillars, obtuse arches' for the nave arcades, he describes 'light lozenge piers having a shaft at the angle with an octagonal capital', supporting 'Tudor' or flattened arches (Kilkhampton). At Launceston St Mary, he lamented the lack of a clerestory, which 'diminishes greatly the effect of the interior', but otherwise approved of the 'spacious' interior of the three-aisled structure, the absence of a chancel arch contributing markedly to that effect. By 1842/3, he had coined the term 'Cornish Perpendicular' to record what he felt was a typical Cornish church, as at Lanteglos-by-Fowey, where he also regarded the three aisles as 'after the Cornish fashion'. Sheviock he considered to be a blend of Decorated and Perpendicular, and the particularly noteworthy window tracery comprised a 'decorated window with a circle on the upper part' – a quite simplistic judgement of the complex patterns found there. In Truro in 1843 we find him displeased with the exterior of St Mary's, 'rather a profusion of ornament [...] & the whole bears evidence of debasement having been re-edified in 1534 [*sic*]'. Inside, he found it even worse – 'devoid of interest, having undergone alterations in the Italian [Renaissance-inspired] style'. By the time Glynne returned to Cornwall in 1849, he had revised his architectural terminology, however, using 'First / Second / Third Pointed' for 'Early English / Decorated / Perpendicular', following the guidance of the Cambridge Camden Society (CCS). Consequently, he describes Zennor as a 'late Third Pointed church of a common Cornish type'; a year later Egloshayle 'is as usual Cornish Third Pointed', with 'piers of the usual form'; and Fowey incorporated First, Second, and Third Pointed features. Yet by 1852 he had reverted to Rickman's original and more widely used terminology,[237] so Maker is 'a late Perpendicular Church' with 'low Tudor arches in each arcade, with the much stilted Perpendicular piers with 4 shafts & alternate hollows'. His descriptions retain this format and terminology until his last visits in 1870.

The typically low-profile, three-aisled church plan, lack of chancel arch, and no clerestory, are, thus, features that Glynne became accustomed to finding; he was, perhaps, even intrigued by their consistent overall character, as a profound contrast to the larger, more individual, and more truly Gothic churches. He was interested in

---

[237] As continually and influentially disseminated in Thomas Rickman's *Attempt to Discriminate the Styles of English Architecture*, which by 1852 was in its fifth edition; see fns 141, 144.

the character of the roofs and their medieval carved wooden bosses and cornices, as at St Ewe (1858), where 'the roofs are coved and ribbed, with bosses of large heads, the interstices pannelled with crosses & square flowers'. At Forrabury (1850), he found 'the roof of the nave is open, that of the chancel meanly ceiled' – disapproving of the manner in which it had been done (mean) and the sense of enclosure (rather than open-ness) that resulted. The number of lights in each window was carefully recorded, and descriptions became more confident, such that at Lanteglos-by-Camelford (1865), the tracery feature similar to that at Sheviock (1842), was now described as a 'singular Flamboyant wheel'.[238] Although soon accustomed to exploring churches 'of the Cornish type', he was ambivalent about their characteristic profile. The contour of Egloshayle (1850) was like 'most Cornish Churches & is far from picturesque, the long unbroken line of wall, without Clerestory & the tall clumsy Tower by no means grouping well', yet at Lanteglos-by-Camelford (1865), 'The body of the Church presents a long bold unbroken line', as if the simplicity and plainness were by now redeeming features. The setting of certain churches also appealed. St Anthony-in-Roseland (1853) was 'in a charming sequestered Churchyard near a branch of Falmouth Harbour'; St John (1849) was 'in a lovely situation, shady & sequestered'; yet on the windswept north coast, Forrabury (1850) was 'very bleak & exposed'.

As Glynne's architectural accounts, and, it seems, his understanding of Cornish churches, became more sophisticated over time, so he began to credit an increased importance to the buildings' fixtures and fittings. Fonts were always carefully catalogued, particularly those of the Bodmin type, and even when less exceptional their form is clearly noted, as with the humble example at Trevalga (1850), where 'the Font is a plain large circular bowl, with moulded stem'. However, he demonstrates little expertise in interpreting sculptures, frequently describing sometimes quite remarkable features just as 'heads', 'grotesques', or 'angels'. At St Thomas-by-Launceston (1840), for example, he noted only a 'South porch of granite with some curious ornamental sculpture on it' for the exceptional Norman tympanum; and elsewhere there was little or no drive to decipher what he saw. In his defence, however, as for the Lysons, such delicate features were frequently covered by heavy coats of whitewash. At Gulval (1843), he found the arcade capitals as having 'sculptured shields & angel figures, but the whole is clogged with thick coats of whitewash'; and on the same tour, at Paul, not only did he find the exterior 'disastrous [...] fain resplendent of its displeasing & low proportions', but 'the interior is scarcely less satisfactory – the whole is glaring with white wash'. Yet at St Austell (1843), although he identified some of the statues set many feet above the ground on the tower (perhaps because they were in full relief?), his interpretative acumen was nothing compared to the Lysons' brave attempts at identifying these figures.

There is a similar analytical naïvety in his notes on stained glass. His accounts of the imagery even in windows as spectacular as St Kew, St Neot, and St Winnow (all 1854), the last 'representing saints with scrolls & also some armorial shields', are beyond

---

[238] Glynne also used the word 'Flamboyant' to describe windows at St Germans (1849), St Just-in-Penwith (1849), and Padstow (1850), although it did not appear to come into common use in England until 1851, and the publication of E.A. Freeman's *An Essay on the Origin and Development of Window Tracery in England* (Oxford/London, 1851). Glynne knew Freeman, so he may have been introduced to the term in earlier conversation, or he may have come across it on his travels abroad – 'gothique flamboyante' – where it was in use well before then. Like his swift adoption of the Cambridge Camden Society's nomenclature, it is symptomatic of Glynne's willingness and ability to use what he considered to be the latest architectural terminology.

cursory.[239] The architecture he experienced, fuelled by his understanding of it as a complex matrix of linear forms, was recorded in an objective and impersonal manner, but paradoxically, such a cool detachment from any architectural context seemed to kindle little or no expression of how a building might have evolved structurally.[240] This principle clearly extended to imagery, as neither did its forms or shapes adhere to particular styles, nor did he attempt to sit sculpture or glass within the frame of reference of the building. That said, he was occasionally moved to comment subjectively; the glass at St Neot, for example, was of 'unusual interest' and 'remarkable' – but there was also a caveat, that 'a large part of the glass is modern' and was only part of a wider restoration of the church, when 'Gothic uniform pues & a Gothic wooden pulpit were erected', features far more appealing to his sense of ecclesiological correctness.

And it is the woodwork and the type of seating – Glynne's 'pues' – that particularly exemplify his sense of ecclesiological righteousness, allied with the views of more pronounced church reformers. Pews had a financial value to the Church, and from a wealthy parishioner's viewpoint they were expressive of a parochial hierarchy, with many large box pews occupied either dynastically or related to landholdings, such privileges often jealously guarded;[241] for the lesser of the parish, it was mooted that they fostered a loyalty to one's weekly place in their church. However, they were also perceived as clogging up and spoiling the proportions of a church interior, and in overcrowded churches, it was slowly dawning anathema that space for many should be used for only two or three.[242] In his notes, Glynne manifests a particular antagonism to 'pues', as in box pews, which were often orientated in a number of directions, instead of facing east, and the non-uniform types and walls of which were often built up to shoulder height (Fig. 9).[243]

St Buryan (1849), he noted, was 'vilely pued', as was Mevagissey (1853). At Mabe (1858), there were 'wretched ugly pues', and at St Veep (1842), 'The body of the Church is full of wooden boxes, alias pues.' He was equally vexed by the

[239] This was also the case elsewhere. The magnificent glass at Fairford (Gloucestershire) (visited before 1840) in its entirety is described in just five sentences (W.P.W. Phillimore and J.M. Hall (eds), *Gloucestershire Church Notes, by the Late Sir Stephen R. Glynne, Bart.* (London, 1902), 31–2); at Eaton Bishop (Herefordshire) (1870), the east window contained 'some ancient stained glass', which is now acclaimed as of outstanding quality (J. Leonard (ed.), *Herefordshire Churches through Victorian Eyes: Sir Stephen Gynne's Church Notes for Herefordshire, with Water-Colours by Charles F. Walker* (Woonton Almeley, 2006), 139); and his notes on the glass in York were equally terse (Butler (ed.), *Yorkshire*, 452–3, for the spectacular glass at All Saints North Street).

[240] This contrasts with the contemporary view expressed by Glynne's nephew in his edition of the *Churches of Kent*, where he wrote that 'Sir Stephen Glynne would at once, as if by instinct, read its architectural history' (see fn. 186). I suggest that Glynne recorded the different architectural styles, but – even if mentally he was able to tease out and understood how a particular building developed – he made few attempts to record any such thoughts in his notebooks.

[241] See, for example, P. Cockerham, 'Views from the Pews: Glimpses of the Material State of the Post-Restoration Church in Mid to West Cornwall', *JRIC* (2022), 42–59, at 53–6; and also, R. Lee, *Rural Society and the Anglican Clergy, 1815–1914: Encountering and Managing the Poor* (Woodbridge, 2006), 43–6, for further case studies.

[242] S. Bradley, 'The Roots of Ecclesiology: Late Hanoverian Attitudes to Medieval Churches', in C. Webster and J. Elliott (eds), *'A Church as It Should Be': The Cambridge Camden Society and Its Influence* (Stamford, 2000), 22–44, at 36–40.

[243] G.W.O. Addleshaw and F. Etchells, *The Architectural Setting of Anglican Worship* (London, 1948), 86–98; W.M. Jacob, 'Sacred Space in the Long Eighteenth Century: Seating in Churches', *Ecclesiology Today* 44 (2011), 3–16.

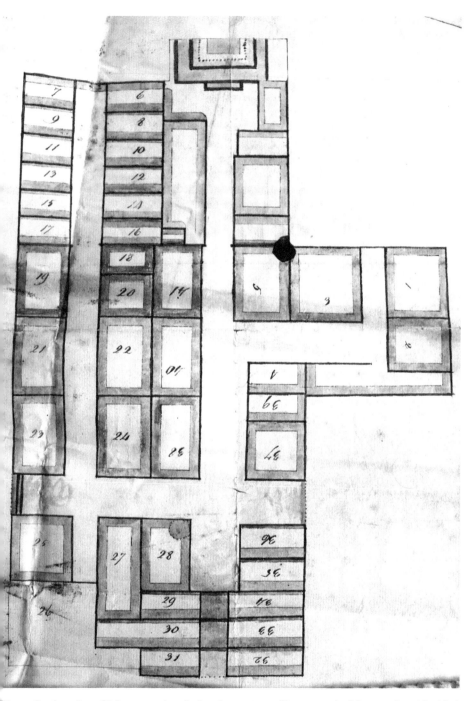

Fig. 9. Seating plan of Manaccan church showing pattern of box pews (1781); reproduced by kind permission of Devon Archives & Local Studies, DHC Diocesan Records, Moger Supplement, PR 338, Rebuilding of Churches, Cornwall, Manaccan.

presence of galleries, as Maker (1852) was 'crowded with pues & galleries', and at Mylor (1849), 'there is much encumbrance of pues & galleries'. Alternatively, at St Ives (1843), the whole of the nave was fitted with 'nice open benches'; at Antony (1849), 'the pues have nearly disappeared & are replaced by nice open benches'; and when visiting Budock (1858), he found 'the pues have been replaced by low open seats'. At Lanteglos-by-Fowey (1842), Glynne found 'very considerable portions of ancient seats, the ends of which present beautiful sculpture in wood'; and at Talland (1850), there were 'many beautiful ancient open benches, the standards exhibiting some excellent specimens of wood carving'.[244] It was not just the preservation of the medieval bench ends in these two churches that satisfied him; it was the retention of low, open seats, which contributed to a sense of space.

However, at no point was Glynne much troubled about the seating needs of the parishioners, which, in Cornwall, had last been addressed in the church building programmes of the late fifteenth and early sixteenth centuries.[245] These structures were now having to cater for a population double or triple their medieval size, and in consequence, wardens sought to install galleries that were also useful for housing an organ, or instruments and singers, previously accommodated in the (usually by then removed) rood loft.[246] Many of these were eighteenth-century constructions of dark wood, usually dominating the west end and obscuring the tower arch, west door, and window – anathema to Glynne.[247] He was concerned not so much with a building's practical function of accommodation, therefore, but almost exclusively with its aesthetics: the simple appearance of the church, and how its architectural and internal visual landscapes influenced, and if possible enhanced, the vertical optics of Gothic-ness. Soaring, lofty Early English was to be preferred, but 'Cornish Perpendicular' sufficed in enhancing the efficient ascent of prayers to the heavens, with the unbroken regularity of the arcades, albeit low, increasing the sense of sacral power as one approached the east end. He deplored the position of the pulpit at Jacobstow (1857), for instance, 'most objectionably placed in the centre' of the main aisle, which underpinned a pre-Tractarian focus on the preacher rather than a liturgical optic on the altar. This is visualised in the delightful caricature of Thomas Rowlandson's depiction of Dr Syntax preaching in the church of Simonsward (St Breward),[248] yet in understanding the satire there is no mistaking the size, prominent position, and elevation of the triple-decker pulpit (Fig. 10).

The congregation, crammed in – apart from the dignitaries, quite comfortably chatting to each other in their own 'manorial' pew – was forced to be within sight

---

[244] Note also, the lack of description of the imagery on the bench ends.

[245] See Mattingly, 'Pevsner', 78–81. There was also a spate of petitions to the bishop in the decades following the Restoration, when churchwardens requested permission to impose specific seating arrangements in their churches, to restore the pre-Commonwealth civic hierarchies disrupted during the Wars; see Cockerham, 'Views from the Pews', 52–5.

[246] F. Bond, *Screens and Galleries in English Churches* (London, 1908), 141–50; and see, for example, the entries for St Gluvias and Truro, quoting the petitions of the churchwardens.

[247] Addleshaw and Etchells, *Architectural Setting*, 98–100; C. Webster, *Late-Georgian Churches: Anglican Architecture, Patronage and Churchgoing in England, 1790–1840* (London, 2022), 112, 127–8.

[248] This print is dated 1806 and was the companion to another print (almost a mirror image) issued in *The Tour of Doctor Syntax in Search of the Picturesque: A Poem* (London, 1812–13?), published by Rudolph Ackermann. See J.J. Savory, *Thomas Rowlandson's Doctor Syntax Drawings: An Introduction and Guide for Collectors* (London, 1997), 42.

of the interior
of St Breward
church in
the early
nineteenth
century, from
a drawing
by Thomas
Rowlandson;
© Image
ID: PAR96J
Album/Alamy
Stock Photo.

Rowlandson Delin.

View of the interior of Simon Ward alias St. Brewer Church
Cornwall

of the cleric, and equally forced to listen to him (or not) discoursing the 'Word of God'. To create such an audio-visual 'preaching box' in the eighteenth century, out of the medieval church fabric, frequently necessitated profound structural alterations so that the clergy and the people might benefit from the theological doctrine then endorsed by the Church.[249] The visual aesthetics of the buildings so converted were generally of little import to the clergy and their parishioners.

Glynne and the Oxford Movement

A gradual dissatisfaction with this type of worship (which of course relied heavily on the charisma and speaking skills of the incumbent), founded on a perceived 'intellectual inadequacy of Evangelical theology', was to form the crux of the Oxford Movement.[250] This was a reassessment of traditional Anglican high church-manship, propagated initially by a handful of such clergy in the university,[251] but that also flourished in the secular environment of a popular medievalism, expressed, for example, in the novels of Sir Walter Scott. Further dissemination of the ideas of church reform was through a series of Tracts, ninety in total, which, in practice, moved towards a focus on a more traditional liturgy, reintroducing elements of Roman Catholic Church ritual into Anglican services. Such Tractarian and ritualist teaching extended to an emphasis on the supremacy of receiving the Sacrament at Mass; the visual emphasis in a church building required adjustment therefore, away from the pulpit (wherever it might have been located), eastwards, following the sacral axis, to the high altar.[252] The purity of the architecture, as the upwards (as opposed to eastwards) flow of simple linear forces, resonated in the purity of the mind and its ability to focus on the liturgy. Ultimately, a church should be a place to move minds, such that, as William Whyte has it, 'buildings should themselves shape spiritual experience'.[253] Hence, in accord with this theological reassessment, Glynne anathematised galleries as dark, brooding structures, which blocked light and obstructed any sense of height and open-ness, and the 'choking' of the nave with large 'boxes' likewise. The same principles condemned the eighteenth-century installation of sash windows, with their flat or rounded tops, wreaking the destruction of pointed apertures, and with tracery replaced by rusty iron bars,[254] as well as the disruption of the roofline by the imposition of skylights,

---

[249] See also Fig. 50a, which shows the pulpit in the middle of the chancel at Lansallos, prior to its reordering.

[250] N. Yates, *The Oxford Movement and Anglican Ritualism* (London, 1983), 8; N. Yates, *Buildings, Faith and Worship: The Liturgical Arrangement of Anglican Churches 1600–1900* (Oxford, 1991), 128–49.

[251] The principal participants were four Fellows of Oriel College: John Keble (1792–1866), E.B. Pusey (1800–82), J.H. Newman (1801–90), and R.H. Froude (1803–36); see Yates, *Oxford Movement*, 11–12.

[252] See G.K. Brandwood, 'Anglican Churches before the Restorers: A Study from Leicestershire and Rutland', *Archaeological Journal* 144 (1987), 383–408, at 397–9; and also C. Webster, '"Absolutely Wretched": Camdenian Attitudes to the Late Georgian Church', in Webster and Elliott (eds), *'A Church as It Should Be'*, 1–21, at 18–21.

[253] W. Whyte, *Unlocking the Church: The Lost Secrets of Victorian Sacred Space* (Oxford, 2017), 70.

[254] Brandwood, 'Anglican Churches', 405–6.

as at Sennen (1849) – all to try and introduce more light to an interior rendered gloomy by the use of so much darkened wood.[255]

It followed that Glynne also had an aversion to the small size of some churches, sometimes compounded by their 'low' profile. Hence, Marazion (1843) was a 'mean & inconsiderable building'; Forrabury (1850) was a 'small mean Church', as also was Cornelly (1858). He equally deplored the poor physical state of some of the churches. Mevagissey (1853) was 'in bad repair & altogether dirty & neglected'; St Levan (1862) was 'neglected' and 'in a very bad state, damp & dirty & having an ugly gallery & rickety pues'; and Minster's interior (1865) was 'in very bad condition, damp, dirty & full of dilapidated pues'. Such a demonstrable lack of care to church fabric was incompatible with his aspiration that the architecture should communicate to the emotions of those enveloped in, and by, the building – something miserably compromised by their low, mean, neglected, dirty, choked, and dark interiors, which were a world away from his ideal model of what a church should be and how its material qualities should articulate to the faithful.[256]

Unsurprisingly, Glynne disliked seventeenth- and eighteenth-century church architecture and fittings, again expressing himself, in the privacy of his notebooks, quite forcibly.[257] St Euny's Redruth, rebuilt (except the tower) in 1770, we consider today as a pleasing building with a charming interior,[258] yet Glynne (1862) found it 'as ugly & uninteresting an edifice as can be imagined'. On his visit to St Gluvias (1849), he dismissed in one sentence the church structure, 'of very base quasi-Italian style', focusing his attention solely on the tower and font. Similarly, at Crowan (1870), he accounts for the St Aubyn mausoleum, erected c. 1779, as 'heavy & ugly', and proceeds to describe the church interior with its 'incongruous modern windows' of the south aisle, which was bizarrely divided from the nave by '2 tall Tuscan columns'.[259] At Falmouth (1843), he was equally damning, the church 'remarkable only for having been built in the reign of Charles II [...] when very few churches were built & those few in no very felicitous style'. Glynne stayed several times at Helston during his tours of the county (1849, 1858) and was

---

[255] At Camborne, for example, in 1725, one Joseph Hosking was paid £26 10s. 'for Building ye Laft' [i.e. gallery], and a further £2 0s. 'for Raysing ye Hinder Seats' so those at the back could hear better; and the following year he was paid another £2 0s. 'for providing and making two windows for the Laft & putting them in', so those in the gallery could now see, KK: X510/1, Churchwardens' accounts and rates, Camborne (1675–1780). The windows can be seen on an early photograph, Fig. 23.

[256] Glynne built four churches on his estates, the last two clearly manifesting these principles. St Bartholomew's, Sealand, Queensferry (Clwyd), by John Douglas (1867), was 'expensively done', like the 'costly touches' found at St John Baptist, Penymynydd, Pentrobin (Clwyd), by John Buckler (1843); see Hubbard, *Clwyd*, 416–17, 420. Equally, not for nothing did Lord Courtenay (1807–88) (later the 11th earl of Devon), write to him 'to ask whether you can recommend to me 4 or 5 good modern ^or even ancient^ Early English churches', for his prospective builder of a new church at Newton Abbot (Devon), J.W. Powell (1827–1902), to study, 'as he lacks experience and observation of good models'; GL, Glynne/Gladstone Ms. 20, letter dated 21 October 1857.

[257] See Bradley, 'Roots', *passim*, for a discussion of the Tractarian movement's disapproval of such architecture.

[258] Beacham and Pevsner, *Cornwall*, 468–9.

[259] M. Symons, 'Bring Up the Bodies: Digging Up the Truth in the Lost Mausoleum at Crowan', *JRIC* (2021), 10–33, who also illustrates the church interior in the 1870s.

content to worship in St Michael's church there, yet he never bothered to record the eighteenth-century building. Hard entablatures supported on Grecian-style columns and 'Venetian' style windows and sashes particularly jarred, echoing his resentment at the panelling out of ceilings in medieval structures, the overall horizontality of these features hindering the vertical view, the vertical ascent of prayer, and ultimately the uplifting of the mind.[260] The numerous effigial slate monuments in the county, popular in the late sixteenth to early seventeenth centuries, were also were ill-tolerated. They crudely but characterfully, and with little sculptural finesse, displayed what Glynne would have termed 'Italianate' influence in their architecture and decoration; moreover, with many of them erected murally, their horizontal architectural strata reinforced the highly objectionable lines of galleries and the tops of box pews.[261] In similar fashion, in contrast to his interest in the fourteenth-century effigies at Sheviock, lying within a sophisticated Decorated architectural arrangement, he ignored Prior Vyvyan's singular Renaissance-inspired tomb (1533) altogether on his first visit to Bodmin (1849); and the equally impressive monument of John Rashleigh (d. 1624) and his son at Fowey (1850) was termed 'gaudy Jacobean', with the numerous large and visually arresting seventeenth-century wall memorials lining the chancel arcades completely invisible to him.

As might be expected, he approved, in the main, of restoration programmes, some of which had been completed before his visits, when objectionable (to him) elements of the interior landscape had been removed, and the Gothic style employed in the rebuilding. St Anthony-in-Roseland (1853) was, therefore, 'a pretty, small cruciform Church [...] the style is Early English [...] the greater part reconstructed, improving on the original', such that 'the general effect of the interior is very solemn and good'. Clearly, 'small' here, did not imply 'mean', with the building's profound verticality emphasised by the open roof and central, open tower and spire. Veryan (1853) was a 'neat Cornish Church in good order & lately well restored', with a new open roof installed, and much reconstruction again having taken place. Glynne possessed no slavish desire (as we do today) to retain medieval structures at all cost, particularly if they had become 'debased' (as at Truro) with time. It was the end result that mattered, especially if it was articulated in an Early English style; hence, the safeguarding of the original structure, in applying the Machiavellian principle of 'the end justifies the means', was of only limited importance.

Ecclesiological development and personal contacts

Glynne's ecclesiological stance is evident from this discussion so far. Before 1840, one of the first Cornish churches he visited was St Mary's Launceston, which bore 'more ornament than is elegant'; one of the last, Menheniot (1870), was 'a fair specimen of a Cornish Church [...] wholly Perpendicular [...] a new screen with parcloses enclose [*sic*] the chancel. The nave is fitted with nice new open seats of pine & the Chancel is laid with new tiles.' While there is greater coverage

---

[260] See Cox (ed.), *Shropshire*, viii–x.

[261] Glynne ignored such monumental sculpture in the main. For example, the complex and opulent slate construction to the Hechens family (1606) at St Stephen-by-Saltash (1852) was dismissed as 'a large mural Monument of slate with the kneeling figure of a Knight', with no attempt to identify the commemorated or describe the rich 'Italianate' architectural setting.

of both architecture and fittings in his later accounts, clearly Glynne's ecclesiological principles were firmly embedded early on, but almost entirely as aesthetic values than with deeply rooted or expressed liturgical concerns. The balance that we encounter, between the viewpoints of an antiquarian and an ecclesiologist, is, early on, firmly in favour of the former; yet later on, it becomes more even, as more attention is given to fixtures and fittings, and their Gothic appropriateness.[262] During the 1840s, increasing degrees of exposure to the liturgical orthodoxies of the Oxford Movement, and their architectural expression propounded by the CCS, undoubtedly nurtured and possibly made him reassess his beliefs, but it seems such processes merely honed his existing convictions, and deepened his passion for visiting – but rarely analysing – churches.[263] After all, his zeal for these activities easily pre-dated the mania for collecting wider data on churches using a printed template / questionnaire, something organised and energised early on in its existence by the CCS.[264] They aimed to record historic structures to a fixed standard, and from an analysis thereof, produce a model for the perfect church construction / reconstruction, to accord with the broad principles of pre-Reformation religion.[265] Theirs was a scheme that was later embraced by sister societies, of which a large number were springing up in the fertile ground of rethinking church functionality and modality in the 1840s.[266] Despite its undoubted

---

[262] This is more easily detected in counties where there is a wider chronological spread of visits, as found in Kent; see N. Yates, 'Sir Stephen Glynne and Kentish Archaeology', in A. Detsicas and N. Yates (eds), *Studies in Modern Kentish History* (Maidstone, 1983), 187–202.

[263] See also, Butler (ed.), *Yorkshire*, 10–14; L. Butler (ed.), *The Church Notes of Sir Stephen Glynne for Cumbria (1833–1872)*, Cumberland and Westmorland Antiquarian and Archaeological Society, Extra Series 36 (Kendal, 2011), 14–18; Parsons (ed.), *Sussex*, xxv–xxix.

[264] R.R. Kenneally, 'Empirical Underpinnings: Ecclesiology, the Excursion and Church Schemes, 1830s–1850s', *Ecclesiology Today* 15 (1998), 14–19.

[265] C. Miele, 'Real Antiquity and the Ancient Object: The Science of Gothic Architecture and the Restoration of Medieval Buildings', in V. Brand (ed.), *The Study of the Past in the Victorian Age* (Oxford, 1998), 103–24, at 120–3. The 'Series of Rough Notes (for correction) of the Churches [...]' carefully compiled from first hand visits, parish by parish, by members of the Exeter Diocesan Architectural Society from the late 1840s to the 1860s, are local evidence of this recording enthusiasm. The data were collated and tabulated for circulation by T.G. Norris, secretary of the society. I am grateful to Stuart Blaylock for clarification on these points.

[266] See S. Piggott, 'The Origins of the English County Archaeological Societies', *Transactions of the Birmingham and Warwickshire Archaeological Society* 86 (1974), 1–15; Whyte, *Unlocking the Church*, 49. Relevant to Cornwall was the foundation in 1841 of the Exeter Diocesan Architectural Society, marked by a paper at its inaugural meeting by one of the secretaries, P.C. Delagarde, 'Observations on the Present State of Church Architecture with Hints for the Regulation of the Society: October 1841', later published in the *TEDAS* 1 (1843), 109–15. Of the 208 individuals in the 'List of Members' of 1843, only fifteen were Cornwall-based, among them Rev. Buller at Lanreath; Rev. Cornish, Kenwyn; Rev. Haslam, Perranzabuloe; Rev. Hocken, Cubert; Rev. Lampen, Probus; Rev. Lyne, Tywardreath; Rev. Scott, Duloe; Rev. Tatham, Broadoak [Bradock]; and Rev. Walker, St Columb. Several of these individuals had already instigated restoration programmes in their own churches by this time; but the unmistakable inference is that such initiatives were driven (unsurprisingly) from Exeter, by the well-connected and well-resourced clergy based there, into the Devon hinterlands. The Tamar, characteristically, proved to be a barrier against the vigour of such influences to be more widely and swiftly adopted by Cornish incumbents.

worthiness, such a regimented, driven, and dogmatic approach could hardly ever have appealed to Glynne, with his well-established habit of flitting in, around, and out of counties, seemingly as the mood took him.

The CCS had been founded in 1839, almost simultaneously with the Oxford Society for Promoting the Study of Gothic Architecture,[267] yet there were profound differences between the two. The Cambridge society was the brainchild of, and later almost hijacked by, two highly opinionated undergraduates, John Mason Neale and Benjamin Webb. They pursued, relentlessly, the 'study of ecclesiastical architecture, and the restoration of mutilated Architectural remains',[268] but in doing so they 'had a seemingly endless appetite for a fight [...] producing pamphlets and letters with uncompromising views, and above all, editing a fierce and opinionated journal, *The Ecclesiologist*'.[269] By contrast, the objects of the Oxford society included the collection of 'Books, Prints, and Drawings; Models of the Forms of Arches, Vaults, &c. [...] and such other Architectural Specimens as the Funds of the Society will admit';[270] clearly, these were gentler, and far less controversial objectives, and, one might surmise, agreeably in alignment with Glynne's own personality. Perhaps his interest in the CCS was piqued by the contents and tone of *A Few Words to Churchwardens*,[271] and he joined, with his brother-in-law Gladstone, in 1841, yet he did not seek admission to the more moderate Oxford society until 1843, again with Gladstone.[272] The 'Proceedings and Reports' of this latter organisation, rather than unrelentingly propagating a High Church agenda within the pages of *The Ecclesiologist*, were put to use, for instance, in recording 'The Drawings of the late Mr Rickman', the author of Glynne's first(?) architectural guide. They were intimately categorised – Norman buildings, Early English piers, Doors, Fonts etc. – in a manner that could have fuelled Glynne's habit of occasionally using his own notes as a data source for creating various tabular analyses. However, while the aim of the Oxford society in this instance was to impose a framework over the mass of the drawings' subject matter, and publicise what they contained, Glynne's analytical motives are more obscure.[273]

---

[267] Not to be confused with the 'Oxford Movement'. The society, whilst upholding the principles of the theological revisionists, did so almost silently.

[268] 'Laws' of the CCS, published by C. Webster (ed.), *'Temples [...] Worthy of His Presence': The Early Publications of the Cambridge Camden Society; The Complete Texts of Eight Important Pamphlets Published between 1839 and 1843 with a Critical Analysis* (Reading, 2003), 47.

[269] Whyte, *Unlocking the Church*, 50. Typical among these pamphlets were *A Few Words to Church Builders* (Cambridge, 1841), and *A Few Words to Churchwardens on Churches and Church Ornaments* (Cambridge, 1841), for which see Webster (ed.), *Early Publications*, 133–88, 193–208.

[270] Taken from *The Rules and Proceedings of the Oxford Society for Promoting the Study of Gothic Architecture* (Oxford, 1840 [*recte* 1839]), rule II.

[271] This publication, typical of Neale and Webb's output, discourses many unshakable beliefs in quite inflexible language: 'About pews and galleries it is hard to speak [...] They have spoilt more churches than perhaps any other things whatsoever', 11–12.

[272] *Proceedings of the Oxford Society [...] Gothic Architecture* (Lent Term, 1843), 5.

[273] For example, NLW, Glynne of Hawarden Ms. 187 (unpaginated) contains a double-page spread of the dimensions of all aspects of the cathedral churches he had visited, which was supplemented by numbers of prebendaries, archdeaconries, and parishes, hence complicating linear dimensions with endowed positions and ecclesiastical personnel. Whether he was trying to determine a relationship between the age, dimensions, capacity, and overall design of

Glynne attended the seventh annual meeting of the Oxford society on 23 June 1846, to hear a paper by A.J. Beresford Hope entitled 'The Present State of Ecclesiastical Art in England', Hope being both a founder member of the CCS and an MP (1841–52), occupations coincident with Glynne.[274] Moreover, with Hope's Cambridge links, it is not surprising that also at the meeting were 'several leading Members of the Sister Society, till lately connected with Cambridge', among them Neale and Webb.[275] Can it be purely coincidental that Glynne was thereafter persuaded to join these two firebrand clergymen – a most unlikely combination, Glynne being an Oxford man some twelve years their senior – in editing the Ecclesiological Society's *Hand-Book of English Ecclesiology*, published in 1847?[276] Glynne's practical involvement was probably minor, although perhaps important financially – albeit he was on the cusp of bankruptcy – but as a respected gentleman antiquary and MP he would definitely have widened the book's appeal and authority. It is also signal that the 'Appendix', comprising 118 pages of county-by-county descriptions of churches, relied heavily on Glynne's knowledge and notes. Many details appear of Cornish churches he had visited and that might not otherwise have been known. Neale, after all, wrote that 'Cornwall can boast little of Catholicity: it is deluged with Wesleyanism and every other kind of schism; and the "revivals" are the fruitful springs of all manner of iniquity.'[277] Doubtless he cultivated an equally dim view of the county's church architecture.

This lengthy discussion of Glynne's ecclesiological ideals and influences, and his contacts in the two formative university societies and the cluster of archaeological societies emerging at this time, aims to contextualise his views, how they evolved, and how they were reflected in his notes – his resignation in tolerating the 'Cornish Perpendicular', for instance. He was ultimately, however, utterly independent in how he pursued his interests and how he expressed himself in the privacy of his own writings. For example, despite his endorsement of the *Hand-Book* and his initial adoption of its terminology – First, Second, and Third Pointed etc. – he swiftly reverted to the nomenclature with which he felt more comfortable, influenced no

a building and its ability to accommodate ecclesiastical hierarchies, is, perhaps, a possibility. Butler, 'Sir Stephen Glynne', 96, proposes a 'Darwinian' motive, in trying to uncover the evolution of 'the church' on a wider basis, such that the larger churches suggested the survival of the fittest, yet the philosophy remains obscure.

[274] *Proceedings of the Oxford Society [...] Gothic Architecture* (Easter & Trinity Terms, 1846), 12–32.

[275] For the dissolution of the CCS and the crisis of 1845 precipitating it, see J.F. White, *The Cambridge Movement: The Ecclesiologists and the Gothic Revival* (Cambridge, 1962), 117–55. In the absence of meetings in Cambridge, it is not unexpected to find Neale and Webb in Oxford, not least to fire up support for their newly founded, and London-based, Ecclesiological Society.

[276] Butler (ed.), *Yorkshire*, 23 note 25, recorded a dinner held in Oxford by the architectural historian E.A. Freeman (1823–92), to which Glynne, Neale, Webb, and Archdeacon Thomas Thorp, as leading members of the Ecclesiological Society, were invited; such networking would have increased the pressure on Glynne to join editorial forces in the production of the *Hand-book*. This book appeared a year before the amalgamation of the teachings of the Oxford Movement and their practical interpretation by the Ecclesiological Society, in *Hierurgia Anglicana: Or Documents and Extracts Illustrative of the Ritual of the Church in England after the Reformation* (London, 1848). This was to prove an influential book, one doubtless studied by Glynne, and that fully endorsed his ecclesiological sentiments.

[277] J.M. Neale, *Hierologus: A Church Tour through England and Wales* (London, 1854), 221.

doubt not only by Rickman's original work, but also by Parker's *Glossary*, which by 1850 was already in its fifth edition in three well-illustrated volumes.[278] Moreover, his reputation as a solid, reliable, and knowledgeable source of information on churches – both physical structure and government – was given an academic respectability by his election as chairman of the 'Architectural Section' of the Royal Archaeological Institute (1852–74). In this role, he would have taken an active part in editing the institute's publications, as well as liaising with the secretary of the archaeological society of whichever county hosted the institute's summer meeting; and despite his personal reserve, he was a frequent attendee at such gatherings.[279] In 1857, the meeting was based in Chester, where 'the section of Architecture was under the efficient direction of Sir Stephen R. Glynne, Bart., unrivalled in the minute accuracy of his Ecclesiological knowledge';[280] he also exhibited works of medieval art from his collections, and chaired meetings. He would no doubt have enjoyed these antiquarian activities in the company of like-minded individuals; yet the month before this July meeting he was recording churches in Hampshire (seven), Surrey (six), and Sussex (three), in July itself he was in the east riding of Yorkshire (three) and back to Sussex (six), leaving there only the week before the Chester meeting. And as soon as it finished, by 3 August he was in Anglesey (three, perhaps four churches), then south to Worcestershire.

He was very swift to resume his solitariness after these social gatherings therefore, his passion perpetually interrupted – as maybe he saw it – by the demands, as one with 'unrivalled' ecclesiological knowledge, of disseminating his learning. Something of this loneliness of spirit is unconsciously conveyed in his lack of acknowledgement of others, as he went about his business. Admittedly, his notes were written for his own private interest and use, and he had no thoughts on publication;[281] the references to Blight and Lysons in his Cornish notes were purely for himself and did not disrupt his observational objectivity. There is a single reference to a 'woman who shewed the Church' at St Ives, but there is no mention of the myriad individuals that he would, of necessity, have encountered – priests, wardens, sextons etc. – and from whom he would have doubtless learned something of a building's history. The notes crystallise his unwavering focus, forever on the church structure and its aesthetic 'Gothic' qualities, yet they also, subliminally, epitomise the man himself, fulfilled and untroubled in the company of churches rather than human society.

Assessing the antiquarian Church Notes for Cornwall

The reason for publishing Glynne's notes owes much to the growing interest in Victorian churches and restorations. Glynne's volumes often give a clear insight into the appearance of a parish church before the major restorations,

---

[278] J.H. Parker, *A Glossary of Terms Used in Grecian, Roman, Italian, and Gothic Architecture*, 3 vols (5th edn, Oxford, 1850).
[279] 'Obituary', *Archaeological Journal* 31 (1874), 400.
[280] *Archaeological Journal* 14 (1857), 364.
[281] He anonymously contributed some 'Ecclesiological Notes' to *The Ecclesiologist*, on some Yorkshire churches, the published accounts differing slightly from those in his notebooks; Butler (ed.), *Yorkshire*, 24 note 37.

and in a few instances, he is describing a church that has completely gone.[282]
The volumes are also useful as an indicator of developing antiquarian attitudes
and scholarship.[283]

So concludes Lawrence Butler in his seminal 2013 article on Glynne and the
relevance of his church notes today; Butler himself was responsible for editing the
notes for Cumbria, Nottinghamshire, and Yorkshire, this last encompassing a mighty
381 church records made from 1825 to 1874. Yet the publishing sequence started,
as we have seen, when Glynne's nephew printed out the notes for Kent soon after
his death, and these were followed by those for Wales, which appeared serially in
Archaeologia Cambrensis (1884–1902), then Lancashire (1893) and Cheshire (1894),
maintaining a focus on the counties around Hawarden, and edited by clergymen
who had known Glynne personally. Northumberland, Durham, and then Yorkshire
appeared in the journals of the relevant archaeological societies, but the focus then
shifted south with the notes for Wiltshire (1922–3) and Dorset (1923–4), engineered
by J.M.J. Fletcher (1852–1940), historian, rector of Wimborne Minster, and canon
of Salisbury. It was most likely not unrelated to such endeavours that Thomas
Cann Hughes (1860–1948), solicitor, town clerk of Lancaster, and president of the
Lancashire and Cheshire Antiquarian Society, undertook the publication of the
notes for Devon and Cornwall.[284] Devon appeared in thirty-eight instalments in
Notes & Queries (1932–4), and Cornwall in twenty-one (1934–5), Hughes having
copied the notes when they had been removed from Hawarden and deposited in St
Deiniol's Library.[285] They are printed in alphabetical order, each instalment covering
around half a dozen churches only, and although the notes appear as they are in
the manuscripts, there are silent editorial adjustments, they make no reference to
sketches, do not identify the comments on the versos, and lack any kind of historical
contextualisation. And while Hughes presented a copy of the Devon notes to Exeter
public library, and Miss Beatrix Cresswell, there was to be no acknowledged benefi-
ciary of a set of the Cornish notes.

---

[282] Of the 121 churches for which Glynne's observations remain, only around sixteen (13 per
cent) had undergone either partial or complete restoration by the time of his visit: Budock,
Crowan, Cubert, Duloe, Feock, Gunwalloe, Kenwyn, Lamorran, Menheniot, Padstow, St
Blazey, St Columb Major, St Just-in-Roseland, St Mabyn, Tywardreath, and Veryan. And in
several cases, such as Crowan, Kenwyn, St Columb Major, and Tywardreath, there were to
be later programmes – Victorian restorations were long processes – that greatly modified the
buildings, leaving his notes as an interim record. Additionally, for three churches, Marazion,
Mylor, and Tintagel, he made commentaries before and after their restoration.

[283] Butler, 'Sir Stephen Glynne', 103.

[284] One can only speculate on Hughes' motive in producing these two counties, as he seems to
have had no family or professional links to the south-west. An unpublished memoir recorded
that he was an 'ardent and prolific collector of [...] special books and rare pamphlets on
Devonshire, Lancashire and Cheshire'; Cambridge, Pembroke College Library, GBR/1058/
HUT/3/2, undated. Presumably the Devonshire interest sparked his interest in editing
Glynne's notes for the county, followed by Cornwall?

[285] As he clarifies in his introduction to the Devon notes, he had been allowed access to the
notebooks by the then warden of the library, Dr Cunningham Joyce, and he managed to
transcribe those for Devon, Cornwall, Cumberland, and Westmorland: *Notes & Queries* 153
(1932), 328. This national journal should not be confused with the regional journal *Devon &
Cornwall Notes & Queries*, also published at that time.

Recent interest – identified by Butler – has produced a new publishing momentum, however, with Somerset (1997), Shropshire (1997), Bedfordshire (1994–2000), Derbyshire (2004), Herefordshire (2006), Yorkshire (2007), Cumbria (2011), and Nottinghamshire (2020), all (except Herefordshire) produced by the record societies for those counties, and with those for the Norwich diocese proposed for 2025. Each of these editions comprises accurate transcriptions of Glynne's text but are supplemented to a greater or lesser degree by bibliographic details, and essays placing Glynne, the notes, and their regional value, into a wider setting. A unique and accessible archive for these nineteenth-century church descriptions has been created therefore. Principal among them is the work by Chris Pickford on Bedfordshire, who published Glynne's notes as one of five sets of nineteenth-century accounts concerning the history of the church buildings, his aim being 'to present the text of contemporary sources in their original state, to convey a feeling for the times as well as to provide information'.[286]

Cornwall is not blessed with the same richness of documentation as Bedfordshire, yet the Lysons brothers' notes, originating in the first decade of the nineteenth century, and included here, are an important adjunct to Glynne's, as they amplify an overall architectural understanding of a church as a building, together with the added colour of its fixtures and fittings. None of the Lysons' notes for any of the counties they studied have been published; indeed, overall, they have received exceptionally scant scholarly attention, not least, perhaps, because the BL catalogue entries, even now, provide just the barest few lines of information on the entire deposit. These two sets of notes, those of the Lysons made up to half a century before those of Glynne, by virtue of their contrasting nature and the differing intentions of the compilers, are beautifully complementary therefore.

The Lysons made brief architectonic comments, often little more than jottings, but scrutinised details that caught their eye, such as Norman doorways, forms of arch moulding, the decoration and tracery patterns of windows, augmented by rough sketches or, occasionally, by drawings of draughtsman-like quality. Screens and bench ends were also recorded, and fonts were a particular interest, again frequently sketched. Stained glass was also a concern, and there was a prodigious fascination in funeral monuments, or, rather, their inscriptions and heraldry. For the Lysons, these last were freely available primary sources of information, of unimpeachable authority, detailing dynasties, their alliances, manorial holdings, and their descent, each monument a crucial element in their method of unpicking the history of each parish, so they could reconstruct it in an inclusive, holistic manner. This textual focus on monuments also makes clear their limitations in describing the sculptural imagery they encountered; just as for architecture there was a lack of an adequate vocabulary with which to express an aesthetic judgement. They were at the edge of an age of such initiatives, however, following Rickman's *Architecture*, and the first instalment of Charles Stothard's *Monumental Effigies of Great Britain*, both appearing in 1817, and both providing accessible sets of terminology – but both published well after Samuel had toured the country and formulated his observations.[287] As a contribution to their

[286] C. Pickford (ed.), *Bedfordshire Churches in the 19th Century*, Bedfordshire Historical Record Society 73, 77, 79, 80 (1994–2000), part I, viii.

[287] C.A. Stothard, *The Monumental Effigies of Gr. Britain Selected from Our Cathedrals and Churches for the Purpose of Preserving Correct Representation of the Best Historical*

'intensive' historical approach, the notes provided the foundation for Samuel's analysis of Cornwall's 'Ancient Church Architecture', and the following sections, summarising the state of knowledge of these buildings and their contents at the start of the nineteenth century. That said, Cornwall was just one county in their formidable *Magna Britannia* project, and visiting the churches and making brief notes on a county-wide basis was more of a 'tick-box' exercise in acquiring data, supplemented by the printed 'Queries', before their attention, and the *grand projet*, rolled on elsewhere.

In contrast, Glynne adopted a magnificently dilletante attitude to visiting Cornish churches. There was no clear plan, dipping into the county where and when he pleased, and, whilst fitting church visits in around his social duties, as, for example, on the occasion(s) he stayed at Boconnoc, he much preferred his independence. His interests were almost entirely architectural, with his detailed descriptions clinically obsessive over certain features, and using newly published textbooks, he enjoyed a specialist vocabulary with which to record what he saw. Like the Lysons, however, he was unable very well to interpret sculptural or pictorial imagery – yet this seems more due to lack of interest than lack of words. His evaluation of woodwork, for example, was framed by his ecclesiological views, such that although he acknowledged the historical value of medieval bench ends, they were to be praised more for contributing to the formation of an open space, and a coherent sacral axis, as much as their heritage. Monuments, too, and particularly it seems in Cornwall, held only a passing interest; again, like the Lysons, his notes for other counties are more comprehensive. He recognised their Gothic architectural features – the 'fine brass [...] [with] [...] an ogee pinnacled canopy' at Antony (1849) is singled out – but even by 1862 he barely registered one of the finest tomb monuments in the county, the Colshull monument at Duloe, misreading its (clearly legible) date and noting just its 'quatrefoils with shields & sculpture of the Crucifixion', probably because he considered it 'debased' Perpendicular. Such objectivity is also manifest in his approval (compared to the tomb) of the opulent architectural and constituent features of Colshull's chapel inside and out, but he either fails, or does not wish, to connect them to a liturgical chantry function. In the same way, he notes nothing of landed descents, heraldry, manorial rights, and advowsons. Although these families would have influenced the structural evolution of the building he was inspecting, he had eyes only to account for the architecture.

The publication of these two sets of notes, juxtaposed for each parish in alphabetical order, provides us with first-hand observational commentaries on the material structure and state of Cornish churches during the nineteenth century. As Butler noted, these antiquaries visited before the major restorations that took place, in the main, in the second half of that century, and they record buildings, or parts of buildings, that have since been altered, removed, or rebuilt, and in the case of some of Glynne's visits – Towednack (1870), for example – at the very time of restoration. There he recorded on the 'North of the nave the windows have been smashed', yet the east window and those in the south aisle 'have been newly inserted', as an eye-witness assessment of what was effectively a building site. For those churches he encountered soon after their restoration, he provides

Illustrations from the Norman Conquest to the Reign of Henry VIII (London, 1817–32).

a contemporary, ecclesiologically informed, view on what was done. The notes also catalogue fixtures and fittings that have since been repositioned, damaged, or lost. Lysons' account of a graveslab with a cross and kneeling figure at Withiel is not just the only record we have of it but describes a bespoke commemorative composition, almost certainly of Bodmin manufacture and with Vyvyan family connections. Likewise, their numerous sketches of heraldic glass identify just how extensive losses have been; and Glynne's forensic notation of window tracery patterns – and sashes – highlights what has since been replaced. We can infer much from this large body of information therefore about the character and contents of the churches when they were closer to their medieval roots – when they possessed properties of their own, and when they housed a remarkable range of fixtures and fittings that had survived not only the Reformation, but also the not untypical eighteenth-century transformation of a church into a preaching box.[288] Going further, as Reginald Wheatley lamented in 1928:

> One can enter very few Cornish churches without a sigh of regret for its departed glories: the old carved waggon roof ruthlessly pulled down by the last genera-tion and replaced with glaring pitch-pine; the pitch-pine seats instead of the solid oak over three inches thick, with carved bench ends; the loss of the beautiful carved screen, and the stained glass windows.[289]

Editorial comment on the publication of the Church Notes

To read both Lysons' and Glynne's notes in isolation solicits a certain impression of how the churches appeared to them, on their possibly rapid, or perhaps more considered, investigation, of each building. Informative that may be, but I have supplemented the notes with a critical apparatus, aiming to answer the unasked question of how the churches these men saw, described, and sketched have subse-quently evolved into the buildings we see today – or indeed, how the structures the Lysons brothers recorded subsequently developed into what Glynne experienced. This approach is not in any way intended to supplant Beacham and Pevsner's invaluable interpretations in the *Cornwall* volume of the 'Buildings of England' series but is simply aiming to transport these nineteenth-century observations into our own time by tracing the changes that ensued. I make no apology therefore for the number (and sometimes length) of the footnotes, although this consid-erable expansion has necessitated the publication of the notes in two volumes, undoubtedly requiring the tenacity and understanding of the reader. In addition, and in a slightly unorthodox manner, some of the illustrations relate to the notes rather than the main text, chiefly because they demonstrate changes in the fabric documented there, rather than in the primary texts. The first volume comprises

---

[288] It is, however, equally salutary to be aware of how some of these buildings were altered in the eighteenth century, but with that evidence brutally removed by the Tractarians a century later. Glynne's notes on the widespread use of box pews, for instance, confirm what we might suspect, parish by parish, but have little other evidence for proving.

[289] R.F. Wheatley, 'The Architecture of the Cornish Parish Church', in Henderson, *Cornish Church Guide*, 225–34, at 229.

this introduction, and parishes A–L; M–Z, a glossary, bibliography, and index will appear in the second.

Among the principal sources consulted in attempting to contextualise the notes have been the Exeter diocesan records in the DHC, comprising faculties, church-wardens' presentments, petitions, visitation reports, and myriad other papers of interest, dating from before the establishment of the diocese of Truro in 1876.

Secondly, I have quarried the diocesan and parochial records in KK, notably the fascinating accounts of the rural deans' visitations from 1808 to 1827, churchwardens' and vestry accounts, family papers, photographic archives, and the documentation of many of the restoration programmes undertaken during the latter half of the nineteenth century, usually (but not always) found among the parish church deposits.

Thirdly, local newspaper reports have been incorporated, not least for their mild journalistic hyperbole, but also as they often provide a 'before' and 'after' narrative of a church's restoration; frequently they comment on the deplorable material state of the building that necessitated its restoration.[290] They are, moreover, in most cases well over 150 years old, so deserve an appreciation of their own antiquarian value. Although we may sometimes be taken up short by the radical nature of these late nineteenth-century fabric restorations – rebuilds – therefore, it is salutary to encounter just how deplorable the physical condition of many churches was at that time. A case study has been introduced for St Gennys, illustrated from records in KK, all too evidently confirming Glynne's laconic comment in his field notes that 'pillars North lean'. The immediacy of such newspaper reports also solicits an even greater respect for these pioneering antiquaries as they toured the county, setting foot in buildings that in some cases nowadays would be classed as redundant, disused, and even – *quelle horreur* – 'unsafe'.

Fourthly, I have often referred to the records of the Incorporated Church Building Society (ICBS) and highlighted their role in financing many of the restoration projects undertaken in the county.[291] These documents are to be found in the database of archives and manuscripts in Lambeth Palace Library and are indexed online;[292] many of the groundplans submitted to the society as part of a church's grant application are illustrated online.[293] These have been mentioned in the footnotes, but the numerous individual weblinks have not been cited. Where possible, however, unpublished church plans have been included, the majority sketched by Charles Henderson in the 1920s, taken from his manuscript collections for the east of the county. These last are works of art in their own right, frequently incorporating vignettes of particularly appealing features, or with explanatory notes in his quick, precise hand, succinctly articulating why the structure appeared to him as it did. The Lysons / Glynne notes are grounded in architecture, and

---

[290] The British Newspaper Archive has been invaluable, available online at: https://www.britishnewspaperarchive.co.uk/

[291] For a valuable and wider consideration of this topic, see M. Warner, *A Time to Build: Signposts to the Building, Restoration, Enhancement, and Maintenance of Cornwall's Anglican Churches and Mission Rooms 1800–2000* (s.l., 2022), 24–30.

[292] Database of Manuscripts and Archives, Lambeth Palace Library, available online at: https://archives.lambethpalacelibrary.org.uk/CalmView/advanced.aspx?src=CalmView. Catalog [accessed June 2023].

[293] https://images.lambethpalacelibrary.org.uk/luna/servlet/LPLIBLPL~34~34 [accessed June 2023].

in the main comprise austere value judgements that demonstrate little or no emotion – Glynne's ecclesiological views excepting. Without visual aids, they risk becoming an awfully dry read, and only those well versed in a technical vocabulary – despite the glossary at the end of the second volume – might be able to interpret the descriptions adequately. Hence, again where possible, illustrations roughly contemporaneous with the notes have been incorporated from a variety of sources. Such material aims to enable a wider understanding of just how these buildings looked and functioned for the social hierarchies of nineteenth-century congregations and their incumbents.

Lastly, several published works have frequently been consulted, some of which are also available online, but that have not always, because of that very frequency, and for brevity, been acknowledged in the notes. These comprise Boase's *Collectanea Cornubiensia*; Polsue's *Parochial History*, which includes highly reliable transcripts of monumental inscriptions; Dunkin's *Brasses*, and Bizley's *Slate Figures of Cornwall*, recording in illustrated detail much of the county's monumental heritage in those two media; Gray's *Gazetteer* focuses on medieval bench ends and their historiography; Mattingly and Swift's online documentation of *Cornish Stained Glass* comprehensively records both medieval and later material; and the Corpus of Romanesque Sculpture in Britain and Ireland describes and illustrates many architectural features, and in particular, fonts, believed to date from before 1200.[294] The reader is referred to these sources should further information be sought.[295]

Editorial method

The Lysons' notes are alphabetised by parish, with the order of the authors' observations on a building sometimes adjusted to produce a coherent account, rather than precisely to replicate the sequence in which the notebook sheets appear on the folios, as they often vary in their subject matter from verso to recto. Also, probably during the consolidation of the collections prior to the preparation of the 'Parochial Histories', passages of the field notes (chiefly transcripts of monumental inscriptions) in Add. Ms. 9462 were copied verbatim into Add. Ms. 9445. For brevity, these repetitions have not been identified further, as they appear to add nothing of value other than as evidence of a wider amalgamation of the various sources; also, there seems to be no reason why some were copied and others were not. In this edition, the notes in Add. Ms. 9462 precede those of Add. Ms. 9445, for each parish

---

[294] For an overview of this online project, see R. Baxter, 'Changing the Face of Romanesque Sculpture: Prior and Gardner and the Corpus of Romanesque Sculpture in Britain and Ireland', in P. Lindley and M.McN. Hale, *Nationalism, Medievalism and the Study of Sculpture: Prior and Gardner's Account Reassessed* (Donington, 2023), 40–4.

[295] G.C. Boase, *Collectanea Cornubiensia: A Collection of Biographical and Topographical Notes Relating to the County of Cornwall* (Truro, 1890); [J. Polsue], *A Complete Parochial History of the County of Cornwall: Compiled from the Best Authorities & Corrected and Improved from Actual Survey*, 4 vols (Truro/London, 1867–72); E.H.W Dunkin, *The Monumental Brasses of Cornwall* (London, 1882); A.C. Bizley, *The Slate Figures of Cornwall* (Marazion, 1965); T. Gray, *A Gazetteer of Ancient Bench Ends in Cornwall's Parish Churches* (Exeter, 2016); J. Mattingly and M. Swift, *Cornish Stained Glass*, available online at: https://www.cornishstainedglass.org.uk/mgsmed/ [accessed June 2023]; Corpus of Romanesque Sculpture in Britain and Ireland, available online at: https://www.crsbi.ac.uk [accessed June 2023].

where both accounts contain unique information, retaining the chronology of their compilation.[296]

In the main, spelling has been modernised and contractions expanded, except when they are quotes from inscriptions, where expansions are italicised, or when they are very common, such as 'ob.' and 'aet.', for example. Ampersands have been retained when used to signify 'and', and also '&c.' for 'etc.'; and capitalisation has been reproduced, as it adds an early nineteenth-century dignity to these records. Where possible, diagrams of tricked heraldic shields have been described and identified accordingly; where the arms are not attributable they have been listed as 'for ?'. Sometimes, too, the Lysons' identification of heraldic tinctures is incorrect, but the material evidence – dirty and / or broken stained glass, for instance – may have been far from clear, and the depiction of provincial heraldry itself was not an exact science. Sketches, diagrams, and shields are indicated within angle brackets ◇; up arrows ∧∧ denote where one or more words have been added as superscript; and words crossed out, when still decipherable, have been struck through ~~like this~~. When a word or passage written in a particularly villainous hand has defied transcription and its meaning is not clear, this has been indicated using [illegible]. In transcribing the notes, new lines have often been started in an attempt to reproduce their appearance on the page, as they frequently correspond to a new topic being described. Sometimes, however, they divide up a single observation unnecessarily, or appear haphazardly on a sheet, and in such cases they have been allowed to run on in a single paragraph.

Glynne's notes, as for Lysons', are also presented here not precisely as they are written. The bulk of his text is on the recto of each folio, with additional comments on the facing verso, as discussed previously. Here, these supplementary notes have been italicised and placed within angle brackets and are inserted into the body of the text at a point where it makes sense to do so, that is, when the added detail complements the topic under discussion on the recto. Sketches, crossings out, contractions, and superscript entries are indicated as for Lysons' notes, and capitalisation has been retained; similarly, for the most part, spelling has been modernised. Individual quirks, however, such as Glynne's persistent used of 'pues' and 'panneling', for example, have been retained, as has the ampersand and his occasionally unorthodox grammar.

Common to both authors was their frequent use of a dash. Sometimes these have been preserved, but in most cases they have been substituted with punctuation appropriate not only to make sense of the not unusual loose sentence structure, but equally to try and conserve a sense of how these men wrote. One recognises with Glynne, for instance, that his notes were written up almost in a 'stream of consciousness' fashion. Although the descriptions adhere to a certain format and bear little resemblance to the order of observations made in the field – as discernible

---

[296] There is an element of doubt here, as it is possible that the author of the notes in Add. Ms. 9445 – suggested as Daniel – toured Cornwall only in 1805; yet that manuscript incorporates much parochial information that is derivative, and physically written on to the folios, suggesting it was done much later when the notes were being ordered. Among the inclusions are what are presumed to be Samuel's own inscription transcripts. The inference, but not exactitude, is that this manuscript was compiled subsequent to Samuel's own formalised church notes therefore.

15.

Cover'd & open over the Chancel bounded, with a floriated cornice. The North Chapel or Transept opens by a very plain wide arch uncertain character, upon imposts. On its soffit a small niche. Over this arch appear the timbers of the roof in Welsh fashion. The Font is a plain large circular bowl, with moulded stem. The South Porch is rude, with open roof.

Forrabury.   S. Symphorian.   1 Feb 1850

A forlorn looking Church, which like the two last named presents some early features. as it is said do some other Churches near the coast in this part of the County. The situation is very bleak & exposed. the plan is a nave, South Transept & porch, Chancel with North Chapel & West Tower. The work is very rude & there are some singularities. The Chancel opens to the N. Chapel or aisle by very coarse plain semicircular arches upon imposts & there is away odd shaped arch set obliquely as a hagioscope slanting off the angle. On the S. of the Chancel is one lancet window. The E. window of the N. Chapel is a triplet — that of the Chancel very badly mutilated. There are no windows at all on the N. of the nave. No Chancel arch, but part of the rood screen remains, of plain work & much injured. The roof of the nave is open. That of the Chancel meanly ceiled. The interior blocked by pews. The Tower arch is pointed but without moulding

(margin note: perhaps very early.)

from the entries for Launcells, for example – the result is often a long and dense block of writing, divided intermittently by dashes (Fig. 11).

Yet it would be invidious to deny him completely the visual evidence character-istic of his style, not least as the dashes appear to signify new thoughts occurring as he consulted his memory to augment the field book accounts. Samuel Lysons, meanwhile, would dash off (literally) his architectural impressions of a standard Cornish Perpendicular church in a practised shorthand but then devote time to laboriously copying monumental inscriptions, or painstakingly deciphering heraldic glass – none of which really interested Glynne.

Overall, in editing these manuscripts, I have endeavoured to produce a readable and coherent record of each church, as a tribute to the unflagging nature of their authors, the accounts characteristic of how they interpreted what they saw. But more than that, as in doing so, I have also attempted to preserve not so much the similarities but the pronounced differences in the texts. They remain, I hope, indic-ative therefore, of the many dissimilarities – in character, motive, evaluation, and ultimately, purpose – of these industrious nineteenth-century gentlemen antiquaries, who devoted so many years to their compilation.

CHURCH NOTES FOR PARISHES
A–L

ADVENT

Lysons: BL, Add. Ms. 9445, fol. 1r.

Advent Church – Tower with ~~near~~ plain pinnacles, doorway is ornamented with roses & quatrefoils in a deep groove.[1]
Font <sketch> circular on an octagonal pedestal.[2] Columns & arches clustered & pointed – a nave, chancel & two transepts.[3]

ALTARNUN

Lysons: BL, Add. Ms. 9445, fol. 5r.

Alternon – Handsome plain tower with four solid crocketed pinnacles, clustered columns, arches obtuse & slightly pointed, windows large with very little tracery.[4]

---

[1] The south doorway is ornamented with isolated stylised fleurons in the jambs and the voussoirs, which are crisply cut in Catacleuse stone, being the counterpart to the door at Michaelstow, not far away.

[2] This Norman font bowl is now set on a renewed octagonal base, with a bulbous base and a top that acts as a plinth to the bowl. The form sketched by Lysons is simpler and was presumably the original; see Sedding, *Norman Architecture*, 1–2, pl. I.

[3] The roof of the south transept collapsed some time before 1870, and the opportunity was taken not to restore it but to wall it off and insert the east window of the transept under the entrance arch in the newly created wall; Maclean, *Trigg Minor*, ii, 319–20. The church was sensitively restored shortly after, for which see the *WB*, 1 October 1874, 5. For the church as Lysons saw it, see C. Spence, '"Iter Cornubiense," a Relation of Certain Passages which Took Place during a Short Tour in Cornwall', part III, *TEDAS* 5 (1856), 107–17, at 110–11, who found 'On the south side a curious Chapel forms a transept, in which are the remains of a single broken pillar.'

[4] The aisles and east ends have an almost complete set of early sixteenth-century 'South Hams' window tracery, stylistically simpler than the Perpendicular tracery frequently found elsewhere; see H. Colvin, *Essays in English Architectural History* (New Haven/London, 1999), chapter 3, 'Church Building in Devon in the Sixteenth Century', 22–51. The church-wardens' accounts note the replacement of the roof in 1845, and in 1860, 'a new seat, repairs to the Rail, and other work was done in the Chancel by the Ecclesiastical Commissioners', KK: P4/5/2. This paved the way for a wider restoration in 1864–7, as reported in the *RCG*, 18 July 1867: 'The roofs are of the customary Cornish type, and have been thoroughly repaired in oak, with new carved bosses and moulded ribs, of the same character and dimensions as the old work, all old timbers and carving that could in any way be brought into use again being preserved [...] The columns and arcading which were out of the perpendicular have been rebuilt, and the whole of the walls raised twelve inches. All the walls internally and externally have been cleaned and re-pointed, the walls of the body of the church inside westward of the chancel screen being plastered. The windows have been repaired throughout, those of the nave being re-glazed in varied patterns. The font [...] has been raised on a new granite step, inlaid with slabs of red Mansfield stone, and furnished with a granite base [...] The old pulpit has been furnished with a new deal base, the top being repaired and re-used [...] The gallery at the west end of the church has been entirely removed, and the tower arch, of Polyphant stone, and one of the handsomest in the county both for richness and noble proportions, has been thrown into view. The floor of the tower has been raised by three granite steps above the level of the nave, and divided from the same by a wooden screen [...] A new window of Polyphant stone has been inserted on the west end of the south aisle.' A contribution to the cost of the works was made by the 'sale of old silver Plate £9 10s. 0d.', in 1864, KK: P4/5/2.

Font on an octagonal pedestal, square at top, at each corner a head, between the heads a star within a circular round of two serpents, the heads pointed at each other at top with the tongues out.[5]

Figures on the pews in South aisle, a fool, a bagpiper, a fiddler, & 2 warriors, on one a flock of sheep, representations of some game, perhaps not very ancient.

Robert Daye Maker of this worke, William Bokenham Curat, the next rather mutilated[?], no date, nothing else remarkable.[6]

No school at Alternon.

ANTONY

Lysons: BL, Add. Ms. 9642, fol. 19r.

East Anthony – Nave & side aisles, clustered pillars & obtuse arches.

In the Chancel monument for the Lady Jane Carew wife [of] Sir Alexander Carew Baronet, ob. 1679.[7]

Monument for Briget, wife of Richard Carew, ob. 1611.[8]

Slab for the Lady Jane Carew.[9] D° for John Deeble Esq. of Wolsdon house, 1796.[10]

Brass of a lady under an elegant Gothic Canopy with a reticulated head dress & long viel [*sic*] over it, for Margery Arundel quondam Domina de Est Anthony, daughter of Warin Erchdecken Knt., 26. Oct. 1420[11] <sketch of headdress>.

In north aisle an elegant monument with bust & head in bas relief by Thos. Carter London, for Mary, daughter of Sir William Carew, ob. 1731.[12]

In addition, despite the repairs to the pulpit at this restoration, it was replaced in 1913, for £85 7s. 6d., KK: P4/5/2.

[5] Lysons, *Cornwall*, ccxxxiii, notes the font as being very similar to a group of fonts, including Warbstow, which they publish on the pl. opposite (no. 4). See also Sedding, *Norman Architecture*, 5, pl. III.

[6] See Mattingly, *Cornish Churches*, 12–13, who accounts for the appearance of the sheep and the bagpiping shepherd as representative of the parish flock, or church store; the 'warriors' are sword dancers.

[7] This was also recorded by Gilbert, *Historical Survey*, ii, 389, as a 'sumptuous monument' over the altar and comprises a framed inscription tablet of black marble supported on a prominent apron and with a heraldic achievement below; it is on the north wall of the chancel.

[8] This is a small tablet of black marble with an ornamental border; Gilbert, *Historical Survey*, ii, 389, mistakenly records her as the wife of Alexander Carew (she was his mother).

[9] The slab is of black marble, set in the floor between the altar and the east wall of the chancel.

[10] Set in a slab in the chancel floor, the inscription is on a lozenge-shaped plate brass.

[11] Lysons, *Cornwall*, ccxxxv, describe the figure of Margery as 'with the reticulated head-dress and veil'.

[12] If contemporary with Mary Carew's date of death, this was one of the earliest recorded sculptural works by Thomas I Carter of London (1702–56), who early on pursued 'the lower branches of his profession, such as tomb-stones, grave-slabs &c.' However, his work was noticed by Charles Jervas, Principal Painter to the King, who presumably provided Carter with suitable contacts thereafter: Roscoe *et al.*, *Dictionary*, 212, 214.

The Tablet of black marble for Richard Carew Esqr., Nato 1555 pacis presul 1581 Cornub. vice com 1586 in re milit regias vices funto 1586. In Collegium Antiquariorum Elect. 1598, ob. 1620.[13]
[separate sheet] E. Anthony – The verses following were written by Richard Carew of Antony Esq. immediately before his death (which happened the ninth of November 1620) as he was at his private prayers in his study (his usual practice) at four in the afternoon & being found in his pocket were preserved by his grandson Sir Alexander Carew, according to whose desire they are now set up in memory of him: 'Full thirteen fives of years I toyling have o'repast / And in the fowerteenth weary, entred am at last / While Rocks, Sands, Stormes & leaks, to take my bark away / By grief, troubles, sorrows, sicknes did essay, / And yet arriv'd I am not at the port of death / The port to everlasting Life that openeth / My time uncertain Lord, long certain cannot be / What's best to mee's unknown & only known to thee / O by repentance & amendment grant that I / May still live in thy fear & in thy favour dye'.[14]
[separate sheet] In south aisle, handsome monument of white marble by Wilton, for Admiral Thomas Graves & Elizabeth his wife, of Thankes, ob. 1755. Son of James Graves Esq., of Lighthausel in Yorkshire, & Mary, daughter of Serjeant-at-law Herdman, of Stanington in Northumberland. She was sister to Eustace Budgell Esq., of St Thomas, near Exeter, granddaughter of William Gulston, bishop of Bristol &c. Cousin to Mr Addison, ob. 1738.[15]
And a monument for Mary, his first wife [of Thomas Graves].
Monument of Lady Sarah Carew, Lady of Sir John Carew Bart., daughter of Antony Hungerford Esq., of Farley Castle, ob. 1671.[16]
A handsome monument for Sir John Carew of Est Antony, Sir Richard Carew, his son, Sir John ob. 1692, Sir Richard 1703.[17]

Glynne: GL, Glynne notebooks 13, fols 55–6

Antony, SS. Antony & John, 23 February 1849.
A Third Pointed Church of Cornish stamp, the nave and Chancel undistinguished, with aisles to both, a West Tower, & North & South porches. The roofs are low

---

[13] Trans., *Born in 1555, Justice of the Peace 1581, High Sheriff of Cornwall 1586, acted as King's Deputy for the Militia 1586, elected to the Society of Antiquaries 1598*. This is the monument to Richard Carew, author of *The Survey of Cornwall* (London, 1602).

[14] These transcribed verses were added to the mural memorial for Richard Carew by Sir Alexander Carew and were engraved on a separate piece of marble joined to the original slab; see *Richard Carew of Antony: The Survey of Cornwall*, ed. F.E. Halliday (London, 1953), 70–1.

[15] This is an early work by Joseph Wilton RA (1722–1803), comprising a circular inscription panel enclosed by pilasters and a frieze, with a cornice surmounted by urns with Roman rostral (victory) columns and two ships, see Roscoe *et al.*, *Dictionary*, 1388.

[16] Now on the north wall, this is a sumptuous monument comprising an aedicule containing an inscription panel of black marble under a heavy entablature, and with heraldic insignia above and below.

[17] This is now in the tower and comprises an oval cartouche with an inscription, surrounded by an architectural frame supporting what are probably meant to be allegorical figures, though they hold no attributes. The descriptions of the other monuments are published by Lysons, *Cornwall*, 16–18, in their account of the descent of the manor of East Anthony [*sic*], 15–16. Those still extant are cited in detail by A.J. Jewers, *Heraldic Church Notes from Cornwall: Containing All the Heraldry and Genealogical Particulars on Every Memorial in Ten Churches in the Deanery of East* (London, [1888]), 41–60.

pitched, the arcades low, & all of granite, clear of wash or paint. The piers all clustered of the usual form, alternate shafts & channeling, those on the North have octagonal capitals with panneled abacus over them, those on the South circular ones, some of the Northern are flowered & with better mouldings, & the North arcade has more of the Tudor form than the other side. The roofs are plain coved.[18] The windows at the East of the Chancel & aisles are of 3 lights.[19] Those of the North aisle are similar, in the South aisle they are mostly square headed.

[56] The Interior has undergone considerable improvement of late years,[20] the pues have nearly disappeared & are replaced by nice open benches, the standards having panneling. The Chancel is laid with encaustic tiles & fitted with stalls, the ends having poppy heads & some cinque cento carving at the back. There is a fine brass in the Chancel just in front of the sacrarium, representing a Lady in a religious habit under an ogee pinnacled canopy, inscribed 'Hic jacet Margeria Arundell quondam domina de Est Antoni' filia Warin Erchdeken militis qui obiit XXVI° die Octobris anno domini MCCCCXX° Cui anime propicietur deus'.[21]

Several windows are adorned with stained glass in memorial of the dead, & there is a fine new Font, of Third Pointed character, the bowl octagonal & panneled, the stem shafted & set on a high base near the North door. The cover a fine wooden one inscribed 'According to His mercy He saved us by the washing of regeneration'. <*The obituary window at the East of the North aisle is in memory of the Right Honourable R. Pole Carew & Caroline his wife, & Gerald their son, erected by the family A.D. 1847. The 3 side windows of the same aisle are also obituary.*[22]>

The Tower is a crude plain one, with battlement & the South Western corbel table under it has corner buttresses, a square turret at the North East, plain belfry windows, a West door & 3 light window, lancets on the North & South. The whole rough cast. The porches are large & plain, the door mouldings in granite & some fine old iron work on the North door. The Churchyard occupies fine sloping ground & is of great extent.

---

[18]   At some point in the second half of the nineteenth century, the roof was replaced by an arch-braced structure; Beacham and Pevsner, *Cornwall*, 95.

[19]   Gilbert, *Historical Survey*, ii, 388, noted that the 'window over the altar contains the arms of Carew, impaled with Hatch, the arms of Beauchamp, and other stained figures'. J. Furneaux, 'On Antony and Sheviocke Churches', *TEDAS* 5 (1856), 1–5, states that 'the more ancient fragments exhibit [...] the Tudor rose, the wafer, and chalice, &c.' No medieval glass now remains.

[20]   In 1797, there were faculties for two pews, including one for the schoolmaster and scholars to be seated at the front of the gallery, so that they might 'pay more strict Attention to divine Worship'; DHC: DR, Faculty Causes, Cornwall, Antony 4, 1797. The galleries were dismantled between then and Glynne's visit therefore, possibly associated with KK: P7/2/11, of 12 April 1831, which is a proposed arrangement of the pews, with numbers of pews and names of tenements in the body of the church and south and north galleries. This may have been related to the application to the ICBS for 'repairs', but the file is missing; LPL: ICBS 1578 (1833).

[21]   Trans., *Here lies Margery Arundell, once lady of East Anthony, daughter of Sir Warin Ercedekne, who died 26 day of October A.D. 1420. On whose soul may God have mercy.* She married Thomas, the son of Sir John Arundell of Lanherne, but possessed the manor of East Anthony in her own right and died without issue, hence her burial in the middle of what was effectively her chancel.

[22]   For these inscriptions, see Polsue, *Parochial History*, i, 25. This additional note (fol. 55v.) is in the same handwriting as Glynne's main account of the church so is probably not the result of a revisit but information recalled after the account had been initially written up.

BLISLAND

Lysons: BL, Add. Ms. 9462, fol. 21r.

Nave & South aisle. In the [chancel] brass for Johannes Balsam Rector 1410.[23]
In North aisle at its East end[24] basrelief in slate of the Kempes.[25] Font with 4 foils &
shields.[26] South aisle, William Thomas barrister at law, 1665.[27]

BOCONNOC (Fig. 12)

Lysons: BL, Add. Ms. 9462, fol. 20v.

Boconnoc font – of free stone <sketch of font with measurements>.
Fol. 21r. Nave & South aisle <sketch of font & Father Time & cradle from a tomb>.
Clustered pillars & obtuse arches.
In aisle monument for a daughter of Sir Reynold Mohun, 1637.
Slab in nave for Rowland Jeynens, 1602.[28]
North aisle Lord Granvilles [*recte* Grenville's] pew.

Glynne: GL, Glynne notebooks 17, fols 130–1

Boconnoc [23 January 1842].
This Church consists of two equal aisles without distinction of chancel, & a chapel
on the north side. There was originally no steeple, but the bells were hung in a
kind of shed near the Church yard gate, at only a few feet above the ground. A
small octagonal tower has, however, been built ^of granite^ on the South side of
the West front, at the expense of the Honourable G. Fortescue in 1829.[29] The walls

[23] This brass forms one of a cluster of such monuments commissioned by parish priests from
the London brass workshops in the early fifteenth century, the others being at Cardinham,
Padstow, and Warleggan; see W. Lack, H.M. Stuchfield and P. Whittemore, *The Monumental
Brasses of Cornwall* (London, 1997), 16–17, 88, 90, 172, 175.
[24] Lysons distinguished between the south aisle as running the entire length of the church, and
his 'north aisle', which is an eastwards extension of the original north transept, the east ends
flush with each other; see Sedding, *Norman Architecture*, 18–21.
[25] A mural monument of slate commemorating Humfry Kempe (d. 1624), his wife Jane, and
their four children.
[26] Lysons recorded this fifteenth-century font with shields in quatrefoils, but by 1849 a
second, Norman font had been discovered outside, resting 'in an angle formed by the junction
of the Church and tower walls'; see Spence, '"Iter Cornubiense"', part I, *TEDAS* 3 (1849),
205–23, at 219.
[27] See Maclean, *Trigg Minor*, i, 59. He was the owner of the estate of Lavethan following the
Kempe family, commemorated by the slate briefly recorded by Lysons.
[28] For this and the Barnstaple school monument to Penelope Drew, the 'daughter of Sir
Reynold Mohun, 1637', see Cockerham, *Continuity and Change*, 107, pls 86, 192.
[29] It is not clear from whom Glynne derived this date, but as he made several visits to
Boconnoc House and was friendly with the Fortescue family – for which see the 'Introduction'
– one might imagine that his information was correct. KK: P12/2/3, is an undated plan *c.*
1835(?) showing the interior layout of the church including the parish pews, Lord Grenville's
pew, pews for Lord Grenville's and the rector's servants, the clerk's desk, reading desk and
pews for pupils at the charity school. It was drawn by Edmund Tatham 'From Recollection',

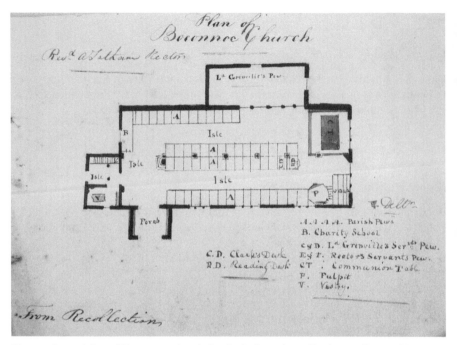

Fig. 12. Groundplan of Boconnoc church (*c.* 1830); from the collections at Kresen Kernow, P12/2/3, plan by Edmund Tatham.

of the Church are of the slaty stone, every window has been mutilated & deprived of its tracery, but those at the East end have been lately restored & adorned with stained glass.[30] The whole Church is of Perpendicular architecture & the labels of the windows are mostly of granite.[31] The two equal aisles are divided by a range of 6 depressed arches upon the same piers as are found generally in this county, & all of granite[32] <sketch of cross-section>. There are two similar arches opening to the North chapel, now the mansion house pew, included there is a portion of elegant

marked at the top 'Reverend A Tatham, rector' (1808–74, rector 1832–74), and shows the recently constructed bell turret. See C. Lorigan, *Boconnoc: The History of a Cornish Estate* (Stroud, 2017), 170. The Hon. George Fortescue (1791–1877) was the second son of Hugh, 1st Earl Fortescue (d. 1841), and although he did not inherit the estates until 1864, he made his home in Boconnoc in 1833–4 and improved the church, house, and estates during his tenure there.

[30] The plan drawn by Tatham indicates mullions in all the windows, including those at the east end, suggesting the 'stained glass' was inserted between the date of the drawing (*c.* 1835) and Glynne's record (1842).

[31] Many of the mullions, hoodmoulds, and labels are original, later incorporated into windows of 1873.

[32] The arcade was rebuilt at the restoration in 1873; see Lorigan, *Boconnoc*, 170–1. O.B. Peter, 'A Visit to Boconnoc', *RCG*, 31 December 1891, 8, noted 'Ancient stonework in the walls is of 16th century workmanship, but subsequent interferences with the building have allowed very little of this to remain. Six granite arches and columns of ordinary type separate the nave from a south aisle of nearly equal length with it, and a short north aisle divided from the nave by two bays of similar arcading, serves as the Boconnoc Chapel. Between the arcade bays of this Chapel is set an old carved wooden screen, a portion of one that was originally at Braddock.'

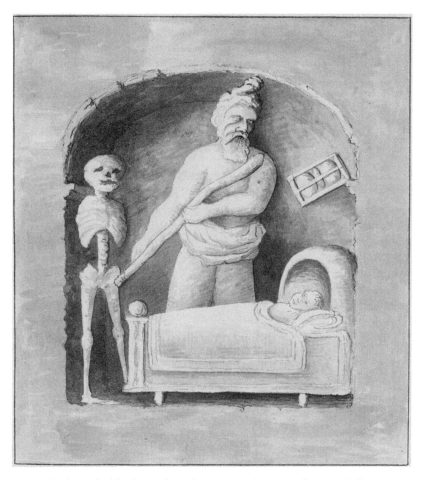

Fig. 13. Sculptured tablet from a funeral monument (seventeenth century), Boconnoc church; © The Bodleian Libraries, University of Oxford, Ms. Gough 224, fol. 180r.

wood screen work, which appears to have formed part of the roodloft.[33] The roofs of both aisles are coved, divided as usual by ribs into pannels & with a sculptured wood cornice. Over one of the piers [131] near the East end is a singular piece of sculpture apparently in plaster, which represents a figure of death standing at the foot of a bed in which is a child, beside which stands a large figure in a ruff bearing a scythe. This seems probably to be of the age of James I (Fig. 13).[34]

[33] Bond and Camm, *Roodscreens and Roodlofts*, ii, 381, record this as having been removed from Braddock church, probably relying on Peter's report (previous fn.); it is of plain early sixteenth-century character.

[34] These figures have been whitewashed over, making interpretation of the material difficult, yet they are a combination of stone and lime plaster, partly carved, partly moulded; see KK: P12/6/1 (1986–9), conservation report. Neither Lysons nor Glynne could make much of these sculptures, but they comprise an unusual representation of childhood death, with the figure of a child in a cradle housed within an arch, while at the head and foot are the figures of Death with a scythe and Time with an hourglass. At the same height over the arcade is the figure of a

The Font is handsome & singular, in form an octagonal cup upon a pedestal of like form, & surrounded by 4 shafts, which have octagon capitals on a level with the rim of the basin, & the whole enriched with curious panneling in geometrical figures &c., the style of the workmanship is Perpendicular but the Early English form is preserved. The Pulpit has fine carving temp: James I. The monuments of the Mohuns have been buried in the vaults.[35] The Church is close to the mansion house on a very steep bank covered with evergreens.

BODMIN

Lysons: BL, Add. Ms. 9462, fol. 21r.

Bodmin Church – large & handsome, Nave & side aisles. 9 arches on each side the 3 next to the east end are not so lofty as the rest but nearly in the same style, on the wooden cornice of the roof of the South aisle near the East end is the following Inscription:
[in Gothic minuscules] An[no] d[omi]ni M° CCCC° LXX° II° / ed[i]ficatuu[m] fuit.[36]
On the roof near the inscription. <sketch of 2 shields>.[37] (Fig. 14)
Pews richly carved with symbols of the Xfixion &c., screen on each side of the Chancel, rich gothic, the lower part, and the part of the seats within the Chancel richly ornamented with carved figures, & arabesque ornaments carved in bas relief.[38]

kneeling lady looking towards this scene. While this is an unorthodox and spatially restricted location for monumental sculpture, these two scenes would have been in full view of the Mohun family as they sat in their pew looking into the nave of the church, directly opposite this north side of the arcade. During the first quarter of the seventeenth century, Sir Reginald Mohun was intent on creating a dynastic mausoleum, marking out the church with various funeral monumental schemes – of which this would have been one – in order to perpetuate a status recognition, and including a new altar of 1621, manifesting a Laudian interest; see Cockerham, *Continuity and Change*, 108, 111, pl. 206. However, from the published pedigree of the Mohun family, it is difficult to identify an individual who died in childhood, and who might have been the raison d'être behind this commemorative imagery; J.L. Vivian, *The Visitations of Cornwall: Comprising the Heralds' Visitations of 1530, 1573 & 1620* (Exeter, 1887), 323–6.

[35] They were on view for Lysons, and also recorded by Gilbert, *Historical Survey*, ii, 913, but clearly Glynne was unable to see them, something mirrored by Polsue, *Parochial History*, i, 72–3, who notes also that 'many of the tablets have been taken down and stowed away in one of the vaults beneath the church'. Perhaps this storage occurred when the belfry was constructed, that is, after Lysons' and Gilbert's visits but before Glynne's, although they were replaced in the church following its 1873 restoration.

[36] Trans., *This was made A.D. 1472.*

[37] Maclean, *Trigg Minor*, i, 151, notes the decoration of the ribs and bosses of the roofs, including these shields, which he found on bosses on the fifth web westward from the chancel arch. Lysons sketched (1) *[argent] a chevron [sable], in chief a label of three points [gules]*, for Prideaux, impaling *[argent] a saltire between four mullets [estoiles gules]*, for Lucombe; (2) *[azure] a chevron between three pears [or]*, for Calmady, impaling Lucombe.

[38] Maclean, *Trigg Minor*, i, 154, records the contract for the manufacture of the pews in 1491, but also that 'many of the old carved bench-ends which were removed from their original position when the church was repewed in 1819, still remain in the church. Some of them have been reworked into screens, and others lie rotting in the parvise chamber.' This repewing was part of a much larger scheme of renewal, as the rural dean reported in 1813 that 'the South Arch in a dangerous Situation as well as the Pillars of the Church. The Southern Wall and the Arch of the West Window are bulging out – the upper part of the Tower in extremely

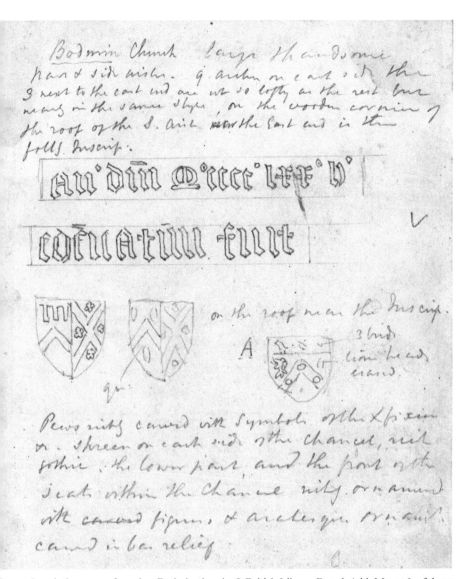

g. 14. Inscription on roof cornice, Bodmin church; © British Library Board, Add. Ms. 9462, fol. 21r.

At the East end of the North aisle is an altar tomb of a hard dark coloured stone having the effigies of a Bishop in pontificalibus with his Crosier on his left side under his arm, his hands joined in prayer. Two Angels supporting his head, one of

bad repair, and should there be frequent ringing it will probably even fall', KK: AD59/74, 139. Gilbert, *Historical Survey*, ii, 627, noted that 'in 1817, the whole of the south aisle of the church, was found to be so enfeebled by age, and otherwise decayed, as to render it necessary for the greater part to be taken down and rebuilt. This was accordingly done', reported in the *RCG*, 25 September 1819, 2. The work extended to rebuilding the west front, removing the Norman doorway there; Sedding, *Norman Architecture*, 23. The original doorway was recorded by William Borlase in 1756. (Fig. 15)

An ancient Saxon door-case at the Western end of the middle Isle of Bodman church. June 24 1756 WB:

Fig. 15. Norman west doorway, Bodmin church (1756), now destroyed; reproduced by kind permission of Devon Archives & Local Studies, DHC, Z19/16/1, 97, drawing by William Borlase.

which holds a shield with these arms (3 fishes) the other the coat [of arms] as A. <sketch of shield labelled A>.[39] Two other angels at his feet with the same shields, round the verge of the slab the following Inscription: 'Hic tumilatur venerabilis Pater Tomas Vivian Megarensis ep[iscop]us hujus q[ui] domus prior qui obiit anno domini M . D . XXXIII primo die Junii cujus ... propicietur deus amen.' Figures of the 4 Evangelists with their attributes [and] symbols carved in alto relievo & 2 shields.[40] [separate sheet] Slab of blue slate. Here lyeth John Vyvyan 1545 a cross on each side of which a shield of arms <sketch of 2 shields>.[41]

---

[39] The 'three fishes' are the arms of Bodmin priory (*azure three fish in pale naiant argent*); the shield 'A' displays *or, on a chevron azure three annulets between three lions' heads erased proper, on a chief gules three martlets argent*, for Vivian of Bodmin.

[40] Trans., *Here lies buried the venerable father Thomas Vivian, bishop of Megarensis, once prior of this house, who died A.D. 1533 on the 1st day of June, on whose [soul] may the lord have mercy amen.* Lysons, *Cornwall*, 34, mention this as a 'remarkable monument'; see Cockerham, *Continuity and Change*, 25–30, pls 16–21.

[41] One shield, *of three birds in fess*, for ?, is inked in on the page; the second shield repeats the arms of Vivian; illustrated by Cockerham, *Continuity and Change*, pl. 1.

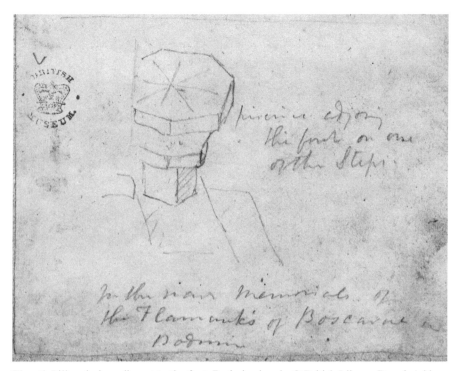

Fig. 16. Pillar piscina adjacent to the font, Bodmin church; © British Library Board, Add. Ms. 9462, fol. 21r.

Piscina adjoining the font on one of the steps <sketch of pillar piscina>.[42] (Fig. 16) In the nave memorials of the Flamanks of Boscarne in Bodmin.[43] Fol. 20v. The north end of North aisle, that is the North aisle of the chancel appears to be of older work than the South part of the Church, and the windows in the same style as the East Window of the South aisle of the Church of St Kewe, which was taken out of the old Church at Bodmin as appears by the account of the building of that edifice in the archives of the Corporation of Bodmin.[44] Some of the carved work of the screens in the Chancel seems to be of the time of Hen. 8, ornamentation in the Holbein style, initials on some of them A.R., T.C &c & Symbols of the Xfixion &c.[45]

[42] This had been removed from the chancel and located adjacent to the font; it was subsequently pierced with a central slit and used as an alms-box.
[43] These slate slabs are fully described by Maclean, *Trigg Minor*, i, 171–2.
[44] The Lysons clearly quarried the town records for this information, which they recorded at length but published only in brief, *Cornwall*, ccxxx, 34. See 'Receipts and Expenses in the Building of Bodmin Church, A.D. 1469 to 1472', ed. J.J. Wilkinson, *Camden Miscellany*, Camden Society NS 7 (1875); and Mattingly, *Churches of Cornwall*, 17–19. This lengthy record is symptomatic of the brothers' desire to pursue their enquiries as deeply as possible into whatever original sources they could uncover at a parochial level, something they do again, for instance, at Constantine.
[45] Fragments remain incorporated into the present stalls and screens. There is a design for the conjectural restoration of one bay of the original parclose screen, based on pieces lying

Fig. 17. Conjectural restoration of one bay of the original parclose screen, Bodmin church (1870?); from the collections at Kresen Kernow, P13/2/59, drawing by Hancock & Co., church furnishers.

[separate sheet] Among the receipts for the building of the parish church of Bodmin from 1469 to Michaelmas 1470 & 1471 'It. recevyd for a window yt sold to the parish of Helland 26s. It. yt recevyd for a window of Seynt Kewa 26s 7d.'

Among the payments, 'Thomas Lucomb glasid the gabell window yn seynt John is Ilde. Bartholomew Trote and Rafe Dyer made the window and glasid next to seynt John. William Olyver of Bodynyell made the next window to that & glasid him. Odo Robyn & Paschoe Robyn glasyd the next wyndow to yn seynt John is Idle. John Wath glasid the wyndow in the south next to seynt John is Ilde. Avery Skeys of Haysportone yef the yre work a yre of the large wyndow yn the south parte the West wyndow there. Summa 9^{li} 18^{s}.1^{d} ob.'

Accounts of the payment for building the belfry at the Bery for a year 12 September 17 Hen. 7.[46]

[separate sheet] Indenture dated 4 December 7 Hen. 7 between Nicholas Glynn of Bodmyn & others & Mathias More Carpynter of the one part & John Carmynowe Esq. & others of the other part – it was agreed that said M. More 'shall make or do to be made fully newe chayrs & seges in iii renges through oute all the body of the said church after the forme & makyng of the chayrs & seges in St Mary church of Plympton and a convenyient Pulpyte after the form & making of the pulpyt in the

in the parvise chamber over the south door, by Hancock and Co., Church furnishers, Bodmin (1870?); KK: P13/2/59. (Fig. 17) See also Mattingly, 'Rood Loft Construction', 88–9, 102–3.
[46] This refers to the Berry tower, the surviving part of the Chapel of the Holy Rood, Bodmin; see Lysons, *Cornwall*, 34–5.

parish church of Mourton in Hemsted to be paid for ye making & workmanship ^4£ to be paid as going for the timber out of Wales 4£ when the said timber be presented to the forsaid burgesses &c.^ of said chairs seges & pulpit 92£. Indenture dated 31 Hen. 8 between Jono Blyghe mayor of the town & borough of Bodmin of the one part the church wardens of the parish church of St Petroc in Bodmyn – containing an inventory of the jewels goods & ornaments of said Church among which were '2 paxes of sylver & gylt & in one of theym one of the thornes that crownyd our savyour ~~Chr~~ Crist. It. a boxe of ev'y (ivory) with a lach of sylver'.[47]

[separate sheet] Old font in Guildhall plain octagonal with inscription imperfect.[48]

[separate sheet] Deu de sa alme eit me[rci] stone found on the site of the priory in Bodmin.[49]

Fol. 21v. <sketch of font with dimensions: 10 x 1' 10 Diameter 3' 5½> of a hard stone of a light brown colour. On the opposite side two figures of animals and heads of animals with foliage.[50]

[separate sheet] <sketch of cross> Four hole cross near the 8 mile stone from Bodmin on Temple Moor.[51]

Fol. 21* Inscription in Bodmin Church taken off 7 Oct 1814 JW [John Wallis] an[no] d[omi]ni M°CCCC° [a space] Vacancy occasioned by the removal of an Image lxx° ii° doma f[ac]t[u]m fuit. <a rubbing of a Gothic minuscule inscription carved in relief on a wall plate>.[52]

Fol. 22r. <sketches> Three arches at the east end <section of pillar> pillars of chancel same dimensions with those of the nave, capitals of the pillars of the nave <sketches of capitals and bases> arches of the nave base of the pillars of the Nave.

[separate sheet] <large plan of the church with dimensions and sketches> windows of the North aisle at the East end from the plan where the roof is lower.

[separate sheet] Windows of Bodmin Church except those of the ^East end of^ North Aisle <sketch of window tracery>.

---

[47] The original document is now lost but was published by L.S. Snell, *The Edwardian Inventories of Church Goods for Cornwall* (Exeter, [1955]), 29–32, from secondary sources (xxii).

[48] Possibly this is a corn measure, noted by Hals; see Polsue, *Parochial History*, i, 78.

[49] These words '[May] God have mercy on his soul' (trans. from Norman French) suggest that a fragment of a thirteenth-/early fourteenth-century gravestone survived in the priory grounds. A Purbeck marble cross slab of similar date can be found lying outside the south wall of the church, as further commemorative evidence of those times; it was recorded by Sedding, *Norman Architecture*, 29.

[50] The font was published by Lysons, *Cornwall*, ccxxxiii and pl. opp.

[51] See Langdon, *East Cornwall*, 46, no. 72; and Preston-Jones and Okasha, *Early Cornish Sculpture*, 174–5.

[52] This rubbing is almost certainly of the same inscription noted earlier (fol. 21r.), which Maclean, *Trigg Minor*, i, 152, noted as carved on the cornice of the northern side of the south aisle. It is not impossible that there were two similar inscriptions, but perhaps more likely that there was an error in transcription, and the 'doma f'c'm fuit' was initially interpreted as 'ed'fi-catuu' fuit'. Lysons themselves altered this in *Cornwall*, 'Further Additions and Corrections', 370, as a result of a letter on the subject on 26 September 1814 from John Wallis jnr, BL, Add. Ms. 9420, fol. 335r. The 'Vacancy' was a gap in the inscription that would originally have been taken up by the presence of a sculptured figure, removed, presumably, at the Reformation.

[separate sheet] St Lawrence chapel divided by 3 arches ^low^ clustered pillars & pointed arches[53] <sketch of foliated capital with 'hollow trough' indicated>.
[separate sheet] Bodmin – found in Mr Gilberts garden which stands on the site of the Priory at 150 yds South East of the church. <sketches of Bodmin Priory capitals, section, window tracery>. Chapel at the east end of the church [St Thomas's] a few yards distant from it, East window large pointed.[54]

Glynne: GL, Glynne notebooks 13, fols 59–61

Bodmin, S. Petrock, 21 February 1849.
A very good specimen of a Cornish Church of the large sort, perhaps the best of this type in the county. It is of considerable length, both nave & Chancel having aisles, which are wide & coextensive, there is a large South porch & a Tower on the North side of the North aisle, not far from the boundary of the Chancel. <*Length of church 151 feet by 63. The date mostly 1470.*[55]> The whole Church appears to be Third Pointed & is in very good condition. The roofs are all of cradle form & no Clerestory [60] with ribs & bosses. The nave is of 6 bays, the arcades have fine lofty arches, with the usual Cornish piers <section of a pier> the shafts having octagonal separate capitals & longitudinal mouldings down the pier between them. Some of the capitals on the North are flowered. <*This Church (formerly belonging to the Monastery) was rebuilt in 1472. In the Eastern end of the South aisle the ribs of the roof are more closely panneled & there are some angel figures.*> There is an ascent to the Chancel. There is a regular Chancel arch, which is unusual in Cornwall, rising on shafts set upon the capitals of the adjacent lateral piers, which are not extended further than the others.[56] There are also arches of division between the aisles of the nave and those of the Chancel. The Chancel is of 3 bays, the arches are rather lower & wider than in the Nave. The windows of the aisles of the nave are of 4 lights; at the West end of the South aisle is one of 6 lights, at the West of the North aisle is one of 5. The tracery is not of the very best kind. The West window of the nave is of 6 lights, the 3 Western gables very wide. The East window of the Chancel is bad & modern, filled with modern stained glass, thought once very fine, but not at all good in reality. <*The East window with its glass was presented to the Church in [vacant].*[57]> The East window of the South aisle is of 6 lights: that of the

---

[53] Maclean, *Trigg Minor*, i, 197, notes that 'the chapel was in ruins in 1814, and was used as a stable: two windows on the south side and three arches which divided the chapel, only, remained then standing', confirming the Lysons' findings. Nothing now remains.

[54] Although roofless, the unusual tracery of the east window, transitioning from Decorated to Perpendicular, survives.

[55] These notes (fol. 58v.) are in Glynne's later handwriting, the dimensions taken from the EDAS notes, DHC: F5/17/2/4, EDAS, series of Rough Notes – sheet 22 (1861); curiously, Lysons, *Cornwall*, ccxxx, publishes the dimensions as 140 feet by 63.

[56] See Mattingly, 'Distinctiveness by Omission', 140–1, who notes that although the building accounts do not mention the construction of a chancel arch, due to the considerable rebuilding of the church from 1469 to 1472, it must date from then.

[57] As Polsue, *Parochial History*, i, 88, relates, this window was the gift of Lord de Dunstanville in 1824 and represents the Ascension. 'Its ecclesiastical appearance is deteriorated, however, by its being divided into square panes', reproducing the prevalent fashion for such glazing patterns. It was subsequently replaced in 1898.

North is of 4. The windows of the South Chancel aisle are of 4, those of the North Chancel aisle of 3 lights.[58] *<In the North aisle of the Chancel is a fine black marble effigy of a Bishop with Crosier, the angels at the head are gone: but shields at the feet. The inscription, Hic tumulatur venerabilis Tomas Vivian abbas Huius Domus prior qui obiit primo die Juni M D XXXIII (to?) Cuius anime propicietur Deus.[59]>* The Interior is handsome & spacious, the pues uniform, no galleries except one at ~~the~~ small one at the West end, in which is a large old Organ.[60] The Chancel is not pued but seated stall wise, the Litany is always said from a Lectern.[61] The Pulpit is composed of pieces of ancient wood carving collected from various quarters.[62] The Font is a magnificent Norman one, of the circular cup form, so often seen in Cornwall, but of unusually large size, set on a cylindrical stem, & surrounded by 4 shafts with capitals on which are sculptured winged monsters <or angels>. On the bowl is a good deal of scroll ^& foliage^ work in high relief with beaded mouldings ~~also~~ & figures of dragons ^below them^. The whole is on a square plinth, ~~with~~ ^the bases of the shafts have^ knobs at the angles, & raised upon two steps. Near the South door, within the nave is an arched recess set rather low down & deep in the wall. *<The Font is engraved in Lysons.[63]>*

[58] The church underwent a series of restorations destroying much of what Glynne noted, in particular the windows and roofs (apart from the south chapel). The *WB* reported a meeting to discuss the situation, 23 January 1873, 12, that 'every time the rain came the water poured in through the roof'; but it was not until 1880 that the nave was partially restored, and 1884 when the church was re-opened a second time, after restoration of the chancel. *RCG*, 26 December 1884, 4, reported that 'some 10 or 11 years ago, the church being then in a shockingly dilapidated condition, the restoration of the western portion was commenced and carried out at a cost of over £3,000, and yesterday marked the completion of the work of restoring the eastern end, the expense of which has been equally as costly […] The three bays in the east end of the north arcade are completely new, and with the exception of two of painted glass, the whole of the windows are either new or have been completely restored, while two memorial windows have been added […] A portion of the ancient oak roof over the east end of the south chancel aisle has been preserved, and with the exception of the other portion of this isle, which has been roofed with oak, the edifice throughout has been new roofed with pitch-pine. The aisles have been taken up and laid with Staffordshire tiles and the flooring of the church with wood pavement completed. The chancel and sanctuary have been paved with encaustic tiles; new choir stalls have been erected […] a new altar of cedar wood has been raised […] On the whole the church has undergone a complete transformation and been in some measure restored to its original pristine beauty.' See LPL: ICBS 7891 (1874–80) for reseating and general repairs, the documentation including a plan detailing what had been completed by 1880 (the westernmost four bays of the nave) and what was yet to be done. For a chronology of the works, see Warner, *A Time to Build*, 94–5.
[59] This and other notes (fol. 59v.) are in Glynne's later hand and seem to be the result of personal inspection of the church fabric on a revisit – for example, a reading of the inscription on Prior Vivian's tomb, which still differs from the more correct version published by Lysons.
[60] This was removed by 1868, exposing the west window, and the organ removed to the north chancel aisle; see Maclean, *Trigg Minor*, i, 153. It is now at the west end of the north aisle. The church was pewed in 1818, following the rebuilding of the south aisle, DHC: DR, Faculty Causes, Cornwall, Bodmin 1 (1818), which includes a seating plan.
[61] Glynne disapproved of the pre-Tractarian practice of not involving the high altar in the performance of the liturgy.
[62] Only the base of the pulpit and a prayer desk now comprise medieval material.
[63] From which source Glynne appears to have later annotated his notes, and see Sedding, *Norman Architecture*, 23–4, pls IX–X.

The Porch is lofty, quite like a Tower, 3 stages in height & embattled, with [an] octagonal turret at the angle. There are 3 canopied ogee niches in front over the door set 2 & 1. The windows of the parvise square headed. This Porch has fine stone groining of late character, with shields & fan tracery. The Priests door on the South of the Chancel has label & spandrels. Its door case within is screened by some fine ancient wood carving brought from elsewhere in which are some [61] shields with emblems of the Passion – IHC & crowned M.[64] The Tower opens from the North aisle by a pointed arch. It is plain Third Pointed, rather bald & wanting in effect, consisting of 3 stages, one set upon the other & gradually diminishing like a Telescope. It has a battlement & 4 pinnacles, no buttresses, the 2 lower stages have plain single windows, with trefoiled heads. *<The pinnacles have an Italian look.*[65]*>* The belfry story has a projecting window of 3 lights flanked by pinnacles. The Tower is of coarse stone masonry with rather finer dressings, altogether rather inferior. There is an indication of a rood turret on the South.

<The Churchyard is spacious, especially on the North & not open to the usual objections of intra mural burial grounds, being so free from dwellings.>

At the East end of the Churchyard is an ancient chapel, now used as a school, dedicated to S. Thomas, & having a Crypt under it. Its East window of 3 lights with the quasi flowing tracery seen at Sherford & elsewhere in Devonshire.[66] The other windows debased, the walls covered with ivy. There are also piscina & sedilia.

BOTUS FLEMING (Fig. 18)

Lysons: BL, Add. Ms. 9462, fol. 22r.

Botusfleming – nothing remarkable.[67]

---

[64] Presumably these were bench ends or panels from the screen, reused at the restoration of 1874–80.

[65] These were set up following the collapse of the steeple in 1699. This and the next note are on fol. 60v.

[66] Glynne had visited Sherford on 24 February 1845 (GL, Glynne notebooks 70, fols 34B–38B). He appears to have in mind the five-branched star shape found in the window tracery there, as well as at Ipplepen, Newton Abbot, Plympton, and Staverton; yet 'although seemingly a Dec. motif, the examples are almost all in a decisively Perp context'; see B. Cherry and N. Pevsner, *The Buildings of England: Devon*, 2nd edn (London, 1989), 45. While Glynne noted the architectural similarities between these examples therefore, he failed to read the Devon window tracery within a wider stylistic chronology.

[67] This comment despite the arcade between the nave and the north aisle formed of four slender octagonal columns of Pentewan stone, the capitals decorated with fleurons, and three of the columns incorporating brackets for statues. The church was noted in 1846 as 'sadly dilapidated, and the walls only prevented from falling by being "shored up" by granite posts', H.M. Rice, 'A Paper on Certain Churches in the Deanery of East, in the County of Cornwall', *TEDAS* 3 (1849), 178–99, at 182–3. A radical restoration took place in 1871–2, prior to which 'some portion of the walls was so dangerously out of the perpendicular, owing to the outward thrust of the roofs, that huge buttresses of modern masonry and large props of granite had to be erected to prevent part from falling. There were the usual old square pews, and unsightly gallery at the western end, blocking the tower arch [...] The roofs are entirely new, all the timbers being visible. The carved bosses of the old roofs that were sound have been carefully preserved, and re-used in the nave roof. A large portion of the walls has been rebuilt. Two new windows have been placed on the southern side of the chancel [...] The pillars and arches

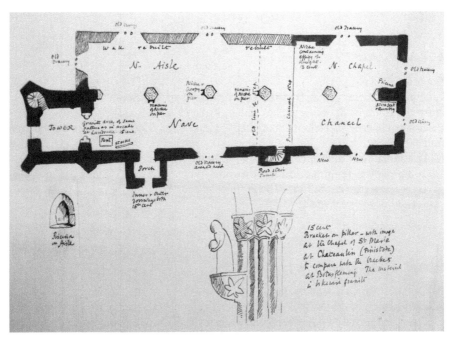

Fig. 18. Groundplan of Botus Fleming church; reproduced with the kind permission of the Royal Institution of Cornwall, Courtney Library, Henderson Ms. 'East Cornwall', 40.

In North aisle monument of Mark Batt Esq., son of Mark Batt Merchant, 1758 & William Batt his son, 1781.
Square font with arches <sketch>.
Slabs in the North aisle for the Pembertons.
John Killinghall Pemberton Esq., Son of William Pemberton Esq., 1789.[68]

of granite have been cleansed from white-wash and the interior walls re-plastered [...] The font, which is a square Early English basin, arcaded in low relief [...] has been cleaned, and now stands on a new base of granite [...] A piscina in the south side of the chancel has been restored according to the remnants of the original which were found; a small rude piscina in southern side of the north aisle, and the entrance to the rood loft are preserved'; *WBCA*, 5 June 1873, 12. See also LPL: ICBS 7337 (1873) for reseating and repairs, including a plan showing the extent of the rebuilding. Heraldic glass recorded by Gilbert, *Historical Survey*, ii, 437, has been destroyed.

[68] This monument is described by Gilbert, *Historical Survey*, ii, 437, as 'a stone', whereas Polsue, *Parochial History*, i, 113, records it as 'two slates' under the gallery, commemorating William and Dorothy Pemberton and their son William, who died in 1773; they have since disappeared. Although Lysons failed to record the tomb with a late thirteenth-century military figure in Purbeck marble, it was noted in their 'Additions and Corrections', 348, as 'lately been discovered, by the removal of a pannel, in a pew'. T. Quarles, 'Opening of the Crusader's Tomb in Botus Fleming Church', *Gentleman's Magazine* (1840 part 2), 31–2, noted it was only visible when the 'rubbish which had accumulated about it' was cleared away.

BOYTON (Fig. 19)

Lysons: BL, Add. Ms. 9462, fol. 23r.

Boyton – August I.
Church with nave, chancel, at the end a prolong of it.[69] South aisle separated by clustered columns & obtuse arches like Egloskerry &c.[70]
Piscina in chancel <sketch of square headed mullioned window,[71] and round-bowled font[72]>.
Marble monument in chancel erected 1731, arms <sketch of shield[73]>.
On a tablet of slate on the tower, arms of Symons, William Symons of Bradridge gave 100£ towards it, ob. 1692. Tower finished 1694.[74]

BRADDOCK

Glynne: GL, Glynne notebooks 14, fol. 58

Bradock, S Mary, 29 January 1854.
A small Church of the usual Cornish Perpendicular character & general arrangement. The plan comprises a body with South aisle, a North chapel, South Porch & Western Tower. There is no distinction of Chancel except a little in the roof as seen within. The arcade has 5 Tudor arches, rather small, with the usual light clustered piers of which the shafts have square capitals – one being ornamented with panneling. The arches & piers are all of granite. The North chapel or Transept open to the nave by

---

[69] It is difficult to understand what Lysons meant by this. The nave/chancel and the south aisle extended eastwards to the same point, although the aisle extended further west than the nave, adjoining the south side of the tower. There is no evidence that in the restoration of 1876–7, the east wall was rebuilt, masking what Lysons might have seen seventy years previously; see the church re-opening reported in *LWN*, 11 August 1877, 4.

[70] Little of this was published in *Cornwall*, 39, although Lysons note the donation by William Symons 'of 100*l.* towards rebuilding the tower of the church; it was completed in 1769, as appears by a tablet on the outside'. This despite their correct record taken directly from the 'tablet of slate' of 1694 as the rebuilding date. The rebuilding preserved the tower arch opening into the nave.

[71] There are three three-light square-headed windows in the south wall that resemble this sketch.

[72] See Sedding, *Norman Architecture*, 38–9, pl. XIV; and the CRSBI online at: https://www.crsbi.ac.uk/view-item?i=3258 [accessed December 2023].

[73] The arms are, *per fess sable and or, a pale counterchanged, three trefoils slipped of the second*, for Symons, impaling *sable, a griffin rampant between three crosses argent*, for ?. This shield surmounts the 'marble monument' to Jane, daughter and heiress of William Symons, widow of John Hoblyn, who died in 1751 (not as the Lysons have it). The inscription also records the generosity of her father in restoring the church from structural decay, and who also 'took care to get ye cure of this parish (rob'd of all by the sacrilege of former ages) supplied whilst living; but having purchased the small Tythes and Altarage of this parish [...] he by his last will restored them to God, giving them forever to the supply and service of this Church'.

[74] Clearly there were several structural issues affecting the church post-Restoration, as in 1677 the chancel was rebuilt, recorded in the churchwardens' accounts as 'Paid ye Massons for Building the Chancel £14 10s. od.', this when seven days' work for the same 'Massons' was paid at 8s. 2d. By 1694, the tower was being reconstructed, church rates for the work levied in 1678 and 1691–2; KK: P16/5/1, churchwardens' accounts 1670–93.

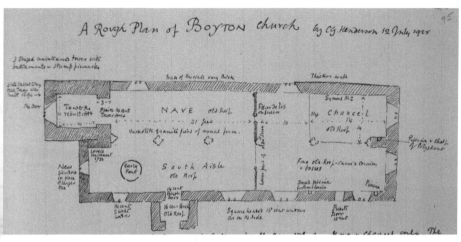

Fig. 19. Groundplan of Boyton church; reproduced with the kind permission of the Royal Institution of Cornwall, Courtney Library, Henderson Ms. 'East Cornwall', 45.

two small flat arches with a square pier, which is a modern arrangement, perpetrated when the chapel was lately repaired & fitted with seats for the Patron.[75] The East window is of 4 lights, the others of 3. The roofs are open, having rudely moulded & sculptured ribs & bosses, & an ornamental cornice.[76] The pulpit is of fine late wood carving, the stalls in the Chancel formed of Gothic carved work brought from elsewhere.[77] The Tower is low & late, without buttress, embattled, with 4 crocketed pinnacles of square form. The arch opening to the nave is obtuse & coarse. The Font a fine one of the Cornish cup form, enriched with rude foliage & heads, upon a circular stem.[78]

[75] Sedding, *Norman Architecture*, 40, describes this as 'a curious twin archway of granite [that] has supplanted the original archway. This comparatively modern erection consists apparently of two seventeenth-century doorways, utilized for this purpose.' However, a plan of the church *c*. 1835 reveals that the north transept was then used as a vestry, with a solid wall (apart from a doorway) separating it from the nave; KK: P17/2/3 (Fig. 20). The archway was created in 1846 to open up the north transept as a manorial pew for the Fortescue family, and it is likely that the north window and the east door to the transept were also made then; KK: P17/5/2, fol. 33v., churchwardens' accounts.

[76] The roof was replaced after discovery of the death watch beetle in the timbers for which a grant was given; LPL: ICBS 11722 (1926–7). The old carvings were reproduced as accurately as possible (information from Church Guide); see also Warner, *A Time to Build*, 98.

[77] The entry for Braddock in *The Diocese of Exeter in 1821: Bishop Carey's Replies to Queries before Visitation; Volume I; Cornwall*, ed. M. Cook, DCRS NS 3 (1958), 7, records 'the building is in good repair excepting the end of the Chancel containing the East Window (which will be repaired this season) & the pews which are very old require repair'. Following this, the church was completely reseated in 1829/30/31, including the 'Rail to Communion and Stairs & Rail to the Pulpit'; KK: P17/5/2, fols 75r. (1829), 18r. (1830), 19r. (1831). Whether this was when the seating was reordered and material incorporated from elsewhere, or whether it was done at another time – for example when the manorial pew was furnished – is impossible to determine.

[78] The unfurling foliage decoration is generally accepted to represent the Tree of Life on one side, and palmettes on the other three; Sedding, *Norman Architecture*, 40–1, pl. XV.

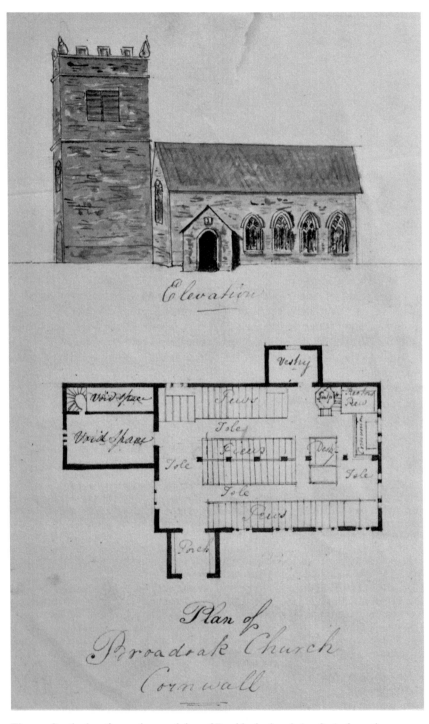

Fig. 20. South elevation and groundplan of Braddock church (*c.* 1830); from the collections at Kresen Kernow, P17/2/3.

The Porch has a Tudor arched labeled door. There is a little old stained glass & some modern & armorial.[79]

BREAGE

Lysons: BL, Add. Ms. 9462, fol. 23r.

Breag – Nave & aisles, Clustered pillars & circular arches, & 2 small Transepts. Windows <sketch of 3 light window> modern font.
Fol. 51r. Pengersick Castle – remains of a tower with one room upstairs pretty entire, with remains wainscot with small pannels, in the upper ones are verses painted in black letter.[80]

Glynne: GL, Glynne notebooks 70, fols 9B–10B

St Breage, July 1843.
A large Church built of granite & consisting of a West Tower, nave & Chancel, side aisles, North & South Transeptal Chapels & South porch. The body as usual low, & the aisles have separate roofs without Clerestory. The Tower has 3 stages in height, & a fine battlement & 4 large crocketed pinnacles set on square panneled pedestals somewhat overhanging the parapet. The buttresses are set at a distance from the angles. The belfry windows are of 3 lights & rather poor character.[81] The west doorway has good mouldings & a label. The west window is of 4 lights. <*The Tower arch is panneled & affords a rich & uncommon specimen.*[82]>
The South porch is of granite ^& embattled^, & entered by a pointed arch springing from octagonal shafts having moulded capitals & panneled. Within this porch is a door

---

[79] The remaining early glass is heraldic, but there is nothing of the sort recorded in the *Diary of the Marches of the Royal Army during the Great Civil War; Kept by Richard Symonds*, ed. C.E. Long, Camden Society (1859), 58–9, who noted: 'In the south-west of the church are many coates in allusion to the Passion–Argent, three nails sable; ladder in bend; and divers more cutt upon the seates in escutcheons.'

[80] See Blight, *West Cornwall*, 71, who cites some of the verses.

[81] Glynne would have seen many windows that were inserted in the late eighteenth century following a lightning strike, as revealed in a letter from the then vicar, Rev. Henry Usticke, to his brother, of 18 January 1762: 'Last Monday about 4 o'clock in the afternoon our tower which if you remember is a remarkably handsome one was rent from top to bottom by a flash of lightning accompanied by a violent shower of hail. It made its way I apprehend in through the belfry window which it shattered to pieces, then up through the Western side of the tower where it struck off the South Eastern pinnacle in a thousand bits, some of which were carried to a great distance into two fields, one on the south and the other on the north side of the church. The cross was likewise struck off from the N.W. Pinnacle [...] The Battlements on the Western and Southern sides of the tower are greatly defaced and for about three fathom above the Belfrey window there is an appearance of being battered with cannon. Every window in the church was shattered to pieces, except ones in the Eastern end of the Church. The walls are opened in four or five places and what is surprising as anything is that through God's Providence no person received any harm'; KK: X1424/49. Borlase, BL, Egerton Ms. 2657, fol. 39v., recorded some heraldic glass in the east window of the 'long' north aisle, but this no longer survives.

[82] This comment on the facing verso is in Glynne's later hand, possibly added after a revisit of the church in 1870, or from Blight's *West Cornwall*, 73, who recorded the tower arch as 'perhaps the finest Perpendicular arch to be found in any of the churches of the district'.

with label & panneled spandrels. The Transeptal Chapels are embattled. The windows are of 3 lights, & rather indifferent tracery.[83] The East windows of the side aisles are of 5 lights, though that of the Chancel has only 3; in some are pieces of stained glass.[84] The windows of the Transepts are particularly bad. The aisles are wide – the divisions formed by a double range of obtuse arches ^(low & narrow)^, 7 on each side, springing from columns of granite, of the Cornish style, having general banded capitals, those on the North having Tudor flowers, lozenges &c. ^& knots^ in relief, sculptured in granite. The Chancel seems to include the 2 Eastern arches, & extends a little beyond the aisles. Over the East portion of the Nave, where was the roodloft, is a painted boarded ceiling;[85] the North Transept has a flat panneled wood ceiling, with the ribs elegantly moulded & foliated, & very fine bosses. The rest of the Church has coved roofs, with ribs [10B] forming pannels with carved bosses, & beneath a flowered cornice. The Chancel roof is rather lower & ceiled. The Transeptal Chapels open to the side aisles by obtuse arches resembling those of the nave.[86]

BUDOCK

Lysons: BL, Add. Ms. 9462, fol. 23r.

Budock – Nave and North aisle & South transept.
In the Chancel brasses of John Killigrew Esq. of Arwenack & Lord of the Manor of Killigrew – he was the first Captain of Pendennis Castle made by K. Henry the 8th, & so continued until the 9th of Q. Elizabeth which year he died, 1567.
Sir John Killigrew Knt. his son succeeded him in the same place by the gift of Q. Elizabeth. In armour bare headed with a beard & ruff his lady with ruff (Elizabeth Trewinnard).
Monument on South wall of chancel with their effigies kneeling in bas relief of Sir John Killigrew of Arwenack Knt., died 26 Eliz., & Dame Mary his wife, daughter of Philip Wolverston of Wolverston Hall, Suffolk; 2nd Killigrew [who] commanded Pendennis Castle Fort since the first erection thereof. John his son married Dorothy, daughter of Thomas Monck of Poderidge, Devon.
John Killigrew grandson of Sir John erected this monument, 1617.[87]
[new paper] On a slab of slate on South wall of chancel.

---

[83] Of the type sketched by Lysons, without tracery and cusping.

[84] There are still some fragments of medieval glass remaining, including an image of the vernicle. It is generally regarded as being unearthed during the restoration of the church in 1890, yet Glynne recorded glass *in situ* well before this.

[85] Presumably originally intended to resonate with the roodloft.

[86] The chancel was restored and lengthened internally in 1880, *TC*, 1 January 1880, 5, reporting: 'As the recess would only admit the altar it was thought proper to appropriate a portion of the nave to the purpose of a chancel; and, accordingly, the chancel now extends to the end the second arch of the nave arcade. Room has accordingly been provided for reading-desk and choir-stalls, which have been tastefully formed of durable pitch pine.' The building was further restored in 1890, unsympathetically, as the *RCG*, 14 August 1890, 6, reported the work principally concerned 'the floor and the aisles, the nave and chancel having been restored most unsatisfactorily about twelve years ago'. The faculty for the repair/restoration is, KK: P18/6/1, 4 December 1890; the plans are KK: P18/6/7, 1889–90. See also, LPL: ICBS 9486 (1890), for reseating and general repairs.

[87] These two Killigrew monuments illustrated by Gilbert, *Historical Survey*, ii, opp. 790.

D.O.M. / Nicholaus Parker / natura munere / generosa et stirpe eretus / virtutis merito / auratus eques creatus / ortu Sussex^s^iensis / occasu Cornubiensis / post plurimos pro Patria Principe / pietate exantlatos labores / hic tandem quiescit Anno 1537 } vivere {cepit
    1603 }   {desi
Nicholaus Burton ejus in praesidia Pendenisiani prefecturae: ~~victori~~ vicarius obiens vices cique propinquitatis amicitiae testamenti vere conjunctissimus perpetuae memoriae ergo moeriens posuit.[88]

Modern font.

Glynne: GL, Glynne notebooks 16, fols 14–15

Budock – S. Budoc, 18 February 1858.
This Church in its present condition offers a very pleasing contrast to the last named [Mabe], being in excellent repair, well cared for & lately having undergone much improvement in its internal arrangements.[89]
The plan is very Cornish, nave & Chancel undivided, North aisle, South transept, South porch & West Tower. The whole late Perpendicular except one lancet window on the South side of the Chancel [15] which marks the existence of an Early English Chancel. The windows have been mostly renewed in Perpendicular character in place of former Venetian ones;[90] & ~~There~~ mostly squareheaded of 3 or 4 lights; those on the North are pointed. The arcade is of a local type & has 7 small pointed arches, the piers of lozenge form with 4 shafts. The Transept is sprawling and awkwardly set on. The Tower arch is plain & pointed, ~~Near on shafts~~ ^that to the^ Transept is pointed on shafts. There is ~~an ogee arch~~ a piscina on the South of the nave ~~near the entrance of the Chancel~~ West end of the Transept. *<The existence of this piscina would seem to point to an altar once placed near.[91]>* The base of the

[88] Trans., *Nicholas Parker, by his nature noble in office, and bred by virtue of his merits, created a knight in the county of Sussex, after many labours in the west of Cornwall, inspired by piety for the prince, rests here at last. The year 1537 he took life, the year 1603 he gave up life. Nicholas Burton placed this in perpetual memory of him dying in the garrisons of the prefecture of Pendennis: the deputy, therefore, yet truly joined together in perpetual memory and the closeness of friendship.* This monument and those of the Killigrews are illustrated and their historical context discussed by Cockerham, *Continuity and Change*, 54, 74–5, 107–8, 110–11, pls 190, 191, 198. The inscriptions are published in *Cornwall*, 48.

[89] The church underwent internal reordering in 1847–8; see LPL: ICBS 4008, for reseating, with new windows, construction of a vestry in the tower, and a gallery for singers and children. Seating plans with open pews, and elevations, are among the documents. There was an additional note that the partition across the entrance to the pulpit and the stalls in the choir should be removed, perhaps to allow better access to the 'free' seats.

[90] Gilbert, *Historical Survey*, ii, 790, records that these were inserted in 1776, and at the same time 'the old pews [were] removed, to make room for modern ones'. KK: P22/4/1 is a volume of the parish rates and accounts, with, at the front, the 'Disbursements for Rebuilding the Church', 1778–9. Glynne saw these 'Venetian' windows replaced by new Perpendicular-style tracery set within the original fifteenth-century frames. *The Ecclesiologist* 12 (1851), 436, commented on the changes and concluded that they were only partially successful in restoring the church from its previously 'modernised' state, where among other depredations, 'a wretched wooden vase' was still used as the font.

[91] Glynne thought the location of this piscina identified a nave altar close by, just west of the entrance to the transept, and possibly co-eval with it as the earliest part of the cruciform

rood screen remains, & is richly carved & has traces of colour, it presents niches & fine carving of foliage, each niche containing a painting of a Saint.[92] The pues have been replaced by low open seats & a new open roof has been made.[93] The South doorway within the porch has an obtuse arch and some curious quasi feathering in granite, the jambs also of granite ^with panneling^. There is an Organ on the floor near the west end. *<The Chancel occupies 2 bays, separated by the roodscreen.>* The Tower is embattled, has corner buttresses & 2 string courses, 4 flattened ungraceful pinnacles, the belfry windows labelled, a small West window of 3 lights & doorway with continuous mouldings.

The vestry is a detached building near the Church yard gate, & has an ogee niche built into the wall.

The North doorway is labelled.

CALLINGTON (Fig. 21)

Lysons: BL, Add. Ms. 9462, fol. 24r.

Callington – Curate – Revd. John Messenger, Revd. Mr John Russel South-hill, Revd. Mr Penwarne at St Germans.[94]

Callington – a daughter Church to Southill – it is a perpetual Curacy.

~~In a~~ ^Under an arch between the chancel and the^ north aisle of the Chancel an altar tomb of alabaster much enriched with gothic tracery, at the foot of the tomb these arms with the garter *<sketch of shield>*. Effigies of a Knight in long hair, plate armour, round at the toes, lion at his feet, helmet, crest & lambrequin under his head: the crest a King's head. Mantle of the order of the garter, collar with the George pendant, hands joined in prayer. Lord Roos [*sic*] said to have been the founder of the Church.[95]

church. This additional comment, and the second one (fol. 14v.) as well as the numerous corrections, suggest a second visit was made, perhaps in 1862 when he was at Gwennap, or 1863 when he was at Feock and Perranarworthal.

[92] See Bond and Camm, *Roodscreens and Roodlofts*, ii, 382; and Mattingly, 'Rood Loft Construction', 76, 86, 88, 103.

[93] This structure replaced the usual ceiled barrel-vault in the nave and chancel, although the barrel-vault was retained in the north aisle.

[94] James Messenger was curate at South Hill and Callington from 1782 onwards, John Russell curate there from 1800, and Thomas Penwarne perpetual curate at St Germans from 1782 to 1822.

[95] This is the tomb monument to Robert Willoughby, Lord de Broke (d. 1502), a few details of whom are given by Lysons, *Cornwall*, 52. It is beautifully made of Midlands alabaster, the best detailed description by A.B. Hutchinson, 'On the Restoration of the Parish Church of St Mary, Callington', *TEDAS* 6 (1861), 312–34, pl. 55, published following the restoration in 1856–9; see also Cockerham, *Continuity and Change*, 15, pl. 6. The tombchest was originally decorated with four shields on each of the long sides and a shield at the upper and lower ends. That sketched by Lysons is quarterly of four, (1) *gules, in the first and fourth a cross crosslet or, second and third a cross moline*, for Willoughby de Broke, (2) *argent a cross fleury gules*, for Latimer, (3) *gules, four fusils in fess argent each charged with a scallop sable*, for Cheyney, (4) *or, within a bordure engrailed, a fess argent*, for Stafford. The crest that Lysons recorded of a 'King's head' is *a Saracen's head affrontée couped at the shoulders proper, ducally crowned or*, for Willoughby de Broke.

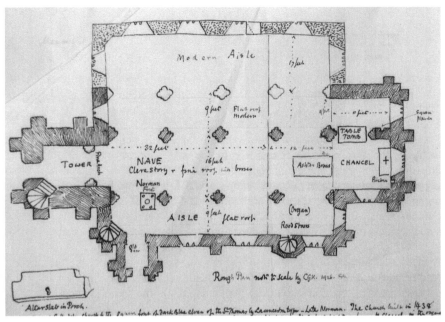

Fig. 21. Groundplan of Callington church; reproduced with the kind permission of the Royal Institution of Cornwall, Courtney Library, Henderson Ms. 'East Cornwall', 67.

Large slab in the nave with brasses of a man in a long gown & his lady, for Nicholas Assheton & Margaret his wife ^'the which Nicholas was one of the'^ the rest is hid by a pew, 1465 (probably the wife) turn over.[96]

> [separate sheet] Assheton qui tumulo Nichola' condit' isto Vulg' cum sensit mite justum miseratum Hic quinquagenis millis interfuit annis hance que ruinosam in q' jacet ipse Capellam Pavit vicinos & egenos & p'eg'nos qui regis et leges & leg' in arte p'itos Conditur et secum judiciale decus nam cum.

Very difficult to read so full of contractions.[97]
<sketch of font> like Altarnun.[98]

[96] The reverse of this paper is blank.

[97] This inscription painstakingly noted by Lysons is on a plate of brass at the feet of the figures of Nicholas Assheton and his wife. The whole of the right side of the slab (including part of the inscription plate) and some of the marginal fillet with the English inscription was evidently covered by a pew encroaching from the north side of the chancel, making their record of the Latin verses incomplete by omitting the ends of the verse lines. A transcription and translation are given by Dunkin, *Brasses*, 16–18, pl. XV. At the restoration, the slab was relaid in the centre of the chancel, and the box pews previously covering it were replaced by benches, and moved back, so the entire slab was revealed: see the 'before' and 'after' plans of the church, and an account of the material changes, in Hutchinson, 'On the Restoration', 321.

[98] See Sedding, *Norman Architecture*, 51–2; it was a relic of the original church, the building enlarged by Assheton in the fifteenth century; see also the CRSBI, available online at: https://www.crsbi.ac.uk/view-item?i=8071 [accessed December 2023].

CALSTOCK

Lysons: BL, Add. Ms. 9462, fol. 24r.

Calstock – nothing remarkable, plain octagonal font. They always decorate this church with yew, box etc. at Easter as well as Xmas. Cothele house in this parish. Mr Foot at Harewood – a pretty seat, his lodge joins the church yard.[99]
Cothele house about a mile South West of Calstock Church.[100]
<sketches of hood mould and stop over square-topped opening with four-centred arches with trefoils in the spandrels> In the hall windows arms of Edgcumbe impaling a lion rampant argent on a field azure semee with fleur de lys. Ditto impaling or a chevron between 3 scallop shells azure. Ditto a ram's head argent horns or on a field sable. The last arms impaling <sketch of arms bendy wavy>.
Fol. 28r. Cotehale – Chapel with Chapel with a screen across,[101] in the east window some remains of stained glass, the annunciation, union rose – arms <sketch of coat of arms[102]>.
A small altar piece with a painting of the offering of the wise men – folding doors, on one side portrait of a man in ruff & short beard with his merchants mark over him <sketch> aet. 34, dressed in black, not ill painted. On the south his wife in ruff & Mary Queen of Scots cap with the same mark over her, & aet. sue 28 – 1589.
Dining room with tapestry & old furniture, a door behind the hangings leads to the chapel. A small room adjoining with tapestry & curious worked sofa &c., from here a flight of steps into a bedchamber. On the stair case a portrait of Sir Thomas Cothale & Parkinson the botanist.[103] Bed chambers all with tapestry. Drawing room in the tower of a good height with rich tapestry & ebony furniture. Entrance at the corner concealing part of the winding staircase with moulded wainscot.
[separate sheet] Cothale – in the hall window, or a chevron between 3 scallop shells azure, impaling or 3 lioncells sable. <descriptions and sketches of three shields[104]>. Arms of England & France quarterly.
Dimensions of the hall 22 feet by 42. All the doorways and windows of moorstone.
NB The furniture has been mostly picked up by the present Lord Edgcumbe & his father – not, as the old housekeeper says, originally found there.

---

[99] Lysons, *Cornwall*, 53, provides a brief history of this seat, and its descent from the Foote family to 'William Roberts, Esq., the present proprietor and occupier'; Gilbert, *Historical Survey*, ii, 452, has a short description.
[100] Lysons, *Cornwall*, 53, publish some information on Cotehele house.
[101] An interior view of the chapel of *c.* 1840 that shows the screen is in the National Trust guidebook, *Cotehele* (1991), 73.
[102] This comprises a shield of eight quarters: 1, Edgcumbe; 2, *a lion rampant argent, in a field azure, semée fleurs de lys*; 3, *sable a ram's head argent*, for Dornford; 4, *argent, a chevron between three broaches*; 5, *a chevron between three scallop shells azure*, for Tremayne; 6, 7, and 8 not tricked.
[103] John Parkinson was the last great English herbalist and among the first true botanists, apothecary to James I and later botanist to Charles I. The portrait of him identified here is not known to have survived; see *ODNB*, J. Burnby, John Parkinson 1566/7–1650, available online at: https://doi.org/10.1093/ref:odnb/21372 [accessed September 2023]. The portrait of Sir Thomas Cotehele remains in the house.
[104] These repeat the heraldry described already.

[separate sheet] Over the drawing room 2 bedchamber in the Tower one with a very curious bed worked. A mirror in this room of metal, chimney pieces all of moor stone flat arches, roof of chestnut.

[separate sheet] Arms in the hall windows, or a chevron between 3 scallop shells azure, impaling Edgcumbe[105] <sketch>.

Glynne: GL, Glynne notebooks 16, fols 16–17

Calstock, S. [blank], 24 April 1860.

A regular Cornish Church on a lofty site commanding a fine view, entirely Perpendicular constructed of granite, & the common arrangement. There are 3 equal aisles or bodies, with separate roofs and no Clerestory, a South porch & West Tower. The Tower is good, of a sort frequent in the neighbourhood: embattled, with octagonal turrets at the angles which are embattled & rise high, but are not crowned by pinnacles. They rise from the string course below the belfry windows & die into the buttresses which are a little removed from the angles. The belfry windows are double, but plain. The West window is of 3 lights & rather small, below it is a labeled doorway. The porch has a cradle roof and granite doorway with mouldings. The windows of the aisles of the nave are mostly poor, of 2 lights, without foils, either debased or mutilated,[106] but at the West ends of each aisle is a fair Perpendicular one of 3 lights. The aisles do not seem to have been originally carried all along the Chancel. The East end of each aisle is of a sort of Elizabethan chamber, with large square transomed windows at the East of 3 lights. On the [17] North side is a labeled doorway, the East end of each is now separated by walling, on the North forming a vestry.[107] The nave is of 4 bays, the arcades formed of wide four centred arches, the piers of clustered shafts having octagonal capitals. The 5th bay within the Chancel is partially walled. There is no Chancel arch, the roofs of cradle form with ribs &

---

[105] Symbolising the marriage of Sir Richard Edgcumbe (d. 1489) with Joan Tremayne of Collacombe.

[106] In 1784, the rural dean reported the need for 'two windows cleaning or new Glass Repairs to Glass in the East window', suggesting their poor state, DHC: DR, PR 362–4/25/13. DHC: F5/17/2/4, EDAS, series of Rough Notes – sheet 21 (1861), recorded that 'the whole church is in a sad state, choked with pews of all heights [...] encumbered with hideous gallery and collection of rubbish within'. Most, if not all, of the north and south windows were replaced at the restoration in 1867.

[107] This is a private mortuary chapel erected in 1588 for Richard Edgcumbe (d. 1588), whose grave slab was the first monument in the chapel to a member of that family. Others followed, such as two fine wall monuments to Pearse Edgcumbe (d. 1666), Jemima, countess of Sandwich (d. 1674), and several ledger slabs. Clearly, this chapel was closed off to Lysons, otherwise they would have recorded the inscriptions. The chapel has the 'labeled' north door and the flat-topped window noted by Glynne and was intentionally walled off from the chancel (doorway access only) and the north aisle. The south chapel east window is presumably of a similar date as it is almost identical to the Edgcumbe chapel. This space was adapted at the restoration into a vestry by closing off the entrance from the chancel and opening up a doorway at the east end of the south aisle; it was without seats in a plan of 1586–8; see P.L. Hull, 'A Plan of the Seating in the Parish Church of Calstock, c.1586–8, Part II', *DCNQ* 35, no. 10 (1986), 378–9; S. Pittman, 'The Social Structure and Parish Community of St Andrew's Church, Calstock, as Reconstituted from Its Seating Plan', *Southern History* 20.1 (1988–9), 44–67; and KK: P26/2/1, which is a copy of the original plan, dated 24 May 1654.

bosses, & as usual low in proportion to the Tower. The Church is pued & has a gallery.[108]
The East window of 3 lights is fair Perpendicular.
There is a lich gate, & a new granite cross in the Churchyard, in memory of the Trelawney family. On the North is a fine view over the Tamar with Morwell rocks.

CAMBORNE

Lysons: BL, Add. Ms. 9462, fol. 23v.

Camborne ~~font~~ Church, Nave & Side Aisles, Clustered pillars & obtuse pointed arches.[109]
Handsome Altar piece of Sienna marble, white marble & jasper, erected 1761 at the expence of Samuel Percival Esq. of Pendarves, the Lords prayer, belief [i.e. Creed] & Commandments on white marble.[110]
On the south side of south aisle is Lord de Dunstanville['s] seat in a sort of Transept with a hole in the wall to view the altar.[111] <pencil sketch of foliated capital of pillar and its base[112]>
Pulpit richly carved with symbols of the Xfixion & arms of Hen. 7 or 8.
Seats carved as all the Cornish churches have.
[separate sheet] Font – standing now in the grounds of Tehidy[113] <pencil sketch, some lines inked in>.[114]
[separate sheet] <measured sketch of font>.
Fol. 24r. Both angels perfect on this side <sketch of angel's hand holding a shield, six words in gothic minuscules as part of the inscription on the font>.

Lysons, BL, Add. Ms. 9445, fol. 38r.

Camborne Church – Monument of William Pendarves of Pendarves, 1683, married Admonition, daughter of Edmund Prideaux of Padstow, ob. s.p.

---

[108] The gallery was erected following a petition by Frances Wallis; DHC: DR, Faculty Causes, Cornwall, Calstock 1 (1819). The church, 'having been restored in every part with the exception of the roof, was re-opened' in 1867; *RCG*, 17 October 1867, 6. It is not easy to account for the extent of the rebuilding from Glynne's description, although the gallery was removed and the church entirely reseated; see LPL: ICBS 6509 (1866–8), with a floorplan detailing the works to be carried out. Further work on the roofs and tower were planned in 1870, see KK: P26/2/238.

[109] Lysons, *Cornwall*, ccxxx, also notes that the capitals of the piers are ornamented with foliage 'in a manner which is very prevalent in the Cornish churches', pl. opp. ccxxxii no. 2.

[110] The reredos is still extant, comprising panels sculpted in classical style, incorporating swan-necked pediments and cherubs' heads; see Beacham and Pevsner, *Cornwall*, 137. It is no surprise that it was to be ignored by Glynne.

[111] See fns 122, 124.

[112] Published by Lysons, *Cornwall*, pl. opp. ccxxxii.

[113] Presumably as a response to eighteenth-century views on baptism, and the prevailing encouragement to use small basins, this font was removed from Tehidy, where it did duty as a flower container, to the Pendarves estate church at Treslothan. It is of granite with four winged angels holding shields, with an ornamental band bearing an inscription around the bowl; see C. Thomas, *Christian Antiquities of Camborne* (St Austell, 1967), 115–16.

[114] Lysons, *Cornwall*, ccxxxii, pl. opp. ccxxxiv, no. 4.

Sir William Pendarves Knt., 1726, only son of Rev. Mr. Thomas Pendarves of St
Columb, heir to Richard Pendarves of Pendarves. Bust of Sir William in flowing
peruke, & armour.

Mrs Grace Percival (to whom Sir William Pendarves left his estates), daughter of
Rev. Thomas Pendarves, married first Robert Coster Esq., of Truro, second, Samuel
Percival of Clifton, left John, younger son of Dr William Stackhouse of Trehane,
her heir, ob. 1763. She founded a school for 12 boys & 8 girls to read, write & cast
accounts, 12£ p.a.

Sir William Pendarves buried in a copper coffin, so the Sexton – the Sexton says that
he was the first person who raised copper in the county. Query – in hoc?[115]

Inscription of the Pendarves on a slate stone, 1655, name hid.

In Chancel, monument of Anne, relict Edward Acton of Acton, Co. Salop, 1780.

Glynne: GL, Glynne notebooks 70, fols 7B–8B

Camborne, S. Martin, 1843.[116]

A Church of granite, of the usual Cornish style & arrangement, comprising a
West Tower, nave, Chancel with parallel aisles, a South porch & small chapel
also on the South. There has been less mutilation externally than is generally
found in Cornwall.[117] The South porch is low, centred by an obtuse arch, within
it a doorway with Tudor arch, mouldings & foliated spandrels. The Tower is not
lofty, the parapet embattled, at the angles 4 square pinnacles. The belfry window
of 3 lights, like that of Ashford in Kent.[118] *<The belfry windows are Perpendicular
geometrical, as often in Cornwall.[119]>* In the 2^d stage is a narrow trefoiled opening.
The West window of 4 lights with good Perpendicular tracery. The whole ~~exterior~~
is late Perpendicular except a window or two. The roofs are slated. The North
door resembles the South. The greater part of the windows poor, consisting of 4
or 5 plain lights within a wide arch. That at the East of the South aisle has better

---

[115] This was an aide-mémoire for Samuel to verify the information from the sexton; for an
account of the copper coffin, see Thomas, *Christian Antiquities*, 163–4.

[116] Glynne's visit was prior to two severe restorations of the fabric, in 1861–2 and 1878. On 26
December 1862, the *RCG* reported (6), that 'Previous to the late restorations, a west gallery,
projecting as far as the second arch, stretched across the whole width of the Church, and
blocked out the tower arch and west window from the church. This has been removed, much
to the improvement of the appearance of the church; and the area has been thrown into the
body of the church. New roofs have been placed on the chancel, the nave, and the north aisle;
and the square high pews have been replaced with low and open seats.'

[117] This concerned the replacement of traceried windows with eighteenth-century sash-style
windows of wood in the 'Venetian' style, which Glynne detested. In 1704, 10d. was paid by
the wardens 'for 5 sheaves of Reed for mats to stop ye windows […] Paid ye glassier for
Repairing ye windows £2', so the conversion of the windows was a simple consequence of
such rudimentary attempts to make the building weathertight. In the same year, 'Paid Francis
Vivian for ye Reparation of ye Church Roof & to put up ye pinnacles £17 17s.', indicating a
building in failure, KK: X510/1, Churchwardens' accounts and rates, Camborne (1685–1760).

[118] See Sir Stephen R. Glynne, Bart., *Notes on the Churches of Kent*, ed. W.H. Gladstone
(London, 1877), 70–2.

[119] This is an addition later on by Glynne, on fol. 6Bv., perhaps following his 1870 visit to the
county when he called at Crowan, only a few miles south.

tracery & 5 lights – One on the South is of 2 lights, square headed & appears to be Decorated.[120] (Fig. 22)
The roofs are of cradle form *<the bosses carved, & a good cornice of vine leaves &c., running below the ribs moulded>* & there is a Clerestory. The divisions of the aisles formed by 7 low Tudor arches on each side, their piers lozenge in form, with shafts at the points & intermediate mouldings [8B] the capitals have a general band, but the whole is sadly clogged with whitewash.[121] The South chapel opens by a single wide arch on octagonal half shafts. Its ceiling is modern.[122] The pulpit has very good wood carving with shields, emblems of the Passion, in the style of the 17th century.[123]
There is an ascent to the Chancel which includes the 2 Eastern arches.
The whole is closely pewed, at the West end a gallery & Organ. (Fig. 23)
There is a piece of extremely fine wood carving inserted within a pew on the South side, exhibiting panneling & figures of animals & human beings.
The Tower opens to the nave by a plain pointed arch.

[120] In 1710, the rural dean presented 'the South:Isle of the Parish:Church of Cambron as being much out of repair both in the Roof and Walls Thereof, the South door is broken and decay'd, & [...] the whole Church wants very much to have the walls whitened with Lime', DHC: DR, PR362–4/27/I. It took twenty-four years for the problems to be addressed, as in 1734 the rural dean presented, 'The south Isle of Camborne Church rebuilding', but evidently reusing the old masonry and tracery patterns, DHC: DR, PR362–4/27/2. However, these windows were themselves replaced at the 1878 restoration.

[121] The reports of the rural dean in 1819 and 1823 ordered the south wall to be whitewashed, to match elsewhere in the church; KK: AD59/74, 310.

[122] This was converted into a completely new aisle at the 1878 restoration, reported in *TC*, 14 August 1879, 7: 'The principal recent addition to the Church is a new South aisle, 80 feet long, 65 feet broad, and 30 feet high, which is lighted by four three-light perpendicular granite windows and at the east and west ends by two handsome five-light perpendicular granite windows [...] The new south aisle is separated from the old south aisle, which is now the middle aisle, by a noble arcade, similar to the others in the Church, composed of six beautifully carved Troon granite pillars, 6 feet 6 inches in height, with two responds; the eight capitals being pieces of elaborate workmanship. The intervening arches are of the Gothic style, the design of the other arcades having been closely followed, as to maintain a harmony of outline and detail. The roof is of pitch pine and arched similar to the others. [...] The porch attached to the new south aisle has also been rebuilt, the old archway being again utilized in the building, but the roof is entirely new, except the pieces of old carved work, which have been worked on to the ribs.' See LPL: ICBS 8227 (1879), for a new south aisle etc., and a floorplan. In the process, the de Dunstanville pew was removed.

[123] One of these panels contains the royal arms, with a talbot and griffin as supporters, a Beaufort portcullis, and a Tudor rose, suggesting a date in the reign of Henry VII (1485–1509), Thomas, *Christian Antiquities*, 140–2. However, the churchwardens' accounts for 1550 record the sum of £3 'for makyng the polpet', and 12d. paid to William Persth 'for yre[n] work to the polpyt', possibly reusing the heraldic panels and forming an association between the king and preaching, KK: P27/5/2/I, fol. 31. However, work on the structure continued, as in 1711 the wardens' accounts note £2 18s. paid to 'Mr. Johns for [wain]scott [damaged] the pullpet [...] paid for 18 foott of [damaged] for the Stair Case [damaged] & boards for ye Pullpett £1 14s. [...] Paid the Juynur for Making ye pulpett Canopy & Stairs £8 0s.; Spent when the Canopy was putt up 2s. 0d', KK: X510/I. There is no further record of this sounding board.

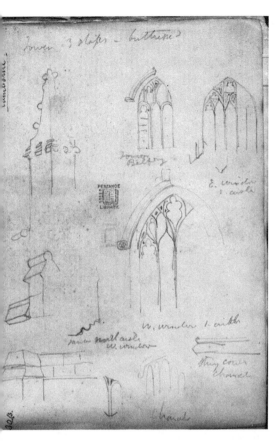

Fig. 22. Tracery patterns in the south aisle, Camborne church (1856); by kind permission of Morrab Library, Ms. BLI/3, fol. 30B, drawing by J.T. Blight.

Fig. 23. Camborne church interior looking west (1858); from the collections at Kresen Kernow, corno5075.

At the East end of the North aisle is the Pendarves pue[124] & a slab of a kind of slate sculptured with armorial bearings & poetical inscription – 1655.[125] There is a turret on the North side that had the stairs to the roodloft.

CARDINHAM

Lysons: BL, Add. Ms. 9445, fol. 42r.

Cardinham Church – new font, old font broken, was square with pointed arches round the side.[126] Clustered columns &c., handsome tower, crocketed pinnacles.[127] In chancel, small brass of ecclesiastic – Hic iacet Thomas Awmarle Rector ecclesie de Cardynan, Rogo vos fratres orate pro me & ego pro vobis in quantum possum.[128] Monument in south aisle, William Glynne of Glynne, Esq., 1664, Nicholas Glynn, 1691, and others, put up by Dennis Glynn Esq., 1699.[129] In north aisle a cross with a top flory and a shield Latin inscription with capitals, no date.[130] [separate sheet] In Cardinham Church a large tombstone, effigy of a man in religious habit, 3 tufts of hair on his head, with a sword by left side, Hic iacet Thomas Aumarle Rector huius ecclie de Cardynham, Rogo vos f'res orate pro me & ego pro vobis in quantum possum.[131]

[124] See LPL: ICBS 5955 (1862), for a new vestry with reseating and repairs, with a floorplan identifying the space occupied by this structure.

[125] As noted by Lysons, referring to a slate slab that Dunkin, *Brasses*, 2, recorded as originally mural, and being brushed over with black lead and then polished appeared to be of cast iron (recorded as such by H. Haines, *A Manual of Monumental Brasses*, 2 vols (Oxford/London, 1861), i, 1, ii, 41). In 1872, it was on the floor close to the organ but is now probably covered. It comprised the crudely incised figure of Alexander Pendarves, kneeling, the arms of Pendarves, and inscriptions in English and Latin recording his death on 30 August 1655 in his twenty-fourth year, transcribed by Polsue, *Parochial History*, i, 185.

[126] This 'old font' has since been repaired, demonstrating the blank arcading on the sides; the one functional on Lysons' visit, an eighteenth-century bowl with a cover, remains in the church.

[127] In 1749, the tower was badly damaged by lightning strike, as reported by the wardens, who 'do hereby humbly Certifye that we have nothing to present, save only the Church & Tower which were lately Damaged by Lightening but […] are now repairing & will be soon finished & sett in good Repair', DHC: DR, Churchwardens' Presentments 37/1.

[128] Trans., *Here lies Thomas Awmarle, rector of the church of Cardinham, I ask you my brothers to pray for me and I will pray for you likewise*; the phrase 'Orate fratres et sorores pro me' would have been familiar to Awmarle from his own celebration of the Mass, and the inscription is thus a *quid pro quo*: you pray for me and I will for you, as an expression of his own humility at the point of his death.

[129] The monument comprises an oval cartouche with an inscription in italics, over which is a large heraldic display surmounted by a semi-circular arch supported by Corinthian columns. Above the whole is a large flaming urn decorated with masks and drapery, while small cherubs rest on the outer edges of the arch and angels in loose low tunics stand at the ends. It is most likely Plymouth work, related stylistically to the large Spoure monument at North Hill (q.v.).

[130] This unrecorded slab, probably late fifteenth century, is mural at the west end of the south aisle and is incised with a cross with thick foliated terminals arising from a plain calvary, with a Latin marginal inscription in Gothic minuscules, albeit with capital letters as well.

[131] Immediately below this entry is 'M.S.S. Mr. Gray', but there is no further reference. Could the repeated transcripts of the Awmarle inscription have been taken directly from this source? The description and inscription are published, Lysons, *Cornwall*, ccxxxv, where the two shields directly under the inscription are also noted; these are *a fess lozengy between three crescents*, probably for Awmarle, the heraldry usually described as *per fess azure and gules, three crescents argent*.

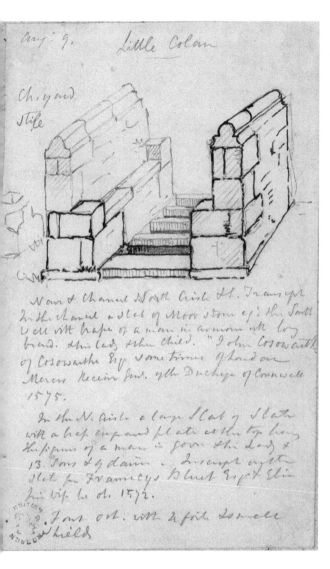

Fig. 24. Church stile, Colan; © British Library Board, Add. Ms. 9462, fol. 27r.

COLAN

Lysons: BL, Add. Ms. 9462, fol. 27r.

August 9 [1805?]
Little Colan – Nave & Chancel, North aisle & South transept.[132]
In the chancel a slab of moor stone against the South wall with brass of a man in armour with long beard & his lady & their children. 'John Cosowarth of Cosowarthe Esq., sometime of London Mercer Receiver General of the Duchye of Cornwall 1575'.[133]

---

[132] The church is not mentioned in Lysons, *Cornwall*, 62.
[133] Gilbert, *Historical Survey*, ii, 670, recorded this brass at the east end of what he thought was the south aisle, rather than the chancel.

In the North aisle a large slab of slate with a brass engraved plate at the top having the figures of a man in gown & his Lady & 13 sons & 9 daughters. Inscription on the slate for Frauncys Bluet Esq. & Elizabeth his wife, he ob. 1572.[134] Font octagonal with 4 foils & small shields. Churchyard stile <sketch of stile>. (Fig. 24)

CONSTANTINE

Lysons: BL, Add. Ms. 9462, fol. 28r.

Constantine – a large Church with Nave & side aisles, & an additional North aisle beyond. In the latter a brass plate with the figure of a man & his wife one son & one daughter, much engraving on it,[135] for John Pendarves Gent. 1616, & Melior his wife, daughter of Richard Gearveis Esq., ob. 1607.
In the North aisle a large brass plate with the figures of a gentleman in a gown & his Lady, & several sons & daughters engraven on it. On a narrow strip of Copper round the Stone – 'Of your Charite praise ye the Lorde for mere goodnes hathe taken to his Infynyte the sowles of Richard Geyeveys Esquier & Jane his wife dowghter of Thomas Trefusis Esquier which God of his greate and Mercie whose bodies lyeth here buryed the second daye of October in the yere of our Lorde God a Thousand fyve hundredth lxxiiii.'[136]
[separate sheet] Plain clustered pillars obtuse pointed arches. In the chancel windows <2 coats of arms sketched[137]>. Book begins in 1569. 1574, first dates of the 12 men.[138] In Northern most aisle <sketch of coat of arms[139]>.
Font plain square.

---

[134] Gilbert, *Historical Survey*, ii, 670, notes this brass in the north or Colan aisle, adjacent to the manorial pew.

[135] This is a relatively simple composition of a man kneeling in front of a prayer desk facing his wife kneeling on the opposite side of the desk, with a son and daughter behind them. A shield of arms is above, and an inscription in Roman capitals below. It is enclosed within a plain stone frame.

[136] The transcript is garbled here. It is possible that the strips on which the Gothic minuscule inscription was engraved were misplaced around the central brass plate, or it may have been misread by Lysons. It should read, 'Of your Charitie praise ye the Lorde for the sowles of Richard Gereveys Esquier & Jane his wife dowghter of Thomas Trefusis Esquier which God of his greate and mere goodnes hathe taken to his Infynyte Mercie whose bodies lyeth here buryed the second daye of October in the yere of our Lorde God a Thousand fyve hundredth lxxiiii.' The brothers' attention was re-called to the brass, with its 'very legible inscription' by Richard Gerveys Grylls, in a letter of 26 June 1812, who goes on to account for the descent of the barton of Bonallack; BL, Add. Ms. 9417, fol. 240r. The brass was restored in 1860 and relaid in its original slab, when, if the inscription was previously disordered, it was rectified.

[137] These show *argent, a chevron between three ?garbs sable*, for Gerveys, and *gules, a bend or*, for ?. Gilbert, *Historical Survey*, ii, 781, noted that 'in the windows are some shattered shields of armorial bearings', but nothing remains now.

[138] Evidently Lysons inspected the parish vestry book, now KK: P39/8/1. This version was copied in 1733 from the original of 1650, including the orders and constitution of the parish made by the twelve men, and their election. See W.B. Mayne, 'Notes on the Church & Parish and Antiquities of S. Constantine (Kerrier, Cornwall)', *JRIC* 17 (1909), 260–73, at 266–8; and C. Henderson, *A History of the Parish of Constantine in Cornwall*, ed. G.H. Doble (Truro, 1937), 216–21.

[139] *Or, a chevron between three scallops azure*, for Tremayne, impaling *a field or*.

Fig. 25. Cornelly church tower and south-west nave, photograph prior to the restoration of 1866; reproduced by kind permission of Michael Warner, from the collections at Kresen Kernow, AD2290/30.

CORNELLY

Lysons: BL, Add. Ms. 9462, fol. 27r.

Cornely – monument of Elizabeth daughter of John Gregor of Trewarthenick[140] <sketch of font with cross & flowers[141]>.

Glynne: GL, Glynne notebooks 16, fol. 8

Cornelly – S. Cornelius, 12 February 1858. (Fig. 25)[142]
A small mean Church, with nave & Chancel, & a small aisle or chapel on the North side of the latter. South porch & West Tower. The Tower is very small & has a whimsical appearance, tapering gradually to the top & consisting of 3 stages, divided by strings, the upper part having a quasi battlement & diminutive pinnacles. The whole Church appears to be of debased period, the windows some square, some pointed have 3 lights, but no tracery.[143] The aisle or chapel belongs to the Gregors & is divided from the Chancel by 2 granite Tudor arches with clustered pair of shafts.[144]

[140] This comprises an oval cartouche enclosing a bust, with an elaborate Baroque-style border with angels, and an inscription for Elizabeth Gregor (d. 1703, aged eighteen).
[141] Although having a venerable appearance, this is post-Reformation naïve work with a Norman base of elvan; see Henderson, *Cornish Church Guide*, 77.
[142] The dilapidated condition is revealed in this photograph, with the tower leaning westwards, a window in the roof to admit light to the west end, and generally poor state of the slates and the masonry. Only one(?) of the tower pinnacles noted by Glynne seems to be visible here.
[143] The chancel was rebuilt in 1866, and a further restoration took place in 1900 when the window tracery may well have been renewed; see LPL: ICBS 10229 (1900–1), for reseating and repairs to the roof, with a floorplan among the documents; see also Mattingly, *Churches of Cornwall*, 23–5.
[144] These are of 1720, the date of the erection of the chapel over their burial vault by the Gregor family of Trewarthenick, the arches mimicking the medieval style of 'clustered' piers found in other Cornish churches. There is a datestone on the exterior west end of the chapel. A petition by

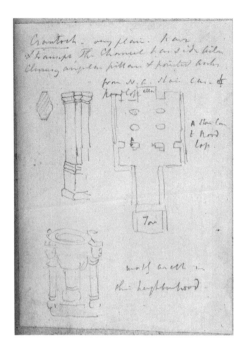

Fig. 26. Groundplan of Crantock church; © British Library Board, Add. Ms. 9462, fol. 27r.

On the North side is a double lancet, possibly original. The walls are covered with ivy, the situation very lonely. The Font is cupshaped on a cylinder.

CRANTOCK

Lysons: BL, Add. Ms. 9462, fol. 27r.

Crantock – very plain. Nave & Transept, the Chancel has side ailes, Clumsy angular pillars & pointed arches.
<sketch and section of pillar, church plan, font> from North Aisle stair case to Rood loft [indicated 'A' on the plan].[145] (Fig. 26)
Small arches in this neighbourhood.[146]

Francis Gregor was because 'ye said Parish Church is very small, not having roome enough therein to accommodate him with proper seats for ^himself &^ his family. And that he hath a mind (with our Consent) to Erect an Isle at his own expense on ye north side of ye said Parish Churche, about twenty two foot in length from East to West and about seventeen foot in breadth from North to South.' The bishop also determined that 'when soe Erected and built We do hereby Assign ^and solely appropriate^ the same to the said Francis Gregor Esq. and his Heirs, as well for seats, as Buriall, as long as he & they shall ^be^ owners and possessers of the Barton of Trewarthenick aforesaid Isle and they repairing the same from time to time at his and their own proper cost and Charge', DHC: DR, Chanter basket D2/53, 10 November 1720. Also see Gilbert, *Historical Survey*, ii, 831, as he describes his evocative journey down 'a long flight of stone steps, overrun with ivy, and other wild plants […] to a door, opening into a commodious vault'.
[145] DHC: F5/17/2/4, EDAS, series of Rough Notes – sheet 23 (1861), recorded that the approach to the pulpit on the south [*recte* north] side, was similarly through a pier, using the old rood stairs.
[146] Relating presumably to the arches of the transepts and not the 'pointed arches' of the chancel aisles. Lysons, *Cornwall*, 69, gives some of the history of this church but does not relate the architecture to its collegiate status, for which see Orme, *Religious History to 1560*, 173–80.

Fig. 27a. Crantock church interior looking east (*c.* 1895); from the collections at Kresen Kernow, P40/2/36.

Fig. 27b. Crantock church interior looking east (*c.* 1895); from the collections at Kresen Kernow, P40/2/36.

Glynne: GL, Glynne notebooks, 14, fols 54–5

Crantock, 4 February 1854.

This is also a Cruciform Church [previous entry was for Cubert], smaller than the last & without aisles ^aisles to the Chancel but not to the Nave^. The Tower at the West end is rude & coarse & of indefinite period. Under the battlement is a block cornice, which in the two Western Counties may belong to any age.[147] There are small buttresses, belfry window single & labeled & slits in the lower stages. On the North East is a stair turret, on the West side a rude door & window. Most of the windows in the body of the Church have been modernised & replaced by sashes.[148]

---

[147] The tower dates from the early fifteenth century, following the collapse of the central tower by 1412; see Orme, *Religious History to 1560*, 177–8.

[148] The rural dean in 1817 ordered 'the Window Frames throughout the Church want painting', suggesting that they were the wooden-sash structures Glynne saw, KK: AD59/74, 245. By 1900, the restoration of the church had started, with 'almost the whole of the internal fittings having been removed. This church is one of the last in which the old-fashioned square pews were to be seen': *RCG*, 11 January 1900, 8. A further note, *RCG*, 17 July 1902, 4, reported that 'no old tracery remained in any of the windows. The east window of the south choir aisle has been restored from four pieces of tracery found buried in the wall.' Two photographs show the nave and chancel looking east, with box pews and the old pulpit, prior to its restoration, much as Glynne would have seen it, KK: P40/2/36 (*c.* 1895) (Figs 27a/b).

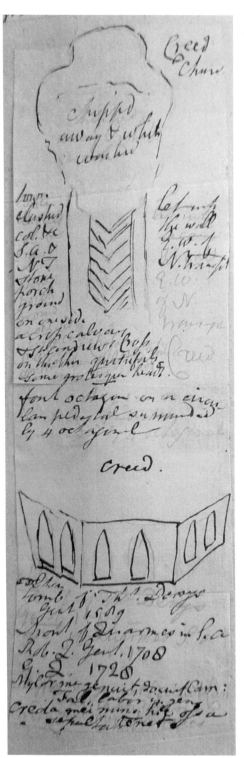

Fig. 28. Piscina and font, Creed church; from the British Library Archive, Add. Ms. 9445, fol. 61r.

There is one on the North side, square headed of 3 lights, & some of a similar kind in the aisles of the Chancel. The Tower arch is obtuse, those opening from the nave to the Transepts rude & of flat form with imposts. The Chancel arch is a plain continuous one.[149] The aisles of the Chancel are very low & narrow & included under the same sloping roof. Between the Chancel & each aisle are 2 wide pointed arches on octagonal piers, with unequal sides. The arches plain & rather mutilated. In these arches are plain wood screens.[150]
The Chancel is long in proportion to the nave. The roofs are coved with ribs. The Font [55] has a plain cup shaped bowl, square at the top, upon 4 legs.[151]

CREED

Lysons: BL, Add. Ms. 9445, fol. 61r.

Creed Church – tower, clustered columns &c., South aisle & North transept, stone porch, groin'd, on one side a cross calvary & St Andrew's Cross on the other, quatrefoils and some grotesque heads.[152] <sketch of the Norman pillar piscina with chevron decoration> chipped away & whitewashed, let into the wall to west of North transept.[153] (Fig. 28)
[separate sheet] Font, octagon on a circular pedestal surrounded by 4 octagonal [columns] <sketch of three sides of the font in crude perspective, showing blind arcading in pointed arches of the font sides>.
Slate tomb of Thomas Denys Gent., 1589.[154]

[149] There are the bases of shafts that once supported the central tower, to the west of the chancel arch; see Mattingly, 'Distinctiveness by Omission', 141.
[150] The remains of these parclose screens were incorporated into new structures at the restoration in 1899–1900; see KK: X272/14/9–11, details of the proposed restoration of the screen (1890). See also, Bond and Camm, *Roodscreens and Roodlofts*, ii, 385: 'There were traces of a very unusual fenestration, the openings not being traceried but left free, the arcaded heads being enriched by a small soffit cusping or cresting surrounding the opening, as at St. Mawgan'; and Mattingly, 'Rood Loft Construction', 85–6, 104. A major part of the refurbishment resulted from the collaboration between the architect, Edmund H. Sedding, and the Pinwill sisters, for which see H. Wilson, *From 'Lady Woodcarvers' to Professionals: The Remarkable Pinwill Sisters* (Plymouth, 2021), 66–75.
[151] Sedding, *Norman Architecture*, 71–2, reported that the four shafts were missing, although the fragments were found in a 'lumber corner and these have been carefully pieced together and put back in their old positions'.
[152] This refers to the bosses and carving of the stone panels making up the ceiling of the porch, one of which bears a calvary next to a cross saltire.
[153] Sedding, *Norman Architecture*, 72–3, pl. XXVII, considered this piscina to be in its original position, thereby suggesting that the north transept was Norman. It is, however, fourteenth century, with the cusped piscina arch firmly of that date, serving the altar on the east wall of the north transept. It seems likely that the pillar piscina was originally in the chancel, moved to where Lysons found it, and then inserted under the piscina arch. It is now free of whitewash.
[154] The slate slab is raised up on a plain and irregular chest, and at the base has a set of verses musing on Death, with the identification of the commemorated at the top, Thomas Denys (d. 1589), his wife Maron (d. 1570), and their eldest son Henry (d. 1602), separated by a heraldic panel. Below is a representation of a fallen tree-trunk 'Truncus Ines', entitled 'Here is the ende of all', symbolising the demise of the family with the death of the eldest son. See Cockerham, *Continuity and Change*, 58, 60, pls 87–8.

Monument of Quarmes in South aisle. Robert Quarmes Gent., 1708, George Quarmes, 1728, 'Mylor me genuit, docuit Cam: Fal: labor ingens / Creda mei nunc hic ossa sepulta tenet'.[155]

Glynne: GL, Glynne notebooks 16, fols 10–11

S. Creed, 12 February 1858.[156]
This Church has two equal bodies, with a North Transept, South porch & Western Tower. The material of firm grey stone & the situation in a secluded Church yard shaded by trees very pleasing.
The whole, as usual, appears to be Perpendicular. Most of the windows on the South side are of 3 lights. The East window of the Chancel a plain one of 4 lights, without tracery, only plain arched lights.[157] At the East of the South aisle a better Perpendicular one of 4 lights, subarcuated. The windows on the North are ~~small, & mostly mutilated~~ squareheaded & labeled. There is an arcade of 5 obtuse arches, more pointed towards the East, with the common clustered piers of 4 shafts with intervals, the capitals octagonal [11] & flowered. The North Transept opens by a Perpendicular arch. In some of the windows are pieces of old stained glass.[158] The roofs are coved & ribbed, with bosses of large heads, the interstices panneled with crosses & square flowers. The West window of the South aisle has some pseudo

---

[155] Trans., *Mylor gave birth to me, Cambridge taught me: I laboured hard in Falmouth: Creed now keeps my bones buried here* – relating to George Quarmes. The inscription is incised on a slab of variegated marble, framed, and with a sculpted heraldic display above.

[156] Twenty-five years after Glynne's visit, the *RCG*, 9 November 1883, 4, reported: 'The church [...] was at one time a fine building, and even now the tower is a good solid piece of masonry, having been rebuilt about 1773, after being struck by lightning. The south porch, the roof of which is composed of St. Stephens stone, ornamented with debased sculpture, is also in a fairly good condition, but all the other walls and the columns of the arcade are considerably out of the perpendicular. The church lies considerably under the ground line, which rises rapidly to the east, and is consequently very damp, a fact which has undoubtedly hastened its decay. The roofs are covered with scantle slates which are very much decayed, and the timbers have literally rotted away, so that the roof is now only supported by the struts.' A programme of restoration including plans of seating before and after the proposed works had been drawn up in 1876, see KK: P41/6/1–3; but perhaps because the estimate was too expensive (£1,800), the church was not repaired until 1905–6, reported in the *RCG*, 26 July, 1906, 5: 'This edifice was for many years allowed to fall into disrepair until it had come to be quite unusable and unsafe [...] Considerable difficulty was encountered when the roof was being dealt with, as it was found that the walls and arcading were much twisted and weakened by age and neglect: these have, however, been completely reinstated, and a typical Cornish parish church, dating from the thirteenth century, has thereby been rescued from decay.' The faculty is KK: P41/6/6 (1904).

[157] This is of 'South Hams' tracery, suggesting a date well into the sixteenth century; see Colvin, *Essays*, 40–1; Mattingly, 'Pevsner', 79–80; Mattingly, *Churches of Cornwall*, 25–7.

[158] Gilbert, *Historical Survey*, ii, 859, recorded 'figures of four of the apostles', and the remains of the glass suggest that originally there was Marian and Christocentric imagery, in accord with the 'Jesus altar' and the image of St Mary Magdalen, both of which were related to chantry or guild provisions; see C. Henderson, 'The Ecclesiastical History of the Four Western Hundreds of Cornwall', part 2, *JRIC* NS 2.4 (1956), 105–210, at 122–3. There was also a tablet 'nine inches square' with a scene of the Annunciation in the south aisle – perhaps an alabaster – but nothing of a flamboyant screen base; was it hidden from view at that time?; see *JRIC* 7 (1883), 53.

Decorated tracery.[159] The Font is Early English, the bowl octagonal, with Early English arches, flat & small, on each face, upon an octagonal stem & 4 legs set on a square base.
The Porch is good – has fine stone ribbed roof of waggon form, the ribs are moulded. The outer doorway is of granite, having clustered shafts with square imposts foliated. The porch has stone benches & externally is ornamented with pinnacles. The ribs are ornamented with large heads & the interstices panneled in [the] form of cross or with square flowers.
The Tower is embateled & has 4 large octagonal pinnacles crocketed of good appearance & Perpendicular character. The belfry windows of 3 lights rather meagre & without foils. The West window also poor & of similar character.[160]
The interior has the old fashioned pues & west gallery.[161]

CROWAN

Lysons: BL, Add. Ms. 9462, fol. 27r.

Crowan Church – Nave & side aisles, between nave & north aisle <sketch of capital with angel bearing shield[162]> & obtuse pointed arches, other shields of 3 fishes & the fish arms impaling those in the chancel.[163]
Brasses on slabs, one with oval helmet & a long sword with arms & no inscription, arms impaling the fishes.
Another of a knight in armour & his lady, filia & heres Johannis Tremnere de Lannevet qu*i* quidem Gulfrid ob ... 1400.[164]
Monument near the end of North aisle by Wilton, for Sir John St. Aubyn, ob. 1772, member for the County & arms St Aubyn Esq., ob. 1794.[165]

[159] This is an interesting comment, with Glynne correctly attributing the cusping of the tracery arches to a later period – the Cornish Perpendicular – than might immediately have been suggested by the design.
[160] Although the rebuilt tower appears to resemble its medieval predecessor, Glynne justly noted the 'Perpendicular character' of the structure; see Gilbert, *Historical Survey*, ii, 859, for an account of the lightning strike and its structural consequences.
[161] These were removed at the 1905–6 restoration.
[162] The arms are of St Aubyn, *ermine, on a cross gules five bezants.*
[163] This refers to the arms of Kemyell, *argent, three dolphins naiant sable*, on the capitals, the impalement recording the marriage of Geoffrey St Aubyn with Elizabeth Kemyell, heiress of Clowance in Crowan, in the late fourteenth century. The only reference to the church by Lysons, *Cornwall*, 72, is that it contains 'several memorials of the family of St. Aubyn'.
[164] Trans., *daughter and heir of John Tremnere of Lanivet, the which Geoffrey died [...] 1400.* These are probably the brasses to Geoffrey St Aubyn (engraved *c.* 1420) and his wife, and Geoffrey St Aubyn II (engraved *c.* 1490) and his wife Alice; see Dunkin, *Brasses, passim,* to unravel their fate. Before their nineteenth-century decimation, they were all illustrated by R. Polwhele, *The History of Cornwall: Civil, Military, Religious, Architectural, Agricultural, Commercial, Biographical, and Miscellaneous,* 7 vols (Falmouth/London, 1803–8), iv, pls between 118 and 119, with a view of the chancel floor where the brasses originally lay.
[165] These two monuments are to John St Aubyn 4th Bt, MP (d. 1772) by Joseph Wilton, and to James St Aubyn (d. 1794), a small wall tablet on the south wall of the north chapel; see Roscoe *et al., Dictionary,* 1389. Sir John was MP for Launceston 1747–54, and then for the county from 1761 until his death.

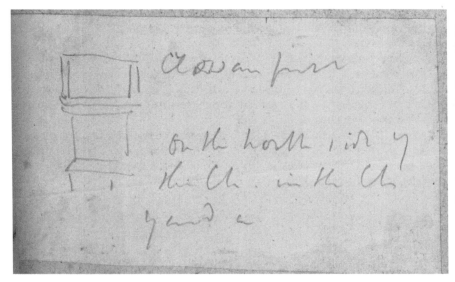

Fig. 29. Font bowl and pillar support, Crowan churchyard; © British Library Board, Add. Ms. 9462, fol. 27r.

[separate sheet] Crowan font on the north side of the Church in the Church yard[166] <sketch of font>. (Fig. 29)

Glynne: GL, Glynne notebooks 16, fols 58–9

Crowan, S. Crowena, 11 February 1870.
This Church is large but has been somewhat modernized.[167] It consists of nave with North and South aisles, chancel with North aisle, West tower & South porch. The South aisle of the nave is short and has [59] incongruous modern windows, having been rebuilt within the last century and is divided from the nave by 2 tall Tuscan

---

[166] Had the font been ejected from the church as an eighteenth-century reaction to its baptismal use? See fn. 171.

[167] The *CT* reported on 25 April 1860, 4, that 'nearly the whole of the interior of the church has been put in good repair, the fine granite piers and arches, which had been enveloped in successive coats of white-wash, have been deprived of their unnatural covering and newly worked over. The tower arch now shows itself in somewhat of its pristine beauty, and the ancient tracery of the west window has been restored and appropriately filled with chaste stained glass, as a memorial to a near relative of the Incumbent.' Reports of subsequent restorations retrospectively noted the church at the time of Glynne's visit as having 'the St. Aubyn pew, occupying nearly the whole of the chancel, was a huge erection of polished oak, not with carvings by a master hand, which would have saved it from all restorations, but plain and unsightly, the work of some long-forgotten village carpenter. The nave was separated from the south aisle by two (I believe, formerly, three) lofty columns of the Tuscan order, painted drab, to heighten the effect produced by their juxtaposition to a perpendicular arcade. The church was covered with a low barrel roof, divided into squares by plain braces and purlins, with ornamental bosses at the intersections, the blank squares between plastered and white-washed. The windows too, plainly showed the prevailing mania which existed in this country, during the whole of the eighteenth century, from which perhaps, no county suffered more than Cornwall, and in Cornwall, no parish more than Crowan', *CT*, 1 October 1878, 6.

columns of granite.[168] *<The South aisle is not carried along the Chancel.>* The North aisle remains in its original condition. The North arcade of the nave has 4 wide pointed arches on octagonal pillars, that of the Chancel has 3 much smaller arches on clustered piers, of Tudor form almost round, that near the West being the smallest.[169] On the capitals both in nave & Chancel are angel figures bearing shields with the arms of St Aubyn. There is no Chancel arch – the Chancel is modernized & the East end rebuilt without a window.[170] The North aisle has memorials to the St Aubyn family. There is a gallery in the North aisle and the church is pewed. The nave has the waggon roof with ribs and bosses. The Tower arch is a plain pointed one – the Tower is of granite of 3 stages with unfinished battlement & 4 pinnacles. There are no buttresses. The West window of 4 lights & good Perpendicular, the West doorway has a hood, the belfry windows of 3 lights, of the pattern which resembles Decorated work but which is clearly Perpendicular. The windows of the North aisle have been mutilated. The Font is Norman.[171] On the North side appears the projection for the roodstairs.

<The South porch is modern like the aisle.[172] There is a Priest's door in the Chancel and a closed North door.[173] The tower is 70 feet high, and has clock & 6 bells. There

---

[168] A seating plan of 1666 (DHC: DR, Chanter 11035, part II) records a building comprising a north aisle, chancel and nave of equal length, and a south transept, the arches into which were supported by a pillar, demonstrating the remains of an original cruciform shape. At some point between 1666 and 1830, but probably at the end of the seventeenth century, the west wall of the south transept was removed, and the building extended towards the south porch as an aisle, the new arcade supported by the Tuscan columns noted by Glynne. Before 1860, the EDAS found the nave 'windows of "wardens" pattern throughout, mere sashes!', the 'south aisle of most miserable character with "wardens" windows and dilapidation. All the monumental brasses have disappeared, some before the late repairs', DHC: F5/17/2/4, EDAS, series of Rough Notes – sheet 25 (1862).

[169] Henderson, 'Ecclesiastical History', 129–30, suggests that the arcade was originally formed of regular arches, but towards the end of the fifteenth century necessitated by the installation of a rood screen across the north aisle and chancel, two large arches were substituted by three smaller ones to match the distance, being those identified by Glynne as of 'Tudor form'.

[170] The chancel and north aisle east windows were blocked off in 1746 as Glynne found; see A. Ridgewell, *A History of Crowan Parish Church* (1990), 20–2, illustrating the medieval roof with ribs and bosses noted by Glynne, and which was replaced in 1872.

[171] The much-repaired bowl of the font is probably twelfth or thirteenth century with a modern supporting pillar, but the four grotesques at its base seem to have been carved out of a different type of granite, similar to the finer-grained variety from which the pillars of the north arcade are derived, so perhaps these are early fifteenth century as well? See Sedding, *Norman Architecture*, 76, pl. XXVIII. The font sketched by Lysons in the churchyard shows the current basin, supported by a single shaft on an angled base, but there is no hint of any sculpture. One suspects that Glynne would have recorded the grotesques if they were then present as the font base, so perhaps the entire plain structure was removed from the churchyard into the building, and then, at a later point, the grotesques substituted for the plain base?

[172] LPL: ICBS 983 (1828–32), for reseating the south aisle and constructing a gallery, the documents including a floorplan and elevation, showing the porch with a flat leaded roof and a balustrade of moorstone, which are what Glynne noted. The aisle was later replaced by a completely new structure, with a new arcade, façade, and porch (1872, 1891), see Warner, *A Time to Build*, 128–9. These additional comments (fol. 58v.) appear to be contemporaneous with Glynne's notes on the church.

[173] Neither of these survived the 1872 restoration.

is an Organ. In the Churchyard on the North is a granite mausoleum, heavy & ugly, of the St Aubyn family.[174]>

CUBERT

Lysons: BL, Add. Ms. 9462, fol. 29r.

Cubert – Nave & South aisle, North & South Transepts.
Nave & aisles separated by pillars with these capitals & semicircular arches <sketch of capital, column base and section>. (Fig. 30)
A plain low spire. Church stands surrounded by corn fields.
Very flat arch under the South window of South Transept;[175] pointed arch with clumsy clustered pillars at the entrance of North Transept.[176] <sketch of font>

Glynne: GL, Glynne notebooks 14, fols 53–4

Cubert – or S. Cuthbert, 4 February 1854.
This Church with its conspicuous spire in a very elevated site is seen at a great distance in the ~~adjoining~~ surrounding country. The plan is cruciform, of the kind frequently seen in Cornwall. The nave & Chancel have each a South aisle, & there are North & South Transeptal Chapels. The tower at the West end is surmounted by a stone spire. The whole of the Church has lately undergone a considerable restoration, & the walls are partly rebuilt.[177] Some parts are Decorated, the Chancel almost wholly so having windows of that character, at the East end of 3 lights, others of 2 lights. There is also a 2 light Decorated window in the South Transept. The other windows are Perpendicular with a few exceptions of restored Decorated ones. The arcade is also Perpendicular & Cornish, that of the nave is of 6 bays, the arches low & obtuse, the piers clustered, having fair capitals of foliage &c, & all of granite. The Chancel occupies 2 bays with similar arches. The Transeptal Chapels open to the nave by fair Decorated arches on

---

[174] Following a petition of 3 June 1779, 'Whereas Dame Elizabeth St. Aubyn the Widow and Relict of Sir John St. Aubyn [...] have humbly requested Leave and Licence for erecting a Mausoleum or Place of Interment in the Church Yard [...] on the North Side and to join partly with the North Wall of the said Church Yard to Contain in Height twenty-eight feet in Depth thirty Feet and in Breadth thirty Feet', a faculty for its erection was granted, DHC: DR, Faculty Causes, Cornwall, Crowan 1 (1779). It was demolished *c.* 1872. For a full history of this enigmatic structure, see Symons, 'Bring Up the Bodies', 10–33 (noted at p. 75).

[175] This is a tomb recess, but no sepulchral marker remains now.

[176] The 'clustered pillars' are of Catacleuse stone; this arch was retained in the mid nineteenth-century restoration.

[177] 'On the 10th April, 1848, this ancient edifice was visited with a most severe thunder storm, which not only shattered the spire to its very foundation, but so injured the fabric, which was in a very dilapidated state before, that it was determined to restore the church throughout. Accordingly, about two years since, the spire was once more raised to rather more than its original height'; *RCG*, 5 November 1852, 5. Glynne visited just after the remainder of the church had been restored, LPL: ICBS 4197 (1849–53), for rebuilding the church, with a floorplan in the documentation. In addition to the steeple, large portions of the walls were rebuilt, and new windows inserted in the north and south transepts, the chancel and south aisle; however, the south-eastern window in that aisle is labelled on the plan, 'This window to be spaired.' According to the *RCG* report: 'All the stone work has been cleaned, and the walls re-plastered, whilst [...] the seats are all new, low and open' – Glynne's 'neat open benches'.

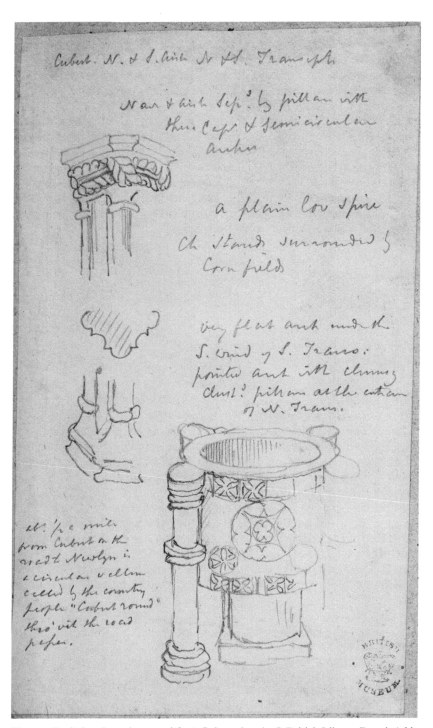

Fig. 30. Capital, column base, and font, Cubert church; © British Library Board, Add. Ms. 9462, fol. 29r.

clustered shafts. There is no Chancel arch, that to the tower is small & plain. The roofs are coved with ribs & carved cornices.[178] There is a small piscina on the South side of the Chancel. The Chancel is fitted with stalls, the nave has neat open benches.

The Font is a curious one, the bowl octagonal & sculptured upon a cylindrical stem surrounded by 4 legs which have capitals ^ranging with the rim^ & also mouldings like joints, ranging with the base of the bowl.[179]

There is a South porch, within which is a Perpendicular door of granite, with label & panneled spandrels. There are no windows at all on the North side of the nave. The Tower is small & may be of Decorated [54] character, but appears to have been for the most part rebuilt.[180] There is a Decorated West window & no buttresses. The spire is a sort of broach, but the line of demarcation between the tower & spire is scarcely seen, & when seen from some points, it has the effect of rising at once from the ground. The distant effect is better. The site is very exposed & commands an extensive view. There is a plain Cross in the gable.

CURY

Lysons: BL, Add. Ms. 9462, fol. 29r.

Cury – Church Nave & North aisle & South Transept with opening to the altar. Clustered pillars, obtuse pointed arches <sketch of font>.
Fol. 28v. <sketch of South door[181]>.

Glynne: GL, Glynne notebooks 16, fols 63–4

Cury (Co. Cornwall), S. Corentinus – 10 February 1870.
This Church has nave with North aisle, South Transept & Chancel, with a South Porch & Western tower, chiefly of the Cornish Perpendicular but with some earlier & remarkable features. Like others of this district, it was probably once cruciform, the North Transept having given way to an aisle. The South doorway is a very good Norman one having much & varied ornament. <*Blight, p. 30.*[182]> The door case is square & the tympanum above has curious ornamentation & a kind of zig zag is carried all down the jambs. The arch has one order of shafts, in its mouldings appears a kind of intersecting chevron & a hood with a course of round knobs. Down the outer jambs is a kind of embattled ornament.[183]

The rest of the Church is almost wholly Perpendicular, but there is a window of 3 lights at the end of the Transept which has a Decorated character & that at the East

---

[178] The roofs were only repaired at the start of the twentieth century; Sedding, *Norman Architecture*, 79. For a chronology of all the repairs, see Warner, *A Time to Build*, 129–30.

[179] Described and illustrated by Sedding, *Norman Architecture*, 78, pls. XXX, XXXI.

[180] Glynne is correct, with the west window also rebuilt, and therefore judged by him to be of a Decorated 'character', and not the original construction.

[181] Illustrated in Lysons, *Cornwall*, pl. opp. ccxxviii, no. 3.

[182] Glynne appears to have incorporated the details given in Blight's book, which he acknowledges (fol. 62v.), into his own record of the church, rather than supplementing his notes at a later date, as he had done until now.

[183] Further described and illustrated by Sedding, *Norman Architecture*, 89–90, pl. XXXIII. For recent analysis of this doorway and the font, see the CRSBI, available online at: https://www.crsbi.ac.uk/view-item?i=7569 [accessed December 2023].

Fig. 31. Drawing of two light window, Cury church (1826); reproduced by kind permission of Vicqui Pollard-Enys, from the collections at Kresen Kernow, EN/2533.

end of the North aisle resembles that in the same place at Sithney & is curious & elegant – of 4 lights with tracery of rather geometrical character, the splay of the arch (which is rather depressed in shape) being curiously filled with quatrefoil ornamentation, the quatrefoils set in pannels.[184]

The windows generally are of 3 lights unfoliated, one ~~of~~ on the south has 2 pointed lights surmounted by a label.[185] (Fig. 31)

The arcade of the nave has 6 small depressed arches, of late date, upon light piers of the common form with shafts & intermediate mouldings – the [64] capitals of the shafts being sculpted in granite. The North aisle roof is of waggon shape, that in the

---

[184] In addition, there is a piscina on the south-east end of the north aisle, indicating an altar was once here. The richness of the window tracery and surrounding frame, together with the gracious proportions of the arcade itself, suggest this area may have served as a chantry chapel, probably for the Nanfan family, as these features are repeated at Padstow where they also likely had a chantry; see Mattingly, 'Pevsner', 76, 78.

[185] A drawing of 1826 shows this window (the only two-light structure in the building) as a much more elaborate composition, presumably replaced at some point before Glynne's visit; KK: EN/2533.

nave is modernised.[186] The seats are mostly open, but with some pues. There is no Chancel arch, but the Chancel is raised on a step & includes 1 arch of the arcade. <*The rood door may be seen on the North now closed.*[187]> The East window is a fair new one of Perpendicular character. The Chancel is in good condition, fitted with stalls & laid with tiles. On the South of the altar is a piscina, plain & oblong in form with round orifice. On the South of the Chancel is a trefoil headed single lancet much splayed. At the junction of the Chancel & Transept is a very curious hagioscope formed by a large chamfer of the angle supported by a detached shaft from which small arches are carried to responds of similar character. Externally the wall has been thickened into 2 rude rounded projections, one of which contains a small oblong window.[188]
The Font has ^a round^ bowl on a central pillar & 4 slender shafts, on the bowl a circular form of ornamentation as at St Levan, filled with stars and triangles. The 4 shafts reach to the top of the bowl & are of fine polished marble.[189] The Tower arch is pointed & plain, on moulded imposts. The Tower is Perpendicular, of 2 stages with embattled parapet & 4 square mutilated pinnacles, it is of very good granite masonry & has no buttresses, at the North West is a taller pyramidal pinnacle.[190] The belfry windows of 2 lights mutilated. The West doorway has hood moulding on head corbels, as also has the West window. The porch is modern & closely adjoins the West wall of the porch [*recte* transept].
There is a fine Churchyard Cross, unusually tall.[191] <*3 bells.*>

DAVIDSTOW

Lysons: BL, Add. Ms. 9462, fol. 29r.

Davidstow – nave & side aisles. Chancel with a screen between – pillars & arches as usual <sketch of font on a stepped base>.

---

[186] The original curved wagon roofs are known from a drawing of the proposals for reseating the church and gallery in 1836, when permission to build in the Bochym aisle was granted by Stephen Davy on 8 July 1836; KK: RH/1/994; and LPL: ICBS 2031 (1836) for enlargement and gallery. Previously, the rural deans had commented on the state of the aisle, 'Bochim Aisle in a dirty state and out of Repair' in 1811/12/13, KK: AD59/74, 271. By Glynne's visit, evidently the nave had been reroofed, and at the restoration of 1873–4, just after Glynne's visit, 'The whole of the north wall has been taken down and rebuilt; the roof of the north aisle has been repaired and branded inside, being enriched with finely carved oak bosses; the roof of the nave, chancel, and Bochym aisle has been entirely reconstructed; the church reseated and fitted; and every window re-glazed'; see *WDM*, 18 July 1874, 2.

[187] For the opening up of this and discovery of several fragments of medieval alabaster work in the staircase, possibly once forming part of a reredos, see A.H. Cummings, *The Churches and Antiquities of Cury & Gunwalloe in the Lizard District* (London, 1875), 18–24.

[188] Illustrated, Blight, *West Cornwall*, 31–32. These features may indicate the start of construction of a south aisle, indicated in the will of John Skewis (1543), but which project was abandoned in the face of religious legislation outlawing processions in 1547; see Mattingly, *Churches of Cornwall*, 27–9.

[189] The sides of the bowl are decorated with quatrefoils and sexfoils in light relief, similar to those at St Levan; the corner shafts of polished marble are modern, and as the central pillar and base are of a type of granite that is not the same as that of the bowl, possibly these also are replacements; see Sedding, *Norman Architecture*, 89–90, pl. XXXIV.

[190] See Rogers, 'Church Towers', 187–8.

[191] During the early part of the nineteenth century, this cross lay in a ditch on the churchyard boundary with its base stone lying nearby. On 16 May 1849, it was re-erected in its base-stone (now lying below the ground surface) where Glynne noted it; see Langdon, *West Cornwall*, 28, no. 34.

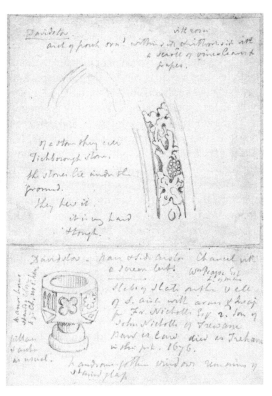

Fig. 32. Font and sculptural decoration, Davidstow church; © British Library Board, Add. Ms. 9462, fol. 29r.

Slab of slate on the wall of South aisle with arms & Inscription for Francis Nicholls Esq., 2^d son of John Nicholls of Trewane, Barrister at law, died at Trehane in this parish, 1676.[192]

Handsome gothic windows, remains of stained glass.[193]

William Pearse esq., Lord of Manor. House stands close to ye Church, no other house.[194]

[separate sheet] Davidstow – Arch of porch ornamented within side ^with roses^ & without side with a scroll of vines, leaves & grapes <sketch>, of a stone they call Tichborough stone, the stones lie under the ground.[195] They hew it. It is very hard & tough. (Fig. 32)

[192] See Cockerham, *Continuity and Change*, 153, pl. 242. The inscription records that he 'was buryed in his seate', presumably close to the location of the slate in the south aisle. The family was based in Trewane, St Kew, but, as the second son, Francis settled at Trehane in Davidstow.

[193] Originally, in the east window of the south aisle there was a shield with the Five Wounds, and others with armorial devices; in the north aisle were flowers, lions' heads, lions' heads with lilies proceeding out of their mouths; and in the east window of that aisle were the head of an angel and a lily pot, suggesting a representation of the Annunciation – and perhaps originally a more extensive programme of the life of the Virgin, see Spence, '"Iter Cornubiense"', part II, *TEDAS* 4 (1853), 285–93, at 288–9; and *The Chantry Certificates for Cornwall*, transcribed etc. L.S. Snell (Exeter, 1953), 21–2. Only armorial fragments remain, now in the tower west window; and it may be that fragments of sculptured canopy work remaining in the church also originated from these chapels.

[194] This is the Churchtown Barton house, just to the west of the church, which Lysons, *Cornwall*, 76, noted as 'inhabited by labourers'.

[195] The stone is Catacleuse, retaining the crispness of the sculptures. On fol. 50r., on the same piece of paper as the notes on Otterham church, Lysons records: 'Touchborough quarry. Large

Glynne: GL, Glynne notebooks 16, fols 66r.–v.

Davidstow, S. David, 7 February 1870.
A large Cornish church of the prevailing Perpendicular type, unhappily much dilap-idated & the interior scarcely fit for divine service. It is one of the most spacious & handsome churches in the Deanery but now sadly out of condition.[196] The plan includes Chancel, nave North & South aisles, South porch & West Tower, mainly Perpendicular. The West window of the South aisle is of 3 lights & apparently of Decorated character, the other windows are Perpendicular, mostly of 3 lights, but that at the East end of the North aisle is a large fine one of 5 lights. The East window has been wretchedly mauled.[197] The Chancel includes one bay of the arcade, & is carried one bay beyond it.
The arcades have each 5 Tudor shaped arches on piers of the usual Perpendicular type, tall & elegant. The capitals octagonal & have some foliage. The roof is of the common waggon kind with tie beams. *<The nave is very wide. The South aisle does not quite come up Westward to the Tower.*[198]*> There are some very fine old bench ends in the nave & South aisle, exhibiting some remarkable wood carving, figures, heraldic shields &c. The Chancel is partly enclosed by ancient wood screens[199] & there are indications of the rood stairs on the North side. The Tower is a very plain one blocked by a [66v.] singing gallery. The Font has an octagonal bowl, alternate sides terminating in a chamfer point which projects & on a circular stem.[200] The South porch doorway is good, the arch having good mouldings with bands of foliage & grapes, but much decayed. The porch has a cradle roof & the South doorway

tumulus 24 paces in circumference at the base, like the Keep of a Castle, about ½ mile north of Davidstow Church. About 300 yards North East of it are 2 tumuli, on the South West side at 100 yards distant, are many banks and ditches like the remains of buildings.' This refers to the Tich Barrow, a round barrow cemetery situated close to the summit of a prominent hill in Davidstow known as Tich Barrow Beacon. Excavations in 1979 recorded undisturbed deposits, including a retaining kerb of flat laid stones, so it is possible when the Lysons visited that such granite 'moorstones' as were used for the building of the church were thought of as having come from this barrow.

[196] On the reopening of the church after its restoration in 1876, the *NDJ*, 27 July 1876, 3, reported: 'An idea of its [previous] condition may be gathered from the fact that, so broken was the roof in many places, that, in the event of a shower of rain during divine service, the members of the congregation were under the necessity of opening their umbrellas to escape wetting.' A faculty for restoration of 19 March 1875 identified the structural deficiencies, including 'that the Arcade between the Nave and North Aisle was about Fifteen inches out of the perpendicular'; see Warner, *A Time to Build*, 131.
[197] The rural dean in 1825 noted: 'The Chancel Window is out of the Perpendicular, the Walls and Roof of the Chancel much out of order, to be examined & repaired', so it may be following this directive that the window was 'wretchedly mauled'; KK: AD 59/74, 10.
[198] This comment (fol. 65v.) appears contemporaneous with Glynne's notes on the church.
[199] Spence, '"Iter Cornubiense"', part II, 289, detailed the chancel and parclose screens, with linenfold decoration and figures of saints, the remains of one saint still visible. The survival of a parclose screen suggests that it enclosed a chapel of the 'ffraternitie of our ladye of Dewstowe', also evidenced by the remains of the Marian glass in the five-light east window of the north aisle, and see fn. 193. During the restoration, the old screen was adapted and placed across the entrance to the tower, but much was destroyed.
[200] Sketched in 1869 by 'J G F.', KK: AD2824/17/7.

within the porch, has label & flowered moulding & panneled spandrels. The North doorway now closed has somewhat similar ornamentation.[201] The Tower is lofty but rather rude, is buttressed on the square, has parapet not crenelated & 4 broken pinnacles. It is of 3 stages, has square turret on the North side with slit lights, a closed West door and mutilated Perpendicular window of 3 lights, belfry windows of 2 lights.[202]

DULOE

Lysons: BL, Add. Ms. 9462, fol. 30r.

Duloe – Church lofty Nave & North aisle & transepts, Clustered pillars with obtuse arches, very large font with trefoil shields & other Gothic tracery.
2 arches between Chancel & North aisle richly ornamented with foliage of vines & grapes, under the arch next the chancel lies the effigies of a Knight in plated armour carved in stone with a collar of SS, a bas relief of the Xfixion at the ^west^ end of the altar tomb, 4foils & shields on the other sides, on a large slab of ^Purbeck^ marble the following inscription in black letter 'Hic iacet Johannes Colshull miles quondam domini de Tremenhert et patronis huis Ecclesie qui obiit xviij° die mense marcij Ann° domini millesimo CCCC lxxxiij Cuius anime propicietur deu[s] Amen'.[203]
A large altar ~~monument~~ tomb for John Killiow of Westnarth.
A slab with effigy in bas relief [separate sheet] for Mary Arundell, daughter of Thomas Arundell Esq., 1629.
Screen of rood loft.[204]
Fragment of brass in Chancel of a Knight in plated armour, oval helmet, holding a hart in his hand inscribed IHC.[205]

---

[201] This was rebuilt at the restoration when it was enclosed and converted into a vestry.
[202] The church was almost entirely rebuilt in 1875–6, leaving only the west tower without alter-ation other than new pinnacles at the corners, and being repointed, as specified in the sentence of consecration of 1 July 1876, KK: P46/6/1. The *NDJ* (*v.s.*) continues: 'The church has been rebuilt in a style in which the lines and features of the ancient building have been faithfully preserved, and the old materials have been used as much as possible [including the capitals to the nave piers]. The work has been well and satisfactorily executed, and the church and its approaches now present a vastly improved and exceedingly pleasing appearance [...] The roof, built of pitch pine, is arched and open, some of the old oak roof having been worked in in the bordering [i.e. cornice].' For a plan of the church post-restoration, see KK: P46/6/2, dated July 1876; an inscription in the porch records the work.
[203] Trans., *Here lies Sir John Colshull, once lord of Tremenhert [Tremadart] and patron of this church, who died 18th day of the month of March A.D. 1483. On whose soul may God have mercy Amen.* Lysons published this account almost verbatim, *Cornwall*, ccxxxvi. The tomb was moved to the middle of the north chapel during the restoration of the church so that the organ could be accommodated in the chancel, where Glynne found it in 1862; see Cockerham, *Continuity and Change*, 14–15, pl. 5; for Colshull himself, see J. Whetter, *Cornish People in the 15th Century* (Gorran, 1999), 1–9; and for a historical contextualisation of Colshull and Duloe, see Mattingly, *Churches of Cornwall*, 29–31.
[204] Presumably this refers to the screen across the chancel and north chapel, the south side of the chapel enclosed by the Colshull tomb and a parclose screen; see Mattingly, 'Rood Loft Construction', 104.
[205] There is no sign of this brass now, almost certainly lost at the restoration of the church. Gilbert, *Historical Survey*, ii, 934, noted it as 'a brass effigy of a man in armour, apparently

Alicia Milles, daughter of Jeremiah Milles, vicar, ob. 1766.[206]
Richly dressed effigy in bas relief in slate, stuck up against South wall by Chancel, for Ann, daughter of Nicholas Coffyn, in a rich fine Elizabethan dress.[207]

Glynne: GL, Glynne notebooks 16, fols 39–40.

Duloe, S. Cuby, 20 August 1862.
The Church consists of a nave & Chancel, each with North aisle, & North & South Transeptal Chapels, the tower being set adjacent to the latter. The Church is in a very nice condition, having recently undergone a careful restoration, with partial reconstruction.[208]
The tower is very rude & plain with little architectural character, surmounted by a pointed ^tiled^ roof. It has neither string course nor buttress, the windows small, those on the East trefoil headed lancets.[209]
There is as usual no Chancel arch, nor marked separation of Chancel. The nave is of 4 bays, the Chancel of 2, & the arcade uninterrupted is of granite with four-centred wide arches well moulded, on clustered piers, of which the shafts have well moulded capitals with Tudor flowers. The chapels open each to the nave by Tudor shaped arches.
The arches in the Chancel are narrower than in the nave, the mouldings filled with square flowers, the piers light, with good mouldings carried down between the shafts,

of great antiquity, and is probably meant to represent one of the Coleshill family'. Either Sir John's grandfather, John Colshull (d. 1413), who founded the family's seat in the parish via a marriage with the heiress of Tremadart, or Sir John's father, another John Colshull (d. 1418?), might be candidates for having had this brass laid down, with 'plated armour, oval helmet' characteristic of military effigies of that period; see Whetter, *Cornish People in the 15th Century*, 1–2.

[206] Jeremiah Milles (bap. 1672, d. 1746), vicar of Duloe (1704–46), was the father of Jeremiah Milles (1714–84), the well-regarded antiquary, dean of Exeter, and collaborator of William Borlase; see *ODNB*, D.A. Brunton, Isaac Milles (1638–1720), available online at: https://doi. org/10.1093/ref:odnb/18749 [accessed October 2023]; and J. Simmons (ed.), *English County Historians* (Wakefield, 1978), 88–9.

[207] This slate is now fixed to the north wall of the north chapel.

[208] Plans of the church before and after the restoration of 1859–60 demonstrate the scale of the works on the walls and windows, the removal of all the box pews, and the reseating of the north chapel, which was largely occupied by an enormous pew for the Bewes family; KK: P51/6/2–3. (Colour Plates 1 & 2) The *RCG*, 13 September 1861, 6, records the restoration: 'The church consists of a nave (60 by 19), chancel (38 by 16), north aisle (60 by 14), and north chancel aisle (23 by 14). Transeptal chapels on the north and south, the latter now used as a vestry, and parted from the nave by an elegant glazed screen. There is also a handsome south porch (9 by 9). The tower, which is of two stages, and contains several of the original early English windows, is at the south of the south transept, and is about 21 feet square, and heavily buttressed. It is now capped by a pyramidal and slated roof. The above arrangement has not been deviated from in the present restoration; but it has been found necessary to rebuild the south, east, and west walls, and the whole of the south transept and south porch [identified by the differences in colour on the 1860 plan]. A new slated roof has been put on the whole of the church, and is as nearly as circumstances permitted a copy of the original. The fittings and seats are of memel timber varnished; the pulpit of carved oak [...] the chancel has been arranged choirwise, with stalls and subsellae [...] The ancient screens have been repaired. A small Scudamore organ, by Allen, of Bristol, occupies a place in the chancel to the eastward of the stalls.' See also LPL: ICBS 5553 (1860), for restoration work.

[209] The tower was originally of three stages, but having started to incline towards the north, the uppermost stage was removed in 1861; Polsue, *Parochial History*, i, 304.

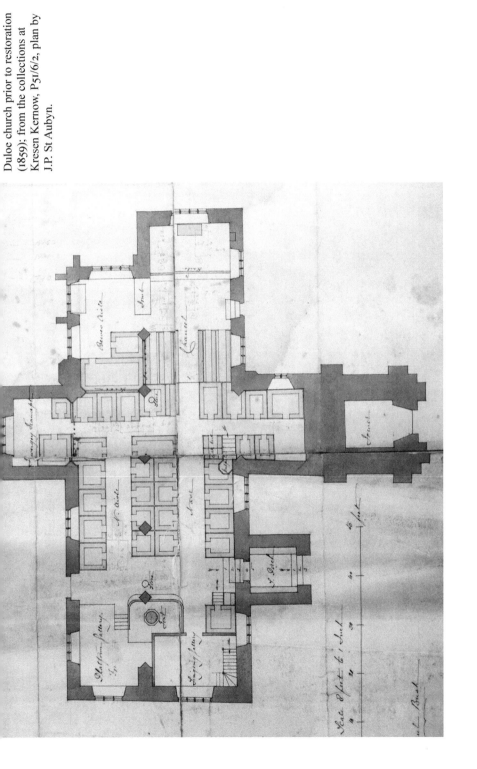

Duloe church prior to restoration (1859); from the collections at Kresen Kernow, P51/6/2, plan by J.P. St Aubyn.

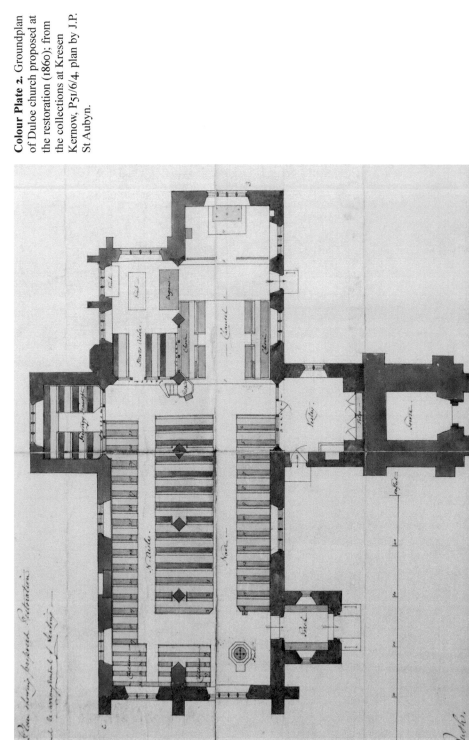

Colour Plate 2. Groundplan of Duloe church proposed at the restoration (1860): from the collections at Kresen Kernow, P51/6/4, plan by J.P. St Aubyn.

alternately enriched with vine foliage carried all down in wreaths. The West respond has 4 shafts with sculptured grapes beneath the capitals. There is a pointed [40] arch between the North aisle of the nave & that of the Chancel. This aisle or chapel is enclosed with good Perpendicular wood screenwork having pretty tracery & foliaged cornice. There is on the North side a rood turret & door with steps opening by a Tudor arched door. The windows are all Perpendicular mostly of 3 lights, those at the West of the nave & East of the Chancel have 4 lights, also that at the East of the North chapel. Those in the Chancel & chapel have shafts internally with capitals & foliage & bases.[210] The South wall has been principally rebuilt, but the Northern is old. The roofs are also new, of cradle form. The seats of the nave of pitch pine, low & open. The Chancel is stalled & contains a Scudamore organ, the altar is of oak.
On the South is a trefoil headed piscina, which may be earlier than the rest of the church. The pulpit is of wood & low. The Font is Perpendicular, a large octagonal bowl, panneled with quatrefoils.[211] The North chapel belonged to the family of — & contains several tombs.[212] One altar tomb panneled with quatrefoils containing shields & sculpture of the Crucifixion on the West side bears some effigies, circa 1403, one black marble effigy of a Lady 1590, an altar tomb 1600 & an incised slab with shields & coarse female figures 1629.[213] The exterior of this chapel is embattled & has crocketed pinnacles set on the buttresses of late Perpendicular work; a stair turret with gargoyles & pierced quatrefoils for openings, on the apex is the figure of a monkey.[214]

EGLOSHAYLE

Lysons: BL, Add. Ms. 9462, fol. 30v.

Egloshayle – Nave & South aisle & North Transept, clustered pillars & pointed arches <sketches of font and capital[215]>.

[210] The difference in the windows, and the survival of the internal shafting to the window arches noted by Glynne, despite the 1861 restoration, is because the west end of the nave was rebuilt in 1693, see DHC: DR, PR362–4/298: 'Wee [...] doe certifie that wee did bargen for taking downe of the west end of the parish church of Duloe, and the rebuilding of it, att the rate of seaventeen pounds & teen shillings the works will bee finished as wee believe about fortnight hence in witness whereof we have here unto sett our hands this eight and twenty day of July 1693. The signe of Bartholomew Lyne, The signe of John Lyne, Masons who tooke the worke of the aforsaide.'
[211] The decoration is similar to the side panels on Colshull's tomb, suggesting it was presented to the church by Sir John at the same time as his chantry chapel was constructed; Whetter, *Cornish People in the 15th Century*, 7.
[212] In Glynne's time, it belonged to the Bewes family of West-North in the parish, who funded most of the restoration and had the seating between the Colshull tomb and the screen arranged to face the chancel, duly approved of in *The Ecclesiologist* 21 (1860), 127.
[213] Glynne erred in noting the date on the Colshull tomb as '1403'; the 'Lady 1590' is a mural slate slab to Ann Smith (d. 1592), the 'altar tomb 1600' commemorates John Killiow (d. 1610) and his wife Dorothye (d. 1600), and the 'coarse female figures 1629' is a double effigial slate slab to Mary Arundell (d. 1629).
[214] See Mattingly, 'Pevsner', 76–8.
[215] This is a crude sketch only and hardly distinguishes the decoration, showing the square bowl supported on a thick single shaft, barely narrower than the bowl itself. The (original) central shaft now is more slender and has four modern piers at the corners; see Seddon, *Norman Architecture*, 93, pl. XXXV.

Pulpit against the North wall of the nave, half of an octagon, way to it from the North Transept.

At one end of the weathering of the door [i.e. the label] at the West end of the Church under the tower <sketch of angel holding shield with linked hearts, for 'I Loveybound'; and an inked-in rubbing of inscription[216]> at the other end <sketch of shield[217]>.

[separate sheet] Stone pulpit at Egloshayle <sketch of pulpit with dimensions[218]> 3 like this <detail of dependent tassels> bottom of the right hand side of the middle compartment <tassel with foliage detail>.

Glynne: GL, Glynne notebooks 14, fols 11–12

Egloshayle, S. – 4 February 1850.

This Church ~~has~~ is rather irregular – has a Chancel & nave with South aisle continued all the way, a North Transept, & a short North aisle contiguous to it, ^North^ & ~~a~~ South Porches, & Western Tower. The South ~~front~~ side presents a long unbroken front, with some large subarcuated Third Pointed windows of 4 lights. The East window of the same aisle is of 5 lights & similar style. The East window of the Chancel has lost its mullions.[219] On the North of the Chancel & in the North Transept are square headed & late of 3 & 4 lights. On the North side of the nave are some [12] plain coarse double windows with obtuse heads of this kind <sketch> probably late in character. The whole Church is as usual Cornish Third Pointed, the walls chiefly of coarse moorstone, with some admixture of granite. The arcade on the South is uninterrupted, of 6 bays, the piers of the usual form, the shafts having separate octagonal capitals & a general band. *<The roof of the South aisle of cradle form with good bosses.>* On the North one arch, similar to the others, opens to the Transept & another to the aisle of the Chancel. The roofs are coved, with ribs &

---

[216] This sketch, recording the contribution of John Lovibond, vicar, to the construction of the tower, and that of the pulpit, are published, *Cornwall*, pl. opp. ccxxxii. The rubbing is mistakenly labelled 'St Just'. Lysons also note (82) the monument to Sir John Molesworth as 'without date', and 'some memorials of the family of Kestell'.

[217] While the sketch is faithful to the original, it is difficult to identify these arms. It is an impalement of, on the dexter, *three birds 1, 2 and 3, all reversed,* impaling *a chevron between three birds heads erased.* The arms of Kestell are *argent, a chevron sable between three falcons proper, belled or, strapped of the second,* which appear as the first quarter on a shield of six quarters on a mural slate monument to a dynasty of the family, dated 1581. The fourth quarter is *three birds' heads erased, 2 and 1,* but this coat remains unidentified. See Maclean, *Trigg Minor*, i, 418–9, pl. XV. The sculptured arms are most likely a confabulation of Kestell heraldry therefore, and, with the 'I Loveybound' inscription sculpted on the other side of the west door of the tower, probably celebrate the combined forces of the Kestell family and the vicar in the tower construction. Lovibond was dead by 1477–8, implying the tower was started earlier than that, and probably coincident with the construction of the bridge at Wadebridge of the 1460s–70s. See A.G. Langdon, *Wade-bridge: Notes on the History of the Fifteenth Century Bridge* (St Agnes, 2012), 15–21.

[218] Published by Lysons, *Cornwall*, pl. opp. ccxxxii.

[219] The 'East window of wood with square panes of glass', DHC: F5/17/2/4, EDAS series of Rough Notes – sheet 22 (1861). The chancel and south aisle had been taken down *c.* 1528 and rebuilt in the same matching style; see Mattingly, 'Distinctiveness by Omission', 153–4, 157–8, for the construction contract.

bosses. The Pulpit is a pretty one of stone, nicely panneled ^& with foliage^. The Font has a square bowl.

The North Porch is plain, has an open ribbed roof & a crude outer door.[220]

The South Porch has an outer door with jambs of granite & an open roof. The inner door has a flat arch set in a square, & over it a blank niche. There is a Priests door on the South of the Chancel. The Tower is of 3 stages & follows the common Cornish pattern – the buttresses are removed from the angles ^& have 6 set offs^ & there is a square turret at the North East. There is a battlement & 4 short pinnacles, the belfry windows of 3 lights. *<The tower said to have been built 1490. 82 feet high. 5 bells.[221]>* On the West side a small 3 light window & a door with arch mouldings, & a hood upon corbel figures of angels bearing heraldic shields. *<In the moulding of the West door is the figure of a serpent, above the door an ^is a^ heraldic shield.[222]>* The second stage of the Tower is very blank. The contour of this & most Cornish Churches is far from picturesque, the long unbroken line of wall, without Clerestory, & the tall clumsy Tower by no means grouping well.

In the Church yard, on the North side are 2 granite Crosses, lately restored.[223]

The Font has a square bowl, perhaps Norman.

[220] This was removed at the restoration of the church in 1867 and the doorway filled in. The *RCG*, 3 October 1867, 7, reported that 'the Church had become thoroughly decayed, so that restoration was absolutely necessary [...] The church now consists of nave, north transept, south aisle and porch, with a lofty tower at the west end. From time to time the rich old carved seat ends were cut away to make room for the huge square boxes which were formerly so popular. The roof was some years ago partially renewed, but the slates were laid upon the decaying timbers, which were too feeble to support the superstructure [...] The whole roof of the nave and transept has been removed, and an entirely new one of Memel deal substituted with inner arches of timber, supported by elegant braces of an archlike form. The east windows, where the wooden frames were totally decayed, have been replaced by a beautiful perpendicular window of five lights, with granite mullions. The old unsightly pews have been swept away, and low open seats of uniform shape have been laid throughout the building. The whole of the aisle is paved with the best Minton's tiles. The font has been restored, and the fittings of the chancel are of wainscot oak, with richly carved screens that separate the chancel from the south aisle.' See LPL: ICBS 6561 (1866/9) for reseating, new windows, and repairs to the walls and roofs, the documentation including a plan. The masonry of the east wall of both chancel and south aisle suggests that it was completely rebuilt at that time with matching tracery in the windows; if the chancel window was 'of wood', it is likely that both windows were reconstructed using the original (*c.* 1528) south-east window as the model.

[221] Glynne probably derived these additional comments (fol. 11v.) from DHC: F5/17/2/4, EDAS, series of Rough Notes – sheet 22 (1861), published well after his visit in 1850.

[222] At the point of the arch, this is not a shield but a triangular-shaped decorative head with a ?mitre on top.

[223] See Maclean, *Trigg Minor*, i, 406–7; Langdon, *North Cornwall*, 29, nos. 29–30.

EGLOSKERRY

Lysons: BL, Add. Ms. 9462, fol. 30r.

Egloskerry[224] – Church with nave & South aisle separated by Clustered pillars with very obtuse arches.[225] <sketch of capital> (Fig. 33)
In the Chancel a marble monument for Paul Speccott of Penheale, armiger, ob. 1644. John Speccott of Penheale, 1677. Honora relict of John, 1692. Paul son of John Speccott, 1671. John Speccott son & heir of said John, 1705.[226]
On a slab of black marble in the chancel on a raised tomb, an inscription for Grace the wife of Paul Speccott of Penhale, one of ye daughters & Coheirs of Robert Halswell, son & heir of Sir Nicholas Halswell of Halswell, Co. Somerset, 1636.[227]
North transept for the Penhele estate. In the window the mutilated figure of a merchant[228] <sketch>.

---

[224] Something of what Lysons would have found is described in an account of the restoration: 'The old building was dark, damp, and full of dry rot. High pews, "three decker" pulpit, large squire's seat with a wooden canopy resting on four Corinthian columns. An altar tomb blocking the Chancel, pit for the Communion table to stand in, walls having more than a foot out of the perpendicular, with ivy growing through them at many points, plastered uneven ceilings decorated with dormer windows, and a gallery blocking the tower arch, all served to make the building anything but a suitable one for prayer and thanksgiving'; *CDP*, 21 May 1887, 4. The report continues: 'The change wrought by the work done is very great [...] The South wall has been rebuilt, the Chancel raised, the windows reglazed, the whole church reseated, the aisles tiled and the roofs renewed or repaired throughout [...] Old monuments and sculptured stones, which before lay hidden, or almost so, have been utilised to decorate the walls with great taste and judgment. All the fittings of the Church have been renewed.' The chancel east window was renewed, modelled on the east window in the south aisle, DHC: F5/17/2/4, EDAS, series of Rough Notes – sheet 26 (1863). The Penheale manorial pew, demolished at the restoration, was mentioned in a petition of 1734: 'The dimension of the seat intended to be built by John Speccott of Penheale Esqr. in the parish Church of Egloskerry the plot thereof by measure from the fore parte of the fore seat belonging to Penheale from North to South is in breadth five foot and halfe and in length from West to East seaven foot and halfe', DHC: DR, Petitions PR517/257. The fact that this was only 'intended' suggests that it had not been erected (Speccott had died in 1705), but the measurements cited were used to define the size of a pew for the 1734 petitioner, Christopher Baron of Treludick, Esq. However, the presence of a large canopied, manorial pew in the Penheale aisle, noted by Gilbert, *Historical Account*, ii, 525, confirms that something extravagant was built, possibly by a later occupant of the manor, its Corinthian columns matching those of the Speccott wall monument nearby? See fn. 226.

[225] Lysons later compared the 'obtuse' or flattened form of the arches in the arcade with those at Boyton.

[226] This mural monument is now in the south aisle and comprises a tablet of pale marble bearing a very faint inscription, set within an aedicule framed by two Corinthian columns, a sculpted apron below and an entablature above, topped by a wreathed oval shield. Funeral armour associated with this monument remains on display in the church.

[227] The Speccott family settled at Penheale in the early seventeenth century, purchasing the estate from the Grenville family of Stowe. The family died out with the death of John Speccott in 1705, as noted in the genealogical inscription on this now dismantled tomb monument; see J.L. Vivian, *The Visitations of the County of Devon: Comprising the Herald's Visitations of 1531, 1564, & 1620* (Exeter, 1895), 706–7; and D. Colville, 'Penheale: The Rebirth of a House', *JRIC* NS 10.3 (1989), 267–82.

[228] This enigmatic alabaster figure is now housed in a recess (?purpose-built at the restoration) in the east wall of the south aisle (where there were also brackets and the remains of

Egloskerry Church ...

In the Chancel a marble mon[ument] for
Paul Speccott of Penheale arms.
ob. 1644. John Speccott of P. 1677.
Honor relict of John. 1692
Paul son of John. S. 1671.
John S. son & heir of S' John. 1705.

On a slab of black marble in the chancel on a
raised tomb, an inscription for Grace the wife of Paul
Speccott of Penheale one of the daus & coh. of Rob.
Halswell son & h. of S' Nich. H. of Halswell
Co. Soms. 1636.

N. transept for the Penheale Isle.
In the window the mutilated fig. of a merchant
an opening from the Lord's Aisle to
the Altar.

Font.

pillars &c. of moor stone.

... arg.
in the N. window of
Transept.

4 miles from Launceston
12 from Camelford

Fig. 33. Font, monumental effigy and architectural details, Egloskerry church; © British
Library Board, Add. Ms. 9462, fol. 30r.

An opening from the Lord's aisle to the altar &c.[229] <sketch of standard Perpendicular window>. Font <sketch> pillars &c. of moor stone. In the North window of Transept <sketch of shield[230]>.
4 miles from Launceston, 12 from Camelford.

FALMOUTH

Lysons: BL, Add. Ms. 9445, fol. 85r.

Falmouth Church – Sophia, wife of John Yorke Esq., of Richmond, Yorkshire, daughter of Sir John Glynne of Hawarden, died on her passage from Lisbon 1766.[231] Richard Lockyer Esq., of Bombay, Late of Lisbon, ob. 1789.[232] Richard Russell, one of the aldermen in the Chamber of the town, date worn.[233] Memorie Sacrum, Magistri Thomae Corker, Qui ob. 10mo, 7^{bris}, An^o D. 1700, Aetate suae 31mo. Qui iacet hic iuvenis fuit Anglis gloria et Afris / Hinc Oriens, illis Martia facta gerens, / Maenibus a Gambiae qui pulso Vindice Mauro / Imperium asservit, non Sibi, Sed Patriae. / Huc rediens Ebur atq*ue*, Aurum, Pretiosaq*ue*, Ligna / Transtulit, heu – moriens non Sibi, Sed Patriae. / Imaturus obit, praereptus funere iniquo, / Damna Simul tristes Afer, et Anglus habent. / Marmora nunc celebrant, meruit majora, Sibiq*ue*, / Staret in aeternum, hoc Aureus Ipse loco.[234]

glass, suggesting a possible chantry function); it was previously noted 'in the window' of the Penheale aisle, the north transept (Gilbert, *Historical Survey*, ii, 525), which is presumably where Lysons found it. Previous attempts at identification have been confused, relating it to individuals associated with the parish long before the date of the figure of *c.* 1500. The choice of alabaster for a monumental effigy, made and imported from Chellaston (Derbyshire), implies an elite patron of means, and although the identity is uncertain, it may have represented Edward Hastings, Lord Hungerford, lord of Penheale (d. 1508). He is reputed to have been buried in the Blackfriars, London, but, if true, that does not preclude the installation of a second tomb at Egloskerry; see Cockerham, *Continuity and Change*, 15.

[229] Referring to a squint between the north transept and the chancel, removed at the restoration.

[230] Lysons blazons the sketch as, *sable, six mullets [pierced] argent, 3, 2 and 1,* for Bonville of Trelawny, in Pelynt, which family's descent terminated in Cecily, the daughter of William, Lord Bonville (d. 1460), and his wife Katherine, daughter of Richard Nevil, 5th earl of Salisbury. Cecily's stepfather was William, Lord Hastings, owner of Penheale – hence the link of this family with the glass here.

[231] Sir John Glynne, 6th Bt (1713–77), was Sir Stephen Glynne's great-grandfather and responsible for the building of the castle on the Hawarden estate. Sophia was one of his thirteen children and died without issue, her body buried at Falmouth after her arrival there on a 'Packet' ship. In the sixteenth century, state letters and dispatches were known as 'the Packet', a term that came to be applied to the boats that carried them; these, by the eighteenth century, were built with a finer hull than average in order to give extra speed and sailed regularly between Falmouth and America, the West Indies, and India.

[232] This is a tablet on the south wall of the church; the Yorke monument is a mural tablet on the north wall.

[233] Presumably this was a floorslab; it is not recorded elsewhere and no longer exists in the church.

[234] Trans., *Sacred to the memory of Master Thomas Corker who died on September 10th, 1700, aged 31 years. The young man who lies here was a glory to both the English and the Africans. Setting forth from this place, performing deeds of war, when defending the Moor from the well-known fortifications of the Gambia, he claimed supreme authority not for himself but for his fatherland. Returning here, he brought back ivory and gold and precious timber. Dying, alas, untimely not only for himself but for his country, he perished, carried too soon away by*

Glynne: GL, Glynne notebooks 70, fols 8B–9B

Falmouth – Charles Martyr [1843].
This Church is remarkable only for having been built in the reign of Charles II when Falmouth was erected into a separate parish, & a period when very few churches were built, & those few in no very felicitous style.
The Church in question bears a general resemblance in style & arrangement to the Cornish Churches, but is a bad & debased edition of these. It has a West Tower & a body with equal side aisles. The Tower is not square & though lofty, of coarse workmanship & has a very unsightly appearance.
The body is very low, but the Chancel a little loftier than the rest, though without architectural division.[235] The windows are very poor & ugly, mostly of 5 lights with plain Perpendicular mullions, in some parts of 2 heights. Some windows have been altered. The Eastern decidedly Venetian.
The interior is heavy, & sadly blocked up with pues & galleries, though attempts have lately been made to improve the arrangements, but not yet with success as regards the removal of pues.[236] The Chancel has however been much embellished, & a handsome lectern & gilt eagle desk provided.[237] The division [9B] of the aisles formed by ugly pseudo-Grecian columns supporting an entablature. The Font is of marble on a mahogany stem.[238] In the West gallery a large Organ. The daily service is carried on in this Church.[239]

an iniquitous death. Africans and English sadly suffer the loss together. Marble tablets now honour him; he deserved greater things, and that he should stand for ever in this golden place.
This is a spectacular sculptured mural tablet on the north wall of the church. It incorporates many coloured marbles and comprises an oval cartouche bearing the inscription supported on a wide apron, while above is a heraldic achievement inclined away from the wall towards the viewer, the better to recognise the arms.
[235] The chancel was altered in 1706 and extended eastwards in 1812; there was an extension westwards in 1749, all documented in DHC: DR, Faculty Causes, Cornwall, Falmouth 1, 3, 6. In 1726, the bishop was petitioned regarding the expansion of the church to the north and south: 'That the said Town & Parish is grown very populous and that the Parish Church there will not hold or contain the Inhabitants thereof, And whereas the said Minister, Churchwardens & Principal Inhabitants of Falmouth aforesaid Have supplicated our leave to erect two new Isles (to wit one on the North and the other on the south sides of the said Church there) to contain each twenty foot square by taking in so much of the Churchyard belonging to ye said Church', DHC: DR, Chanter Basket D2/131.
[236] Prior to Glynne's visit in 1870, the improvements had always been piecemeal. As the *FP*, 12 March 1898, 5, has it: 'There are probably very few churches in the "first, last, and best county in England" which have undergone such variety of alterations as Falmouth Parish Church of King Charles the Martyr. Erected in the middle of the seventeenth century, it was from time to time added to, whilst the interior underwent many changes. Historical records show that what one generation built and approved of a succeeding generation disapproved of and demolished. Hardly any of the changes sensibly affected the character of the church, however, and few of them enhanced its appearance. During the past twelve months the structure has once more been in the hands of the builder, who has repaired the ravages made by time's defacing hand, and, practically speaking, has re-built the church.' See Sedding, *Norman Architecture*, 303–4, for an account of the restoration in 1897–8; and Warner, *A Time to Build*, 148–9.
[237] This still remains in the church.
[238] This is carved with detail similar to that on the credence table of 1759; Beacham and Pevsner, *Cornwall*, 187.
[239] Presumably because there was an ever-changing congregation, consequent upon the town's flourishing maritime trade.

FEOCK

Lysons: BL, Add. Ms. 9445, fol. 86r.

St Feocke – clustered columns, tower detached like Gunwalloe <sketch of font>. Revd. Mr Symons.[240]

Glynne: GL, Glynne notebooks 16, fols 43–4

S. Feock, 22 August 1863.
This Church is Perpendicular of the Cornish sort, consisting of a nave & Chancel undivided with South aisle, North Transept & South porch. The belfry is situated at some distance West of the Church & is a low square Tower with pointed roof, of very plain character, set upon a sudden eminence rising at the outskirts of the uneven Churchyard. It has no architectural character, but is picturesque from being covered with ivy. There are 3 bells. <*Low detached belfrys occur also in Cornwall at Gwennap, Talland, Lamorran.*[241]>
The Church was repaired & put into good condition in 1844.[242] The arcade within is of granite, & has 6 Tudor-shaped arches on light piers of the usual kind <sketch> with octagonal caps & there is nothing to mark the Chancel but a better kind of roof coved with ribs & bosses & a cornice of foliage. The Transept opens by a wide Tudor arch on shafts. The windows are all Perpendicular mostly of 3 lights. The East window has shafts with capitals of foliage & some of the windows have stained glass, mostly new.[243] One window on the North is square headed. The seats are mostly open; there is an organ on the ground at the West end.[244] The Font is a new one [44] of black marble, having some Norman ornament.[245]
The Sacrarium is laid with pretty new tiles, & the Decalogue &c. are in black letter. The South porch has doorways of granite, the inner having an obtuse arch,

[240] Vicar of Feock 1799–1828; his monument is in the church.
[241] This note (fol. 42v.) is typical of the kind of categorisation that Glynne enjoyed.
[242] As reported in *The Ecclesiologist* 4 (1845), 241–2, involving 'part of the south wall, and the east, and part of the north walls, and the north transept, have been carefully and strongly rebuilt after the original design, and the whole roof relaid. Internally an unsightly gallery has been removed, and the square pews destroyed [...] The whitewash has been scraped from the pillars, arches, and walls, and the latter washed with stone colour, and ornamented with appropriate texts rubricated. Most of these were discovered when the whitewash was removed, and have been restored.' See LPL: ICBS 3445 (1844–5) for reseating, reroofing, and general restoration, with a floorplan demonstrating the total saturation coverage of the new benches, to the extent of twelve schoolchildren accommodated on the step of the sanctuary. Presumably also at this time was destroyed the 'Rood-Loft of the South-Isle, [where] are the King's Arms – C.R. 1638', noted by Tonkin, CL: Tonkin Ms. C, 2.
[243] No medieval glass survives now, but Gilbert, *Historical Survey*, ii, 807, noted 'some few remains of painted glass, which are here and there dispersed in its Gothic windows'. He quotes Hals and Tonkin's record of glass including the figure of St Feock, and those 'of a man and woman, and behind them several children, all in the act of adoration', hence, a donor window of some kind. See the replacement tracery (post-1844) of the east windows of the chancel and south aisle, KK: EN/2533/3.
[244] Possibly it had been in the gallery until that was removed.
[245] It is not in fact 'new', but a Norman work of Catacleuse stone with crisply sculpted ornamentation; see Sedding, *Norman Architecture*, 123–4, pl. XLIX; see also CRSBI, available online at: https://www.crsbi.ac.uk/view-item?i=5941 [accessed November 2023].

with good mouldings, the inner one flowered. In the Churchyard is a nice ancient cross.[246] The Churchyard occupies a curious hollow or basin, shaded with fine trees, but with some uneven ground & the appearance of the Church sunk in the hollow & its detached belfry, is rather remarkable. Over the Chancel a new Spirelet has been placed.[247]

FORRABURY

Lysons: BL, Add. Ms. 9462, fol. 33r.

Forrabury – very small mean Church in form of a X, with circular arch between the nave & each transept. Opening from North transept into the Chancel [i.e. squint]. Cross without the churchyard on the south side. Church stands on a rocky eminence very near the Sea.

Glynne: GL, Glynne notebooks 14, fols 15–16

Forrabury, S. Symphorian, 1 February 1850.
A forlorn looking Church, which like the two last named [Tintagel and Trevalga] presents some early features, as it is said do some other Churches near the coast in this part of the County. The situation is very bleak & exposed, the plan is a nave, South Transept & porch, Chancel with North chapel & West Tower. <*The arch to the South Transept is very plain & semi-circular – perhaps very early.*> The work is very rude & there are some singularities.
The Chancel opens to the North chapel or aisle by very coarse plain semi circular arches upon imposts & there is a very odd shaped arch set obliquely as a hagioscope, & cutting off the angle.[248] On the South of the Chancel is one lancet window.[249] <*In*

---

[246] Langdon, *Mid-Cornwall*, 32, no. 35.
[247] This was removed at a subsequent restoration in 1875–6, which despite the earlier efforts was essentially a rebuilding of the entire church. *RCG*, 5 August 1876, 5: 'The new Church [...] is situated within the churchyard and is slightly larger than the old building which it has replaced – the nave has been widened and the chancel lengthened, and – what would improve many other Cornish Churches – the walls are heightened. The most remarkable thing in the general appearance of the interior of the building are the chancel arches – a rare feature in the neighbourhood. Three pointed arches of two orders, supported by clustered columns and labelled caps and bases, divide the chancel from the nave, and this together with the increased length of the chancel, give the Church an unique and remarkably good appearance [...] there is a small south chancel aisle. The north aisle is of two bays, and the south aisle of the whole length of the Church. A south porch has been re-built, but all the old doorways have been re-inserted in the new building; and most of the old windows have been restored and used again, there being only two entirely new ones, and these are in the west end. The roofs are entirely new – open pitch pine, with principals about five feet apart and with windbraces; and the seats are like-wise of pitch-pine; except the chancel stalls, which are of oak.' The sentence of consecration of this rebuilt church is KK: P64/2/5 (1876).
[248] The large size of the hagioscope, enabling direct vision of the altar from the box pews in the north transept, can be seen on the plan of the church following a visit made in 1866 by Maclean, *Trigg Minor*, i, pl. XXII.
[249] Maclean, *Trigg Minor*, i, 591–2, pl. XXII, verifies Glynne's description of the church, although, 'since 1866 [...] scarcely a vestige of the old work remains'. His groundplans of *c.* 1874 reveal the extent of the restoration, KK: EN/2053. The *WMN*, 8 October 1867,

*the Church yard is a large cross.*²⁵⁰> The East window of the North chapel is a triplet, that of the Chancel very badly mutilated.²⁵¹ There are no windows at all on the North of the nave. No Chancel arch, but part of the roodscreen remains, of plain work & much injured. The roof of the nave is open, that of the Chancel meanly ceiled. The interior blocked by pues. *<Some ancient bench ends remain with varied emblems.*²⁵²> The Tower arch is pointed but without moulding. [16] The Tower is remarkably plain & has no window, door or any other opening. The porch adjoins the South chapel & is entirely of stone, with moulded pointed outer door. The ground rises considerably on the North side. The Font has a circular bowl of porphyry, carved in cross lines.²⁵³

FOWEY

Lysons: BL, Add. Ms. 9462, fol. 31r.

Fowey church – large handsome tower with rich pinnacles, & ornamented with bands of Gothick tracery. Nave & side aisles separated by shapely pointed arches

---

2, reported: '[The church] was very small and the necessary enlargement has, of course, much changed its character, the north transept having been embodied in a new aisle, and the chancel lengthened.' Financial details of the 1866–8 restoration are contained in the churchwardens' accounts, including the minutes of a vestry meeting on 8 September 1866: 'That this Meeting formally recognises the duty of enlarging the Parish Church of Forrabury on account of the insufficiency of the accommodation for the congregation'; KK: P65/5/1. Another scheme for reseating the church had been planned in 1853, yet it did not take place, presumably because no grant aid was obtained, LPL: ICBS 4167 (1853). An earlier project had already been considered by the EDAS, who remarked that it was 'wholly deficient in ecclesiastical character, and […] the same increase in accommodation might be supplied by a re-arrangement of the seats, without destroying any of the present walls', 'Quarterly Report […] 1849', *TEDAS*, 3, 202. Perhaps this provoked a rethink by the parish, which was then rejected by the ICBS, or the ICBS followed suit with the EDAS views on what was proposed.
²⁵⁰ By Glynne's visit, this had been removed from outside, where Lysons found it, to inside the churchyard; see Langdon, *North Cornwall*, 34, no. 38.
²⁵¹ Gilbert, *Historical Survey*, ii, 579, found the interior of the church with 'its windows darkened by iron bars'; and in 1819 the rural dean ordered the 'window frame and shutters to be repaired and Glass to be cleaned and repaired'; KK: AD59/74, 146. Spence, '"Iter Cornubiense"', part III, 108, writing only a few years after Glynne, noted that 'the eastern window of the Chancel is a late and frightful insertion, made of Delabole slate. The ancient window, a triplet of unequal lancets, lies in the Church yard.'
²⁵² The church once contained many ancient bench ends and a screen, but subsequent to the restoration in 1867 the few ends that were saved were worked into an altar, credence table, and pulpit; see Gray, *Gazetteer*, 19–21. The screen has not survived but was replaced by an example noted by members of the EDAS who visited the church in 1897, as 'modern and inartistic', with the equally pithy comment that the old bench ends 'when taken out, were reserved by the then Rector; it is a pity that reservation did not mean conservation', H. Reed, 'Churches of Boscastle, Trevalga, and Tintagel, Cornwall', *TEDAAS* 3rd series 1.3 (1899), 186–99, at 191. Glynne's additional notes (fol. 14v.) suggest a revisit to the church, perhaps at the same time as I suspect he called again at Tintagel, in 1870; Forrabury is less than four miles from Tintagel and six from St Teath.
²⁵³ In 1813, the rural dean recommended that the font was to be 'scraped and repaired and painted', but probably, and thankfully perhaps, it was never done, KK: AD59/74, 145.

on octagonal piers, no Capitals. In South aisle monument of Thomas Graham Esq., 1792, & his wife [Susannah, d. 1789].[254]
On a slab, brasses for man & his wife, he is in long gown beard & ruff. Robert Rashleigh & Agnes his wife & children (date gone).[255]
[separate sheet] In the North aisle in a window on a slab of slate, In memory of Mary the Daughter of Sir Peter Courtney of Trethurffe, ob. 1655, grandaughter to Jonathan Rashleigh of Menabilly.
In the North aisle a very large and handsome monument with the effigies in alabaster in a long gown beard & ruff lying on a pillow richly ornamented, the lower part of the monument richly ornamented with fine flowers & shields of arms for Jonathan Rashleigh of Menabilly Esq. ^1675^ & his family <sketch of shield[256]>. Some verses under read thus 'Yet at his death but daughters 6 one son he had no more / all them to purtrare [i.e. bodily decay] under here because fit space was none / The Son whose only Charge this was is therefore set alone', a port merchant. Pillars of the Corinthian order all of veined marble. Monument for John Rashleigh Esq. 1624, John Rashleigh junior 1624.[257] Turn over.[258]
[separate sheet] Slab – Tablet for Thomas Trefry Esq., Counsell at law, 1635. Other brasses without inscription.[259] And another tomb with a slab of Free Stone, figure in armour with sword & dagger, monument only cut in outline, John Treffry Esq. 1590.[260] In nave – monument of John Goodall merchant, 1686, & his son ~~Richard~~ William with effigies.[261]
Brass ^with effigies^ for Alice wife of John Rashleigh Esq., ob. 1591, he himself died 1580.[262]

[254] This mural monument comprises a white marble pyramid supporting an urn, with an inscription below.

[255] All that now remains of this brass of c. 1580 is the figure of Robert Rashleigh. Two groups of children and the figure of his wife Agnes, the inscription plate and most of the marginal inscription are all lost; see Lack, Stuchfield, and Whittemore, *Brasses of Cornwall*, 41–2.

[256] This of a cross, with 'a lion' indicated in the centre; relating to the Rashleigh tomb of 1624, the arms are those of the family, *sable, a cross or between a Cornish chough argent, beaked and legged gules in the first quarter, in the second a text T of the third, in the third and fourth a crescent of the last.*

[257] This is a London-made marble monument with the recumbent full-length figure of Jonathan Rashleigh set upon a tombchest, one short side of which bears the kneeling figure of his son. It is a work of 1624, yet above the tombchest, but not physically bonded, is a mural tablet set under an entablature supported by Corinthian columns, with a pediment ornamented with a heraldic achievement, and an inscription to Jonathan Rashleigh (d. 1675). Lysons appears to confuse the two inscriptions, and incorrectly allocates the 1675 date (perhaps as an afterthought, as the date is added as superscript), to the tomb monument. See Cockerham, *Continuity and Change*, 120, pls 228–30.

[258] The reverse of this sheet is blank.

[259] These are most likely the small figures of civilians, two male and two female, which had lost their inscriptions but were mid fifteenth-century brasses of the Treffry family; see P.D. Cockerham, 'The Early Treffry Monuments at Fowey: A Re-appraisal', *Church Monuments* 10 (1995), 20–36.

[260] This slab of Pentewan stone is now mural; see Cockerham, 'Treffry Monuments', 27–9.

[261] Now in the sanctuary, this mural double effigial monument is a fine example of Plymouth craftsmanship. Two kneeling effigies of the father and son face each other across a prayer desk, the elder marked out by his wearing the robes of office of the newly established Mayor of Fowey.

[262] This brass is a separate monument for Alice Rashleigh, wife of Robert, who was memorialised on the brass noted by the Lysons previously.

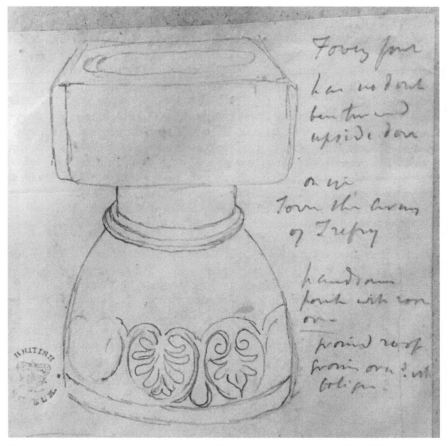

Fig. 34. Inverted font, Fowey church; photo Christian Steer, from the British Library Archive, Add. Ms. 9462, fol. 33r.

Fols 31r., 31v., 32r.[263] <sketches of windows, pinnacles etc. of Place house, drawings of house> Place, Fowey – flight of steps to ye church. Many coats of arms in the north window of the hall.[264] Entrance to the hall by a stair case, unaltered. Place House in Fowey – on ye north side of the church.

Fol. 33r. Fowey font has no doubt been turned upside down[265] <sketch>. (Fig. 34) On the tower the arms of Trefry. Handsome porch with room over, groined roof, groining ornamented with foliage.

---

[263] This is a copy of the print of Place published by Lysons, *Cornwall*, ccxlii, and opp. ccxliii; see the additions in the 1830s by Joseph Treffry, C. Bristow, 'The Building and Decorative Stones of Cornwall', in Holden (ed.), *The Distinctiveness of Cornish Buildings*, 40–55, at 49–50.

[264] These were earlier recorded by Richard Symonds in 1644, see the *Diary of the Marches of the Royal Army during the Great Civil War; Kept by Richard Symonds*, ed. C.E. Long, Camden Society (1859), 68–9.

[265] Of Catacleuse marble, and similar to that at Feock, this is now set on a modern base; see Sedding, *Norman Architecture*, 130, pls LI, LII; see also the CRSBI, available online at: https://www.crsbi.ac.uk/view-item?i=5650 [accessed June 2023].

Fig. 35. View of Hall Farm Chapel(?); reproduced with the kind permission of the Royal Institution of Cornwall, Courtney Library, Henderson Ms. 'East Cornwall', 260A.

Place house, arms of Eight E.N., lion & dragon, arms with lion & motto che sera sera. <sketch of shield[266]>. Fol. 34r. Foy is a considerable & flourishing town built of stone, some built on the side of a steep hill & along the river. Old Crown in Fowey with arms of Trefry – they say it was a monastery – query? Polperrow is a town most singularly situated on a very small portion of level ground between two very steep rocky hills – stone houses. In those, hanging gardens above the town – stone houses. <sketch of small battlemented tower> remains of a chapel on the hill – ruins of considerable buildings.[267] (Fig. 35)

[266] The motto of the Russell family, dukes of Bedford, see C.N. Elvin, *A Hand-Book of Mottoes* (London, 1860), 229. The shield is split per pale with only the dexter side tricked, *argent a lion rampant gules, on a chief sable three scallops argent*, for Russell. The motto of the Treffry family is 'Whyll God Will'; see Gilbert, *Historical Survey*, ii, pl. 6, 894, where he noted it on the chimney piece in the hall, dated 1575.

[267] This may be the small tower of the medieval chapel at Hall Farm, Lanteglos-by-Fowey; for a contemporary description, see Gilbert, *Historical Survey*, ii, 901.

Glynne: GL, Glynne notebooks 13, fols 61–3

Fowey – S. Finbarrus, 30 January 1850.
A fine Church in some points exhibiting work of a superior kind to what is usually found in Cornwall. It consists of a nave & Chancel undivided, North & South aisles, South porch & West Tower. *<The Church is said to have been partly rebuilt in 1336, & again in 1466.*[268] *>* The South aisle is wide, & continued to the East end, the North aisle, which is much narrower & has a lean to roof, is ends one bay short of the East end.[269] The nave is lofty & has the appendage, unusual in this county, of a Clerestory continued quite to the end of the Chancel. The Tower is a very fine lofty one, of Third Pointed character, erected in 1466.[270] It has a battlement & 4 octagonal panneled pinnacles at the angles, corner buttresses, & is 3 stages in height, divided by horizontal bands of panneling. There is also a panneled band near the base, & some small pinnacles are set on the buttresses. The West door has good continuous mouldings & panneled spandrels, containing quatrefoils; over it a window of 4 lights. The North aisle is plain, without parapet, & but little seen, being very near to the great Mansion of the Austens, called Place House.[271] The South front which is conspicuously seen, has an embattled parapet & pinnacles on the buttresses. [62] The South porch is curious from having its entrances on the East & West walls & not on the South front. This seems to arise from the steepness & sudden rise in the ground. The East & West doors of the porch are of singular character, late & not very pure ^the arch depressed^ the outer moulding has a kind of spiral ornament, at first sight resembling Norman, the inner is on shafts with octagonal sculptured capitals. *<The hoods of the porch doors have square flowered corbels.*[272]*>* The porch has a parvise & a battlement, & a stone groined roof, with central boss, the ribs from shafts at the angles & are moulded. The door leading into the nave has panneled spandrels & over it a niche with a rose in the apex. In one of the angles of the porch is a benatura on a shaft.
The interior is very lofty & handsome. On each side a fine tall arcade, apparently Middle Pointed (probably ^of^ 1336.) There are 4 lofty arches with continuous orders, carried down octagonal columns without capitals resembling those at Lostwithiel. The Clerestory windows are Third Pointed of 3 lights <sketch> but only appear on the North. Those of the North aisle also of 3 lights, are of very similar character. Those of the South aisle are of 4 lights, Third Pointed, without foliation; the rear arches have shafts with octagonal capitals. The East window of the Chancel of 5 lights, Third Pointed & pretty fair. There is an ascent to the Chancel by 3 steps, the only mark of distinction. The Chancel opens to the South aisle by only one arch which is wide, of Tudor form, springing from shafts with octagonal capital & sculptured granite abacus.

[268] This is in Glynne's later handwriting (fol. 60v.); possibly he gleaned this from Lysons, *Cornwall*, III; see also Henderson, 'Ecclesiastical History', 166.
[269] This was extended to the east end to accommodate the vestry and organ at a restoration in 1876; see fn. 273.
[270] See Mattingly, 'Pevsner', 76, 81, for confirmation of this approximate date.
[271] Curiously, Glynne visited Fowey the day after the burial of Joseph Thomas Austen, who had assumed the name and arms of Treffry in 1836 from his uncle William Esco Treffry (d. 1779). Evidently the house was still associated with the Austen family rather than Treffry; see also Lysons, *Cornwall*, 110–11.
[272] This addition (fol. 61v.) is in handwriting very similar to the account of the church, so is probably contemporaneous with his original account.

The East window of the South aisle is of 5 lights[273] & below it is the sacristy.[274] The roof of the centre aisle is coved, panneled with ribs & bosses & angel figures in the cornice. That of the South side is flat & plainly panneled.[275] The Tower arch is a lofty [63] one with mouldings & shafts, partly masked by a Western gallery.[276] The Pulpit has Jacobean carving.[277] The Font is early, a circular cup having round the upper part a course of star & rude flower.[278] There are a few post-Reformation brasses & a gaudy Jacobean Monument.[279] The Church is pued.[280]

GERMOE

Lysons: BL, Add. Ms. 9462, fol. 34r.

Germo Church – Nave & South aisle, clustered pillars & obtuse arches, North & South Transept.[281]

[273] The church was reroofed in 1867, KK: P66/5/1. Nine years later, there was a major restoration, when the sacristy, at the east end of the south aisle, was remodelled into accommodation for worshippers, and its east window was rebuilt with four lights rather than the five that Glynne saw; LPL: ICBS 7740 (1874–6), including a floorplan. See the *RCG*, 5 August 1876, 5, which reported the reopening of the church: 'Those who knew the grand old church in its decayed state can best speak of the worth of the work that has been accomplished; but the eye of the most ordinary observer must be struck with the extreme neatness and we may say cleanliness [...] A very necessary and judicious addition has now been made in the shape of the lengthening of the north aisle eastward through the chancel, thus providing a vestry and a place for the organ. With this exception, the whole work has been one of restoration. The church has been reseated throughout, the body with pitch pine and the chancel with stalls of wainscot oak, left, as usual, in its unvarnished state to be mellowed by age [...] There are several new windows, that in the east end being especially worthy of notice.'
[274] The groundplan (LPL: ICBS 7740) of 1876 shows no evidence of a sacristy, with the Treffry chapel filled with benches set hard against the family tomb monuments and communicating directly with the chancel.
[275] The nave roof can be dated to 1526x51, whereas that of the south aisle is earlier, as it was extended eastwards when the five-light window was inserted, to form a chantry chapel for the Treffrys and accommodate the tomb of Sir John Treffry (d. 1500), his brother William (d. 1504), and William's wife; Vernacular Architecture Group (2022) Dendrochronology Database [data-set]. York: Archaeology Data Service [distributor], available online at: https://doi.org/10.5284/1091408 [accessed January 2023]. See also Mattingly, 'Distinctiveness by Omission', 151–3; and Mattingly, *Churches of Cornwall*, 34–5.
[276] This was removed at the 1876 restoration.
[277] It is dated 1601 and is decorated with panels of round-headed arches containing arabesques, perhaps from the cabin of a Spanish galleon; see Cockerham, *Continuity and Change*, 57, pl. 83.
[278] Clearly by Glynne's time the font had been righted from when Lysons described it.
[279] The 'gaudy' monument' is most likely the effigial tomb to John Rashleigh, discussed above.
[280] These are shown on a groundplan of the church in 1843, LPL: ICBS 3288 (1843), with 'Mr Treffry's aisle' in the south chapel, and 'Mr Rashleigh's aisle' in the north-east of the nave, both identified. As early as 1821, it was noted that 'Church Seats not in good repair & many so large & private Property, that the poor inhabitants are unable to attend Church', Cook (ed.), *The Diocese of Exeter in 1821*, 23. See also a letter of 30 August 1843 from Rev. John Kempe at Fowey to William Rashleigh of Menabilly, mentioning attempts to improve the pews in Fowey church, CL: RASH/4/319. The large family pews/aisles were swept away in 1876.
[281] See E.W. Godwin, 'Notes on Churches in Kerrier and Penwith', *Archaeological Journal* 18 (1861), 231–52, at 248–52, for a description of the church before its restoration, as it would

Fig. 36. 'St Germoe's Chair', Germoe churchyard; © British Library Board, Add. Ms. 9462, fol. 34r.

On the North East side of the Church yard against the hedge is a kind of recess with a stone seat, which the Country people call the chair of Germo Rex of Cornwall[282] <plan with dimensions & sketch, with two corbel heads>. (Fig. 36)

GERRANS

Lysons: BL, Add. Ms. 9462, fol. 34r.

Gerrance – Nave, South aisle & North Transept. Clustered pillars, Stone Spire.[283] Monument in South aisle for Edward Hobbs of Tregassa & Jenefore his wife, ob. 1718. John Thomas of Nanshuthall, Armiger, Nepos & haeres, erected in 1732[284] <sketch of font[285]>.

have been seen by Lysons; and for an account of the early cruciform church, see Sedding, *Norman Architecture*, 152–4.

[282] Lysons, *Cornwall*, ccxxix, describes the 'chair [...] in the Saxon style', although it is clearly medieval. See Blight, *West Cornwall*, 77–8; S. Rundle, 'Cornish Chairs', *JRIC* 14 (1901), 384–93, at 389–91; and Henderson, 'Ecclesiastical History', 170.

[283] The church that Lysons saw was almost entirely rebuilt in 1849–50 after the roof was destroyed by fire in 1848; Warner, *A Time to Build*, 157. The *RCG*, 30 May 1851, 5, reported: 'The new church at Gerrans is rather a faithful restoration of the old building than what would be called new in design, for, although the tower and spire are the only portion allowed to remain, the great object of the inhabitants appears to have been to reproduce what had fallen to decay. It had been utterly dilapidated, unfit for public worship, and incapable of satisfactory repairs [...] It consists of a north and south aisle, with small north transept; the chancel separated by a light and appropriate screen. The seats, which are convenient and roomy, are open throughout, an arrangement we are glad to see generally observed in our new churches, and in reseating the old ones. The east windows are fitted with neat stained glass, and all are very good.' As *The Ecclesiologist* 10 (1850), 246–7, commented, 'the very stones of the church's Debased piers and arches having been replaced, and the old windows, so far as possible, used again [...] we have here, an old church – of no great merit, to be sure – exactly re-produced, and fitted up in better style and taste'. See also KK: P70/2/2–3, rebuilding and enlargement of Gerrans Church (1849–50); and LPL: ICBS 3833 (1846–50), including a floorplan.

[284] This elaborate monument, recorded by Polsue, *Parochial History*, ii, 73, as the only one then in the church (were others destroyed at the rebuilding?), is by John Weston of Exeter; see Roscoe *et al.*, *Dictionary*, 1372. Gilbert, *Historical Survey*, ii, 842, found it protected by an iron railing (now gone) and in the north aisle. Yet the south aisle was the area in the church specified in an episcopal petition on 6 June 1732 by 'John Thomas of Tregolls Gent. [who] Sheweth, that your Petitioner is desirous to Erect a Monument in Memory of Edward Hobbes Gent. and Jenefer his wife deceased in the Parish Church of Gerrans [...] in an Angle in the South East Isle there Eleven feet in height and six feet in breadth, the erecting of which will be no way Prejudicial to the Walls of the said Church or any persons Right'; DHC: DR, Chanter basket D2/239. Permission was granted in March 1732/3 (Chanter basket D2/240).

[285] The sketch does not show the four round pillars, one at each corner, that support the bowl today and are probably contemporary with the restoration; see Sedding, *Norman Architecture*, 155–6; and the CRSBI, available online at: https://www.crsbi.ac.uk/view-item?i=15269 [accessed June 2023].

GOLANT (ST SAMPSON)

Lysons: BL, Add. Ms. 9462, fol. 7r.[286]

St Sampson – has a south aisle, clustered pillars, obtuse arches, plain octagonal font. Well adjoining the church porch.

GORRAN

Lysons: BL, Add. Ms. 9462, fol. 36r.

Gorran – Nave & South aisle & North transept, clustered pillars obtuse arches <sketch of font>.
Some slight remains of stained glass in ye East window of South aisle.[287]
Monument in Chancel for Richard Edgcumb de Bodrugan Esq., younger son of ^Sir^ Richard ^de Mount^ Edgcumb Knight, ob. 1655.[288]
Church not paved.[289]
12 seines – 3800 hogsheads of pilchards. They call the parish Gorran & the town Lewarren. Gorran haven is a fishing town.[290]

Glynne: GL, Glynne notebooks 14, fol. 44

Gorran – S. Gorran, 1 February 1853.
A Church of true Cornish character, with a nave & undivided Chancel each with South aisle, a North Transept & Western Tower. The whole, as usual, is Perpendicular. The arcade within consist of 8 arches, 3 of which are in the Chancel, the piers are clustered, with 4 shafts having octagonal capitals & intermediate mouldings down them. There is a pointed arch, very plain opening to the Transept & to none to the Chancel. The roofs are coved & separate with ribs &

---

[286] This note is written on a sketch of the 'Tristan' or Castledore stone, perhaps made on Samuel's route to Golant from Fowey; see Okasha, *Corpus*, 91–6.

[287] There are remains of medieval glass in the same window: the head of an apostle or Christ, and some inconclusive fragments, presumably part of the scene of taking down Christ from the cross, recorded by Tonkin; see Gilbert, *Historical Survey*, ii, 847.

[288] This dark marble wall monument with an Italian-style frame is now in the nave. Its Plymouth origin is suggested by a letter from Philip Edgcumbe (cousin of the deceased Richard) to Pears Edgcumbe Esq. (brother), dated 17 December 1655, a few days after Richard's funeral at Gorran, in which he related: 'I have taken course [...] to speake unto the stone Cutter of Plymouth aboute makinge some monum[en]t for your brother', KK: ME/3037.

[289] That is, the floor was strewn with rushes on beaten earth. The rural dean commented in 1813 that 'the flooring of the Church sunk and uneven', and in 1820: 'Walls in many parts of the Church covered with Green Mould [...] very damp & covered with Green mould all around the Communion Table & under the East Window', symptomatic of the lack of stone flooring, KK: AD 59/74, 195.

[290] As this information is written on the note of Gorran church, it must have been acquired on his journey by conversation in the village, rather than from a correspondent or documentary research.

bosses.[291] The windows mostly of 3 lights. ~~That~~ Those at the East ^& West^ of the South aisle of 4, & over it [*sic*] a square sculptured stone. The East window of the Chancel is mean of 3 lights. There is a lancet on the East & West sides of the Transept, perhaps early.[292] On the North of the Chancel there are no windows. The Vista of the Church is long & undivided. The Font is of the Cornish make, the bowl cup shaped, upon a cylindrical stem, surrounded by 4 shafts on raised octagonal bases, with heads for capitals. On the bowl is some rude foliage sculpture, tracery, shields & initials.[293] The base is raised, the age doubtful. The South porch is embattled & has crocketed pinnacles. The Tower is a fine lofty one of granite, of 3 stages, divided by strings & embattled, having crocketed octagonal pinnacles: a labeled West door & 4 light window, & belfry windows of 3 lights.[294]

GRADE

Lysons: BL, Add. Ms. 9462, fol. 36r.

Grade – in form of a Cross, between Chancel & North aisle of Ditto on the wooden Cornice is the following inscription [in Gothic minuscules], Domi*n*is Johannes Role me fieri fecit A^o d^i M^o CCCC^o LXXX° VI^{to}.[295]

---

[291] The *WMN*, 23 April 1867, 2, reported that 'Gorran Church is in a very dilapidated state. The roofs have been allowed to remain unrepaired for a considerable time, and a correspondent informs us that he was at Gorran on Saturday, and got on the roof, when he found that the roofing felt placed over the holes was blown aside by the wind, and there were pools of water in the church.' In 1869, there was a partial restoration, reported by the *RCG*, 13 November 1869, 5: 'The wood work of the roof of the south aisle has already been erected, and many of the principals in the nave and chancel have been put together during the past week. Most of the beautiful carved panels of the old pews have been preserved, though a few have unavoidably been destroyed in taking down the old roof of the church. No doubt when the parishioners again assemble for divine worship in the church of their forefathers they will regret the effect of the beautiful roof should be marred by the unsightly appearance of the pews.' The roof continued to deteriorate, as the *RCG*, 14 August 1875, 8, reported that 'the debris of the old roof and a winter's rain found out all the weak places where they lodged, and sunken graves, disjointed seats, and rotten floors, left the present vicar no alternative, in the interest of the barest decency, but to set himself to the work of a complete restoration'. See LPL: ICBS 7704 (1874–7), for reseating/repairs, replastering, and repairs to walls. The roofs were eventually replaced in a severe restoration programme of 1890–5; Warner, *A Time to Build*, 161.

[292] These are from the early cruciform building.

[293] Considered to be Norman in origin, reworked in the fifteenth century to incorporate the arms of the Bodrugan family of Gorran, *argent, three bendlets gules*; see Sedding, *Norman Architecture*, 158.

[294] Curiously, Glynne made no comment on the large number of ancient bench ends then in the church.

[295] Trans., *Sir [lit. Lord] John Role had me made A.D. 1486*. J.J. Rogers, 'Notice of the Cradle Roof of Grade Church, in Cornwall, A.D. 1486–7', *TEDAS* 6 (1861), 147–50, recorded that 'the roof [...] is neither lofty, nor richly carved, nor in good condition; but it is interesting on account of the inscriptions upon the cornice [...] and from its having remains of colour upon the principals of the Chancel & north transept'. The roof was destroyed at the demolition/restoration of the body of the church, despite Rogers's plea at the end of his article (50) that 'the Rector, Rev. F.C. Jackson, has shewn so much taste and judgement,

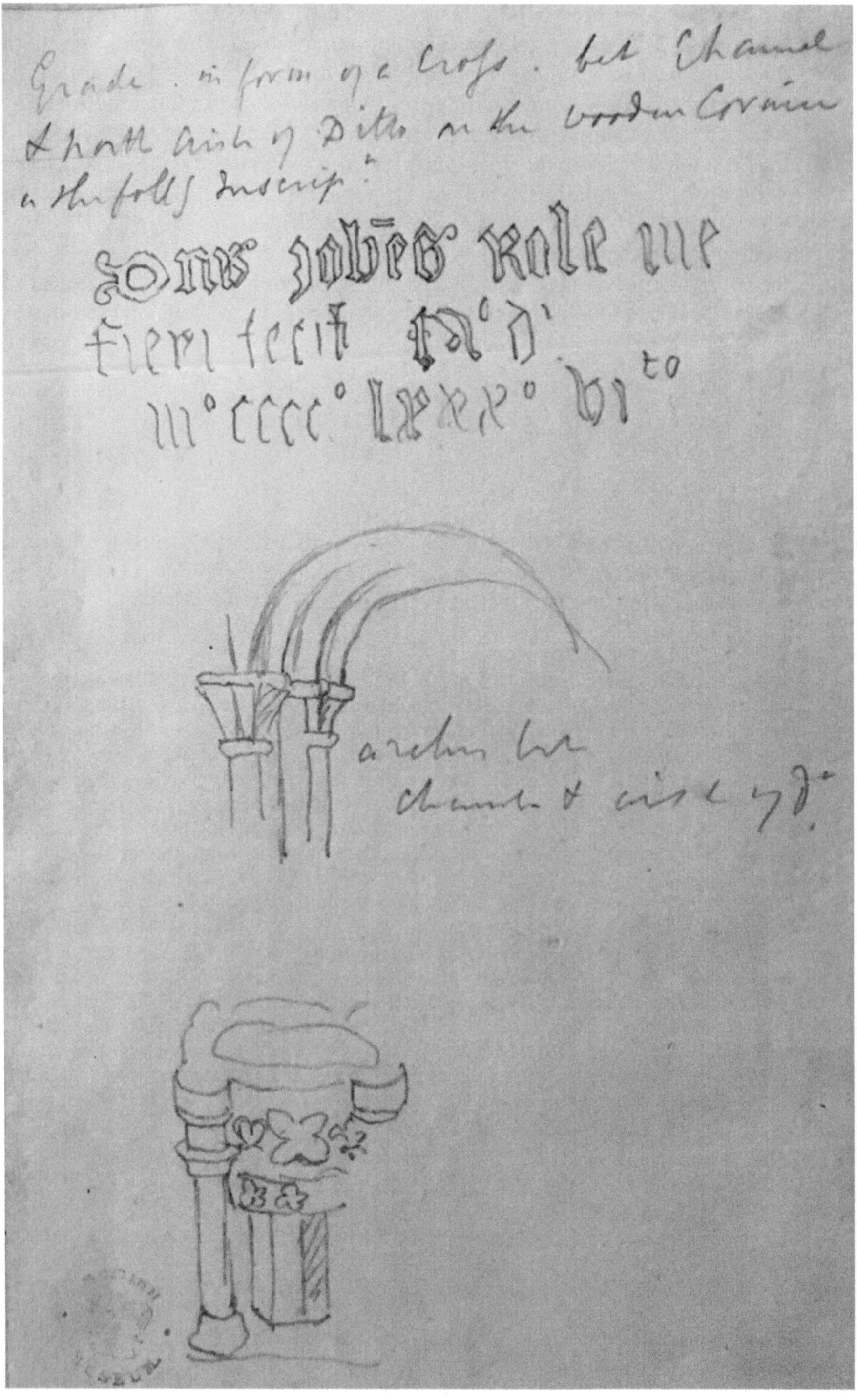

Fig. 37. Inscription and font, Grade church; from the British Library Archive, Add Ms. 9462, fol. 36r.

Arches between Chancel & aisle rounded <sketch of arch with pier and clustered capital; font>.[296] (Fig. 37)

Glynne: GL, Glynne notebooks 13, fols 50–1

Grade – S. Grade, 17 February 1849.
This Church bears much resemblance to others in the district in its style, but somewhat varies in form. It is cruciform with West Tower & South porch, the Chancel having a North aisle, but the nave none. The Transepts are large in proportions & do not open by arches. The tower is Third Pointed & embattled, with 4 crocketed pinnacles & divided by one string.[297] There are no buttresses, the West window of 3 lights, those of the belfry of 2 & the West door closed. It opens to the nave by a very rude arch of obtuse form, on imposts. Most of the windows are late, some square headed & debased. The East window, of 3 lights, & the East some of the North aisle transept of 2, have a Middle Pointed look, but doubtful. The East window of the North aisle is fair Third Pointed. The roofs are open & cradle, with ribs, & a nice cornice to some part. [51] The ribs at the crossing, are arranged so as to intersect & have bosses.[298] There is a hagioscope in cutting off the angle between the South Transept & the Chancel, having a central pier at the angle & lighted by a small square-headed window.[299] The Chancel is divided from its aisle by 2 small arches, 1 obtuse, the other clumsy pointed, but both of Third Pointed period, with the usual Cornish pier having shafts with separate octagonal capitals. In the Western pier is a square aperture.[300] The Font is large, the bowl a circular cup, on a central octagonal stem surrounded by 4 shafts detached, with capitals & bases. On the bowl is some curious ornamental star like panneling & foliage, of Middle Pointed or Third Pointed character marking the continuance of an early form of Font at an advanced period.[301]

as well as liberality, in his restoration of the Sister Church of S. Ruan Minor, as to afford a guarantee that the architectural features of that of Grade will be carefully and skilfully preserved, if he should be encouraged to undertake its restoration'. See Godwin, 'Churches in Kerrier and Penwith', 234–8, including a plan and a sketch of window tracery. A rubbing of the inscription dated 1837 is now in the North Devon Athenaeum: Harding Mss, third schedule, box 2C.

[296] Lysons, *Cornwall*, 25, notes monuments to the Erisey family and a transcription of the inscription to Hugh Mason (d. 1671), the latter contained in a letter from the incumbent of Mullion church, Rev. William Willcock, to Daniel Lysons of 16 December 1813, BL, Add. Ms. 9420, fols 381r.–382r.

[297] See Rogers, 'Church Towers', 188.

[298] Indicative of the cruciform plan at the time of the roofing, similar to Landewednack, only two miles distant.

[299] See J.J. Rogers, 'Notices of Certain Lynchnoscopes, or Low Side Windows, Existing in Certain Churches in the West of England', *Archaeological Journal* 11 (1854), 33–7.

[300] This is similar to the aperture found at Ruan Major, but its function in both churches is obscure, other than as a passage between the chancel and a (possible chantry) chapel; see Godwin, 'Churches in Kerrier and Penwith', 236, 332–3.

[301] The font is seen as fifteenth century by Rogers, 'Notice of the Cradle Roof', 148, agreeing with Glynne's appraisal, and 'of a much later date' than the Bodmin group of fonts suggested by Lysons, *Cornwall*, ccxxxiii. Yet Sedding, *Norman Architecture*, pl. LXXII; and Beacham and Pevsner, *Cornwall*, 222, see it as thirteenth century. Possibly it is a fifteenth-century version of the early sculptural form at Bodmin, or nearby Cury, commissioned when the north chancel aisle was added to what was essentially a Norman cruciform building. The decoration is in light relief and crisply sculpted with none of the comparative crudity and heaviness of

There is a brass in the South Transept representing a man & woman of the 15th century.[302] The South porch has a small shallow trefoiled niche on the East wall.[303] At the entrance of the Churchyard is the usual granite grating to exclude the pigs.[304] <Since 1860, Grade Church has been pulled down, all but the tower, & rebuilt on a smaller scale, with only Chancel & Nave.[305] There were inscriptions in the old Church on the cornice of the roof. 'Dominus Johannes Roly me fieri fecit – 1486. Thomas Erysy me fiere fecit 1487'. The original roof ~~had~~ of the North transept had diagonal ribs. There was a brass to James Erisey, his wife & 5 children all in surplices, with inscription, 1522.[306] The West window is not in the centre.[307]>

GULVAL

Lysons: BL, Add. Ms. 9462, fol. 36r.

Gulval – Nave & South aisle & North transept. Octagonal pillars with angels holding shields & plain shields on the Capitals, the arms &c. obscured by whitewash.[308] At the South corner <sketch of font with two additional shields[309]>. Table of Purbeck marble at the East end of South aisle against the North wall.[310]

an earlier date; equally, there is a regularity and evenness in the drawing of the composition, and the supporting pillars are relatively slender, suggesting a later period.

[302] This was known as the Erisey aisle, in which, as well as the brass to James Erisey, Borlase noted two wall monuments to the family, now in the tower; BL, Egerton Ms. 2657, fol. 51r.

[303] Retained on the current south porch.

[304] Despite the rebuilding of the church, this still exists.

[305] Interestingly, Polsue, Cornwall, ii, 109, in 1868, comments that the earlier building was 'considered too dilapidated for repair'. See LPL: ICBS 5752 (1861–3), for rebuilding the church, the documents including a groundplan of the new church. A piece of the original window tracery is loose in the church.

[306] Glynne corrects his earlier dating ('15th century') of the brass but misinterprets the plain gowns worn by the children as surplices: an ecclesiological mistake?

[307] These supplementary notes (fol. 49v.) were probably based on Rogers, 'Notice of the Cradle Roof', passim, as although the paper appeared in the TEDAS in 1861, that society exchanged publications with the Ecclesiological Society.

[308] As noted by Glynne more than thirty years later. Following the visit of the rural dean in 1817, it was 'ordered the Church to be white washed, where the walls are green with dampness', KK: AD59/74, 315.

[309] The shields show a cross fleury and a ?gridiron; illustrated by Blight, West Cornwall, 82. On the font, the sketch shows a shield of Kemyel, argent, three dolphins naiant sable, impaling St Aubyn, ermine, on a cross five bezants (as at Crowan, suggesting a late fourteenth-/early fifteenth-century date – see fn. 162), and an angel holding two superimposed triangles, perhaps forming an 'M' for Maria?

[310] This is the Davile/Harris wall monument of c. 1635, still in the position where Lysons found it, his note amplified in BL, Add. Ms. 9445, fol. 128r. It is made of dark Somerset alabaster, which might easily have been mistaken for Purbeck; see Cockerham, Continuity and Change, 112–13, pl. 208, for its dynastic relevance. Borlase (1748) transcribes the inscription and notes: 'When this Inscr'n was repair'd in 1721 it was copyed very imperfectly', DHC: Z19/16/1, 16, suggesting what we see now is not the original text.

Lysons: BL, Add. Ms. 9445, fol. 128r.

Gulval – Monuments in south aisle, William Daville Esq., 1627, Arthur Harris Esq., of Haine & Governor Protector of Mount St Michael, 1628. John Harris, the heir, put up the monument to his father & grandfather, A.H., Margaret, only daughter of Daville. Harrises of Kynigy in parish of Gulval.
William Harris Esq., 1766. William Arundell Harris, 1792, his widow has a son eleven years of age. Thomas Buckley Esq., 1775.

Glynne: GL, Glynne notebooks 70, fols 2B–3B

Gulval, S. Gulval, July 1843 <*Blight, p. 80*[311]>.
The Church is rather a rude structure, built of granite, in a beautiful church yard shaded with large trees within a short distance of the sea. There has been much mutilation, but the most singular feature about the Church is the great inclination of the Chancel, the East wall of which is not in a straight line.[312] The Church consists of a West Tower nave & Chancel with South aisle continued to the East, a South porch & a North Transeptal chapel. <*Similar to S. Levan in arrangement* [visited in 1862].> The whole is rude Cornish Perpendicular & all the windows have been deprived of their tracery.[313]
The Tower is 3 stages in height & has a battlement & 4 coarse square pinnacles – the belfry window of 3 lights (resembling those of Ashford in Kent[314]) – in the angles of the belfry story ^below the parapet^ are 4 images set in hollows. <*The geometrical tracery seen in windows of Cornish Towers is probably Perpendicular.*> The West window of 2 lights has been mutilated, below it is a doorway with bold continuous mouldings. The tower has no buttresses. Within the plain South porch is a good plain door with arch mouldings. The Tower opens to the nave by a pointed arch rising from half octagonal shafts ^with chamfered imposts^. <*The tower arch has a plain soffit on chamfered imposts, under which is added a moulded arch on octagonal responds.*> The interior exhibits a rare collection of high backed pews. There are 6 rather narrow pointed arches dividing the South aisle, the piers octagonal and rather slender, but with coarse overhanging capitals; in some of which are sculptured shields & angel figures – but the whole is clogged with thick coats of whitewash.

---

[311] These additional notes are in Glynne's later hand and were probably made in 1870 when he revisited the area, after the publication of Blight's *West Cornwall*.
[312] The *CT*, 20 January 1858, 3, recorded that 'the South aisle was entirely rebuilt about 81 years since, when (sufficient precautions not having been taken to relieve the lateral pressure of the roof of the nave and chancel), the columns were thrust into their present slanting position'. In 1781, the royal arms and the board painted with the Ten Commandments were removed, presumably during these works, KK: P77/2/7.
[313] It is likely that the windows had been replaced by eighteenth-century sashes. Following Glynne's visit, there were two restoration programmes, of 1856–8 and 1891–3; KK: P77/2/6–7 for the former, and P77/2/20 for the latter; see also W.W. Wingfield, *Gulval Church and Churchyard Past and Present* (Penzance, 1894), 1–13, for chronological reviews of the changes. As Henderson, *Cornish Church Guide*, 104, has it: 'Its interest and antiquity have fled before the invading forces of modern munificence', chiefly of the banking family of Bolitho.
[314] As per his note on Camborne church.

The North chapel opens to the nave by 2 arches of similar character.[315] <*In the Chancel on the South are piscina & sedilia, & on the North a credence. The first is trefoiled, the others cinquefoiled, all of Decorated character.*[316]>
The roofs both of nave & aisle are coved, with plain ribs forming pannels.[317] The Font is improperly placed in the Chancel,[318] & is rather a curious specimen. The bowl is cup shaped & not large, on a square stem which has 4 shafts at the angles, with the intermediate spaces moulded. ~~At the angles also are~~ On the bowl, corresponding with the shafts, are 4 shields borne by angels, bearing, 1. Chevrons in fess. (2) a cross fleury. (3) a portcullis. (4) 3 fish impaling [fol. 3B] a plain cross. There is a barrel organ. The external elevation is as usual displeasing from the length & lowness of the body. The ground rises considerably on the North side. There are monuments to the family of Harris. There is a late door on the South side near the East end.[319]

GUNWALLOE

Lysons: BL, Add. Ms. 9462, fol. 36r.

Gunwallo – Nave & side aisles, clustered pillars, obtuse pointed arches <sketch of font>.

Glynne: GL, Glynne notebooks 16, fols 64–5

Gunwallow – S. Winwallow, 10 February 1870.
This Church derives its chief interest from its romantic and lonely situation close to the sea, amongst sand hills covered with herbage. It is wholly Perpendicular, and of the Cornish type, comprising nave & Chancel with North & South aisles & South porch. An unusual feature, but seen occasionally in Cornwall, is the low detached belfry, built on the rock against a steep ascent, near the West end of the Church. It has rather a modern character and with a pointed roof, and seen at Talland, Gwennap, St Feock, Lamorran, Mylor. The Chancel roof rises higher than that of the nave & aisles, & the aisles are not carried quite to the East end of the Chancel. The arcades have each 5 Tudor-shaped arches with piers, having the usual arrangement with

---

[315] This was completely rebuilt and incorporated into a north aisle in 1891–3.
[316] These features were subsequently restored in 1856–8; what remains are not necessarily the ancient structures; see the illustration of the original credence by Blight, *West Cornwall*, 80.
[317] This was completely replaced in 1891–3; reported in *TC*, 6 October 1892, 5: 'It was determined to re-roof the whole of the church with new timbers, the design of which was set out with much accordance with the usual Cornish "cradle" or "waggon", roof divided into bays by moulded ribs, the part near the chancel being boarded. Then Mr. William Bolitho, jun., started the idea of building a new transept on the north of the nave, which he proposed as an accommodation for the Bolitho family and to contain records of members of that family who had been buried at Gulval. In addition to this transept the north chancel aisle and the north aisle were built […] This transept and north aisle were roofed in same way the rest of the church.'
[318] Polsue, *Parochial History*, ii, 117, also found it in front of the communion table, although earlier on Lysons found it 'at the South corner'. The EDAS noted that 'it is now in its proper place', DHC: F5/17/2/4, EDAS, series of Rough Notes – sheet 25 (1862).
[319] Despite the rebuilding of the south wall in the 1780s (see fn. 312), this feature survives, comprising a four-centred arched doorway under a square hood mould.

shafts & cavetto, much as at Cury, the capitals sculptured with something like cable moulding. The south aisle has a waggon roof open with good wood-carving. Those of the nave & North aisle are inferior.[320] That of the Chancel is coved and boarded. The interior needs restoration & the arcades are whitewashed.[321] The windows of the South aisle are plain, of 3 lights, merely round-headed, & of a kind often seen in Devon & Cornwall.[322] Those of the North aisle are of 2 lights, ogee-headed with a quatrefoil in the head, having a Decorated look. The last window of this aisle is good Perpendicular of 3 lights, & that of the South aisle similar, with foliage at the points of the cusping.[323] The East window has 3 equal gables.[324] The Font in use has an octagonal bowl of granite, late & possibly modern. The South porch has a fine wood roof, having well carved ribs & cornice [65] of foliage. The doorways both within & without have Tudor arch with imposts ornamented with trefoil panelling in granite. In the Churchyard is a portion of an earlier Font – a circular bowl of Norman design.[325] Some pannels of the rood screen remain, with rude paintings of the Apostles.[326] <Blight, Cornish Churches, p. 35.>

[320] This is perhaps explained in that the roofs of these parts of the church were repaired in the 1820s; for example, the rural dean in 1822 noted: 'Roof of Middle Aisle uncovered'; KK: AD59/74, 277; yet the elevated chancel roof may have been an original feature reflecting the prestige ownership of the chancel by Hailes Abbey (Gloucestershire). Gunwalloe church was a dependent parochial chapel of Breage, and its patronage was awarded to Hailes by the earl of Cornwall in 1246; Henderson, Cornish Church Guide, 105.

[321] Glynne visited the church shortly after a restoration programme had started (1869–71); see A.H. Cummings, The Churches and Antiquities of Cury & Gunwalloe in the Lizard District (London, 1875), 128.

[322] These were rebuilt at the restoration following Glynne's visit but retain the three light 'round-headed' tracery suggestive of the 'South Hams' style; see Colvin, Essays, 22–51. Gilbert, Historical Survey, ii, 771, found them 'heavy' Gothic and strengthened by 'iron gratings', that is, fixings holding small squares of glass.

[323] The remains of the stone tracery of one of these windows was figured by Cummings, Cury & Gunwalloe, opp. 128, with a three-light window, the central light having a high-level transom that formed the base to an uppermost compartment with multi-cusping of the arch above. These fragments were found propped up against the west wall of the churchyard; Polsue, Parochial History, ii, 125, found them 'fixed for preservation to the east wall of the porch'.

[324] 'New roof throughout the church, retaining the carved oak in the south aisle. The chancel was rebuilt and extended eastward two feet. The west wall of nave and a new west window inserted (as also one in chancel). Not one of these windows is comparable to the remains of the original [...] A new window in west end of north aisle, and the stone-work of all the remaining windows restored, and the church reseated. Paving the passages with Bridgewater tiles which took the place of the previous "lime ash". The church was opened with a festival on 5 June 1871'; KK: P78/1/1, notes in the parish register.

[325] This second font is now inside the church, with fluted moulding underneath and arrowhead decoration around some of the bowl, Sedding, Norman Architecture, 166–7. The first font described by Glynne was, as he surmised, a nineteenth-century copy of an earlier model.

[326] The remaining probably sixteenth-century rood screen panels are now mounted behind the north and south doors, each comprising a rich, flamboyant traceried framework above four panels, painted with figures of the Apostles; see Bond and Camm, Roodscreens and Roodlofts, ii, 386.

GWENNAP

Lysons: BL, Add. Ms. 9462, fol. 36r.

Guennap – Nave & side aisles, clustered pillars, square tower tiled on the South side of the Church, detached from it at the extremity of the Church yard. Modern marble font.

Glynne: GL, Glynne notebooks 16, fols 45–6

Gwennap – S. Wenap, 26 August 1862.[327]
A large Church having 3 equal aisles, without architectural distinction of Chancel & a South porch. The belfry is detached & very nearly resembles that of S. Feock, both being at a distance from the Church, but this is situated on the South extremity of the Church yard, touching the outer wall. It has a pointed roof & window to the bell chamber & door below.
The Church is wholly Perpendicular, the Northern & Eastern windows have been recently restored & are of 4 lights. The West window of 3, those on the South are still unrestored, & without mullions, but the hoods externally remain.[328] The arcades on each side are of the usual Cornish Perpendicular character, both as regards arches & piers, the arch mouldings are good, there are 7 arches on each side, of which 2 are [46] within the Chancel, the difference of which is marked by ~~the roof~~ a low stone screen[329] & a slight difference in the capitals of the pillars which in the Chancel have rather richer sculpture.
There is a West gallery & organ.[330] The Font seems new, square bowl of polished granite, with scalloping & inlaid sculpture representing sacred emblems.[331]
The outer doorway of the porch has granite arch mouldings & shafts.
The Church yard is very extensive, beautifully kept & planted with avenues of fine trees.
The pulpit is new, & of granite.

---

[327] Glynne visited just before the start of a restoration programme that continued into the 1880s. See KK: P79/2/2, for a list of subscriptions, accounts, and report of restoration work of 1863; and KK: P79/2/3 for the financial accounts to 1880.
[328] Gilbert, *Historical Survey*, ii, 804, wrote that 'five of its noble window frames have been deprived of their stone mullions, and the remaining fragments, together with other ornamental stone work, seem to exist merely to display the mangling of modern Vandalism. Venetian frames have been substituted for the majestic ones which have been removed, and it may be argued in favour of these spoliations, that additional light has been obtained in the churches so metamorphosed, instead of the prevailing gloom [...] About forty years ago, the author of this work remembers when very young, to have seen these windows nearly filled with stained glass, and the figures of male and female saints caught his particular notice.' Shortly after his account was published, the rural dean reported in 1822 that 'the roof of Middle Aisle in a very defective state, Ends of Rafters quite decayed and the Lead also in a very bad state', KK: AD59/74, 279, suggestive of a more generalised fabric decay.
[329] This was removed by the incumbent in 1871; see *WMN*, 8 May 1871, 4. 'Successive restorations in the eighteenth and nineteenth centuries are responsible for the removal of practically everything of interest'; C.C. James, *A History of the Parish of Gwennap in Cornwall* (Penzance [1949]), 30.
[330] See LPL: ICBS 637 (1825–6) for a west gallery, the documents including a floorplan.
[331] Glynne noted it correctly as granite, whereas Lysons thought it was marble, perhaps uncertain of its highly polished finish.

Fig. 38. Font sides, Gwinear
church; from the British
Library Archive, Add. Ms.
9445, fol. 130r.

GWINEAR

Lysons: BL, Add. Ms. 9445, fol. 130r.

Gwyniar – Monument of Elizabeth, wife of John Arundell Esq., of Sithney, daughter
of Tobias Lanyon of Gwinnear.[332]
Pinnacles – tower, at one corner a turret, at the others plain pinnacles. 2 aisles,[333]
clustered columns &c.
Font octagonal with a circle on pedestal <sketches of the font sides[334]>. (Fig. 38)

[332] This comprises an inscription incised in lower-case Roman script on a white marble panel
framed by a plain black marble/slate frame. It commemorates Elizabeth Arundell (d. 1683);
see Gilbert, *Historical Survey*, ii, 699.
[333] Lysons did not note the additional chapel as a northwards extension to the north aisle,
despite it opening to the aisle via three bays with piers of the standard type.
[334] The font bowl was restored in a pseudo-Norman style with the date inscribed on it of 1727,
but the circular shaft and the base are original; see Sedding, *Norman Architecture*, 160–1.

GWITHIAN

Lysons: BL, Add. Ms. 9642, fol. 36r.

Gwythian – nave, chancel, south aisle[335] & small north Transept. Capitals with the scroll of foliage. Clustered pillars, font square, covered up with board.[336]
Standard fig trees in the Church yard grow about in several parts of the parish 'like thorns' or such like said the sexton.
Church stands close to the sand.[337] Quatrefoils &c. under the battlements of the Tower.

ILLOGAN

Lysons: BL, Add. Ms. 9462, fol. 37r.

St. Illogan[338] – nave & aisles, plain clustered pillars on the north of the chancel. Basset chapel with brasses of John Basset Esq. & his wife & children on the wall, 1603.[339]

[335] The EDAS noted that the chancel was rebuilt in 1782 with 'roundheaded east window and flat ceiling [...] the roof thrown open in 1859. Previous to this all the windows in the church, except one, were roundheaded, or square', DHC: F5/17/2/4, EDAS, series of Rough Notes – sheet 26 (1863). The church was radically rebuilt in 1867 to return it to a cruciform shape and is now quite unlike the building noted by Lysons. The *RCG*, 2 May 1867, 8, reported: 'In order to restore the church to its original form, the late Third Pointed [Perpendicular] south aisle and arcade have been taken away and a new south transept built; with the exception of the arcade all remains of value or interest had been long ago demolished. The shafts, capitals and bases of the arcade have been preserved, and used in the construction of a new Lych-gate. The whole of the north and south walls of nave, the transepts and a portion of the Chancel have been rebuilt. The old First Pointed [Early English] arch into the north transept (which was of sandstone) was found to be in a very crumbling condition, and unfortunately there was no possibility of retaining it [...] The old aumbrye or recess in the north transept has been faithfully restored. The new arch into the chancel is of two orders [...] The end window of the south transept is new, of three lights, with First Pointed [Early English] tracery. The side windows of chancel are of two lights, the pointed heads being filled in with circles and trefoil cusps [...] The three-light east window, erected a few years ago, has been retained [...] The old north and south doorways have been rebuilt. The outer doorway of porch is new. The tower has been reopened, and the fine arch – a regular Cornish tower arch – thrown into view. The tower floor is new and the pinnacles of tower have been thoroughly repaired. The roofs of nave, transepts, and chancel are entirely new, of red deal, unstained.' See Mattingly, 'Distinctiveness by Omission', 141–3.
[336] Most likely this was an eighteenth-century reaction to the font's appearance; see Sedding, *Norman Architecture*, 165. At the 1867 restoration, four supporting shafts of serpentine were added.
[337] Remarked upon by Lysons, *Cornwall*, cxcix, 130: 'The church-town would have shared the same fate [of being subsumed by sands], had it not been prevented by the timely exertions of the church-wardens, who, with all possible expedition, caused large plantations to be made of a species of rush.' The rural dean ordered in 1812 that 'the Trench outside the Church to be cleared up, and the Church Yard (which is very foul) to be broke up and cleared of weeds. Recommended to plant the Sand outside the Church fence with rushes, to prevent it filling the Trench', KK: AD59/74, 319.
[338] The church was completely rebuilt in 1846 to the south of the old church, which had been acknowledged by the parishioners as beyond repair, KK: X434/1 (1838–45). The body of the old church was demolished, leaving the tower as a landmark; KK: P88/2/1, are elevations etc. for rebuilding Illogan church and retaining the old tower as a part of the new building (1844–5), which was an idea later abandoned in favour of a completely new church. See LPL: ICBS no. 3546 (1844–7) for the rebuild, with plans in the documentation. For a description of the old church, see DHC: F5/17/2/4, EDAS, series of Rough Notes – sheet 25 (1862). The opening of the new church was reported in the *RCG*, 6 November 1846, 3.
[339] Borlase, BL, Egerton Ms. 2657, fol. 46r., recorded this monument as 'in Tyhydy Chancel [...] formerly on the floor'; it is now on the east wall of the north aisle of the new church.

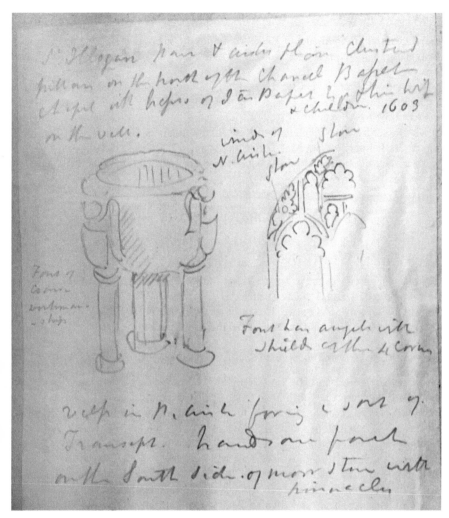

Fig. 39. Font and architectural details, Illogan church; from the British Library Archive, Add. Ms. 9462, fol. 37r.

Font of coarse workmanship. Font has angels with shields at the 4 corners[340] <sketch>. (Fig. 39)
Recess in North aisle forming a sort of Transept, handsome porch on the South side of moor stone with pinnacles <sketch of window of North aisle incorporating carved spandrels>. <Cross sketch> on the South side of the church, another stump of a smaller one.[341]

Gilbert, *Historical Survey*, ii, 688, found the church a 'venerable Gothic edifice, indebted for most of its ornaments, to the Basset family, many of which are interred, within a spacious vault, under the northern aisle'. Lysons, *Cornwall*, 144, noted only that the church and churchyard contained Basset family monuments.

[340] This was considerably reworked during the 1846 rebuild (possibly using the early fifteenth-century font at St Ives as a model) and sited in the new church.
[341] See Langdon, *West Cornwall*, 44, no. 62.

Lysons: BL, Add. Ms. 9445, fol. 132r.

Illogan Church, monuments of Basset of Tehidy in this parish.

John Basset Esq., 1603, brass figure & his wife, daughter of Sir Francis Godolphin, Knt.

Monument of Francis Basset Esq., 1769, father to Lord Dunstanville, with a medallion.

John Collins M.A., Rector of Redruth [erected a] monument of his wife, daughter of Mr Basset by Mary, daughter of Rev. John Pendarves, & sole heir of her uncle Alexander Pendarves Esq. Mrs Collins ob. 1743.

In Churchyard, John Pendarves Basset, grandson of Lord Dunstanville, 1739, aged 25. King Charles letter.[342]

JACOBSTOW (Fig. 40)

Lysons: BL, Add. Ms. 9462, fol. 36r.

Jacobstow Church – Nave & Aisles with a chancel. Remains of rich stained glass in East window of South Aisle & Chancel.[343]

Font like Warbstow. Pillars &c. like ye other Cornish Churches.

Tower handsome with pinnacles & ~~4foils~~ tracery at the base.

Glynne: NLW, Ms. 185 (unpaginated field notebook [1857])

Jacobstow – Tower Cornish, on [illegible] no buttresses, battlement, 4 crocketed pinnacles, stair turret at North East, base swells for quatrefoil panel at base.

Porch embattled, granite. Spandrels foliage, continuous mouldings. Inner plain, niche over it. Porch stone vaulting, all white wash.

Windows, 3 light Perpendicular Cornish, 4 lights East of aisles, pointed; Chancel window – properly [illegible] aisle. East end mauled.

Octagonal turret preserved North, 1 bay. Tower, West doorway, labeled and spandrels, West window 3 lights. 2nd stage Tower has on West, octagonal niche.

Pued. Arcades, 4 late Perpendicular Tudor piers <sketch of cross-section> coved roofs of aisles, ribs & bosses, centre is more altered, ribs gone. Pulpit badly placed in centre. Remains ancient wood seats, perhaps ends of benches & mounted high.[344] East window internally has Decorated mouldings & shafts, fine, capitals moulded, octagonal bases; tracery altered; very good mouldings. All internally clogged white wash.

Font fine <sketch> square, square stem, 4 heads at angles, wheeled circles each face, and dragons heads over wheels; shaped stem.

---

[342] This did not survive the move of fittings from the old to the new church.

[343] None of this remains, but Lysons' comment is expanded by Gilbert, *Historical Survey*, ii, 563 'The windows were formerly beautified with a variety of stained glass, among which were several shields of armorial bearings [...] The last of these ornaments was destroyed about the year 1814, "merely", as the parishioners say, "because it darkened the church".'

[344] This 'mounted high' comment is puzzling, although as box pews were introduced in 1830, perhaps some of the bench ends were incorporated into their partitions, suggested by Glynne's later written-up notes; see fn. 348.

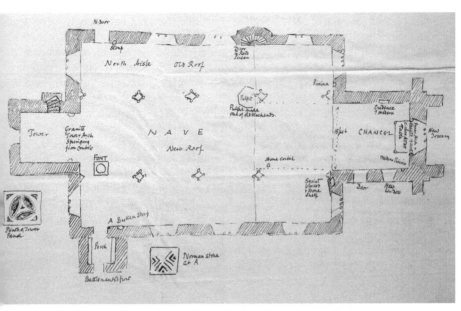

40. Ground plan of Jacobstow church; reproduced with the kind permission of the Royal ~~titution~~ of Cornwall, Courtney Library, Henderson Ms. 'East Cornwall', 173.

Stoup inside North door. An old Chest. 2 light belfry window. Grove of firs. Tower smooth masonry, roofs slated, low.

Glynne: GL, Glynne notebooks 14, fols 68–70

Jacobstow, S. James, 23 January 1857.
This Church is wholly Perpendicular, has a nave & Chancel with North & South aisles, West Tower & South porch. The windows of the usual Cornish type, of 3 lights, except those at the Eastern extremities which are of 4. The Chancel extends a little Eastward of the aisles & its East end has been rather mauled. There are 4 arches on each side of the body, of Tudor shape & late, the piers of common form <sketch>. The roofs coved, having ribs & bosses [69] those of the aisles rather better than of the central space. There are ~~traces of~~ Decorated mouldings in the East window internally, & of very good character, with shafts having moulded capitals & octagonal bases, but the tracery has been altered.[345] The whole of the interior is much clogged with whitewash.[346] There is a rood turret on the North side.[347]

[345] The shafts, capitals, and bases remain, although the rest of the window was replaced in 1886.
[346] As encouraged by the orders of the rural deans in 1814, 1824, 1825, KK: AD59/74, 15–16.
[347] At the restoration in 1886, 'on opening up the rood-loft stairs the body portion of a knight formed of plaster was found; the head was gone, and is said to have been squared off and built into the west wall [*sic*] of the chancel, which was rebuilt within the memory of an old mason. It is said by an old inhabitant that in rebuilding the north chancel wall some eighty years ago the heads of many monuments were then used as building material', *RCG*, 13 August 1886, 6. In 1824, the rural dean ordered: 'The East Wall of the North Aisle must be taken down several feet & built up again', perhaps relating to this memory, KK: AD59/74, 16.

Some remains of ancient carved seats may still be seen, but with ugly modern deal all about them. The pulpit is most objectionably placed in the centre.[348] The Font is a curious one of a Cornish kind, & perhaps early. The bowl square, having heads at the angles of the upper part, & formed downwards into a kind of cup shape, dying into a short octagonal stem. On each face is a circle containing a kind of wheel or star & over it a dragons head.[349] <sketch> Within the North doorway is a stoup. The South porch is wholly of granite & embattled, its roof is a good stone vault now whitewashed.[350] The outer doorway square headed, having foliage in the spandrels & continuous mouldings. The inner door plain, & over it a dilapidated niche. The Tower is regularly Cornish & of granite, without buttresses & tapering – it has a battlement & 4 large octagonal crocketed pinnacles – at the North East a stair turret. The base swells out & along it is a panneled band.[351] The West window of 3 lights & under it a labeled doorway with spandrels. On the West side of the Tower in the 2nd stage is an ogee canopied niche. The belfry windows of 2 lights. The masonry of the Tower very smooth & fine. There is a fine [70] ancient chest in the Church. The East end of the Chancel mantled in ivy. In the Church yard a fine grove of firs.[352]

KENWYN

Lysons: BL, Add. Ms. 9445, fol. 148r.

[348] 'In 1830 the late rector, the Rev. John Glanville, took down the old oak benches, and they were sold in lots, and in their place arose the square horse-boxes and the three-decker pulpit which have been removed this year', *RCG*, 13 August 1886, 6. Like Glynne, the EDAS noted 'a central mass of the clerk's desk, reading desk, pulpit', Glanville clearly favouring a pre-Tractarian approach to preaching, DHC: F5/17/2/4, EDAS, series of Rough Notes – sheet 27 (1864). Perhaps the pulpit's location was also in response to the rural dean commenting in 1738, that 'the floor of the Alleys uneven & a great pit nigh ye pulpit not paved – the reading desk so narrow that ye minister cannot kneel, (made so upon ye account of an infirm minister)', DHC: DR, PR362–4/30/3.
[349] See Sedding, *Norman Architecture*, 167–8, pl. LXXV.
[350] Prior to the restoration, the porch was 'nearly three-quarters of an inch thick in whitewash, so that the carving could not be seen', *RCG*, 13 August 1886, 6.
[351] As noted by Lysons, and comprises mouchettes in roundels and quatrefoils in squares.
[352] The restoration of the church commenced in April 1886. 'The builder [...] has torn down some portions of the fabric [...] There are several parts of the fabric which it was thought first would not need rebuilding, but on closer observation the builder found that these parts must be attended to in order to make the church thoroughly "weather-tight"', reported the *WT*, 27 April 1886, 6. 'The church has been reseated; the windows have been repaired and reglazed, all, with the exception of the tower window, with cathedral glass; the nave roof has been entirely renewed; the aisle roofs have been reslated and releaded; and the stonework has been cleaned down and repointed. The east and south chancel walls have been rebuilt on their old lines; two new windows have been traced in them; the floors have been relaid and renewed. The chancel floor has been tiled throughout. The pulpit is new, except the panels [made from bench ends] [...] The north aisle and the chancel were in such a dangerous condition that they would soon have fallen [...] A small portion of the screen now serves as a chimney ornament in a cottage hard by'; *RCG*, 13 August 1886, 6. A grant was made for general repairs (LPL) ICBS 9009 (1885–6)), including a plan of the new church and a sketch of the tracery of the east window of the north aisle, demonstrating its precariousness before it was renewed.

Kenwyn Church – tower with crocketed pinnacles, south aisle & north transept, clustered columns. Modern porch. On the capital of the middle column leading to transept, angels, on the capital of the East pilaster a very reduced figure of a bishop with his hands raised up.[353]

Glynne: GL, Glynne notebooks 17, fols 152–3

Kenwyn [1843].[354]
This Church is beautifully situated on an eminence, the tower forming a fine object among the trees. It is not however a very interesting structure & entirely of late Perpendicular work of the most ordinary Cornish kind. It consists of a West Tower, a nave with South aisle, & North & South Transeptal chapels.[355] The tower is of granite, 3 stories high with battlement & 4 square pinnacles panneled & crocketed & having the small embattled moulding. The belfry window of 3 lights & ugly, the West doorway has a label & trefoils in the spandrels. The buttresses are [153] not at the angles but set near to them. There is no distinction of Chancel & the nave is divided from the aisle by 6 obtuse Tudor arches, the piers lozenge with mouldings & small shafts having individual octagonal capitals. The Transeptal Chapels each open to the nave by wide single Tudor arches on clustered shafts, some having the capitals sculptured with figures.
Many of the windows have been modernised, & those which have escaped are of indifferent tracery.[356] The two equal East gables have the windows of 5 lights, with contracted arches.[357] The exterior is very ordinary. The South porch is very large, its entrance by a pointed arch on octagonal shafts. The interior is neat but bare; there is a small organ. The Font is square upon 4 round legs & a square plinth. The Churchyard is of unusual extent, and on the North side of the Church is carried

---

[353] These unusual capitals were left unchanged at the restorations.

[354] 'The church was enlarged in the fifteenth century [now considered more likely in the sixteenth century], but a series of bad restorations from 1820–62 has contrived to deprive it of all interest'; Henderson, *Cornish Church Guide*, 117. The rural dean reported in 1812 that 'the Roof of Chancel much out of repair and admits wet, & the roof of the Church in general wants repair, the walls & roof of the Church in general wants repair, the walls & roof of Tregavethan Aisle out of repair, and also the rails of the Pulpit Stairs'. In 1818: 'The Pillars & South Wall considerable [*sic*] out of perpendicular and should be immediately inspected'; KK: AD 59/74, 201. Gilbert, *Historical Survey*, ii, 809, noted the church 'has been lately taken down, and is re-building upon an enlarged plan'. See LPL: ICBS 82 (1818–20), for enlargement. In 1765, Borlase noted: 'Over the door of the Tregavethan Ile, Kenwen Church, there is an Inscrn. much defac'd by the Masons in order to smooth the face of the stones', BL, Egerton Ms. 2657, fol. 105r. This no longer exists.

[355] The south transept is a structure completely of the 1820 restoration; see the groundplan with the ICBS papers. The north transept and tower were left virtually unaltered at that time, although the walls of the south aisle, the south porch, and the east ends were all rebuilt. 'Much space is gained for new pews (which will be free-sittings) by reducing the number of Pillars' in the arcade, although this never happened as presumably a financial step too far. The north transept was eventually rebuilt in 1855 by the owner, J. Ennis Vivian; DHC: F5/17/2/4, EDAS, series of Rough Notes – sheet 29 (1866).

[356] Glynne visited before a second major rebuilding in 1862; see KK: P98/2/18/1–10, 23, 25–7, for financial accounts and correspondence etc.

[357] *The Ecclesiologist* 4 (1845), 241, noted 'two new east windows of early perpendicular work have lately been put up', presumably after Glynne's visit; see Warner, *A Time to Build*, 192.

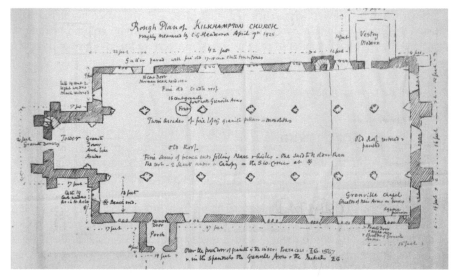

Fig. 41. Groundplan of Kilkhampton church; reproduced with the kind permission of the Royal Institution of Cornwall, Courtney Library, Henderson Ms. 'East Cornwall', 206.

over several acres, which being on very uneven ground & planted with large trees presents a striking appearance.

KILKHAMPTON (Fig. 41)

Lysons: BL, Add. Ms. 9462, fol. 38r.

Kilkhampton – August 2 <sketch of font with shields[358]>. (Fig. 42)
Nave & side aisles, large & handsome. Clustered pillars & obtuse arches.
Windows all uniform <sketch of tracery>.
About ¾ of a mile west of Kilkhampton Church are the remains of a Strong fortress called the castle hill – consisting of an oval monument, very steep, divided into three parts by 2 steep ditches <sketch[359]>.
Fols 37v., 38v. <sketches of South doorway, one measured with sections[360]>.

Lysons: BL, Add. Ms. 9445, fol. 151r.

[Inscriptions on the monument to Sir Bevill Granville of Stowe (d. 1643), erected in 1714 by his grandson George, lord Lansdowne, published verbatim, *Cornwall*, 166.]

---

[358] Lysons highlights four shields (1) *gules, three clarions or*, for Grenville, (2) *three fesses dancetty impaling two chevrons*, (3) *two chevrons impaling two chevrons*, (4) *a saltire*. For this sixteenth-century font, see Henderson, *Cornish Church Guide*, 123; no mention is made of the font cover shown in Buckler's drawing.

[359] This is the site of Penstowe Castle, a late Norman motte and bailey construction; see Henderson, *Cornish Church Guide*, 122.

[360] Published by Lysons, *Cornwall*, ccxxvii, and pl. opposite. The four orders of this doorway are described by Sedding, *Norman Architecture*, 173–4, pls LXXVII, LXXVIII; see also A. Woodcock, 'Beasts and Beakheads: Romanesque Sculpture at Morwenstow', in P. Holden (ed.), *Celebrating Pevsner: New Research on Cornish Architecture* (London, 2017), 41–8, at 43–4, 46; and the CRSBI, available online at: https://www.crsbi.ac.uk/view-item?i=7062 [accessed September 2023].

Fig. 42. Font in Kilkhampton church (1827); from the British Library Archive, Add. Ms. 36360, fol. 161, drawing by John Buckler.

Fig. 43. Monument to Sir Bevill Granville, Kilkhampton church (1827); from the British Library Archive, Add. Ms. 36360, fol. 162, drawing by John Buckler.

Monument surrounded by warlike instruments, at the bottom a helmet reversed with two battleaxes stuck into it, one on each side, supposed to allude to the manner of Sir Bevill Granville being slain.[361] (Fig. 43)
Memorials of the families of Orchard of Aldercombe, Waddon of Tonacombe & Westlake of Elmsworthy. Col. Orchard of Hartland Abbey representative of former & owner of Aldercombe [illegible].[362]

Glynne: GL, Glynne notebooks 17, fols 74–5

---

[361] It is attributed to the sculptor Michael Chuke (1679–1742), who worked under Grinling Gibbons at Stowe House; see C.J. Easter, 'Michael Chuke of Kilkhampton and a Call to Arms', *Church Monuments Society Newsletter* 16.1 (2000), 7–10; and Roscoe *et al.*, *Dictionary*, 273.
[362] Published in brief, *Cornwall*, 165–6, but with no elaboration of the illegible text. There survive monuments to Richard Westlake (d. 1704), of Emsworthy, gent., and Sarah Cottell (d. 1727), of Aldercombe, but none to the Waddon or Orchard families. Probably they were lost at the restoration in 1860, see fn. 364.

Fig. 44. Kilkhampton church interior looking east (1827); from the British Library Archive, Add. Ms. 36360, fol. 157, drawing by John Buckler.

Kilkhampton [before 1840].
This is a light & handsome Church consisting of a West Tower, & a nave & Chancel with coextensive aisles, & no Clerestory. The whole is Rectilinear, excepting a South doorway which is of rich Norman work. The Tower is of 3 stages, embattled & crowned with 4 crocketed pinnacles, the West doorway has a label, & over it is a window of 4 lights. The other windows are numerous & mostly of 4 lights, & of very plain character.[363] There is a plain South porch, & the Chancel has a small South door, over which is a stone tablet with a canopied niche & shield bearing the Granville arms. The Interior is spacious & presents no distinction of nave & Chancel – on each side are 7 Tudor arches with light lozenge piers, having a shaft at each angle with an octagonal capital. (Fig. 44)
The Tower opens by a fine lofty arch. The roofs are coved & divided into panneled compartments by ribs having at their points of intersection rich foliated bosses.[364]

[363] As Lysons noted, these are without elaborate tracery, as the latest type of Perpendicular window design of the 'South Hams' style. Their date is probably just pre-Reformation; see Colvin, *Essays*, 22–51.
[364] Glynne visited the church twenty years or so before its restoration in 1860. According to a press report on the restoration, he would 'have beheld a mournful sight – the deep-stained granite columns, the high-pewed chancel, the defaced and fast decaying oak carving, and the lavish indulgence in white and yellow wash, would have wearied his eye, and chilled his heart; whilst the classic architecture which blocked up the east end, and surrounded the Holy Table with ornaments by no means of Christian type or character, would have offended his taste'; *RCG*, 28 September 1860, 6. The report continues: 'It is gratifying to see all these blemishes

There are many ancient bench ends enriched with beautiful [75] wood carving & tracery, on one of which are figures of Moses & Aaron. The pulpit has some good carving of a later date.[365] The Font is octagonal, panneled with shields. There is a fine monument to Sir Beville Granville who died in 1714 [*recte* 1643, erected in 1714].

LADOCK

Lysons: BL, Add. Ms. 9445, fol. 159r.

Ladock Church – tower, clustered columns & North aisle & South transept. No monuments[366] <sketch of font with floral panels[367]>

LAMORRAN

Lysons: BL, Add. Ms. 9445, fol. 165v.

Lamorran[368] – very small church, nave & small North transept, in which a large monument against the north wall, 9 or 10 feet high, all of wood, with kneeling figures

now removed, and the ancient sanctuary shining forth in all its early beauty [...] The feeble parts of the main walls have been rebuilt; the roof stripped, boarded, and re-covered with new slate; the plaster and whitewash have been removed: the pews dethroned and replaced by new carved oak standards and seats; and the beautiful and richly-carved cradle roof of oak opened to public view, cleared of the plaster ceiling which concealed it. The Chancel also has been re-modelled, the cumbrous and inappropriate Grecian work removed, and the side Chapels have been parted off by traceried and carved oak screens [...] The whole of the East end has been rebuilt, and three rich traceried windows in granite hare been inserted in place of the old round-headed ones, which were dilapidated.' The following year it was reported that 'the new wood carving is sumptuously and well executed, and bears comparison with the old with considerable advantage. At the communion end of the church the restoration and additions are abundant and elegant. The numerous windows, with colours "richly light", chiefly memorial, shed a dazzling, though "dim religious light", and in conjunction with the beautifully tiled floor, and elaborate screen, give quite an aspect of gorgeousness to this part of the edifice'; *NDG*, 1 October 1861, 4. In 1859, the parish secured a mortgage of £400 towards the costs of repair, KK: P102/6/1.

[365] Glynne did not record the large reredos (now gone), which was, according to Gilbert, 'presented to the church by the master builders of the earl of Bath's magnificent mansion at Stowe, and is truly handsome', *Historical Survey*, ii, 548. However, perhaps Glynne confused imagery on the reredos with that of the pew ends, as Gilbert's description continues: 'It contains the portraits of Moses and Aaron', whereas the bench ends incorporate no such figures.

[366] Gilbert, *Historical Survey*, ii, 828, agreed: 'The interior of Ladock Church is extremely plain, not even a single monument has been raised against its walls.' However, a tomb slab, perhaps once in the churchyard, is now mural inside the south porch, to Nicholas Cornelius (d. 1632), which bears a recumbent skeleton, and a skull and bones sculpted in flat relief; see Cockerham, *Continuity and Change*, 80, pl. 151.

[367] See Sedding, *Norman Architecture*, 176–7.

[368] In 1760, Rev. Samuel Gurney, rural dean of Powder, visited Lamorran and reported 'the Chancel of Lemorran, now Mr. Bedfords, as Being Quite Ruinous', DHC: DR, PR 362–4/28/17; yet seven years later, the rural dean Rev. James Walker reported that he could not get to Lamorran 'but by water, & therefore was obliged to defer seeing it till very lately. The Church there is nothing amiss in worth taking notice of, ^or^ that is not promised to be amended [...] but I have wrote Mr. Bedford by this Post concerning it, & doubt not (as he is a man of honesty) he'll soon set all matters right which I have desired him to do soon, as I am persuaded you will enquire after it again', DHC: DR, PR 362–4/28/19. Quite how 'ruinous' the chancel was in 1760 is difficult to

in bas relief like those in slate with inscription in capitals, under which are coats of arms John Verman Esq., lord of manor, Patron of advowson, 1658 & his wife Catherine, daughter & co-heiress of John Trehane of Trehane, 1665.[369]
Turret detached, font circular & plain on one short pedestal & four small circular pillars with heads rather as at St Wenn.
Arms over church door, 2 bends ([illegible] the Coat of Verman).[370]

Glynne: GL, Glynne notebooks 16, fol. 8

Lamorran – S. Moren, 12 February 1858.
A small Church, cruciform in plan & without a steeple, lately much renovated & partially rebuilt.[371] The roofs appear new & have a ridge crest. The Chancel arch looks Early English, with shafts having abaci, the arches to the Transepts pointed & quite plain. The windows are squareheaded Perpendicular in the nave, in the Chancel Decorated; the East window of 3 lights <sketch> some new stained glass & a little old appears in the windows.[372]
There is a low ivied shed-like building in the Church yard, which contains 3 large bells, almost on the ground.[373]
The situation is most lovely: amidst woods on a picturesque creek of Falmouth Harbour.

assess, although clearly there were serious structural issues with the building at that time. Rev. Thomas Bedford was rector 1759–1803, with, therefore, responsibility for the upkeep of the chancel.

[369] There is some confusion here. There was no north transept at this date but only a southern one, and the monument is an oblong slate plate within a wide wooden frame, sculpted in flat relief with effigies, inscriptions, and shields, located on the south wall of the transept. One inscription mentions John Verman as 'Dominus de Lamorran et hujus Eccliasiae Patronus', hence Lysons' note of the advowson. Shortly after John Verman's death, the manor was conveyed to William Walrond of Bradfield, Esq., as part of the marriage of his eldest son to Mary, John Verman's daughter, DHC: 1926B/W/T/31/8 (1660).

[370] These arms were later removed. The heraldry is likely not that of Verman but of the Halet family, lords of Lamorran in the fourteenth century; see fn. 372.

[371] Gilbert, *Historical Survey*, ii, 835, recorded the original church as an aisleless structure, with a small transept on the south side. Following alterations in 1845 under the supervision of Lord Falmouth's Steward (Polsue, *Parochial History*, ii, 388), further restoration plans were publicised in *The Ecclesiologist* 15 (1854), 359. William White, architect, was to add a north transept 'matching that on the south side, and to build a small vestry between the new transept and the north side of the chancel. As the existing chancel is not larger than a sanctuary, and the building cannot be extended eastwards, Mr. White treats the present chancel as a sanctuary, inserting a sanctuary arch which will spring from detached circular shafts [...] the new chancel will be guarded on three sides by low screens [...] Mr. White has raised the roofs to a good pitch, and has altered the windows into good Pointed ones of early tracery.' Much of what Glynne saw – the Early English 'chancel arch' – was completely new therefore, for which see Mattingly, 'Distinctiveness by Omission', 140, 145–6.

[372] The medieval glass comprises several fragments from a Golgotha, an inscription in early sixteenth-century(?) *textura*, and a shield (reversed) with *two bends*, possibly for de Halet (*or, two bends sable*), hence associated with the arms over the doorway.

[373] This belfry was left virtually unrestored during the work on the church in the mid nineteenth century.

LANDEWEDNACK

Lysons: BL, Add. Ms. 9462, fol. 38r.

Landewednack – Nave & North aisle & South transept, with opening to the altar. Clustered pillars & Circular arches. South door with chevron moulds &c. Circular arch filled up & a pointed door under it. Much obscured by a thick coat of whitewash <sketch of arch>.
Fol. 38v. <sketch of font[374]>. (Fig. 45)

Glynne: GL, Glynne notebooks, 13 fols 49–50

Landewednack – S^t nnty ui S. Winwolas 17 February 1849. ⟨*Blight, p. 53 &c.*[375]⟩ This Church has a North aisle along both nave & Chancel which are quite without separation, a South Transept, West Tower & South porch. There is the prevailing Cornish type, but with some earlier features, which make this Church more interesting than most in the county. The porch touches the Transept & has some nice stone groining, the boss enriched with an angel bearing a scroll. There are also shield bearing angels, supporting the corner ribs. The porch has a plain rough battlement, & internally stone benches. The South door is Norman with one order chevroned, the other exhibiting a series of square tesserae with various sculptures, some with circles, some with chevrons, but not uniform.[376] There are shafts to the inner member only. <*The Norman door arch is remarkably lofty.*> Within this Norman arch is inserted a Third Pointed door with panneled spandrels. The Tower is plain Third Pointed with battlement & 4 crocketed pinnacles, divided by one string, having a west window of 3 lights, & belfry window of 2, & no buttresses. <*The tower is without buttresses; 3 bells. The tower arch has plain soffit. The bells all ancient.*[377]> The Tower arch is a rude pointed one on imposts, & the Tower has thick walls.[378] The roofs are cradle & ribbed, the ribs of the North aisle more enriched, & ribs crossing opposite to the Transept.[379] There is an arcade of 5 obtuse arches, with the usual piers of Third Pointed character <sketch>, the shafts having octagonal caps. The whole arcade of granite and not painted.
[50] There is a hagioscope cutting off the angle between the Transept and Chancel having a detached pier with mouldings & square capital, also a late mullioned square headed window lighting the hagioscope.[380] The East window is of 3 lights apparently

---

[374] Lysons, *Cornwall*, ccxxxiii–ccxxxiv, pl. opp. ccxxxiv, no. 1.

[375] The supplementary notes relating to this church (fols 48v., 49v.) are consistent with Glynne's reading of Blight, *West Cornwall*, 53–7, following his visit. For example, Blight illustrates the high Norman doorway (55) and mentions the three bells (56), illustrating the founders' marks, which details prompt Glynne's additions.

[376] Sedding, *Norman Architecture*, 182, pl. LXXX, describes the outer voussoir as decorated with characteristic zig-zag patterns and the inner one with simple devices such as three concentric circles, redolent of the Trinity, a cross in a circle, and a single decorative pattern.

[377] E.H.W. Dunkin, *The Church Bells of Cornwall: Their Archaeology and Present Condition* (London, 1878), 24–5, 29, notes the pre-Reformation inscriptions on the bells.

[378] The EDAS noted that 'the vicar, Mr. Robinson, has restored the chancel and opened up the tower arch', DHC: F5/17/2/4, EDAS, series of Rough Notes – sheet 28 (1864); Polsue, *Parochial History*, ii, 391, notes that the work was done in 1862.

[379] That is, in the bay of the nave opposite the transept, the ribs run diagonally, extending over the wider space, as would have been the case at Grade.

[380] The original window had a central mullion that is now missing, as is the stone step outside the window. The north face of the capital above the pillar forming the hagioscope was altered

Fig. 45. Font in Landewednack church (1746); reproduced by kind permission of Devon Archives & Local Studies, DHC, Z19/16/1, 62, drawing by William Borlase.

Middle Pointed. That at the East of the aisle is of 4 lights, Third Pointed but at first sight having a Middle Pointed look.[381] On the South side is one Middle Pointed window of 2 lights. On the North, the windows are of three lights, Third Pointed, with foliations but no tracery. The South Transept end window is Third Pointed of 3 lights, that on the East side of 2. *<The East window of the aisle has its cill extended as a sedile.*[382]*>* In some of the windows are pieces of stained glass.[383] There is a rude piscina on the South of the Chancel & a small niche in the Transept. The Font is a very remarkable one, the bowl a circular cup on a central octagonal shaft & 4 surrounding ones of wood *^reaching to the top of the bowl^*.[384] The whole covered with a curious inscription. *<The font is of the 13th century, the inscription I H C D Ric Botham me fecit*[385]*>*.

at some point. Perhaps this was to accommodate the structure of the rood screen, but it might have been at the start of the opening out of the transept into an aisle. Some of this space was later occupied by a seventeenth-century stone inscription tablet with an ornamented pediment. See Blight, *West Cornwall*, 53–4.

[381] Glynne's view is that this was a Perpendicular window constructed so as to appear more ancient; Beacham and Pevsner, *Cornwall*, 265, write that this is an original fourteenth-century window, but Glynne, in the context of the ?sixteenth-century construction of the north aisle, is more persuasive. The situation might be complicated by the reuse/recombination of pre-existing tracery.

[382] No longer present, presumed removed in the 1860s on the insertion of the glass in that window.

[383] No ancient stained glass remains; see Borlase's account, BL, Egerton Ms. 2657, fol. 48r., who noted 'the remainder of a very good female figure painted in the Glass'.

[384] The bowl is now supported by late nineteenth-century columns of dark serpentine, but they do not reach 'up to the top of the bowl', merely supporting the four bulbous protrusions. In Glynne's day, was the entire structure painted, to mask the contrast between wood and stone? Whatever the case, it is possible that the original structure was damaged – perhaps in the Civil Wars? – and replacement wooden legs installed in the eighteenth century.

[385] This is copy of a 'Bodmin-style' granite font, the bowl almost square in plan with large bulbous additions to form four corners, the whole curving down below as the corners form rough capitals to the legs. The inscription is in Lombardic script in relief, itself an antiquated form of text at that time, and reads: 'IHC [quatrefoil] D(OMINUS) RIC(HARD) / BOL /

Fig. 46. Pen and ink drawing of the interior of the north side of Landewednack church (*c.* 1875?), currently hanging in the church, probably by J. Romilly Allen; reproduced by kind permission of the Parochial Church Council of St Wynwallow, Landewednack.

The walls are of rough stone. On the North is a square rood turret.[386] (Fig. 46) The ground of the Churchyard is uneven and the view beautiful.

HAM / ME FECIT', trans., *IHC, Sir [lit. lord] Richard Bolham made me*. He was rector from 7 August 1404 to 28 February 1415/16, F.C. Hingeston-Randolph, *The Register of Edmund Stafford (A.D.1395–1419): An Index and Abstract of Its Contents* (London, 1886), 27. It is possible that the presentation of this font marked the start of a fifteenth-century construction period. See also, C.H.I., 'Granite Font in Landewednack Church', *Gentleman's Magazine* 76 (November 1806), 1017, figs 5, 6; and Godwin, 'Churches of Kerrier and Penwith', 243.
[386] This is now erased. The *RCG*, 25 July 1879, 4, reported a visitor who 'found men engaged pulling down a portion of one of the side walls. On closer examination I observed that they had removed the doorways and stairs that once led to the rood loft. It appears a recess is to be built, instead to hold an organ. The antiquarian, who visits the Lizard, will regret this change as these relics of the past revealed many a line of history to him. He will now need a revised guide book to tell the church's history. But, I suppose, as the rood loft had been long ago removed, it was considered the stairway was no longer any use in the church, and ought to be relegated to the region of the worthless [...] it is only in keeping with other changes within the church.' The rebuilding effectively removed the window of the North aisle wall outwards, reinserting it into the new wall, the join marked externally by brickwork. An undated drawing in the church made prior to these changes shows the entrance to the rood stairs and their exit at loft level, together with the north wall of the aisle and a corbel support for a chancel arch. The last is puzzling, although the drawing is initialled 'JRA', most likely John Romilly Allen (1847–1907), a notable archaeologist, artist, and fieldworker, and its veracity is almost unquestionable. Was this arch a nineteenth-century pastiche, inserted by the vicar when he 'restored the chancel' (see fn. 378), and that

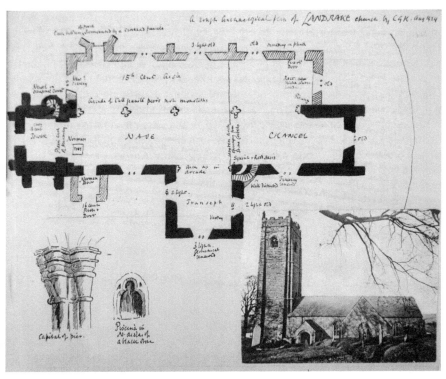

Fig. 47. Groundplan of Landrake church; reproduced with the kind permission of the Royal Institution of Cornwall, Courtney Library, Henderson Ms. 'East Cornwall', 220.

LANDRAKE (Fig. 47)

Lysons: BL, Add. Ms. 9462, fol. 38r.

Landrake – in the Chancel a brass against the Wall of Edward Courteney Esq., 2[d] son of Sir William Courteney of Powderham, 1509[387] <sketch of font[388]>.

Glynne: GL, Glynne notebooks 14, fols 28–9

Landrake, S. Peter, 28 May 1852.
The plan is a Nave & Chancel each with North aisle continued to the East end, a South Transeptal chapel, North ^& South^ porches, & West Tower. The latter is

was later removed, as the support of such an arch purely on corbels seems unlikely, apart from its strange position eastwards of where a rood screen would have been?

[387] Originally on the north side of the chancel, intentionally, perhaps, in proximity to the Easter Sepulchre, this brass has been taken up from its slab and is now mural on the north side of the sanctuary.

[388] Listed by Lysons, *Cornwall*, ccxxxiii, as belonging to the same group as Altarnun, Callington, Jacobstow etc.; Sedding, *Norman Architecture*, 186, pl. LXXXII; see also the CRSBI, available online at: https://www.crsbi.ac.uk/view-item?i=10960 [accessed December 2023].

tall & resembles that of St Stephen, 3 stages in height, with buttresses not set at the angles, an octagonal turret at the North East, battlements & 4 pinnacles.[389] The belfry windows of 2 lights. The West window of 3, & below it is a door. The North porch is shallow & has its pediment flanked by diagonal crocketed pinnacles of granite. The door has mouldings in granite, with label & panneled spandrels. The Northern windows are Perpendicular of 3 lights. [29] Some others are of 2 & 3 lights, & some mutilated. The South door is of granite.[390] The arcade within is Perpendicular, of 4 bays, the arches depressed, & the piers much resembling those at S. Stephen's. There is no distinction of the Chancel[391] & the Church is entirely pued. *<The Font is Norman, has a square bowl with geometrical patterns on the sides & heads at the angles. The base octagonal. In the South Transept is an ogee piscina. In the North aisle a trefoliated piscina[392]>*

LANDULPH

Lysons: BL, Add. Ms. 9462, fol. 38r.

Landulph[393] – Font octagonal on 5 pillars.[394]

LANEAST

Lysons: BL, Add. Ms. 9445, fol. 167r.

[389] Gilbert, *Historical Survey*, ii, 416, comments: 'The church tower, is a very conspicuous building, and has been rendered truly venerable, by the combined injuries of time and weather.'

[390] Strangely, Glynne fails to note the Norman appearance of the south door, perhaps confused by the incorporation of a pointed arch to match the opening of the porch when it was added in the sixteenth century; see Sedding, *Norman Architecture*, 184–5, pl. LXXXI. The church was restored in 1877, reported in the *WMN*, 26 July 1877, 4: 'In the present restoration the wagon-headed roof, corresponding in pattern to a portion of the ancient roof remaining in the north aisle, has been adopted throughout the building [...] The interior of the church has, in fact, been completely transformed [...] Chancel and nave, aisle and transept, have been reseated, the chancel with oak stalls having simple carved ends, and the rest of the church with pitch pine [...] the transept and the porch have been entirely rebuilt [...] five of the windows in the south aisle are also new; the mullions being of Polyphant [...] the ancient granite doorways of the porch have been reused'; see LPL: ICBS 7904 (1875–7), with a plan of the church post-restoration.

[391] In the 1850s?, it was noted that 'the chancel arch has disappeared, but traces of rood loft remain'; DHC: F5/17/2/4, EDAS, series of Rough Notes – sheet 21(1861). A chancel arch was added at the 1877 restoration using the existing thin stone shafts and capitals; see Mattingly, 'Distinctiveness by Omission', 139.

[392] This addition (fol. 28v.) is in similar handwriting to Glynne's church description.

[393] The published account, Lysons, *Cornwall*, 171–3, contains details of the brass to Theodore Paleologus (d. 1636), 'descended from the Imperial line of the last Christian Emperors of Greece [...] He departed this life at Clyfton [Landulph], the 21st of January 1636.' This information was derived from a letter from Rev. Francis Vyvyan Iago FSA, rector of Landulph, to Daniel of 12 January 1814, BL, Add. Ms. 9418, fols 79r.–81v.

[394] This comprises a restored Norman base supporting the basin, inscribed and dated 1660; Sedding, *Norman Architecture*, 187.

Llaneast – handsome tower with sold crocketed pinnacles, architecture very like Alternon,[395] font exactly the same,[396] clustered pillars with quatrefoil ornaments.

LANHYDROCK

Lysons: BL, Add. Ms. 9462, fol. 40r.

Lanhydroc – Church, Nave & side aisles, clustered pillars & obtuse arches. Two tablets of verses in Latin & English on slate with arms over <sketch of shield of four quarters[397]> G.C., motto: Cala-rag-wethlow.[398] George & Jane Carmynowe, the English lines begin thus 'The Care of myne I owe to Car-myn-owe'. Two slabs on the floor for George Carmynowe of Paulmaugan Esq. & Jane his wife, sister & heir of George Lower, he died 1599, she 1509 [*recte* 1609].[399] In the North aisle, Monument for the Lady Essex Speccot, youngest daughter of John Earl of Radnor, ob. 1689.[400] Font plain & octangular. Cross in Lanhydrock Church yard <sketch>.[401] The house lies close to the Church on the South East side.

Glynne: GL, Glynne notebooks 17, fols 132–3

Lanhydrock [26 January 1842]. The Church is close to the mansion, a singular quadrangular building of granite, resembling a College, one side occupied by a Gatehouse. The date 162. appears in various parts, but the style is more that of Elizabeth. [133] Probably in this remote district the more ancient style continued longer in use. The building does not seem to

---

[395] Inasmuch as the arcade is of the same low, four-centred arches, and the window tracery not dissimilar, but with more cusping and decoration at Laneast.

[396] As published, *Cornwall*, ccxxxiii, grouped with Altarnun and others; see the CRSBI, available online at: https://www.crsbi.ac.uk/view-item?i=9735 [accessed December 2023].

[397] Only the upper two of these quarters are blazoned by Lysons, with dexter quarter of *azure a bend or, with a label of three points*, for Carminowe, and sinister, *sable a chevron between three roses argent*, for Lower, the whole noted in full by Borlase: BL, Egerton Ms. 2657, fol. 227r.

[398] Although the Cornish language has been recently used to create mottos for civic and personal heraldry, this motto in Cornish for the Carminow family (trans. *A straw for a tale-bearer*) is the only medieval example now known.

[399] The 'two tablets of verses in Latin and English', form a mural memorial to George Carminowe and his wife Jane Lower, presumably erected close to the floor slabs marking their graves and creating a commemorative ensemble. The grave slabs no longer exist, no doubt removed at the 1887–8 restoration.

[400] It was the death of this lady, three weeks after her marriage to John Speccott of Penheale (d. 1705), from smallpox that he had initially contracted, that ultimately led to the failure of the Speccott dynasty, as recorded at Egloskerry, see B.D. Henning, *The History of Parliament: The House of Commons 1660–1690*, 3 vols (London, 1981), iii, 462. Her monument, the slate tablets with the Latin and English verses, and the grave slabs of George and Jane Carminowe associated with them, are recorded by Lysons, *Cornwall*, 174.

[401] See Langdon, *Mid Cornwall*, 35, no. 42; and Preston-Jones and Oshaka, *Early Cornish Sculpture*, 158–9.

have been finished. There is a fine gallery with enriched stucco ceiling & cornice.[402] The Church may be coëval with the house & is of the latest Gothic, almost debased but quite uniform.[403] A small structure of 3 equal aisles with a Western tower embattled, & with 4 square pinnacles, the whole of granite but without buttresses. There is a South porch, the door of which has an enriched spandrel, the roof sculptured in wood with a cornice. Within there are two ranges, each of 4 Tudor arches, with low granite piers resembling those at Boconnoc. The windows all of 3 lights with late tracery, some with shafts. The interior neat & pleasing though small – it contains a barrel organ.[404] In the Church yard is part of an ancient cross.

LANIVET

Lysons: BL, Add. Ms. 9462, fol. 38r.

Lanhivet – Nave & side aisles, plain clustered pillars & pointed arches. Windows all uniform[405] <sketch of 3 light standard Perpendicular window>.

---

[402] The east range of the house was demolished in 1784 to create the E-shaped house Glynne saw (and we see today). The earliest date carved on the house is 1634, when the cross passage was installed into the sixteenth-century side passage house. Other dates carved into the mansion are 1642 on the south range and 1651 on the gatehouse, so presumably Glynne made an error here. It is also difficult to understand his comment about the house being unfinished – unless he is referring to the fact that part was knocked down to create a more fashionable and salubrious dwelling. See P. Holden, 'Situation, Contrivance, Receipt, Strength and Beauty: The Building of Lanhydrock House 1620–51', *JRIC* (2005), 32–44.

[403] Glynne's description of the 'late tracery' of the windows, and the 'latest Gothic' architecture (i.e. very late Perpendicular), probably influenced his opinion on their date of construction as contemporaneous with the house. In addition, the plasterwork in the church would have resonated with that in the gallery in the house, and perhaps also to the plasterwork royal arms. Yet the church appears to have been built in the late fifteenth/early sixteenth century by the Augustinian priory of St Petroc in Bodmin, to whom the church belonged; see Henderson, *Cornish Church Guide*, 129.

[404] In 1818, Gilbert, *Historical Survey*, ii, 637, noted that 'the interior, however, requires great improvements, in order to render it a suitable appendage to the establishment of its illustrious patron', describing the Radnor pews occupying the east end of the south aisle. Correspondence to and from Charles Agar (1769–1811) in 1808 concerns an estimate for repairs to the church, and although one was eventually forthcoming, for £384 18s. 4d., it was deemed too high, and as one of the craftsmen suggested that the old seats in the church were unrepairable, it was pointless to prepare an estimate; KK: CL/5/371/6/29, 33, 34, 80 (April to December 1808). DHC: F5/17/2/4, EDAS series of Rough Notes – sheet 23 (1861), recorded that 'the present state of substantial repair seems to date from 1820', and indeed, in 1821, the church was reported as 'in the highest state of possible repair – it has been new seated entirely at great expense', Cook (ed.), *The Diocese of Exeter in 1821*, 39. The church was restored fully in 1886–8, including the extension of the chancel eastwards to allow for the installation of an alabaster reredos under the new window, and there was possibly much other rebuilding; see P. Holden, *Lanhydrock* (Swindon, 2007), 38–9.

[405] Gilbert, *Historical Survey*, ii, 638–9, records the windows as 'of the Gothic order, strengthened by stone tracery, and iron work'. Evidently there were no eighteenth-century sash windows installed here, and at the restoration in 1863–70 only the east window of the chancel was replaced. See T.Q. Couch, 'Parochialia: Lanivet', *JRIC* 1.4 (1865), 71–81, who noted that before the restoration, 'perennial streams soaked through the roofs and coursed down some of the pillars; mosses and fern luxuriated in the crevices of the walls and windows; the pillars were dangerously out of the perpendicular'; the *WB*, 21 October 1864, 6,

At the East end of South aisle, Tablet with the effigies of an old Gentleman in ruff & long beard praying with this inscription,
John} Courtney {Esq} was buried ye {first} day of {March 1559
Ric} {gent.} {sixth} {December 1632
These lived and dyed both in Tremere / God hath their souls their bones lie here / Richard with Thomsen his lov'd wife / Liv'd 61 years then ended lyfe.[406]
[separate sheets] <sketches of cross[407]>.
Fol. 39r. <sketch of St Benet's[408]> Lanhivet – lofty cross in the Church yard on the North side of the Church, of moor stone, with braid[?] ornament engraved on it much obscured, a mark on the East side: about ~~10 feet high~~ 9ft 8in high <sketch of east side of cross[409]>.
<sketch of cross[410]> This cross is near the Church at the west end.
[separate sheet] Lanhivet August 8 [1805?] <sketch of font> Cross on the west side of the church in the church yard <sketch of tall standing four holed cross, the shaft decorated with foliated scrollwork, dimensions recorded>.
On a stone on the north side of the church <four letters of an inscription[411]>.
Ancient cross on the North side of the church at 10 feet high the cross of which is not pierced. It is covered with ornament much defaced by time, a man on the East side.[412]

LANLIVERY

Lysons: BL, Add. Ms. 9462, fol. 38v.

Lanlivery – August 14. In the North Transept against the East wall, 2 fragments of sculpture in alabaster, one of the resurrection of our Saviour with the soldiers

noted that 'the church had been allowed to fall into such lamentable decay that little besides the walls is capable of restoration. The old barrel roof will be replaced by an open wooden one; the singing gallery removed; the old pews, of every size and shape, will give place to uniform open benches, and various other improvements will be made, or tasteless additions swept away.'

[406] This slate monument recording two generations of the Courtney family, and the social status of each, is now set against the north wall, moved probably at the restoration, when the south chapel was converted into a vestry, LPL: ICBS 6296 (1863–71), for reseating, new roof, and repairs to the walls, and also see KK: P110/6/1, for a plan of the church in 1865.

[407] This is the churchyard cross on the west side; see fn. 410.

[408] Published, Lysons, *Cornwall*, opp. ccxxxvii, where it is styled a 'monastery of St Benet's [...] of which there are considerable remains, now occupied as a dwelling-house; the tower of the church is also standing'. There is no evidence that this was ever a monastery but most likely a roadside chapel, still with much remaining late fifteenth-/early sixteenth-century work remaining; see Henderson, 'Ecclesiastical History', part 3, *JRIC* NS 3.2 (1958), 211–382 at 287–9; Orme, *Religious History to 1560*, 303.

[409] Langdon, *Mid Cornwall*, 37, no. 46; Preston-Jones and Okasha, *Early Cornish Sculpture*, 159–61, illus. 114–18, 362–65.

[410] Lysons, *Cornwall*, ccxlv; Preston-Jones and Okasha, *Early Cornish Sculpture*, 161–3, illus. 119–23.

[411] This stone is built into the north wall of the church; see C. Thomas, 'A Second Inscribed Stone from Lanivet Church', *Cornish Archaeology* 55 (2016), 181–4. Whether it was in the ground at that time and later incorporated into the masonry, or whether it has been in its current place for a longer period, is not known.

[412] This seems simply to repeat the note made on another sheet of paper, on the same folio.

guarding the sepultures, the other of the general resurrection as it [illegible] several bodies rising out of their coffins.[413]
Font octagonal with 4 foils & shields
On a slab in the Chancel, a cross florée with a shield hanging to it, charged with a chevron between 3 dolphins (for Kendal) on ye Cross Ihc in text, on a label at the bottom the date 1547 [*recte* 1517], with the Inscription around the edge 'Sub hoc sap (qu?)o pr mitvr corpus Gualteri Kendall qui decimo tercio die julii anno infra scripto morbo periit'.[414]
Fol. 39v. An ancient Cross, thrown down at the cross road near Llanlivery, close to the Turnpike road leads from Lostwithiel to St Austell.
NB The inscription on the stone pillar near the turnpike gate between St Austell & St Blazey, not legible, quite obliterated on the south side where there is a square neat, & nearly so on the north, but I could not judge it so well for want of sun shine on it <sketch of cross with dimensions[415]>.

Lysons: BL, Add. Ms. 9445, fol. 168r.

Lanlivery – Church tower with handsome crocketed pinnacles, clustered columns, south aisle, north transept, font octagonal with gothic tracery. Several of for of [*sic*] Kendall of Pelyn, Walter Kendall, 1744, Walter Kendall, 1696; some others on the floor, worn, Walter Kendall, no date of death with cross flory & their arms.[416]
In north transept on the wall, two rich pieces of bas relief, in one a soldier in armour is lying on the ground his hand supporting his head, another is drawing his sword – I think it is the resurrection – the other is certainly figures rising from their graves, & one of them appears to be a bishop.[417]

Glynne: GL, Glynne notebooks 16, fols 47–8

---

[413] Gilbert, *Historical Survey*, ii, 878, notes that 'in the small northern aisle are the remains of a once elegant monument, representing the resurrection'. While this is possible, it is more likely these sculptured fragments were from a medieval alabaster altarpiece. Lysons found them on the east wall, i.e. above where an altar would have been, with the window over raised up to accommodate it. For *comparanda*, see F. Cheetham, *English Medieval Alabasters* (Oxford, 1984), 272–81 (Christ's Resurrection), 315–6 (Resurrection of the Dead). This decoration suggests the transept was originally a private chapel, entered through a doorway (reworked) on the east side. Pieces of an old screen were noted in the north transept and the chancel, DHC: F5/17/2/4, EDAS series of Rough Notes – sheet 29 (1866). There are no signs of the alabasters or the screen now, although a photograph of the alabaster is in the collections of the CL, Truro.
[414] The inscription is in Roman capitals and reads 'CORPVS GVALTERI KENDALL QVI DECIMO TERTIO DIE JVLII ANNO INFRA SCRIPTO MORBI PERIIT SVB HOC SAXO PREMITVR', trans., *The Body of Walter Kendall who died on the 13th day of July in the year below written, lies under this slab*. See E.L. Cutts, *Manual for the Study of the Sepulchral Slabs and Crosses of the Middle Ages* (London, 1849), 71, pl. XXX.
[415] This cross was removed in 1840 and re-erected in Boconnoc Park by the Hon. S.M. Fortescue. This is the earliest illustration and reference to it and identifies the cross-roads where it formerly stood as being the staggered junction between Lanlivery and Fowey on the Lostwithiel to St Austell turnpike road. See Langdon, *East Cornwall*, 20, no. 24.
[416] This contradicts the earlier? note with the inscription transcribed and the date suggested.
[417] This is a more comprehensive description of what can only be the alabaster panels, published Lysons, *Cornwall*, ccl.

Lanlivery – S. Brevita, 23 August 1862.[418]
A large & handsome Church, conspicuously situated on a lofty eminence & a good
specimen of the local Perpendicular Church. It has a spacious nave & Chancel
undivided, with North aisle running to the East end, a North Transept, a South
porch & fine lofty West Tower. The material is almost wholly granite, the body
long & rather too low for the stately Tower. The windows in the nave are pretty
uniform Perpendicular of 3 lights: those at the East of the Chancel & its aisle also
Perpendicular, but of 4 lights & not similar. On the West of the ~~nave~~ South aisle[419] is
one of 3 lights having [48] something of a Decorated character. The arcade dividing
the aisle has ~~wide~~ 6 wide arches & clustered piers all of granite, the latter are of
the accustomed make with square tablet capitals, of which the Eastern have more
sculpture, in the others are flowers rudely cut. Both nave & Chancel have coved
roofs, with ribs & bosses, & cornice ornamented with angels bearing shields.[420]
The tower arch is lofty & good, on clustered columns having circular capitals. The
Transept is long & sprawling, cut off from the body, in neglected condition & not
used. It has some earlier work at its North end, a good Decorated window of 3 lights,
& on the East side a plain 3 light window, perhaps late Perpendicular. There is a rood
turret in the angle of the nave & Transept. The Font has an octagonal bowl with
quatrefoil pannels containing shields, on an octagonal panneled stem. The interior
is pewed & unimproved.[421]

[418] This church has recently undergone a thorough archaeological appraisal, in which Glynne's
account is named as one of the few important sources for the church's appearance before
a restoration scheme was launched, lasting from 1865 to 1880; see W. Rodwell, 'Lanlivery
Church: Its Archaeology and Architectural History', *Cornish Archaeology* 32 (1993), 76–111.
For documentation and plans, including proposed north and south elevations, and elevations
for a new window, fireplace, and door in the vestry (north transept), see KK: PIII/2/14–15
(1864).

[419] Here Glynne evidently revises his opinion of the arrangement of the church, from a nave
and north aisle to a nave and a south aisle, complicated by the parochial use of the south aisle
as the nave and chancel.

[420] These are now replacements of the originals; see the report on the restoration in the *RCG*,
13 October 1888, 5: 'The old roof, of oak – an exceedingly fine example – having become
dilapidated beyond repair, it was resolved on restoring it to its original state […] All the timber
is English oak, unvarnished, and the carving thereon the facsimile of the original [including]
carved wall-plates, ribs, purloins, and bosses – the latter being particularly effective.' Only
the south aisle retains any visible ceiling woodwork, and no angels remain on the cornice.
On 5 May 1724, the parish renewed a contract with John Geach and John Hunt, helliers of St
Sampson parish, 'to keep the roof of the said parish Church in good order […] [and] […] to
wash the Church with white lime once every 3 years' for £1 15s. p.a., KK: PIII/5/1. The sum
was less than half paid for a similar service in Camborne church, recorded in 1713 (and other
years) as being £3 19s. 8d, although it was a three-aisled structure compared to just the two at
Lanlivery, KK: X510/1.

[421] In 1730, the wardens' accounts record the payment of £10 5s. for 'the Carpenter's bill
for making ye Seats', with £2 13s. for 'timber & drawing boards for ye Seats', presumably
constructing the box pews encountered by Glynne, KK: PIII/5/1. DHC: F5/17/2/4, EDAS
series of Rough Notes – sheet 29 (1866), records 'square pews, about to be altered?' The pews
were replaced according to the seating plan proposed in 1864, KK: PIII/2/13–15 (undated but
1864). *The Ecclesiologist* 27 (1866), 187, termed the church 'miserably bepewed', prior to its
restoration. The wardens' accounts register the heaviest expenditure for the years 1862–7,
consistently reliant upon a penny rate; the annual total raised was halved in 1868 and thereafter, when 'Voluntary Contributions in lieu of Church Rate' were collected, but presumably
by that time the need for extra funds for restoration had disappeared, KK: PIII/5/4.

The Porch has fair doorways, the external with granite mouldings & label & coved roof with ribs & foliaged cornice.

The grand & lofty Tower is seen at a great distance, from its elevated position. It is placed at the West of the North aisle, though the Southern terminates in what is used as the Chancel.[422] It is of fine granite masonry, has 2 string courses, & an embattled parapet with 4 large octagonal turrets at the angles capped by crocketed pinnacles, which are chamfered off at the string below the belfry windows into angel corbels. The Western belfry window has 4 lights, the others 3, the buttresses are not set at the angles of the tower, & at the North West angle is a stair turret pierced with elegant ~~quatrefoiled~~ openings, some labeled, some exhibiting sculpture.[423] The West window has 4 lights, with hood on block corbels,[424] the West doorway labeled.

LANREATH (Fig. 48)

Lysons: BL, Add. Ms. 9462, fol. 39r.

Lanreth – Nave & South aisle, clustered pillars & obtuse arches.

In the Chancel a very rich monument for Charles Grylles Esq., Counsellor at law, 1611, erected by Jonathan Gryles Esq. his son & heir, 1623.[425]

The effigies of him & his wife (small) kneeling on the altar tomb fronting the Chancel, with canopy over them supported by Corinthian pillars. 4 sons & 4 daughters under all. Monument fronting the Church.[426]

Arms of Gryles on the pews ~~all round~~ in the Chancel, & ^East^ end of the South aisle, which is separated from the other part by the screen of a roodloft which also crosses the nave & is enriched with foliage &c. on the cornice, & gilt.[427]

Fol. 38v. <two sketches of font with enlargement of the foliage detail[428]>.

Glynne: GL, Glynne notebooks 14, fols 61–2

Lanreath, S. Manarck, 31 January 1854.

---

[422] That is, the south aisle was used as the body of the church, the west end of the original nave contiguous with the tower.

[423] Described by Rodwell, 'Lanlivery Church', 99, as 'the south-west corbel bears the finest sculpture, an enchanting pair of lions facing one another, flanking a wheat ear. The south-east corbel has two complete crowned human figures, in "flying" posture, holding a head between them. The two northern corbels depict angels, flanked by crude human masks.' The odd lion/ wheat symbolism may reflect the legend of St Brivita, patron saint of the church, rumoured to have helped the residents with their agricultural endeavours.

[424] That is, they were perhaps intended to be carved but the work was not done.

[425] A. Bizley, 'The Grylls Monument at Lanreath', *JRIC* NS VII part 3 (1975/6), 211–19; Cockerham, *Continuity and Change*, 84, pls 160–1. A large paper woodcut of the monument, taken from Polwhele's work, forms fol. 166 of BL, Add. Ms. 9445.

[426] Presumably this is intended to mean that the monument faced into the church from its location set against the south wall of the chancel.

[427] Gilbert, *Historical Survey*, ii, 917, found the 'rood-loft or screen, was at first curiously carved, painted, and gilded, but it is now so much injured, that it is difficult, if not impossible, to ascertain the subjects which it once exhibited'.

[428] Published by Lysons, *Cornwall*, pl. opp. ccxxxiii.

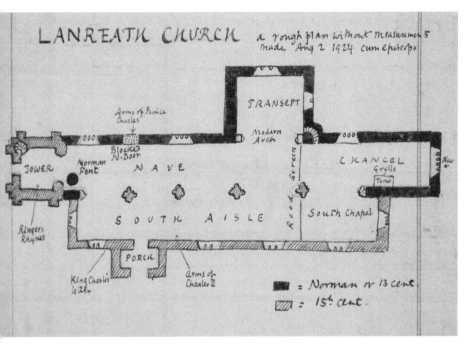

48. Groundplan of Lanreath church; reproduced with the kind permission of the Royal
~~Ins~~titution of Cornwall, Courtney Library, Henderson Ms. 'East Cornwall', 243.

Fig. 49. Interior view of Lanreath church (1870); from the collections at Kresen
Kernow, corn03755.

The plan is a nave & Chancel with parallel South aisle, & a North Transept, a West Tower & South porch, all of the Cornish Perpendicular except some part of the Chancel, which has some indications of Decorated work. The Chancel extends a little beyond the aisle. There is a granite arcade of 5 bays, of Perpendicular character, with the usual ~~arcade~~ clustered piers with 4 shafts & intermediate mouldings, the shafts have square capitals sculptured with rude flowers & bases nearly similar. The roofs are coved & plastered, with ribs & bosses.[429] The Tower arch is tall & good, upon shafts, that to the Transept is very poor & plain. The Chancel includes one bay, the division is marked by a fine rood screen of wood, which extends across the aisle as well as the nave & is of 5 arched compartments of 4 light tracery with 4 cornices of foliage & all well moulded. The lower part panneled. *<There are figures of Saints painted in the lower pannels of the screen on the South side, on which side the cornices also are painted & gilt.[430]>* The rood doors appear high up both on the North & South. The windows on the South are of 3 lights, except the East window of the aisle, which is of 4 lights & rather poor character. On the North the windows are of 4 lights & rather flat arches. The East window of the Chancel is of early Decorated character of 3 lights, & filled with some pretty good modern stained glass.[431] On the North of the Chancel is a square headed window of 4 lights.[432]

The Font is a very fine one of Norman work. The bowl is circular covered with rude foliage or flowers, in shape something resembling shells. The stem has chevron ornament & a toothed band.[433]

---

[429] Sedding, *Norman Architecture*, 199, noted that 'the plaster has been removed from the ribs in the nave, where the defective timbers have been made good with others of the same material. In the case of the north aisle, the fine roof of which is also of late fifteenth-century workmanship [perhaps early sixteenth century?], the ceiled ribs were in sufficiently good repair to render restoration unnecessary. In the case of the nave, however, where the plaster had to be removed, Mr Bodley did not replace it; and, moreover, in the south aisle [...] he boarded the panels in preference to replastering them.' See also KK: P113/2/51, Papers Relating to Church Restoration (1887–1938).

[430] See Bond and Camm, *Roodscreens and Roodlofts*, ii, 389, who noted: 'A late vicar had a portion of these panels [...] cleaned off, and invited the parishioners to be responsible for the removal of the rest – which, to their credit, they refused to do.' Plans for the restoration of the screen, and the clergy and choir stalls, are KK: P113/2/38–9 (1904–5). See also Mattingly, 'Rood Loft Construction', 76, 87–8, who discusses the surviving imagery.

[431] In 1867, Polsue, *Parochial History*, ii, 34, recorded this window filled with glass relating the birth, baptism, and Crucifixion of Christ, given by the Rev. Pering Cornish; this was later replaced.

[432] The church was restored in 1887–8, reported by the *RCG*, 27 January 1888, 4: 'The church is a fine example of the Cornish-Perpendicular, and is chiefly remarkable for the fact that the old screen remains, though in a somewhat maimed and decayed condition. The restoration of this screen, which stretches right across the church, has not yet been taken in hand, owing to the lack of funds [...] The present work has been mainly the thorough restoration of the roof and the reflooring of the church. The timbers of the roof of the nave and chancel are now left open, displaying fine carved bosses and massive ribs. The roof of the aisle has been ceiled between the ribs, and ornamented with stencil work upon a chocolate ground. The principal addition to the church has been a magnificent east window [...] Nearly all the windows have been newly glazed, and the walls have been replastered throughout.' Fig. 49 shows the ceiled roof of the chancel prior to restoration.

[433] See Sedding, *Norman Architecture*, 196–7, pl. 83. The font is significant in that the decoration breaks away from the usual type and displays an artistic individualism, perhaps encouraged by the use of Catacleuse stone rather than granite; see A. Woodcock, 'Beasts and

The Tower is of moorstone, 3 stages in height & embattled, with 4 fine octagonal crocketed pinnacles, the buttresses are not set at angles, the belfry windows are of 3 lights: also the West window, below which is [62] a door with label & panneled spandrels. The porch has a coved roof, its inner door with a Tudor arch & label with a niche over it.
In the Chancel is a rich monument to some of the Grylls family AD 1623, the canopy on Corinthian columns, with 2 kneeling figures & 8 children.

<Lanreath, over the boys
The last died first, the first & all the rest
With children store, the living God hath blest
Who praise his name that blessed father store[434]
And hope ^in^ bliss to bless him ever more.
Over the girls
One died a child, the rest all childless died
And yet with child, in child birth Heaven denied
Base ^earth^ their souls or issue should detain
An Rare things are shewn, but straight shut up again.[435]>

LANSALLOS[436]

Lysons: BL, Add. Ms. 9462, fol. 40r.

Large square font with some rude flowers &c. on the side. Nave & side aisles clustered pillars pointed arches, no monuments.[437]

Glynne: GL, Glynne notebooks 13, fols 64–5

Lansallos, S. Allsoys, 30 January 1850.[438]

Beakheads: Romanesque Sculpture at Morwenstow', in Holden (ed.), *Celebrating Pevsner*, 41–8, at 43.
[434] This line should read: 'Who praise his name, that blessed hath their store.'
[435] These verses (fol. 61v.) were probably written on the verso facing the church description because they were supplementary to it, and his retention of the verse form would not have fitted into the otherwise densely written page. His other comment (fol. 60v.) seems to be contemporaneous with the description.
[436] An arson attack in 2005 resulted in the partial destruction of the chancel and side chapel roofs.
[437] Equally, Gilbert, *Historical Survey*, ii, 917–18, recorded no monuments other than some ledger stones to the Mellow family. The fourteenth-century stone figures of a man in armour and his lady – possibly of the Hywysch family based at their mansion of Raphael – and the effigial slate slab to Margery Budockshide (d. 1579), all found in the church today, were excavated from under the chancel floor during restoration work in the 1880s. For plans of the church in 1884, see KK: AD2467/P/7/9, showing the original church layout with the pulpit placed centrally in the chancel, accompanied by box pews (Fig. 50a); and KK: AD2467/P/7/3, showing the proposed layout filled with open benches, and the renewal of several windows, including the east window (Fig. 50b).
[438] Probably contemporaneous with Glynne's visit, the chancel was reported 'of most meagre character, a mass of dirt and desolation, the very slates have muck laid on, to keep

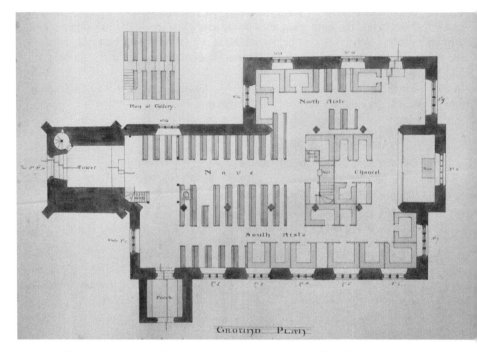

Fig. 50a. Groundplan of Lansallos church prior to restoration (1884); from the collections at Kresen Kernow, AD2467/P/7/9, by Richard Coad, architect.

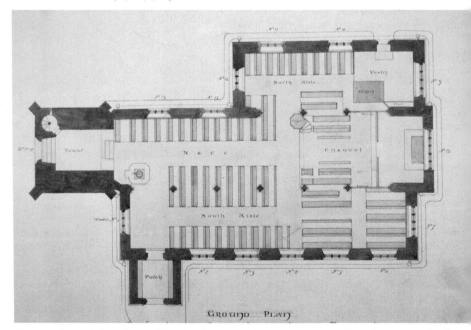

Fig. 50b. Groundplan of Lansallos church proposed post-restoration (1884); from the collections at Kresen Kernow, AD2467/P/7/3, by Richard Coad, architect.

A Cornish Church of the usual arrangement, except that the North aisle is only a short one, more of a Chapel attached to the Eastern portion only. There is a West Tower & a South porch. The whole is Third Pointed. The Tower lofty & rather good of its kind, having a battlement & 4 crocketed pinnacles of octagonal form, 3 stages in height, the buttresses angular, the belfry windows of 3 lights of a common Cornish type. The West window is rather similar, above it a canopied niche with large finial, containing the bracket of a statue. The West door has a labeled Tudor arch the label returned with square foliated blocks. The lower parts of the buttresses have panneling, some of which has the wavy pattern. The Chancel is undistinguished & the South aisle is continued to the East end. The arcade has Tudor arches with piers resembling those at Talland, the shafts have large granite abaci on the capitals. The North chapel has wide Tudor arches opening to the body, with plainer piers. The roof of this chapel is unfinished & left open. The roofs of the other aisles are coved, & ribbed with bosses.[439] The windows of the South aisle of 3 lights have mostly lost their tracery, that at its East end is of 4. There are some [65] square headed ones on the North & a small labeled Tudor arched door. The East window of the Chancel is a very bad modern one.[440] There are some fine old carved open benches, some of the standards having beautiful wood sculpture with panneling & tracery.[441] The Font has a square bowl & seems early: on each face a cross & 4 round holes.[442]

LANTEGLOS-BY-CAMELFORD

Lysons: BL, Add. Ms. 9462, fol. 40r.

Lanteglos – Nave & South aisle separated by clustered pillars. North Transept.

them in place?'; and in the south aisle, 'The hoods [i.e. hood moulds] remain but not a single original window', DHC: F5/17/2/4, EDAS, series of Rough Notes – sheet 24 (1862).

[439] In 1813, the rural dean reported that 'the Church has lately been new ceiled, the floors in the Aisles new laid and are now level – A new one of the little North Aisle has been built', which is how they were found by Glynne nearly fifty years later; KK: AD59/74, 113–14. The roofs were further repaired in the 1920s by E.H. Sedding; see KK: P114/2/1, a report on the state of the fabric (1908), and P114/2/2, subsequent correspondence (1911); see Warner, *A Time to Build*, 206–7. The fire and subsequent restoration facilitated dendrochronological analysis of the timbers, with the south aisle the earliest at 1483x1508, the north aisle at 1507x32, the nave at 1514, the porch at 1510x35, and the chancel at 1519–44. See Vernacular Architecture Group (2022) Dendrochronology Database [data-set]. York: Archaeology Data Service [distributor], available online at: https://doi.org/10.5284/1091408 [accessed July 2023]. As Mattingly, *Churches of Cornwall*, 48–9, has it, 'like many other Cornish churches, Lansallos was still a building site in the 1540s'.

[440] This was replaced at the 1884 restoration, when the tracery of the other windows noted by Glynne as 'mostly lost' was repaired/renewed.

[441] The pews were also dated by dendrochronology at 1507x32 (see fn. 439); and as they incorporate a range of designs with Gothic arches and Renaissance-inspired features, they demonstrate the relatively early adoption of Italianate influences, as on Prior Vyvyan's tomb in Bodmin of the 1530s.

[442] Glynne's description sits awkwardly with the actual decoration briefly (but correctly) noted by Lysons. See Sedding, *Norman Architecture*, 201, pl. LXXXV; and the CRSBI, available online at: https://www.crsbi.ac.uk/view-item?i=8696 [accessed December 2023]. The four corner supports seen today are modern.

Fig. 51. Font and church notes, Lanteglos-by-Camelford; from the British Library Archive, Add. Ms. 9462, fol. 40r.

Light Gothic windows at the end of the Chancel & South aisle <sketch of font[443]>. (Fig. 51)

Glynne: GL, Glynne notebooks 16, fols 33–4

Lanteglos (Co. Cornwall) by Camelford, S. Lanty, 25 October 1865.
A Perpendicular Church of the Cornish type, consisting of 2 long equal aisles, a North Transept and Western Tower. The 2 East windows are of 5 lights, one having a singular Flamboyant wheel in its head, the other very good Perpendicular. The other windows are of 3 lights, some having lost their tracery, but others on the South retain pieces of good stained glass.[444] There is no division of Chancel, the arcade is of 6 Tudor shaped arches on light piers <sketch> with 4 shafts having octagonal

---

[443] The sketch has two additional vignettes, one of a circular panel on the font, the other (probably) of the circular tracery in the chancel east window, as a comparator, and suggesting a similar date be ascribed to the two. The only published information was that the church contained 'a memorial for Digory Wallis, of Fentonwoon, who died in 1560', *Cornwall*, 182, supplementing their note of this seat. The monument was in the churchyard but was not found on a recent (2021) visit; see Maclean, *Trigg Minor*, ii, 311.
[444] Several probably late fifteenth-century biblical figures, emblems, and armorials survive, but their significance in a glazing programme is unclear; see J. Mattingly and M. Swift, 'The Medieval Glass of St Julitta, Lanteglos-by-Camelford, Cornwall', in *St Julitta's Church Lanteglos-by-Camelford: The Restoration of a Medieval Church, Discovering 800 Years of History, a Collection of Papers* ([Lanteglos], 2020), 73–82.

caps with foliage. To the Transept opens a very ugly obtuse arch on imposts, & in the Transept is one square headed window of 2 lights. The arch to the Tower is a very rude pointed one on imposts. The roofs are coved, with ribs and bosses forming panneled compartments, & a carved cornice.[445] There are 2 sedilia in granite on the South of the Sacrarium having continuous mouldings, & above a band of ornamental sculpture with vine leaves, grapes & scrolls. The Font is a fine one, the bowl octagonal, the sides having varied panneling, some with quatrefoils, some with the wavy Flamboyant sculpture, resembling the tracery of the East window. The stem is octagonal & panneled & raised on 2 steps. The Tower is without buttresses & tapers, divided by 2 strings, has battlement and 4 short square pinnacles. At the North East is a stair-turret, the belfry windows of 3 lights with the Cornish circles in the tracery. The West Window of 3 lights and mutilated.[446] [34] The West doorway has a contracted arch & hood on corbel heads. The whole is of granite. The South porch is good Perpendicular & has both doorways of granite, labelled, with finely panelled spandrels. The arch mouldings good – over the inner door is a canopied niche. The body of the Church presents a long bold unbroken line. The Church yard is retired and lies low.

LANTEGLOS-BY-FOWEY

Lysons: BL, Add. Ms. 9462, fol. 40r.

---

[445] As also recorded in the early 1850s, by Spence, '"Iter Cornubiense"', part III, III.
[446] In 1730?, the rural dean noted that 'one Seat under the Gallery and another near it not fix'd; The Wortheval's seat at the Eastern end of ye South Isle out of Repair; The Cover of ye Font broken […] The Southern Door decay'd […] Window broken […] North side of the Chancel and part of the floor out of [repair]; The Roof of the Church shatter'd by the Storm', DHC: DR, PR 362-4/31/3. There were clearly many structural issues, although by 1818 Gilbert, *Historical Survey*, ii, 591, reported that 'the interior of this church has of late undergone considerable improvement'. The church underwent further restorations in 1865 and 1870 that effectively sanitised the interior, as Maclean, *Trigg Minor*, ii, 308, recorded that 'the old seating had been long removed before the restoration', and that the north wall of the transept had been rebuilt and a new window introduced, as well as new windows in the west end of the south aisle and in the tower. See the plan of the restored church c. 1870, KK: EN/2053. That the 'old seating' had been removed before Glynne's visit is clear, as in 1717, 'James [Prideaux] who hath a Considerable Estate in the parish of Lanteg[los] […] at his own expense erected a seate or pew [in the] [Chanc]ell of the said Church of Lanteglos Contayning six feet and three [inches] in length and five foot and Eight inches in Breadth and situated in the middle of the Chancell of ye said Parish Church between ye Communion Table and a seate belonging to the Minister', DHC: DR, Petitions Chanter Basket D2/3 (considerably damaged). If such a seat had been in the church in this location when Glynne visited, his notes would surely have conveyed his dismay on its inappropriate location. J.D. Sedding wrote to the *WMN*, 20 March 1871, 4: 'I cannot refrain from expressing my regret that in the recent restoration of Lanteglos Church […] it was thought right to remove the flight of steps to the altar, and thereby destroy for ever a most unusual feature in a church of that size. This old arrangement was known in the neighbourhood as "quite like a cathedral!" and that it was coeval with the remainder of the chancel may be attested by the same mouldings being used to the sedile and windows.' The presence of this 'flight of steps' would have been highly unusual in a parish church of this type, when just one or two would have been the norm. Was it, therefore, something introduced in the 'considerable improvement' noted by Gilbert in the early nineteenth century? See also J. Mattingly, 'Lanteglos-by-Camelford Church in Historical Documents', in *St Julitta's Church Lanteglos-by-Camelford*, 47–56.

Lanteglos – Nave & side aisles, octagonal pillars plain with circular arches.
In North aisle a Monument for Captain Benjamin Young of the Royal Navy, he was
pretty tall of stature &c., ob. 1649 [*recte* 1749] <sketch of font>.
[separate sheet] Lanteglos – In the South Aisle in the wall an obtuse arch much
enriched, under it an altar tomb in (Slab of Moorstone) with the Brass Effigy of a
Knight in armour, plated armour, oval helmet long sword, lion at his feet.
'Hic jacet Thomas de Mohun & Johes Patris ejus filius & heres Reginaldi de Mohun
Millitis & Elizabethe uxoris sue filie & heredis Johi Fitzwilliam militis qui …
Thomas obiit die – mens – anno dom M CCCC. Quor &c.'
Arms in the east window <sketch of shield[447]>.
On a slab underneath the brasses effigies of a Knight in plated armour & his Lady.
John Mohun Esq. & Ann his wife daughter of Richard Code ^armigeri^ fil' & heres
William Mohun Esq., his wife one of the sisters of Edward Courtney Earl of Devon,
which John & Ann died September within 24 hours 'ex infirmitati vocat' Sudye anno
dni 1508'. 2 coats [of arms].
Pew richly ornamented with the Mohun arms.

Glynne: GL, Glynne notebooks 17, fols 127–9

Lanteglos by Fowey – [25 January] 1842.
This large Church is in a very solitary situation on an eminence not very accessible
from the most populous parts of the parish, & having only one habitation ^near it^
(a farm house inhabited by bitter dissenters).[448]
The Church is much neglected & out of repair, but is very spacious, consisting of
3 equal aisles wide, but low, after the Cornish fashion, & a very massive but rude
Tower at the West end of the nave, partly but not wholly engaged with the side
aisles.[449] The style is the Cornish Perpendicular, but with some earlier indications.[450]
The material is a rough dark slaty stone. The Tower has no buttresses, but is very
plain, something in the Welsh style, with a rude battlement, & a square headed
belfry window with label. [128] The South doorway is rude, with pointed arch upon
imposts. The Tower opens to the nave by very large rude pointed arch & by two
smaller ones to the side aisles, upon string piers, above the latter is an Early English
string course. The nave body is divided from each aisle by a row of 5 wide & very
obtuse arches, upon octagonal columns of rude workmanship, the whole of which
lean outwards & appear to be very insecure.[451] The windows present rather ordinary

---

[447] A*zure, two bendlets or*, for Fitzwilliam.
[448] This is a rare expression of Glynne's dislike of non-conformists.
[449] Could this have been so constructed with the idea of building a spire on top, intended as a
maritime marker?
[450] Also surmised by Sedding, *Norman Architecture*, 204, pl. LXXXVI. One of the jambs
is inscribed with 'XP' (Chi-Rho) as the sacred monogram symbolising Christ. Its presence
suggests reuse of the stone from an even earlier church on site; see H. O'Neill Hencken,
'Inscribed Stones at St Kew and Lanteglos by Fowey, Cornwall', *Archaeologia Cambrensis*
90 (1935), 156–9, who dates it as not later than the eighth century.
[451] The reopening of the church post-restoration is fully reported in the *RCG*, 22 February
1906, 4: 'Its tower, strong in appearance, was so ruinous that the peal of six bells (locally
famous for their tone) could no longer ring. The northern wall bulged outwards dangerously.
The roof gaped, and admitted the rain and the birds: the timbers had been braced together
with beams and iron ties, the former uncouth, the latter rotten with rust. A gallery, unused,

tracery, some square headed, some with obtuse arches of 3 and 4 lights. That at the East of the South aisle contains some fine fragments of stained glass.[452] The roofs are ribbed & semi circular, with some bosses.[453] The floor is paved with a kind of slate, & the whole has an appearance of neglect & decay, the more striking from the spacious dimensions of the Church. There are very considerable portions of ancient seats, the ends of which present beautiful sculpture in wood, but many have been strangely disfigured by green & blue paint! Many have very fine tracery & various emblems, & along the bases is a series of quatrefoils. In the South aisle is the ancient pew of the Mohuns bearing the date 1632, with sculpture in wood & arabesque

dirty and decayed, blocked the belfry arch. The east window might have served for a garden frame: the walls and arches were punctually and annually white washed at Easter for some forty years: and in the body of the church bench-ends of the fifteenth and sixteenth centuries, and seventeenth century panels of exquisite design, had been mixed up indescribably with high box-pews and patchwork of the cheapest carpentry [...] The work of restoration involved considerable care, for the north arcade was leaning towards the aisle about twelve inches, and it was held in that position by several iron tie-rods, and even the north wall was affected by the outward thrust of the roof. All the fourteenth and fifteenth century roofs were found in their original position, although, of course, they had been seriously dislocated by the giving way of the north arcade. They have, however, been very carefully repaired in "situ", and the arcade has been partially straightened, without even lifting the roofs. This one of the few churches which have escaped the usual plastering up of the roofs, such a common method during the last two centuries of obscuring the defective woodwork. Not only were all the old roofs in their original positions, but also the old carved bench-ends, and some very interesting Jacobean carved high pews, with their panels enriched with heraldic devices [...] The whole of the floor had to be dealt with. It was found to be honeycombed with vaults, and concrete had to laid over the entire area. Oak block flooring has been laid on the spaces occupied by the medieval benches, which have been most carefully repaired [...] Two piscinas were found concealed behind modem plastering. Two recesses were discovered in the north wall, probably for the reception of figures or shrines. The original west entrance under the tower, which had for many years been blocked, is now opened out. The precipitous slope of the ground from west to east, on which the church is built, may be realised from the fact that the ground is no less than twelve feet above the level of the tower floor. The difficulty of approach has been met by the construction of twelve steps outside the west door, and seven steps within the church to floor level. It is prolonged [sic] to rehang the bells, and the tower has been strengthened for the purpose. The pinnacles, which were found in the churchyard, have been restored to their original position. Much remains to be done to complete the repairing of the medieval and Jacobean seating.'

[452] Four figures in the upper tracery of the east window, to the north and representing the Coronation of the Virgin, the Virgin Mary, and St Anne, seated and enthroned; and to the south a semi-kneeling angel facing the standing figure of the Virgin, as the Annunciation. Of fifteenth-century date, these figures were probably part of a life cycle of the Virgin commissioned when a chantry chapel was constructed at the east end of the south aisle with a private entrance just to the north of the altar on the east wall, where the tomb and brass of Thomas de Mohun was installed. John Thomas Austen of Place, Fowey, wrote to Daniel Lysons on 8 May 1814, noting that 'there is one Quarter'd sh'd of 6 Coats in painted Glass [...] however I could not make it out exactly without a Ladder [...] in the same window was an inscription in painted Glass let us pray for the Souls of Mohun [...] & Sir Wm Trevanion K^{nt}. who caused this Window to be glazed', BL, Add. Ms. 9416, fols 67r.–v.

[453] In 1754, an 'Agreement to keep in repair the roofs of the parishioners' part of the church' was drawn up with William Honney, hellier of Lanteglos (KK: P116/6/2), but by 1822 the rural dean reported that 'the Roof is plaistered against the pin neatly but not ceiled. The parish object to the ceiling on account of the additional expence of it, & from the difficulty of doing it without removing many of the irons & cross beams which have been carried across the Church to keep together the outward Walls'; KK: AD59/74, 116. Evidently the structural situation continued to deteriorate over the rest of the century.

patterns, also shields with the arms of Mohun, Fitzwilliam &c. all painted. There is also another grand pew of the same character which belonged to the Grenvilles.[454] Under a window in the South aisle is a Perpendicular tomb[455] under a canopy with feathering & surmounted by a cornice of the Tudor flower, on this is the brass figure of an armed knight with inscription. This commemorates Sir Thomas Mohun; the inscription is given in Lysons – date 14..[456] There is another brass on a flat stone with the figures of Sir John Mohun (grandson of the above), his wife & 8 children, with an inscription also given by Lysons (1508).[457] [129]

The Font is of granite of square form with some rude Norman foliage, the corners of the basin being rounded off into the cylindrical shaft which supports it, & is set upon a square base.[458]

The Chancel has no arch of division, but extends beyond the aisles.

In the Church yard is the shaft of a cross in granite, surmounted by a four sided kind of tabernacle with sculpture representing the Virgin Mary, the Crucifixion, St Peter &c., & a cornice containing the nail head ornament.[459]

Glynne: GL, Glynne notebooks 64, p. 1 [n.d.]

---

[454] This is depicted on a watercolour of the church interior prior to restoration, exhibited in the church. In 1877, W.H. Rogers noted 'a fine old manorial seat in this (Mohun's) aisle dated 1608', and he blazoned the complex heraldry 'illustrative of the descent of Mohun of Cornwall and an alliance with Chudleigh', *The Antient Sepulchral Effigies and Monumental and Memorial Sculpture of Devon* (Exeter, 1877), 118–20. In 1866, J.P. St Aubyn prepared a seating plan, which took no account of the Mohun and Grenville family pews in the church accommodation, and although the ICBS were approached for a grant, LPL: ICBS 6242 (1864–8), the scheme did not go ahead. The seats and the medieval bench ends were reorganised by Sedding in his restoration of 1904–6 and placed at the west end of the south aisle, with other woodwork completed by the Pinwill company, KK: P116/2/6; and see Wilson, *Pinwill Sisters*, 84–8. Any bench ends retaining the 'green & blue paint' were cleaned at that time.

[455] The tombchest and canopy are constructed of a coarse-grained limestone. Sedding, *Norman Architecture*, 208, notes that the moulding of the Purbeck marble tomb slab is continuous on all four sides, suggesting that it was originally more prominent under the canopy than currently, where one edge is built into the wall.

[456] Lysons, *Cornwall*, ccxxxvi. The painting on the back of the tomb is not a Resurrection scene, as usually identified, but the image of Christ as the Man of Sorrows, censed by angels. John Thomas Austen also informed Daniel (see fn. 452) that this painting was recently 'whitewashed over', BL, Add. Ms. 9416, fol. 67r.; and see Gilbert, *Historical Survey*, ii, 898.

[457] The brass is actually to John Mohun, Esq., as per the inscription Glynne recorded in notebook 64. Lysons, *Cornwall*, 184, cites the most basic information from the inscription.

[458] The font basin is of Pentewan stone with an upper edge ornamented with a nail-head moulding, supported by a Purbeck marble shaft and base; illustrated by Sedding, *Norman Architecture*, pl. LXXXVIa.

[459] This was discovered in 1838 in a trench beside the western side of the church wall, perhaps buried to save it from Reformation destruction. It is a four-sided Lantern cross with the Crucifixion on the northern face, the Virgin Mary and Child on the opposite face, the remaining two sides bearing single figures, possibly Sts Peter and Paul. Glynne's 'nail-head ornament' is a combination of ogee-pointed arches and panels in combination with four-centred crocketed tracery; see A.G. Langdon and A. Preston-Jones, *Illuminating Our Lantern Crosses: A Catalogue of Late Medieval Cornish Lantern Crosses and Related Stone Sculpture* (Truro, 2022), 83–8.

In East window of South aisle stained glass with arms of Mohun, quartering Chichester, Courtenay, Haire, Fitzwilliam &c.[460] In the South aisle near East end a tomb under canopy enriched with feathering & surmounted by cornice of Tudor flower. On the tomb is the brass of a Knight in armour & an inscription on the border of brass, running thus,

> Hic jacet Thomas de Mohun de Joh'annes pater ejus, filius et heres Reginaldi de Mohun Militis et Elizabethe uxoris sue filie et heredis Joh'annis FitzWilliams Militis, Qui … (sec[und]us frater Johannis ultimi domini de Mohun et)[461] … Thomas obit … die mensis … anno domini Millesimo CCCC … quorum animabus propicietur Deus. Amen.[462]

On a flat stone in the floor near the above the effigies in brass of John Mohun his wife & 8 children, inscribed – date of death 1508.

> Hic jacent tumulata corpora Johannis Mohun armigeri, et Anne uxoris eius filie Ricardi Code armigeri et qui [quidem] Johannis fuit filius et heres Willielmi Mohun armigeri ac Florencie uxoris eius unius sororum Edwardi Courtenay Comitis Devonia et qui q'dem Johannis et [sic] Anna obierunt mense Septembris infra viginti ^quatuor^ horas ex infirmitate dicta sudore vocata Sud[or]e[463] Anno Domini M V^c VIII quorum animabus propicietur Deus. Amen.[464]

John Mohun was grandson of Thomas first named.
Near this is a fine pew, (1632 date) enriched with arabesque sculpture panelling and armorial bearings of Mohun.[465]

---

[460] This expands Lysons' record of the glass (fn. 447) and identifies the heraldry found on the Mohun monuments, described by Dunkin, *Brasses*, 14, 23.
[461] It is uncertain why Glynne inserted this line of the inscription in parentheses, unless it was then covered by the masonry of the wall/canopy – or whitewashed.
[462] Trans., *Here lie Thomas de Mohun, and John his father, son and heir of Reginald de Mohun, Knight, and Elizabeth his wife, daughter and heiress of John Fitz William, Knight, who [...] second brother of John, the last Lord Mohun, and the said Thomas died [blank] day of the month of [blank] AD 1400 [blank]. On whose souls may god have mercy. Amen.* The inference from this inscription and the generic figure of a man in armour on the tomb is that this was intended as a dynastic monument within a Mohun chantry, commemorating Thomas de Mohun and his father, which discoursed textually and heraldically their high-status lineage affiliations.
[463] This amendment to Glynne's initial interpretation, from 'dicta' to 'vocata' may well have been made after consulting Lysons, *Cornwall*, 184, where this (correct) reading is provided.
[464] Trans., *Here lie buried the bodies of John Mohun, Esq., and Anne his wife, daughter of Richard Code, Esq., and who the said John was son and heir of William Mohun, Esq., and Florence his wife, one of the sisters of Edward Courtney, earl of Devon, and the said John and Anne died in the month of September, within twenty-four hours [of each other], from the illness called the Sweating Sickness, AD 1508, on whose souls may god have mercy.*
[465] Although not specifically noted by Glynne, the size of some of these box pews was considerable. For instance, in 1716 a petition was sent up by nine parishioners, who 'hath no seat or Pew within the said Parish Church, for themselves to sit in, wherby they are rendered incapable of attending the divine service of the Church with that Reverence & devotion that they ought, Our Parish being very populous & the seats in our Parish Church being at publick times generally very full, & we do farther humbly Certifie your Lordshipp that there is a vacant plott of ground by the Bellfry between two Pillars being in length thirteen foot &

LAUNCELLS (Fig. 52)

Lysons: BL, Add. Ms. 9462, fol. 38r.

Lancels – Handsome Gothic Church, nave & side aisles separated by handsome clustered pillars, obtuse arches. Seats richly ornamented with carved Gothic tracery, the symbols of Xifixion &c.
Rude paintings of Apostles &c. on the base of a screen[466] <sketches of pier and capital, font>.
Glazed tiles with raised figures of lions, birds, gryphons etc. & roses.[467]
Mr Jones's seat & park near the Church.[468]

Lysons: BL, Add. Ms. 9445, fol. 167r.

Lancels church – Monument of John Chamond, ob. 1624, his figure in armour, recumbent & with a ruff.[469]
Henry Spoure Esq., ob. 1666, married the daughter & heir of Edmund Speccott of Anderton.[470]

Glynne: NLW, Ms. 185 (unpaginated field notebook [1857])

Launcells – 3 equal aisles / South Porch / West Tower, rood protruding on North at 1 bay. 3 light Perpendicular <sketch> roof slated. Tower like Bridgerule, 3 strings diminished, battlement, 4 crocketed pinnacles.
West door obtuse, granite, continuous [moulding?], 3 light window.
Pretty remarkable site, very steep, woods & water.
<sketch of oblong moulding> in 2nd stage of Tower. Large Porch outer door on imposts. Stoup to Porch. High evergreens on pillars remarkable. Arcade, 5 Tudor late granite & mouldings, light shafts <sketch> granite Tudor flowers on capitals. Full of open seats, whole of body &c., neat paneled tracery, shields and emblems, Crucifixion / Passion, Lily [illegible]. Various initial letters to shields, & leaf scribed all round.
All paved of tiles, forms of [illegible] tiles glazed <sketch> swans, fleur de lys, Holy lamb.

---

breadth four foot four Inches fit & convenient for the erecting & building a seat or Pew for the above nam'd to sit in time of divine Service', DHC: DR, Presentments Chanter Basket DI/13.
[466] The screen no longer survives.
[467] None of this detail was published in Lysons, *Cornwall*, 185–6.
[468] This refers to the Barton of Launcells, 'which had been for a considerable time in the Orchard family, was leased by the late Paul Orchard, Esq., for a long term of years, to the late Rev. Cadwallader Jones, and is now the seat of Joseph Hawkey, Esq., who married his widow', Lysons, *Cornwall*, 185.
[469] For the dynastic significance of this monument to the Chamond family, see Cockerham, *Continuity and Change*, 90, 93, 96, 103, pl. 168.
[470] This was a mural slate tablet but is now lost; see P. Cockerham, '"Hoc sub sepulchro dormit pulchellus puer": Edmund Spoure's Commemoration of His Son and Heir Henry, at North Hill (Cornwall)', *Church Monuments* 36 (2022), 130–78, at 166–7, pl. 20.

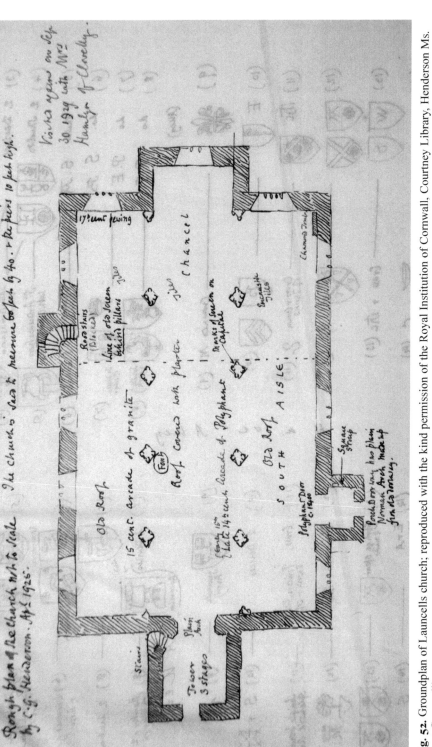

Fig. 52. Groundplan of Launcells church; reproduced with the kind permission of the Royal Institution of Cornwall, Courtney Library, Henderson Ms. 'East Cornwall', 274.

Cradle roof aisles, ribs & bosses. Font cup shaped, carved rope round top, on cylindrical & square base. East 3 windows of 4 lights. Quantity of glazed lights. Plain Tower arch concealed.

Glynne: GL, Glynne notebooks 14, fols 71–2

Launcells, S. Andrew, 21 January 1857.
An excellent specimen of the Cornish Perpendicular Church, especially as the interior retains the ancient benches & is altogether in good preservation & neat condition.
The Church has 3 equal aisles or divisions, with a Western Tower & large South porch. The Tower much resembles that at Bridgerule,[471] in its battlement, pinnacles & division by strings into 3 tapering stories. The second stage has an oblong moulded opening. The Porch contains a stoup, the outer door has imposts. The Tower arch is plain. The roofs slated. *<The West doorway of the Tower has an obtuse arch. The material granite.[472]>*
The windows are all of 3 lights except ~~that~~ those at the East of the aisles which are of 4, and very much of one pattern. The interior is light & pleasing. The arcades are each formed by 5 Tudor shaped arches with good mouldings, the piers of the usual form but having Tudor flowers in their capitals, the whole of the granite untouched by whitewash.[473] The roofs are coved, ~~the~~ with ribs & bosses, the latter enriched with shields, scrolls & initial letters.[474] The pavement of every part abounds with [72] original encaustic tiles. The benches are entirely open & ancient, presenting excellent specimens of enriched carved ends: square topped & abounding in rich & varied sculpture, tracery, shields, the emblems of the Crucifixion & Passion, ~~Litres~~ Fleur de lys &c. ~~Holy Lambs.~~ On the tiles appear fleur de lys, Holy Lambs & figures of birds.[475]

[471] Bridgerule (Devon) is less than four miles away from Launcells; see Cherry and Pevsner, *Devon*, 212–13.
[472] Glynne's additional comment (fol. 70v.) seems contemporaneous with his church description, and it appears in his field notebook with the other information – yet the doorway is rounded, not a flattened 'obtuse' arch.
[473] However, in 1768 it was ordered that 'the wall near the Belfry to be white washed', DHC DR, PR362–4/30/2; and in 1814 and 1824 the rural deans ordered that 'the Church must be White washed'; KK: AD59/74, 21–2. Perhaps this was never carried out effectively, and although the Chamond tomb was covered in whitewash in the Georgian period, this may have demonstrated more an iconoclastic motive than one of 'cleanliness', see *The History of Christianity in Cornwall AD 500–2000*, exhibition catalogue, Royal Institution of Cornwall (2000), 30.
[474] Curiously, in 1909, it was reported that 'the nave and chancel roofs are tunnelled from end to end with plaster, so that none of the woodwork is visible. The aisles and porch have also had their panels ceiled', Sedding, *Norman Architecture*, 212, confirmed by Henderson in 1925 and 1929; CL, Henderson Ms. 'East Cornwall', 274. This must have taken place at some unrecorded point between Glynne's visit and the early twentieth century therefore. Sedding also noted that 'the church is much in need of repair', as it was never modernised during the nineteenth century. It was only in 1932 that moves were taken to restore the fabric; see *WMN*, 27 September 1932, 8; Mattingly, *Churches of Cornwall*, 51–2.
[475] These are typical of Barnstaple ware; see L. Keen, 'A Series of Seventeenth- and Eighteenth-Century Lead-Glazed Relief Tiles from North Devon', *Journal of the British Archaeological Association*, 3rd series 32 (1969), 144–70; see the sketches of the bench ends in CL, Henderson Ms. 'East Cornwall', 275.

The Font is early, the bowl of cup shape, round the top a rope moulding the stem cylindrical on a square base.[476]
The Church is very beautifully situated on steep ground amidst wood & streams. The interior from its tiles & carved benches is remarkably beautiful – the columns were wreathed with evergreens placed there at Xmas.

LAUNCESTON, S. MARY MAGDALENE

Lysons: BL, Add. Ms. 9462, fol. 42r.

Nave & side aisles, clustered pillars & very obtuse arches
In the South aisle Monument of the Rev. William Bedford,[477] Charles Bligh alderman, & often mayor, 1716.[478]
Family of Lawrence.[479]
Font octagonal.
In North aisle a brass plate on the floor for Giles Pinfold of Minchin Hampton 1745, aet. 40.[480]
A splendid monument for Granville Pyper Esq., & Richard Wise Gent., Aldermen of Launceston both buried at Bath. Granville died at Bath 1716, Richard who died at Launceston 1726 chose to be buried with him – juxta cineres domini amantissimi & charissimi.[481] Executed by John Weston, 1731.[482] Two orders of pillars Corinthian & over the composition of veined white & black & yellow marble, in the upper part statues of Faith Hope & Charity, busts on the top on each side with inscription. [separate sheet] Justice & Faith – poorly executed.[483]

---

[476] Described by Sedding, *Norman Architecture*, 210–1; and see the CRSBI, available online at: https://www.crsbi.ac.uk/view-item?i=8149 [accessed December 2023].
[477] This monument to Rev. William Bedford, rector (d. 1737), was in fact commissioned in 1787, after the death of his sons Charles and John in 1786 and 1787 respectively. They succeeded him as curates of the church, between them serving seventy-three years in office, Gilbert, *Historical Survey*, ii, 505.
[478] The Bligh monument, an inscription plate set within a richly decorated border, was petitioned for in 1731, 'Whereas Elizabeth Blight is desirous to erect [a] Monument in Memory of her Father & Mother deceased [...] of three Feet & half [in height] & seven Feet in Length to be fixt on a Jam, or Peer or the [south side] of the Church, ye erecting of which will be no way prejudicial [...] Walls of the said Church, or to any Persons Right', DHC: DR Petitions Chanter Basket D2/230. The licence was granted the following year, Chanter Basket D2/231.
[479] This refers to a large wall monument also in the south aisle to Arthur and Charles Lawrence, both of whom died in 1780, Arthur aged twenty-five years, and Charles aged twenty-two, commemorated by an elegy on their deaths; see Gilbert, *Historical Survey*, ii, 506.
[480] This is now mural in the north aisle.
[481] Trans., *next to the ashes of the most loving and most dear*. The inscription continues, contextualising the quote from it made by Lysons.
[482] This monument is unsigned and only hesitantly attributed to Weston. It may well have been Lysons' viewing of the monuments to Edward Hobbs (d. 1718) at Gerrans, and Henry Scobell (d. 1727) at St Blazey, which Weston signed, that he also attributed this monument to him; see Roscoe *et al.*, *Dictionary*, 1372–3.
[483] This massive monument has been the subject of much scholarly attention, not just because of its form and composition, but more from its commemoration of two men, the one (Wise) as manservant and later secretary to the other (Piper), and their evident desire to be buried together in the same vault in Bath Abbey. The monument provoked controversy at the time

Prior of Launceston.[484]

Richard Vyvyan of Tresmarrow, 2nd son of Sir Richard Vyvyan of Trelowarren, Barrister at law & Recorder of Launceston, 1771, & Philippa his wife, daughter & heiress of Hugh Pyper Esq., 1771. & [separate monumental inscription] for Hugh Pyper Esq. of Tresmarrow, eldest son of Philip Pyper Esq., & grandson of Sir Hugh Pyper, 1754.

Monument with effigies kneeling at the East end of North aisle, for Col. Sir Hugh Piper Knt., Lieutenant Governor of the Royal Citadel & Island of Plymouth, Captain of the Castle of Exon, Constable of the Castle of Launceston, one of his Majesty's justices of the peace for the Counties of Devon & Cornwall, an alderman & Representative in Parliament for the Borough of Dunhevid.[485] He served in the Civil Wars as an Ensign, Lieutenant & Captain under Sir Richard & Sir Beville Granville, Kts, at the siege of Plymouth, the battles of Stratton & Lansdown, where he was wounded in the neck & thigh & shot thro' the shoulder. His Estates were sequestered by the rump Parliament for his Loyalty to his Master & injured Sovereign King Charles the 1st, he died July 24 1687, aet. 76.[486]

[separate sheet] Monument for Captain Philip Piper his son.[487]

Gothick pulpit very richly ornamented with sculptured foliage.

Round the lower part of the Chancel on the outside on shields, 'Ave Maria gracie plena Dominus tecum sponsas [sic] amat sponsam maria optimam partem ^3^ legit [elegit] o quam terribilis ac metuendus est locus iste vere aliud non est hic nisi domus dei et posta celi'.[488] This inscription begins from the small door on the south side & runs round to the west end of the church <sketch of arcade with inscribed shields>.

There is a very mean tower at the South West corner.

regarding its proximity to the Piper pew and its dislocation of the town authorities from their pews, because it was planned to be erected 'over the seat where the Town Clerk of the said Burrough and part of the Two seats where the Burgesses or Assistants of the said Burrough usually Sitt when in the Church', DHC: DR, Chanter basket D2/178, 5 March 1728. However, an episcopal licence was granted 10 May 1729, DHC: DR, Chanter basket D2/179. For a discussion of the 'queer' nature of this monument, see A. Bray, *The Friend* (Chicago/London, 2003), 211, 230–4.

[484] This heading seems out of place here.

[485] For his civic and parliamentary career, see Henning, *House of Commons 1660–1690*, iii, 247.

[486] This inscription is published in Lysons, *Cornwall*, 190, unlike the other inscriptions he transcribed. The monument collapsed in the 1930s, and only the figures, part of the inscription, and the prayer desk before which the figures were depicted kneeling, survive. Permission for the space to be occupied by the monument was granted by the borough in 1678, who 'give and graunt unto Sr Hugh Piper Knight Deputy Governour of Plymouth and one of the Aldermen of the Burrough aforesaid and to his heires for ever for a burying place one parcell of grownd in the parish Church of St. Mary Magdalen within the said Burrough lying and being in the Chancell of the said Church on the North-East side of the said Church which is now rayled in by the said Sir Hugh Piper, and where Phillipp Piper Esq. lately deceased sonne of the said Sir Hugh Piper lyeth interred Contayning Fifteen Foote in length and six foote and half in breadth or thereabout', DHC: DR, Chanter basket D1/1. It was duly confirmed by the Consistorial Court on 30 August 1686. See also O.B. Peter, *Sir Hugh Piper: The Knighted Son of Launceston, and His Descendants* (Launceston, 1904).

[487] The inscription panel to Philip Piper (d. 1677) is now mounted murally in the south aisle, under that of his father.

[488] Trans: *Hail Mary full of grace, the Lord is with you. The bridegroom loves the bride; Mary has chosen the better part; Oh how terrible and fearful is this place, yet there is nothing else here except the house of God and the entrance to Heaven.*

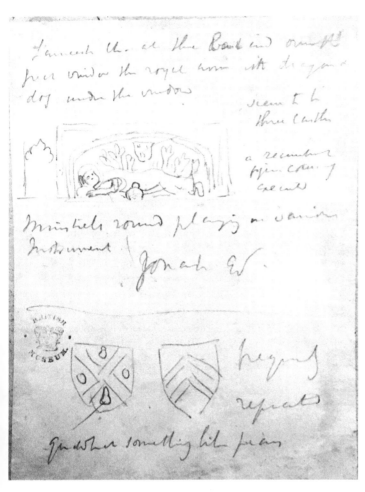

Fig. 53.
Sculpted figure
and heraldry,
Launceston St
Mary; from
the British
Library
Archive, Add.
Ms. 9462,
fol. 40r.

Fol. 40r. Launceston Church – At the East end over the great window, the royal arms with dragon & dog, under the window a recumbent figure crudely executed[489] <sketch of figure with shield> seems to be three castles <identifying the charges on the shield[490]>. (Fig. 53)

[489] This refers to the recumbent figure of Mary Magdalene sculpted in low relief in a separate slab of granite positioned under the east window, and to which the inscription around the church alludes. The figural iconography has been variously interpreted, but Mattingly, *Churches of Cornwall*, 54, suggests she is represented as a Good Friday penitential figure creeping to the cross.

[490] The stone is now decayed, and it is difficult to give a precise interpretation of the heraldry, although R. and O.B. Peter, *The Histories of Launceston and Dunheved, in the County of Cornwall* (Plymouth, 1885), 307, named the charges as 'a chevron between three bells'. This combination was incorporated on shields found on medieval church bells in the county (Dunkin, *Church Bells*, 33, 36, pl. II), and also had an acknowledged Exeter basis as such (D.H.B. Chesshyre, T. Woodcock *et al.* (eds), *Dictionary of British Arms: Medieval Ordinary*, 4 vols (London, 1998–2014), ii, 298). One might speculate that with these arms celebrating music, and in the context of the penitential figure of Mary Magdalene, this was a reference to the indulgence published by Bishop Lacy in 1440 of forty days granted to all penitents

Minstrels round playing on various instruments. Jonah <sketches of shields>[491] frequently repeated, query where[?] something like pears [for the charge on the Kelway coat].

Fol. 41r. <sketches of details of the church porch[492] and associated sculptures>.

Fol. 40v. July 31. Door of the White Hart Inn at Launceston <sketch of round decorated arch, with base and capital of column, and a list of parishes>.[493]

Glynne: GL, Glynne notebooks 17, fols 76–8

Launceston [before 1840].

This is a late Rectilinear Church & remarkable for the richness of its exterior, which however has more of ornament than is elegant, & the whole is rather curious than of good character. The Church is large, consisting of 3 long aisles of equal length & height, without Clerestory or any distinction of Chancel ^& the whole embattled^. The Tower is plain, embattled, with a square turret attached, & is singularly placed [77] considerably to the West of the nave & a modern erection intervening between them which contains vestry & other rooms. *<The Tower seems to be the remnant of the original church. The present Church was built in 1540 by Sir Henry Trecarrel & dedicated to St Mary Magdalene.*[494] *There is an inscription*

contributing to the support of the Guild of Minstrels, who were duly sculpted around the principal figure; hence, the rebuilding of the church was an opportunity to refresh the purposes of this indulgence perhaps? See Henderson, *Cornish Church Guide*, 138; and G.R. Dunstan (ed.), *The Register of Edmund Lacy, Bishop of Exeter, 1420–1455*, vol. II (Torquay, 1966), 197.

[491] These are, *argent, two bones in saltire sable between four pears or*, for Kelway, and *argent, three chevronells sable*, for Trecarrel, funded by Henry Trecarrel and his wife Margaret Kelway; see Mattingly, *Cornish Churches*, 52–4.

[492] A drawing of the south porch and window of the south aisle is reproduced in Lysons, *Cornwall*, opp. ccxxxi, with his description of the church.

[493] Lysons, *Cornwall*, ccxxviii, 191, note the doorway, perhaps removed from the priory ruins in 1767 to form an imposing entrance to the inn, when its facade was rebuilt and the interior refurbished; see H.L. Douch, *Old Cornish Inns and Their Place in the Social History of Cornwall* (Truro, 1966), 75. The list of parishes names those in the north-east, extending south-westwards to Blisland and Lanhydrock, presumably as an itinerary.

[494] The period of construction was over three decades, from around 1511 to its termination in 1544 on the death of Sir Henry Trecarrel. There was also 'iij li rec[eptis] ex dono Johan[nis] Arundell milit[is] ad vitriand[um] alter[is] fenestr[am] ib[ide]m hoc anno' (trans., *£3 received from the gift of John Arundell knight to the glazing of the altar window of the same this year*), taken from the borough accounts for 1543–4, KK: BLAUS/172, identified by Peter and Peter, *Launceston*, 183–4. The sum donated seems quite large in comparison to the 20s. paid to a glazier in Chagford, in 1531, for a new window; and 23s. 6d. paid to a glazier for 'glassen of ye church wyndows & ye church howsse & a glasse over ye rodlofft', in Stratton in 1564, and there will doubtless be other *comparanda*; see *The Church Wardens' Accounts of St Michael's Church Chagford 1480–1600*, trans. F.M. Osborne (Chagford, 1979), 108, and *Stratton Churchwardens' Accounts 1512–1578*, ed. J. Mattingly, DCRS NS 60 (2018), 112. This donation probably marks the *terminus ante quem* for the church construction. For example, before this date, in 1534, there is a receipt for windows brought to the church, each window itemised by weight, KK: BLAUS/76; and in 1538, progress had continued such that an agreement was drawn up relating to 'all suche leddes, cisternes, pipes and gutters [...] according to the patente and facion of the leddes of the churche of Buckland, w^tin the countie of Devon', taking their model from an example that presumably the officers of the borough had successfully seen in action, KK: BLAUS/75. No medieval glass remains in the church now, as in 1646 it was replaced: 'For putting up in sundry windows 100 foote of new glass at 7d. the foote, £2 18s. 4d., more for 24 foote of french glasse at the higher end of the churche

in Latin, running all round the Church.[495]> There is a large South porch, ^having windows with crocketed ogee canopies^ which together with the walls of the Church is covered with a series of panneling, with sculpture representing shields, niches, foliages &c. ^The buttresses also have crocketed pinnacles.^ Immediately under the East window is a piece of sculpture representing St Mary Magdalene, ^(recumbent beneath an arch)^ to whom the Church is dedicated. The whole has a rich & singular effect.[496]
The Interior is spacious & light, the windows very numerous & all of 4 lights ^except the East window which is of five lights^. The divisions of the aisles are formed by a double row of Tudor arches, 8 in each row, which have light lozenge piers each with 4 shafts having octagonal capitals, some of which have the square flower.[497] ^The want of a Clerestory diminishes greatly the effect of the interior.^ The roofs are coved & divided by ribs into panneled compartments, the ribs have fine wood carving, & the bosses at their points of intersection very rich – there are also wood figures from which the ribs spring. The Pulpit has excessively beautiful wood carving, divided into compartments each having an ogee arch with feathering & the spandrels filled with elaborate foliage. There are also rich & beautiful bands of foliage with vine leaves & grapes, both above & below, & the pedestal supporting the pulpit has fine panneling. The Font is [78] of granite, of octagonal form diminishing towards the base upon an octagonal pedestal.[498] The Church is neatly pewed & has a large Organ.[499]

Glynne: GL, Glynne notebooks 64, fol. 2 [before 1840]

at 9d. ye foote £00 18s. 4d.', KK: BLAUS/413. It is curious to note that at this date the 'higher end' of the church still carried a certain prestige, requiring the glass to be 'French' and of higher quality.
[495] Glynne revisited Launceston in 1858 probably adding these notes on fol. 76v.
[496] Fully described by Beacham and Pevsner, *Cornwall*, 288.
[497] In 1838, the granite pillars and windows were cleared of whitewash, so if Glynne visited after this date (as is likely) he would have appreciated the quality of the carving; Warner, *A Time to Build*, 210. After Glynne's visit, the church was restored in 1852–3, as reported by the *RCG*, 7 January 1853, 6: 'It will be remembered by those who have formerly visited this church, that although its exterior was so handsome (the granite stones being elaborately carved in various devices), yet the interior used to present a desolate appearance, the pillars leaning very much, and hideous boxes of pews of all shapes and sizes bearing the usual testimony to the depraved taste of the last half-century. The church has been now entirely renovated, all the pillars taken down, the roof is a new and most substantial one (the cost of which was partly met by a grant from the corporation fund left to them in trust for the purpose), and the seating also re-arranged in uniformity and regularity, whereby 100 additional sittings have been gained for the poor.' LPL: ICBS 4335 (1850–3) gave a grant towards reseating and repairs including plans before and after restoration. The plan prior to the work shows the pattern of high pews, with the pulpit, desk, and clerk's seat in the central aisle in front of the altar.
[498] This was a post-Reformation structure, mounted on a Norman base ornamented with grotesques; see Sedding, *Norman Architecture*, 214–5, pl. LXXXVII; and the CRSBI, available online at: https://www.crsbi.ac.uk/view-item?i=8217 [accessed December 2023], who question whether the original structure associated with the base was brought to St Mary's church from another location.
[499] The history of the organ (1718–24) is related by Peter and Peter, *Launceston*, 322–5, together with the building of a new loft in which to accommodate it, for which also see DHC: DR, Petitions Chanter Basket D2/28 (1718).

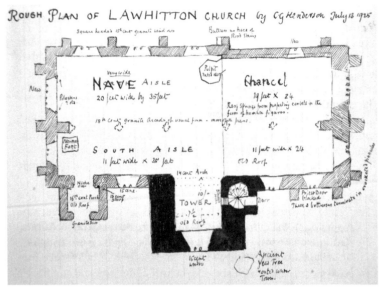

Fig. 54.
Groundplan
of Lawhitton
church;
reproduced
with the kind
permission
of the Royal
Institution
of Cornwall,
Courtney
Library,
Henderson
Ms. 'East
Cornwall',
284.

Launceston – Church built from the ground in 1540 by Sir Henry Trecarrel & dedicated to St Mary Magdalene. Inscription round the whole Church in Latin. Tower detached & more ancient, belonged to the Chapel of St Stephen.

LAWHITTON (Fig. 54)

Lysons: BL, Add. Ms. 9462, fol. 42r.

Lawhitton – small Church, tower on South side,[500] Nave & South aisle, font like Warbstow &c.[501]
In the Chancel on the North side of the altar a monument in artificial stone by Coad & Sealy with Sarcophagus &c. for Richard Coffin Esq., ob. 1786 [*recte* 1796], the family resided for many generations at Hexworthy in this County. He was Son of Edward Bennett & Honour his wife, daughter of Richard Coffin of Portledge, Devon, dying without issue, in him ended the lineal descent of the family of Bennet & Coffin.[502]

---

[500] The tower originally stood at the end of the south transept before the south aisle was added.
[501] See Sedding, *Norman Architecture*, 222–3, pl. XCII, for a description of the font, although it was not included in the list made by Lysons of fonts similar to that at Warbstow; see also the CRSBI, available online at: https://www.crsbi.ac.uk/view-item?i=5005 [accessed November 2023].
[502] This monument, now mutilated, was described by Gilbert, *Historical Survey*, ii, 498, as 'representing a recumbent female effigy, pointing at the following inscription, which is placed between the figures of two boys' – the inscription transcribed being that fairly accurately published by Lysons. The figure of the female was the Coade *Mourning Girl*, who could be depicted reclining on a cornice, or as here, on a sarcophagus. It is also accompanied by putti, illustrating one of the pitfalls of making up monument designs from stock units made by the Coade workshop, in that the putti are too large in scale for the figure of the girl; see A. Kelly, *Mrs Coade's Stone* (Upton-upon-Severn, 1990), 249. What remains

A slab in South aisle for Richard Bennett Esq., Counsellor at Law 1619.[503]

LELANT

Lysons: BL, Add. Ms. 9462, fol. 43r.

Lelant Church – Nave & side aisles. Clumsy clustered pillars & pointed arches, one arch at the west end between Nave & North aisle clumsy round pillars originally 3' 1" high in the shaft.[504] Door in North aisle & a staircase in North wall. <sketches of Norman capital & later capital with leaves> some plain.
Font modern.
Ancient Cross on the outside of the Church yard at the West end of the Church with a coarse Crucifix on one side <sketch> the South side, <sketch of high cross> in the Church yard.[505]

Lysons: BL, Add. Ms. 9445, fol. 181r.

Lelant Church – Hugh Pawley 1721.[506]
Stephen Pawley Gent., 1635, figures on slate of himself & wife kneeling, & behind them eleven children.[507]
A slate monument with figures in memory of William Praed Gent., of Grenchrow [*sic*] with three daughters, 1620.[508]

has been conserved and mounted murally in the church. The dynastic detail is recorded by Lysons, *Cornwall*, 193.
[503] A floor stone in slate, this, with others to the Bennet family, such as Robert Bennet (d. 1683), is now poorly preserved.
[504] This refers to the remains of the original Norman arcade, of which only the westernmost arches survived, as also identified by Glynne. The arch was probably walled up when the church was enlarged in the fifteenth and sixteenth centuries and the remainder of the Norman arcade substituted by the routine 'clustered pillars and pointed arches' of the Cornish Perpendicular – although it also suggests that the proposed Perpendicular aisle was never finished; see Blight, *West Cornwall*, 83–4; and Sedding, *Norman Architecture*, 223–5, pl. XCIII.
[505] See Langdon, *West Penwith*, 32, nos. 40–1, where both crosses are easily recognisable from Lysons' sketches.
[506] This is a polished marble slab with an inscription in Roman letters set underneath a heraldic display. The inscription commences: 'This Marble Stone was placed here in the year of our Lord 1713', yet it records the deaths of Hugh Pawley (1721) and his wife Judith (1698), so is presumably in error for '1723', erected by one of their four surviving children.
[507] The inscription on this slate slab is unclear due to the desquamation of the surface, but it bears two shields, one of Pawley (*or, a lion rampant sable, on a chief dancette of the second three mullets argent*) impaling Tresteane (*azure, three stone pillars argent, on a chief vert as many lapwings proper*), the other quartering Arundell(?). William Borlase tricked the arms and deduced the families commemorated by the monument and their mutual related status; he found it in the south chancel. See BL, Egerton Ms. 2657, fol. 18v.
[508] This slab is cut in higher relief, so the desquamation of the surface has caused fewer disruptions to the inscriptions. Borlase found the slate in the north chancel; BL, Egerton Ms. 2657, fol. 18v. The Praed family was settled at Trevethow, Lysons, *Cornwall*, cxlvii. William Praed had married Prudence, the sister of Stephen Pawley, relating the two families and perhaps providing a motive for the commission of two very similar commemorative slate slabs.

Glynne: GL, Glynne notebooks 70, fols 5B–6B

Lelant Uny, St. Uny [1843].

A Church of the usual Cornish arrangement – a West Tower, nave & side aisles with separate roofs continued to the East end & a South porch. The general features are Perpendicular but there are Norman portions near the West end of the nave. The Tower is embattled, with 4 modern pinnacles & a polygonal turret on the West side. There is also a poor West door & 3 light window, the belfry windows are also of 3 lights. The North aisle is carried to the West wall of the Tower. The Northern windows are modernised in a wretched fashion, ~~and~~ as indeed are most others about the Church,[509] that at the East end (which presents 3 equal gables) is of 4 lights.[510] There is a North door closed, with a label & panneled spandrels. The South porch has a gable & is entered by a small obtuse arch springing from half octagonal shafts. Above it a canopied niche. Within the porch is a handsome doorway with good mouldings & surmounted by a label, the spandrels containing very elegant panneling. Within the arch moulding is the 4 leaf flower. The interior, as usual is low. On each side are 6 arches of somewhat dissimilar shapes, mostly wide & some with rather straight sides. Most of the piers have 4 shafts clustered in diamond form with intermediate mouldings, the capitals ^general^ octagonal ^& plain^, but in one instance on the South side there is some very good foliage on ~~the~~ a capital. The 2 Western arches on the North side are remnants of an earlier building, the piers very short & thick, of circular form, one arch semi-circular, the other pointed, but very rude & plain, & Westward of the last arch is a considerable portion of original wall.[511]

[6B] There is a fine coved roof, with ribs forming panneled compartments & elegant bosses.[512] There is a turret on the North side with door that led to the rood steps. In the South aisle of the chancel is a small Tudor arch door with label. The Font is a panneled octagon bowl.[513] In the West gallery is a barrel organ.

[509] In 1845, these sash windows were replaced by two light windows with stone mullions, and much of the church cleaned of whitewash; see *The Ecclesiologist* 10 (1850), 356. Glynne pasted a copy of this report on the church improvements opposite his account of it, on the verso of fol. 4B.

[510] This window was replaced by one of three lights at a restoration in 1872–3. The *RCG*, 9 August 1873, 5, reported that 'the fabric is very interesting, as it contains portions of Norman and thirteenth century work which were left, when the last re-building took place in the 15th century. Mr J. D. Sedding, the architect, has retained the latter – 15th century – in all his designs [...] Unfortunately an east window, quite out of character with the rest of the church, filled with painted glass of about thirty years ago, rather offends the eye, but the architect has made the best of the evil by raising the window and thus making the chancel and nave somewhat higher than they were before.' See also LPL: ICBS 7512 (1872), for repairs following gale damage; and notes of the restoration etc. in KK: P120/1/4, register of baptisms (1846–1901). The questionable glass has since been replaced (1973) by a window designed by M.C. Farrar Bell FRSA MGP, which is nationally renowned for its design and features.

[511] Drawn in elevation by Godwin, 'Churches in Kerrier and Penwith', 338–9.

[512] The roofs of the chancel and north aisle were completely replaced at the 1872–3 restoration. Prior to this date, the *RCG*, 5 March 1870, 5, reported that 'Lelant parish church [...] is in a very bad state, and has half-decayed square boxes for seats. The arcades and walls are in good condition, and the windows are in a fair state, but the roof is little better than was that of the daughter church of Towednack. Some very heavy pieces of the roof have recently fallen down.'

[513] The font at that time was most likely eighteenth century. Lysons noted it as 'modern', and the EDAS also noted it as 'octagonal, modern, rather poor', DHC: F5/17/2/4, EDAS, series of

LESNEWTH

Lysons: BL, Add. Ms. 9445, 181r.

Lesnewth – church in form of a cross, tower with plain turrets. Font octagonal on an octagonal pedestal. Church very mean and almost sunk in the ground.[514] The top of the roof nearly on a level with the churchyard style – a very steep descent from it[515] <sketch of font[516]>.

LEWANNICK

Lysons: BL, Add. Ms. 9462, fol. 43r.

Lewannick – Nave & side aisles, clustered pillars there but the South Chancel & Nave have the capitals ornamented, obtuse pointed arches.[517]

Rough Notes – sheet 25 (1862). J.H. Matthews, *A History of the Parishes of Saint Ives, Lelant, Towednack and Zennor, in the County of Cornwall* (London, 1892), 91, recorded that the 'ancient font' had been ejected from the church probably in the eighteenth century, replaced by the 'modern' version, but the original was restored to the church in 1889 having been found in a farmyard broken into two. See also the CRSBI, available online at: https://www.crsbi. ac.uk/view-item?i=9113 [accessed December 2023].

[514] The church as Lysons saw it was almost completely rebuilt roughly sixty years later, with the ancient cross-shape replaced by a simple nave and chancel with a vestry to the south; see Maclean, *Trigg Minor*, ii, 411–12, pl. XLI. The *RCG*, 4 October 1866, 7, reported: 'The old church was in the early English style of architecture, with nave, aisle, chancel, south porch, two transepts, lofty square tower, and handsome carved roof. The church having fallen into a state of decay, resolution was come to re-erect it […] In rebuilding the church the old plan has not been thoroughly adhered to, the north chancel, in consequence of the dampness of the soil, having been done away with […] The building now comprises nave, chancel, south transept, and tower. The chancel and tower are separated from the nave by arches of massive masonry, the tower arch being old work. On the north the chancel, is an old Norman window, with a deep recess, in which fits a stone slab, supposed to have been from an altar from its bearing five crosses carved on it; it will now be used as a credence table. On the opposite side of the chancel the old piscina has been restored […] The south transept is separated from the chancel by two arches, the centre support being a massive granite pillar, said to be of the Norman period. The arches are filled in with an ornamental screen, the transept used a vestry […] The windows have all granite jambs, mullions, and tracery; some are new, but where possible, the old stone has retained […] The font has been restored and a new base supplied. The roof of the church is open […] The old stone has been used up in the building, and the south porch, about which there was some old work, has been carefully restored, and the old quoins have been refixed without any dressing all.' See KK: P121/5/1, churchwardens' accounts; and the faculty for rebuilding, DHC: DR, Faculty Causes, Cornwall, Lesnewth (1865).

[515] Because of the setting of the church in the landscape, a frequent direction from the rural deans was 'earth round the church to be repaired', repeated annually, 1821–3; KK: AD59/74, 153.

[516] This shows the original font base, replaced at the restoration.

[517] The EDAS noted that the 'chancel is ruinous', DHC: F5/17/2/4, EDAS, series of Rough Notes – sheet 21 (1861). The church suffered a devastating fire in 1890, following which some features were replaced, as reported in the *RCG*, 20 November 1890, 6: 'The only portions of the edifice not destroyed by the fire were the external walls, portions of the columns which divided the nave from the aisles, the font, an ancient cresset stone, the roofs over the two porches, the vestry, and a part of the reredos. All the rest of the timber work, all the internal fittings, and the timber work and bells in the tower were destroyed […] The beautifully carved and moulded south aisle arcade columns of Polyphant stone, which the fire had cracked

Fig. 55.
Groundplan
of Lezant
church;
reproduced
with the
kind
permission
of the Royal
Institution
of Cornwall,
Courtney
Library,
Henderson
Ms. 'East
Cornwall',
303.

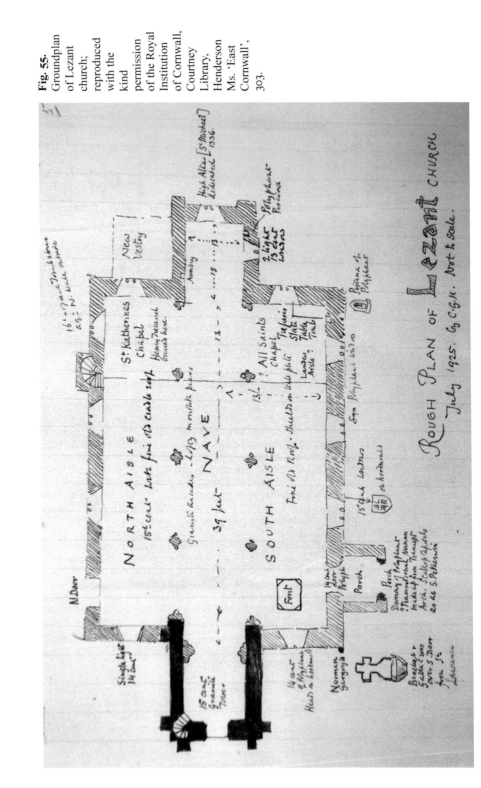

ROUGH PLAN OF LEZANT CHURCH

July 1925. By C.G.H. Not to scale.

The door of the Nave enriched with vine leaves ^in a large channel^ pointed arch.[518]
Font octagonal on one side a labyrinth or ornamentation &c.[519]

LEZANT (Fig. 55)

Lysons: BL, Add. Ms. 9462, fol. 43r.

Lezant – Handsome moor stone Church, Nave & side aisles.[520]
Monument in South aisle against the wall, with effigie of a lady in ruff,[521] also a slate
tomb beneath with these arms[522] <sketch of heraldry, font[523]>.

LINKINHORNE

Lysons: BL, Add. Ms. 9462, fol. 44r.

and slit in every direction, and the injured granite columns of the north arcade, have been
faithfully reproduced [...] With the exception of a small portion of the wall which adjoins
the south porch, none of the external walls have been rebuilt. The new roofs are of the exact
contour of the old ones [...] The former seats, fixed 350 years ago, were of massive oak,
having carved ends, some of them terminating with representations of kneeling angels; these
seats, unhappily, were all burnt [...] The foundations of the fine old Norman font had sunk,
and the font itself had become cracked by the heat. It has now been raised to its original level
on the floor and re-lined with lead.' See also KK: P123/2/5–7, photographs of the church
before and after the fire.

[518] This refers to the tower doorway, which has multiple mouldings made of Polyphant stone
and a tall crocketed ogee arch with elongated finials to the sides, which survived the fire; see
Gilbert, *Historical Survey*, ii, 486–7.

[519] Sedding, *Norman Architecture*, 232–3, pl. XCVI; and see the CRSBI, available online at:
https://www.crsbi.ac.uk/view-item?i=4238 [accessed December 2023].

[520] That is, the aisles do not extend eastwards flanking the chancel. A letter from Rev. Charles
Mayson of 1812 details the destruction of medieval glass and window tracery in the latter half
of the eighteenth century; BL, Add. Ms. 9419, fol. 18r., discussed in the Introduction.

[521] This is the large mural monument to Mary, the wife of Robert Rashleigh (d. 1621), comprising
the reclining figure of a lady in a dress and large ruff, set within an aedicule, topped by a lozenge
with the arms as sketched by Lysons; see Cockerham, *Continuity and Change*, 90–2, pl. 166. The
monument bears no inscription now and none is recorded, so identification is from the heraldry
of Rashleigh (Quarterly, *sable, a cross or, between a Cornish chough argent, beaked and legged
gules*, in the first quarter, in the second, *a Saxon 'T' of the third*; in the third and fourth quarters
a crescent of the last; on the cross in chief a rose) impaling *argent, a chevron between three
spindles sable*, for Trefusis. The only match fitting this heraldic alliance is of Mary, the daughter
of Thomas Trefusis Esq., of Lezant, who married Robert Rashleigh of Fowey; see Vivian,
Visitations of Cornwall, 391–2 (Rashleigh), 467 (Trefusis).

[522] *Argent, a chevron between three spindles sable*, for Trefusis. Although there is no person-
alised inscription on this monument – only a set of verses to the Trefusis family – it is to
Thomas Trefusis (d. 1606) and his wife Mary Coryton, their two sons and two daughters;
see Cockerham, *Continuity and Change*, 59–64, pls 99, 107. This and the Rashleigh tomb
dominated the east end of the south aisle as a dynastic mortuary chapel.

[523] This was originally square and of the Altarnun type, but the corners (bearing heads?)
have been trimmed down, leaving four panels with decorated roundels; Sedding,
Norman Architecture, 236; and the CRSBI, available online at: https://www.crsbi.ac.uk/
view-item?i=8850 [accessed December 2023].

Linkinhorn – a handsome church of Moor stone. Nave & side aisles, in the North aisle monument for Richard ~~Saltwell~~ Saltren gent. ~~1705~~ of Exwell in this parish, 1708, & others of his family.

And of Edward Kneebone.[524]

Clustered pillars, enriched capitals[525] <sketch of capital and font[526]>.

4 miles from Callington.

LISKEARD

Glynne: GL, Glynne notebooks 17, fols 126–7[527]

Liskeard [1842].

This is a very spacious Church, altogether on a grand scale & wholly of Perpendicular work except the Tower which is mean & low in comparison with the body & also of an earlier period, having small narrow windows with obtuse heads arranged in 3 stages which are divided by string courses, & under the battlement an Early English corbel table[528] beneath which is a cornice of small arches.[529] The nave is very lofty

---

[524] Lysons, *Cornwall*, 196–9, published a detailed account of the parish taken chiefly from a Ms. account by W. Harvey of 1727, which was later published by J. Polsue, *A History of the Parish of Linkinhorne from the MS. of W. Harvey* (Bodmin, 1876), although it contains almost no information on the church *per se*. The Lysons' information on this parish was amplified by a letter of 9 June 1807 from James Coffin, BL, Add. Ms. 9416, fols 326r.–327v. For a mid nineteenth-century description, see Rice, 'On Certain Churches in the Deanery of East', 190–1.

[525] This refers to the capitals of the south arcade, made up of trefoils, quatrefoils, and flowers, with crested decoration.

[526] Sedding, *Norman Architecture*, 241; the font is of the Altarnun type.

[527] Lysons, *Cornwall*, 201, mentions simply: 'In the parish-church at Liskeard, is a memorial for Joseph Wadham, who died in 1707, "being the last of that family, whose ancestors were the founders of Wadham College in Oxford"', with no details on the church building. No manuscript notes of the building survive.

[528] Drawings of these corbel table heads suggest these are Norman rather than Early English, as Glynne has it, KK: X1148/4/2.

[529] Gilbert, *Historical Survey*, ii, 950–1, states: 'It had two square towers in the time of Henry VIII, one on each side, but it appears they were taken down in 1627, and one erected at the west end, which is rather low, and crowned with battlements.' Sedding, *Norman Architecture*, 242–8, expands on this with detailed descriptions of the (now replaced) single tower, and that there were originally 'two square towers', as they appear in a map of the coast from Land's End to Exeter (1539–40), now BL, Cotton Ms. Augustus I, I, 35, 36, 38, 39. For reproductions, see Lysons, *Cornwall*, between 108 and 109; and S. Doran (ed.), *Henry VIII: Man & Monarch*, exhibition catalogue, British Library, London(London, 2009), no. 210. The tower that Glynne saw was being demolished in 1898, KK: P126/2/27 (1896–8); and KK: X1148/4/1–8, plans and elevations of the old tower and the proposed replacement, as well as the south porch and vestry (1888–1902). A faculty was granted 'to take down the remainder of the tower and rebuild the same, also to erect a Choir Vestry in the small space on the south side of the tower, and to insert a west window to give more light to west end of the Church. To remove an old tower arch in order to allow the deep foundations of the tower to be carried all round without a break, and give space for the font which was at present very inconveniently placed, and to erect a higher tower arch so as not to obstruct the much needed light from the proposed west window. Also to provide a Bell Chamber with a peal of eight bells, and a ringers' chamber on the first stage of the tower so that the floor of the tower might be used as a Baptistry etc.'; KK: P126/2/27/51 (1898).

& has North & South aisles of equal height & width, and an additional aisle on the South, eastward of the porch. The Chancel has also side aisles, but is rather lower than the nave. The interior is grand from its spacious proportions. The nave is divided from each aisle by 5 very lofty pointed arches upon pillars of granite of the form common in this county. The additional South aisle opens by 3 arches of like character, but the capitals are plain. The Chancel has 3 arches on each side, the 2 Eastern of which are filled with tracery apparently of modern work. The South side of the Church has a fine [127] battlement with pinnacles, all in granite.[530] The South porch is large, & has a Tudor arch doorway with panneling in the spandrels, & above the door 3 canopied niches. The North side has a plainer battlement & presents rather an unusual arrangement in a succession of three projecting bays or recesses equal in height with the aisle & set at regular intervals. One forms a porch, the others open to the interior by flat arches & have stone roofs, forming as it were chapels or in the present fashion, pews.[531] The windows on this side have mostly obtuse arches. Those on the South are larger & of better design & execution but all of 4 lights, except those at the extremities which have 5 lights. The East window is of 5 lights, & has shafts to the mullions & to the arch mouldings. There is an octagonal stair turret at the ^South West^ angle of the South aisle. The interior is neat, with regular pews.[532] The pulpit is carved in the style of James I. The Font is of granite, but modern.[533] There is no Organ, or gallery except at the West end.[534]

[530] See Mattingly, 'Pevsner', 74, 77–8.
[531] These were originally constructed as guild chapels; see CL: Henderson Ms. 'East Cornwall', 329–31; and Mattingly, 'Distinctiveness by Omission', 142–3. For the historical background of a chantry chapel in the north aisle, see Mattingly, Churches of Cornwall, 55–6.
[532] Gilbert, Historical Survey, ii, 951, recorded that the interior 'underwent considerable repair a few years ago [1793], when it was entirely newly seated, but many specimens of the ancient carved work have been preserved in the doors of the modern pews'. There is no old woodwork remaining now, perhaps replaced in 1859–60 when the church was reseated, KK: P126/7/2. The church was thoroughly restored in 1879, as reported by the RCG, 14 March 1879, 5: 'The floor, the seats, the walls, the windows and the roofs have been renovated; but the decoration of the chancel has yet to be carried out, and the only cause which hinders this being done at once is the want of the necessary funds. The roofs have entailed no slight labour. All the corbels – which, with the exception of a few in the nave, are new – have been carved.' Ten years later, the chancel was restored, WBCA, 19 December 1889, 2, starting with 'the demolition of the old and dilapidated vestry, and rebuilding on the same site a structure in the 15th century style, to harmonise with the church, the windows, doorways, and other dressings being of granite, interior fittings of oak, and tiled floor [...] The old chancel [...] was very badly arranged, and there was no apparent distinction between it and the other portion of the church. The view of the east end was, moreover, obstructed by the position of the pulpit, which stood on the south side of the nave aisle, near it being the old high pews of the Corporation, whilst on the north side of the nave aisle was a high reading desk, the clerk's desk, and churchwardens pew. These obstructions have now been removed, and a passage carried across the east end of the nave. The old oak pulpit, which is beautiful specimen of carving, and bears date "Anno Domini, 1636", has been rebuilt on a moulded granite base much lower than it previously stood.'
[533] This judgement is odd, as the font is most likely a work of the sixteenth century; Beacham and Pevsner, Cornwall, 310.
[534] A faculty for a south gallery and reseating was obtained in 1792, DHC: DR, Faculty Causes, Cornwall, Liskeard 4. The west gallery was taken down in 1912; KK: P126/7/12.

LITTLE PETHERICK

Lysons: BL, Add. Ms. 9445, fol. 250r.

Little Petherick – small church, low tower, small pinnacles, one aisle, clustered columns. Font octagonal with quatrefoils.[535]

LOSTWITHIEL

Lysons: BL, Add. Ms. 9462, fols 42v.–43r.

<sketches of font, one measured,[536] spire, and section through the hill and Restormel castle>.
Fol. 43r. [separate sheet] Restormel castle – In the chapel a piscina of this form <sketch> ~~part of~~ a pointed arch appears at the west end, with part of the mouldings. Fragment of a window lying with others near the gate <sketch of tracery>. Entrance on the west side <sketch of arch> surrounded by a vallum and a very deep ditch. The area of the castle within is much lower than the top of the monument.[537]

Glynne: GL, Glynne notebooks 17, fols 131–2

Lostwithiel [1842].
This Church has several singularities & in its general features does not resemble the Cornish Churches. It has a lofty body with low aisles, & a Clerestory which is unusual in Cornwall, but no distinct Chancel. The steeple at the West end is a very singular composition, consisting of a square tower short & plain, upon which is set a curious but not inelegant octagon ^lanthorn,^ each side of which rises into a pediment or gable & is entirely filled with fine open tracery, & which is surmounted by a tolerably lofty stone spire. The lower portion of the steeple is Early English, & has 3 plain lancet windows arranged <sketch, showing two windows above a third> & on ~~the~~ its South side is a doorway unusually placed & singular in character, but which is probably Early English, the outer moulding of the arch being stopped in two places by a kind of knot. The tracery in the lanthorn is remarkable & rather foreign, & is probably of a transition style from Decorated [132] to Perpendicular; each side presents a double arch with quatrefoil between the heads, occupying the whole space, but ^at^ about the centre of each side is a band of open tracery with grand quatrefoils, across each side & continued in a line all around this portion of the steeple. In one side the quatrefoil tracery is varied into a wheel or rose, instead of being in a square. Each gable is

---

[535] This brief description of what was then a simple building hardly accords with the appearance of the church today. There were considerable changes introduced, first, by William White, in 1858, with the addition of a new north aisle, followed by the almost complete Roman Catholicisation of the building during the twentieth century under the direction of J.N. Comper, for the patron, Athelstan Riley. See Warner, *A Time to Build*, 222–3, and Beacham and Pevsner, *Cornwall*, 315–16.

[536] Published by Lysons, *Cornwall*, ccxxxiv, and pl. opp., no. 2. Apart from the font, they give no information about the church other than 'a memorial' to Tristram Curteys (d. 1423), perhaps taken from another source, such as BL, Stowe Ms. 1023, fol. 48r.

[537] Described in *Cornwall*, ccxli, 176–7; but the piscina is not mentioned.

Interior of Lostwithiel Church. Cornwall. East View.

Fig. 56. Interior view of Lostwithiel church, looking east (1836); reproduced with the kind permission of the Royal Institution of Cornwall, Courtney Library, Lawrence Ms. 'Watercolour drawings of Lostwithiel Church'.

surmounted by a finial, & in the Spire, are ~~is another~~ other canopied openings, of less elegant workmanship, with the arches on shafts.[538] <sketch of spire> (Fig. 7) The roofs of the Church are modern & of slate. The aisles are low & not wide, most of the ^side^ windows are square headed, those at the West end of each aisle are lancets. The Clerestory windows have contracted arches.[539] The interior is lofty & spacious, & the body is divided from the aisles by 2 ranges each of 5 tall pointed arches, the piers of which are octagonal but without capitals & have rather the appearance of having been altered.[540] (Fig. 56)

[538] Lysons and Glynne saw the spire following repair after a lightning strike in 1757, reported by J. Smeaton, 'An Account of the Effects of Lightning upon the Steeple and Church of Leftwithiel, Cornwall; In a Letter to the Right Honourable the Earl of Macclesfield, President of the R[oyal] S[ociety]', *Philosophical Transactions of the Royal Society*, 50 (1757), 198–204, in which he described 'a great many stones fell upon the roof of the church and several made their way thro both roof and ceiling down into the church, breaking the pews, and whatever they fell upon […] all the windows in the Church were either broken out or bagged inwards'; available online at: https://doi.org/10.1098/rstl.1757.0026 [accessed June 2020].

[539] Glynne visited just after the nave roof had been lowered in 1841, shortening the clerestory windows as a consequence, and converting them from three lights occupying pointed arches to three-light windows with lights of almost equal length. The roofs were again replaced around 1877–9, with the mark of the original roof visible on the east side of the tower and differences in masonry patterns evident on the north side towards the east end; the original window openings can also be traced in places. See Warner, *A Time to Build*, 226.

[540] The easternmost arch was opened out in 1775–6 on the removal of the wall between the chancel and what was then the vestry: 'To take down the walls of the Vestry room, and to turn an arch', see F.M. Hext, *Memorials of Lostwithiel and of Restormell* (Truro, 1891), 82–3.

Fig. 57. East window of Lostwithiel church (1836); reproduced with the kind permission of the Royal Institution of Cornwall, Courtney Library, Lawrence Ms. 'Watercolour drawings of Lostwithiel Church'.

The East window is a very large one of 5 lights with Decorated tracery rather of an early period.[541] (Fig. 57)

The two East windows of the aisles are, in the South a 3 light Decorated one, in the North a triple lancet. There is a very curious Font of octagonal form, the age of which is rather doubtful, but it is probably Early English. It stands on 5 shafts, the

[541] The east window was taken down, repaired, and reglazed in 1843 by the Corporation, October 1843; see CL, G.B. Lawrence, 'Watercolour Drawings of Lostwithiel Church and the Various Monuments, Windows and Internal Fittings [...] 1836', prior to fol. 1, which shows the elegance and simplicity of the tracery and the glass replaced before that restoration; it was reglazed again in 1886 (*RCG*, 28 January 1887, 5). George Bell Lawrence, commander RN, owned much property in Lostwithiel and retained an antiquarian interest in the town. He died in 1846, his wife predeceasing him (1845), and together they are commemorated by a memorial erected in the church 'by their bereaved children'.

Interior of Lostwithiel Church. Cornwall

Fig. 58. Interior view of Lostwithiel church, looking west (1836); reproduced with the kind permission of the Royal Institution of Cornwall, Courtney Library, Lawrence Ms. 'Watercolour Drawings of Lostwithiel Church'.

central the largest, & all clustered & moulded, which rest upon a square basement. On each face of the octagon is rude sculpture representing various subjects in relief, 1. the Crucifixion. 2. a hunter with hawk in hand & blowing bugle. 3. 2 Lions passant. 4. a grotesque animal's head. 5. A square filled with geometrical figures. 6. a dog & hare. 7. as 5. 8. the head of a Bishop.[542] At the West end is a gallery containing an Organ.[543] (Fig. 58)

[542] This is of early fourteenth-century date, the imagery also including a Crucifixion; see Hext, *Memorials of Lostwithiel and of Restormell*, 85–8; F. Bond, *Fonts and Font Covers* (London, 1908), 233, 240.

[543] On the front of the gallery were the royal arms (dated 1760), and to either side the arms of Lostwithiel and those of the earl of Mount Edgcumbe. It was taken down in the 1870s, see LPL: ICBS 8001 (1875–9), 'for general repairs, including reflooring, removal of western gallery and restoration of spire'; and KK: P128/2/17–19, for sketches and specifications on the restoration of the spire (1863). A postcard of the church interior prior to the restoration is KK: P128/2/24.

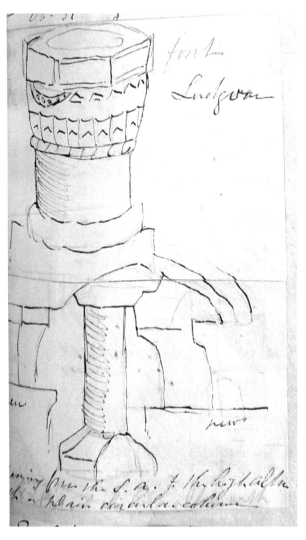

Fig. 59. Font, and a view into the chancel from the south 'aisle', Ludgvan church; from the British Library Archive, Add. Ms. 9445, fol. 187r.

LUDGVAN

Lysons: BL, Add. Ms. 9445, fol. 187r.

Ludgvan <sketch of font[544]>. (Fig. 59)

[separate sheet] Opening from the South aisle to the high altar, with a plain circular column <sketch looking between pews through the opening showing the column[545]>.

---

[544] This appears to be an eighteenth-century font modelled on a Norman example; it was then mounted on a round pillar and not on the hexagonal support of today.

[545] This shows a bizarre circular column supporting the east side of the arch opening into the south transept – perhaps facilitating a squint? – removed when the transept was converted into an aisle; see fn. 548.

Fig. 60. West end of Ludgvan church (1762); reproduced by kind permission of Devon Archives & Local Studies, DHC, Z19/16/1, 136, drawing by William Borlase.

[separate sheet] Annae suae / & per annos propemodum / quadraginta & quinque / uxori, peramatae amanti / amabili, [extremum hoc quaelcunque] grati animi pignus / posuit Gulielmus Borlase, Decessit in Christo / multum desiderata Apirilis 21 die in Ano. 1769, aetatis 66.[546]
On another stone, Etiam sunt depositae reliquie / Annae Mariti Gulielmus Borlase. L.L.D., R.S.S. / perurbani perhumani perquam pii / hujusque parochiae per annos 52 / rectoris desideratissimi / ... necnon ... / scripta / ... ob. 31 August 1772 aetatis 76.[547]

Glynne: GL, Glynne notebooks, 16, fols 5–6

Ludgvan, S. Paul, 16 February 1858.[548]
This Church with its elevated site & fine Tower forms a very conspicuous object – but the rest of the Church is not equal to the Tower. (Fig. 60)

---

[546] Trans., *William Borlase here sets up a pledge of his grateful heart to Anna, his wife for nearly forty-five years, who was deeply loved and his beloved [whatever this end may be], who passed away in Christ, much missed on the 21st of April 1769, aged 66.*
[547] Trans., *The remains of Anne's husband William Borlase L.L.D., R.S.S., were also deposited here, the most pious, most humane of people, and the most loved rector of this parish for 52 years [...] as well as [...] writings [...] he died 31 August 1772, aged 76.* These are approximate transcripts of the inscriptions (some portions are omitted) on the gravestones to William Borlase (1696–1772) and his wife Anne, located side by side in the chancel. As they were collected together with notes on the church and a sketch of the font, it is likely that they were taken at first hand rather than from another source. The Lysons would have recognised the importance of the commemorated individuals, and William Borlase's reputation as an antiquary, historian, and natural historian, together with his legacy of publications and manuscript notes on the county.
[548] Glynne's visit was fifteen years or so after a large-scale rebuild; see LPL: ICBS 2378 (1838–41), concerning the enlargement of the church, the replacement of the south transept and porch with a new south aisle, porch, and west and east windows of two lights. The documents include plans and elevations before and after the works. Glynne's comment that the shafts and capitals of the piers of the south arcade were of 'rather doubtful character' was, hence, quite correct. For an earlier and comprehensive description of the church, see P.A.S. Pool, 'The Parish of Ludgvan in 1770, by the Rev. William Borlase', *JRIC* NS 6.4 (1972), 275–92, at 286–9.

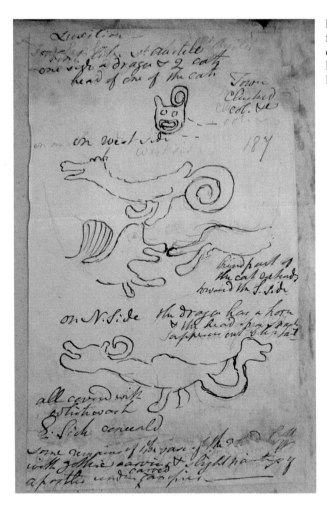

Fig. 61. Sketches of the font sides at Luxulyan church; from the British Library Archive, Add. Ms. 9445, fol. 187r.

The plan embraces 3 aisles of which the Southern is shorter than the others, but all of equal height. The Southern is the widest. The Northern arcade has 6 narrow Tudor shaped arches, with the usual clustered piers, the capitals octagonal & with moulded band. The Southern arcade is of 4 wide arches, with piers differing from the others, but equally with shafts & octagonal capitals, of rather doubtful character. The Chancel includes 2 bays. The roofs are [6] coved. There is a small door on the North corresponding to the place of the rood loft. The windows have all been mutilated.[549] The Font is of Marble or Serpentine, ef the bowl octagonal, with a moulding below it of rope, beaded scroll & toothed, the stem cylindrical & of granite.[550]

[549] As visible in the Borlase drawing of 1762, where the west windows of the north aisle and tower are clearly shuttered. This pattern of fenestration with small square panes was retained into the twentieth century, recorded by photographic glass slides, CL, Hughes Clifton collection, Ludgvan Eccles. External views 1 and 2 (from the north-east). They were replaced by the windows visible today during the 1912–13 restoration; see fn. 552.

[550] This describes the font drawn by Lysons; yet the EDAS recorded that 'as lately as the year 1842, a Wedgwood basin, on the sill of the east window, was used', DHC: F5/17/2/4, EDAS, series of Rough Notes – sheet 25 (1862).

There is a monument to the parents of Sir Humphry Davey.[551] i̶n̶ In the cill of the East window is a slab inscribed, with figures of Parents, 2 sons & 3 daughters, in memory of John Smith Rector 1631 [*recte* John South (d. 1636)].
The Interior has a neglected look[552] & the North wall leans out of the perpendicular.[553] There is a South porch.
The Tower is a very grand one of granite, embattled & having 4 square pinnacles crocketed & panneled. The buttresses are withdrawn from the angles. There are 2 divisions by string courses. The belfry windows of 3 lights. The West doorway labeled with granite arch mouldings & panneled spandrels. The West window of 3 plain lights, without foliation or tracery.

LUXULYAN

Lysons: BL, Add. Ms. 9445, fol. 187r.

Luxilion – Tower, clustered columns &c.
Font like St Austell, one side a dragon & 2 cats, head of one of the cats <sketch>.
On west side <sketches of 'cats'> hindpart of the cat extends toward the South side.
On North side the dragon has a horn & the head appears cut of a part of the tail <sketch>, all covered with whitewash. East side concealed.[554] (Fig. 61)
Some remains of the base of the rood loft with gothic carvings & slight paintings of apostles under carved canopies.[555]

---

[551] This is a mural tablet of white marble bearing an inscription to Robert Davy of Varfell (d. 1796), and Grace his wife (d. 1826), whose remains were buried in the churchyard at the end of the south aisle. They were the parents of the noted scientist Sir Humphry Davy, 1st Bt (1778–1829), the tablet also recording his death at Geneva in 1829. Presumably the memorial was erected by other members of the family to recognise Davy's links with the parish where he grew up.

[552] This was still the case up to the restoration in 1887–8, when the *RCG*, 20 January 1888, 8, noted: 'The interior of the building has been very greatly improved. Formerly it presented an old-fashioned and dingy appearance, but all the old box pews have been removed, and the walls and ceiling replastered and recoloured, so that its aspect is now a bright, clean, and modern one.' In addition, *TC*, 20 October 1887, 5, reported that 'the whole of the old flooring was removed and the vaults and graves which honeycombed the basement (and in which repose such venerated dust as that of Dr. Borlase, the pioneer of Cornwall's antiquarians) were hermetically closed by concrete, so as never again to offend the noses or injure the health of worshippers. The east window has been thoroughly renovated, as have been some parts of the walls, roof, other windows, &c.'

[553] This was not addressed until the early twentieth century, reported by *TC*, 28 August 1913, 2: 'The North wall taken down to the window sill level, and then rebuilt; also the whole length of the wall under ground level underpinned with cement concrete. North Arcade – Old arcade which was very much out of upright taken down, new foundations inserted, and re-built; arches, columns being rectified throughout'; see also Warner, *A Time to Build*, 227.

[554] Lysons was clearly captivated by the liveliness of the designs on this font, yet he merely grouped it with those at St Austell and Newlyn East in the printed account, *Cornwall*, ccxxxiii.

[555] There is no other record of this screen except Gilbert, *Historical Survey*, ii, 870: 'It had formerly a screen, or rood-loft, which displayed full length figures of the apostles, painted and gilded. This ancient screen, with the figures still visible, has been cut to pieces, merely to patch up old seats.' Lysons saw it before this had taken place, therefore. Perhaps the destruction was an economy response to the repeated directions of the rural deans to repair the flooring of most of the seats in the church, from 1810 to 1811; KK: AD59/74, 211. Remnants of the screen, including the figures of St Peter, a jester, and two secular figures, are incorporated into the woodwork of a nineteenth-century side altar in the church; see Mattingly, 'Rood Loft Construction', 89, 92–4, 106.

DEVON AND CORNWALL
RECORD SOCIETY

(Founded 1904)

Officers 2022–2023

President: Dr S. Roberts BA, MA, PhD, FSA, FRHistS

Chairman of Council: Dr Oliver J. Padel MA, MLitt, LittD, FSA

Hon. Secretary: L. Browne BA, Dip. Gen., QG, Member of AGRA Council

Membership Secretary: K. Osborne BA MA PhD AMA

Hon. Treasurer: M. Billings MSc, BA, PGCLT, FCA

Hon. Editor: Dr Catherine R. Rider MA, PhD, FRHistS

The Devon and Cornwall Record Society promotes the study of
history in the South West of England through publishing and
transcribing original records. In return for the annual subscription
members receive the volumes as published (normally annually). For further details
see http://www.devonandcornwallrecordsociety.co.uk/

Applications to join the Society should
be sent to The Membership Secretary, Devon and Cornwall Record Society,
Devon Heritage Centre, Great Moor House, Bittern Road, Exeter, EX2 7NL, or
emailed to membershipDCRS@btinternet.com

DEVON AND CORNWALL
RECORD SOCIETY PUBLICATIONS

Previous volumes are available from Boydell & Brewer Ltd.

A Shelf List of the Society's Collections, ed. S. Stride, revised 1986

New Series

1 *Devon Monastic Lands: Calendar of Particulars for Grants 1536–1558*, ed. Joyce Youings, 1955

2 *Exeter in the Seventeenth Century: Tax and Rate Assessments 1602–1699*, ed. W.G. Hoskins, 1957

3 *The Diocese of Exeter in 1821: Bishop Carey's Replies to Queries before Visitation, Vol. I Cornwall*, ed. Michael Cook, 1958

4 *The Diocese of Exeter in 1821: Bishop Carey's Replies to Queries before Visitation, Vol. II Devon*, ed. Michael Cook, 1960

5 *The Cartulary of St Michael's Mount*, ed. P.L. Hull, 1962

6 *The Exeter Assembly: Minutes of the Assemblies of the United Brethren of Devon and Cornwall 1691–1717, as Transcribed by the Reverend Isaac Gilling*, ed. Allan Brockett, 1963

7 *The Register of Edmund Lacy, Bishop of Exeter 1420–1455, Vol. 1*, ed. G.R. Dunstan

8 *The Cartulary of Canonsleigh Abbey*, ed. Vera C.M. London, 1965

9 *Benjamin Donn's Map of Devon 1765*, Introduction by W.L.D. Ravenhill, 1965

10 *The Register of Edmund Lacy, Bishop of Exeter 1420–1455, Vol. 2*, ed. G.R. Dunstan, 1966

11 *Devon Inventories of the 16th & 17th Centuries*, ed. Margaret Cash, 1966

12 *Plymouth Building Accounts of the 16th & 17th Centuries*, ed. Edwin Welch, 1967

13 *The Register of Edmund Lacy, Bishop of Exeter 1420–1455, Vol. 3*, ed. G.R. Dunstan, 1968

14 *The Devonshire Lay Subsidy of 1332*, ed. Audrey M. Erskine, 1969

15 *Churchwardens' Accounts of Ashburton 1479–1580*, ed. Alison Hanham, 1970

16 *The Register of Edmund Lacy, Bishop of Exeter 1420–1455, Vol. 4*, ed. G.R. Dunstan, 1971

17 *The Caption of Seisin of the Duchy of Cornwall 1337*, ed. P L. Hull, 1971

18 *The Register of Edmund Lacy, Bishop of Exeter 1420–1455, Vol. 5*, ed. G.R. Dunstan, 1972

19 *A Calendar of Cornish Glebe Terriers 1673–1735*, ed. Richard Potts, 1974

20 *John Lydford's Book: The Fourteenth-Century Formulary of the Archdeacon of Totnes*, ed. Dorothy M. Owen, 1975 (with Historical Manuscripts Commission)

21 *A Calendar of Early Chancery Proceedings Relating to West Country Shipping 1388–1493*, ed. Dorothy A. Gardiner, 1976

22 *Tudor Exeter: Tax Assessments 1489–1595*, ed. Margery M. Rowe, 1977

23 *The Devon Cloth Industry in the 18th Century*, ed. Stanley D. Chapman, 1978

24 *The Accounts of the Fabric of Exeter Cathedral 1279–1353, Part I*, ed. Audrey M. Erskine, 1981

25 *The Parliamentary Survey of the Duchy of Cornwall, Part I*, ed. Norman J.G. Pounds, 1982

26 *The Accounts of the Fabric of Exeter Cathedral 1279–1353, Part II*, ed. Audrey M. Erskine, 1983

27 *The Parliamentary Survey of the Duchy of Cornwall, Part II*, ed. Norman J.G. Pounds, 1984

28 *Crown Pleas of the Devon Eyre 1238*, ed. Henry Summerson, 1985

29 *Georgian Tiverton, The Political Memoranda of Beavis Wood 1768–98*, ed. John Bourne, 1986

30 *The Cartulary of Launceston Priory (Lambeth Palace MS.719): A Calendar*, ed. P.L. Hull, 1987

31 *Shipbuilding on the Exe: The Memoranda Book of Daniel Bishop Davy (1799–1874) of Topsham, Devon*, ed. Clive N. Ponsford, 1988

32 *The Receivers' Accounts of the City of Exeter 1304–1353*, ed. Margery Rowe and John M. Draisey, 1989

33 *Early-Stuart Mariners and Shipping: The Maritime Surveys of Devon and Cornwall 1619–35*, ed. Todd Gray, 1990

65 *Devon Parish Taxpayers, Vol. 3, Churchstow to Dunkeswell*, ed. Todd Gray, 2022
66 *The Memoir of John Butter: Surgeon, Militiaman, Sportsman and Founder of the Plymouth Royal Eye Infirmary*, ed. Dee and Mike Tracey, 2023

Devon Maps and Map-Makers: Manuscript Maps before 1840. Supplement to Volumes 43 and 45, ed. Mary R. Ravenhill and Margery M. Rowe, 2010

Extra Series:
1 *Exeter Freemen 1266–1967*, ed. Margery M. Rowe and Andrew M. Jackson, 1973
2 *Guide to the Parish and Non-Parochial Registers of Devon and Cornwall 1538–1837*, ed. Hugh Peskett, 1979, supplement 1983
3 *William Birchynshaw's Map of Exeter, 1743*, ed. Richard Oliver, Roger Kain and Todd Gray, 2019